C: The Complete Reference
Second Edition

C: The Complete Reference
Second Edition

Herbert Schildt

Osborne **McGraw-Hill**

Berkeley   New York   St. Louis   San Francisco
Auckland   Bógota   Hamburg   London   Madrid
Mexico City   Milan   Montreal   New Delhi   Panama City
Paris   São Paulo   Singapore   Sydney
Tokyo   Toronto

Osborne **McGraw-Hill**
2600 Tenth Street
Berkeley, California 94710
U.S.A.

For information on translations and book distributors outside of the U.S.A., write to Osborne **McGraw-Hill** at the above address.

A complete list of trademarks appears on page 803.

C: The Complete Reference, Second Edition

34567890 DOC 90

ISBN 0-07-881538-X

Preface xiii

CONTENTS

Most of the time, writing a book is challenging, tedious, exciting, frustrating, and a lot of work all rolled into one. But the creation of *C: The Complete Reference, Second Edition,* had an extra, almost intangible component. I had been given the mission of creating a complete reference guide to the C programming language. Not just *any* book, but the *complete* book. Whenever I write a book, I try to be thorough, but in this book I had to be even more thorough. It was the word "complete" that kept haunting me. I knew that programmers from around the world would be buying my book because it was the *complete* reference. Finally, I realized, as I'm sure you must, that no one book on C can hope to cover all of its nuances, tricks, and uses. The C language is just too rich and powerful. But I do say this: The writing of *C: The Complete Reference, Second Edition,* was a labor of love. I am confident that you will be pleased with the result.

Is This Book for You?

This C reference is designed for all C programmers, regardless of their experience level. It does assume, however, a reader able to create at least a simple C program. If you are just learning C, this book will make an excellent companion to any C tutorial and serve as a source of answers to your specific questions.

What's New in the Second Edition

For the most part, I have left the basic structure of the book unchanged from the first edition. A couple of chapters have been moved, but the presentation of material within each chapter reflects the original book. Also, much new material has been added, including expanded coverage of graphics.

The major differences between the first and the second editions are caused by conformance to the new ANSI C standard. When the first edition was written, the ANSI C standard, still in its infancy, was being continually changed. Also, at that time no compilers conformed closely to the evolving standard. Therefore, most of the original edition reflected the more common de facto C standard as defined by Kernighan and Ritchie. However, now that the standard is stable, and given the fact that all major C compilers comply with the standard, it seemed time to switch to the ANSI C standard. (Important points and differences between the old de facto standard and the new ANSI standard are still covered by this book, however, so you don't have to be using an ANSI C standard compiler to utilize the book.)

The major changes caused by conformance to the ANSI C standard are function prototyping, which is used throughout the book, and inclusion of all header files. In older versions of C, most header files were not needed for programs to run correctly. However, in order to take advantage of function prototyping, all header files must be included because they contain the prototypes of the standard library functions.

Another change caused by the adoption of the ANSI C standard is that the modern form of function declaration is used. (The older — sometimes called "classic" — form is still explained in detail, but the code examples use the modern form.)

What's Inside

This book covers in detail all aspects of the C language and its libraries. It includes both the old de facto C standard and the ANSI C standard. However, the main emphasis is on the ANSI C standard. The book is divided into five parts, covering

- The C language
- The C libraries
- Common algorithms and applications
- The C programming environment
- C++: C's newest direction

Part One provides a thorough discussion of the keywords, preprocessor directives, and features of the C language.

Part Two discusses the standard C library. Both the K&R and ANSI standard library functions are covered. Also included are some functions common to the DOS programming environment, including DOS calls and graphics. For DOS-specific functions, Microsoft C was chosen for the examples.

Part Three covers some of the more common and important algorithms and applications that all C programmers should have in their toolbox. You will find Chapter 22, which deals with AI problem-solving techniques, particularly interesting.[1]

Part Four covers the C programming environment including such things as interfacing to assembly code, efficiency, porting, and debugging.

Part Five examines C's newest direction, C++. C++ is a superset of C designed to handle the rigorous needs of large projects and to aid in program verification.

There are many, many working functions and programs contained in this book. If you are like me, you like having a lot of routines to draw upon but hate entering them into the computer. It always seems that I type something wrong and spend hours trying to get the program to work. For this reason, I am offering on disk the source code to all the functions and programs contained in this book for $24.95. Just fill in the order blank on the next page and mail it, along with your payment, to

Herbert Schildt
RR 1, Box 130
Mahomet IL 61853

Or if you're in a hurry, just call (217) 586-4021 (the number of my consulting office) and place your order by telephone (VISA and Master-Card accepted).

—HS

---

[1]For a wider assortment of C applications, refer to my book *Advanced C, Second Edition* (Berkeley, Calif.: Osborne/McGraw-Hill, 1988). For those interested in AI, see my book *Artificial Intelligence Using C* (Berkeley, Calif.: Osborne/McGraw-Hill, 1987).

Order Form

Please send me _____ copies, at $24.95 each, of the programs in *C: The Complete Reference, 2nd Edition*. Foreign orders, please add $5 shipping and handling.

_____

Name

_____

Address

_____   _____   _____

City   State   ZIP

_____

Telephone

Disk size: 5 1/4 _____ 3 1/2 _____

Method of payment: check _____ VISA _____ MC _____

Credit card number _____

Expiration date _____

Signature _____

Send to:

Herbert Schildt
RR 1, Box 130
Mahomet, IL 61853

or phone: (217) 586-4021

The C Language

An Overview of C
C Expressions
Program Control Statements
Arrays and Strings
Pointers
Functions
Structures, Unions, Enumerations,
   and User-Defined Types
Console I/O
File I/O
The C Preprocessor and Comments

**P
A
R
T

O
N
E**

The first part of this reference guide presents a thorough discussion of the C programming language. Chapter 1 provides a quick overview of the C language—the more knowledgeable programmer may wish to skip directly to Chapter 2. Chapter 2 examines C's built-in data types, variables, operators, and expressions. Next, Chapter 3 presents program control statements. Chapter 4 discusses arrays and strings. Chapter 5 looks at pointers. Chapter 6 deals with functions, and Chapter 7 discusses structures, unions, and user-defined types. Chapter 8 examines console I/O. Chapter 9 covers file I/O, and Chapter 10 discusses the C preprocessor and comments.

The material in this section (and most of the material in the book) reflects the ANSI standard for C. However, the original C standard as derived from the UNIX version 5 C is also covered, and important differences are noted. The book covers both ANSI and the original C to ensure that you find information relevant to your C programming environment.

An Overview of C

The purpose of this chapter is to present an overview of the C programming language, its origins, its uses, and its underlying philosophy. This chapter is mainly for newcomers to C.

The Origins of C

C was invented and first implemented by Dennis Ritchie on a DEC PDP-11 that used the UNIX operating system. C is the result of a development process that started with an older language called BCPL, which is still in use primarily in Europe. BCPL was developed by Martin Richards, and it influenced a language called B, which was invented by Ken Thompson. B led to the development of C in the 1970s.

For many years, the de facto standard for C was the version supplied with the UNIX version 5 operating system. It is described in *The C Programming Language* by Brian Kernighan and Dennis Ritchie (Englewood Cliffs, N.J.: Prentice-Hall, 1978). With the popularity of microcomputers, a large number of C implementations were created. In a near miracle, the source codes of most of these implementations were highly compatible. However, because no standard existed, there were discrepancies. To remedy this situation, ANSI established a committee in the summer of 1983 to create a standard that would define the C language once and for all. At the time of this writing, the ANSI standard committee is concluding the formal adoption process. All mainstream C compilers have already implemented the ANSI standard. This book fully covers and emphasizes the ANSI C standard. At the same time, it contains information on the old UNIX version of C. In other words, no matter what C compiler you are using, you will find applicable material here.

C Is a Middle-Level Language

C is often called a *middle-level* computer language. This does not mean that C is less powerful, harder to use, or less developed than a high-level language such as BASIC or Pascal, nor does it imply that C is similar to assembly language and that it presents the user with the associated troubles. C is thought of as a middle-level language because it combines elements of high-level languages with the functionalism of assembly language. Table 1-1 shows how C fits into the spectrum of computer languages.

Highest level	Ada
	Modula-2
	Pascal
	COBOL
	FORTRAN
	BASIC
Middle level	C
	FORTH
	Macro-assembler
Lowest level	Assembler

Table 1-1.   C's Place in the World of Languages

As a middle-level language, C allows the manipulation of bits, bytes, and addresses—the basic elements with which the computer functions. C code is very portable. *Portability* means that it is possible to adapt software written for one type of computer to another. For example, if you can easily move a program written for an Apple MacIntosh to an IBM PC, that program is portable.

All high-level programming languages support the concept of data types. A *data type* defines a set of values that a variable can store along with a set of operations that can be performed on that variable. Common data types are integer, character, and real. Although C has five basic built-in data types, it is not a strongly typed language as are Pascal and Ada. C permits almost all type conversions. For example, you may freely intermix character and integer types in most expressions. C performs no run-time error checking such as array-boundary checking. These types of checks are the responsibility of the programmer.

In the same vein, the original versions of C did not perform many (if any) compatibility tests between a function's parameter and the arguments used to call the function. For example, in the original version of C, you could call a function using a pointer without generating an error message, even though that function had actually been defined as requiring a floating-point argument. However, the ANSI standard introduced the concept of *function prototypes,* which allows some of these potential errors to be reported if so directed by the programmer. (Prototypes will be discussed later in Chapter 6.)

C is special in that it allows the direct manipulation of bits, bytes, words, and pointers. This makes it well-suited for system-level programming, where these operations are common. Another important aspect of C is that it has only 32 keywords (27 from the Kernighan and Ritchie de facto standard, and 5 added by the ANSI standardization committee), which are the commands that make up the C language. As a comparison, consider that BASIC for the IBM PC contains about 159 keywords!

C Is a Structured Language

Although the term *block-structured language* does not strictly apply to C, C is commonly referred to simply as a structured language. It has many similarities to other structured languages, such as ALGOL, Pascal, and Modula-2. (Technically, a block-structured language permits procedures or functions to be declared inside other procedures or functions. In this way, the concepts of global and local are expanded through the use of *scope rules,* which govern the "visibility" of a variable or procedure. However, since C does not allow the creation of functions within functions, it cannot formally be called block-structured).

The distinguishing feature of a structured language is *compartmentalization* of code and data. This is the ability of a language to section off and hide from the rest of the program all information and instructions necessary to perform a specific task. One way that you achieve compartmentalization is by using subroutines that employ local (temporary) variables. By using local variables, you can write subroutines so that the events that occur within them cause no side effects in other parts of the program. This capability makes it very easy for your C programs to share sections of code. If you develop compartmentalized functions, you only need to know what a function does, not how it does it. Remember, excessive use of global variables (variables known throughout the entire program) may allow bugs to creep into a program by allowing unwanted side effects. (Anyone who has programmed in BASIC is well aware of this problem.)

A structured language allows you a variety of programming possibilities. It directly supports several loop constructs, such as **while**, **do-while**, and **for**. In a structured language, the use of **goto** is either prohibited or discouraged, nor is it the common form of program control, as it is in BASIC and FORTRAN. A structured language allows you to indent statements and does not require a strict field concept (as some FORTRANs do).

Here are some examples of structured and nonstructured languages:

Nonstructured	Structured
FORTRAN	Pascal
BASIC	Ada
COBOL	C
	Modula-2

Structured languages tend to be modern. In fact, a mark of an old computer language is that it is nonstructured. Today, most programmers consider structured languages easier to program in and easier to maintain.

C's main structural component is the function—C's stand-alone subroutine. In C, functions are the building blocks in which all program activity occurs. They allow you to define and code separately the separate tasks in a program, thus allowing your programs to be modular. After you have created a function, you can rely on it to work properly in various situations without creating side effects in other parts of the program. Being able to create stand-alone functions is extremely critical in larger projects where one programmer's code must not accidentally affect another's.

Another way to structure and compartmentalize code in C is through the use of code blocks. A *code block* is a logically-connected group of program statements that is treated as a unit. In C, you create a code block by placing a sequence of statements between opening and closing curly braces. In this example

```
if (x < 10)   {
   printf("too low, try again\n");
   scanf("%d", &x);
}
```

the two statements after the **if** and between the curly braces are both executed if **x** is less than 10. These two statements together with the braces represent a code block. They are a logical unit: One of the statements cannot execute without the other executing also. Note that every statement in C can be either a single statement or a block of statements. Code blocks allow many algorithms to be implemented with clarity, elegance, and efficiency. Moreover, they help the programmer conceptualize the true nature of the routine.

C Is a Programmer's Language

Surprisingly, not all computer programming languages are for programmers. Consider the classic examples of nonprogrammer's languages,

COBOL and BASIC. COBOL was designed not to better the programmer's lot, not to improve the reliability of the code produced, and not even to improve the speed with which code can be written. Rather, COBOL was designed, in part, to enable nonprogrammers to read and presumably (however unlikely) to understand the program. BASIC was created essentially to allow nonprogrammers to program a computer to solve relatively simple problems.

In contrast, C was created, influenced, and field-tested by working programmers. The end result is that C gives the programmer what the programmer wants: few restrictions, few complaints, block structures, stand-alone functions, and a compact set of keywords. By using C, you can nearly achieve the efficiency of assembly code combined with the structure of ALGOL or Modula-2. It is no wonder that C is easily the most popular language among topflight professional programmers.

The fact that you can often use C in place of assembly language is a major factor in its popularity among programmers. Assembly language uses a symbolic representation of the actual binary code that the computer executes directly. Each assembly-language operation maps into a single task for the computer to perform. Although assembly language gives programmers the potential to accomplish tasks with maximum flexibility and efficiency, it is notoriously difficult to work with when developing and debugging a program. Furthermore, since assembly language is unstructured, the final program tends to be spaghetti code— a tangled mess of jumps, calls, and indexes. This lack of structure makes assembly-language programs difficult to read, enhance, and maintain. Perhaps more important, assembly-language routines are not portable between machines with different central processing units (CPUs).

Initially, C was used for systems programming. A *systems program* forms a portion of the operating system of the computer or its support utilities. For example, the following are usually called systems programs:

- Operating systems

- Interpreters

- Editors

- Assembly programs

- Compilers

- Database managers

As C grew in popularity, many programmers began to use it to program all tasks because of its portability and efficiency. Because there are C compilers for almost all computers, you can take code written for one machine and compile and run it on another with few or no changes. This portability saves both time and money. C compilers also tend to produce very tight, fast object code—tighter and faster than that of most BASIC compilers, for example.

In addition, programmers use C in all types of programming tasks because they like it! C offers the speed of assembly language and the extensibility of FORTH, but few of the restrictions of Pascal or Modula-2. Each C programmer can create and maintain a unique library of functions that have been tailored to his or her own personality and that can be used in many different programs. Because it allows—indeed, encourages— separate compilation, C enables programmers to manage large projects easily, with minimal duplication of effort.

Compilers Versus Interpreters

The terms *compiler* and *interpreter* refer to the way in which a program is executed. In theory, any programming language can be either compiled or interpreted, but some languages are usually executed one way or the other. For example, BASIC is usually interpreted and C is usually compiled. (Recently, however, C interpreters have gained in popularity as debugging aids.) The way a program is executed is not defined by the language in which it is written. Interpreters and compilers are simply sophisticated programs that operate on your program source code.

An interpreter reads the source code of your program one line at a time, performing the specific instructions contained in that line. A compiler reads the entire program and converts it into *object code*, which is a translation of the program source code into a form that the computer can execute directly. Object code is also referred to as binary code or machine code. Once the program is compiled, a line of source code is no longer meaningful in the execution of your program.

auto	double	int	struct
break	else	long	switch
case	enum	register	typedef
char	extern	return	union
const	float	short	unsigned
continue	for	signed	void
default	goto	sizeof	volatile
do	if	static	while

Table 1-2.   A List of ANSI C Keywords

When you use an interpreter, it must be present each time you wish to run your program. For example, in BASIC, you have to execute the BASIC interpreter, load your program, and type **RUN** each time you want to use it. The BASIC interpreter examines your program one line at a time for correctness and then executes it. This slow process occurs every time the program runs. A compiler, by contrast, converts your program into object code that your computer can execute directly. Because the compiler translates your program one time, all you need to do is execute your program directly, usually just by typing its name. Therefore, compilation is a one-time cost, while interpreted code incurs this overhead each time a program runs.

The Form of a C Program

Table 1-2 lists the 32 keywords that, combined with the formal C syntax, form the C programming language. Of these, 27 were defined by the original version of C. These five were added by the ANSI committee: **enum, const, signed, void,** and **volatile.**

In addition, many C compilers have added several keywords that better exploit the memory organization of the 8088/8086 family of processors, and that support inter-language programming and interrupts. Here is a list of the most commonly used extended keywords:

asm	_cs	_ds	_es
_ss	cdecl	far	huge
interrupt	near	pascal	

Your compiler may also support other extensions that help it take better advantage of its specific environment.

All C keywords are lowercase. In C, uppercase and lowercase are different: **else** is a keyword; ELSE is not. You may not use a keyword for any other purpose in a C program—that is, you may not use it as a variable or function name.

All C programs consist of one or more functions. The only function that must be present is called **main( )**, which is the first function called when program execution begins. In well-written C code, **main( )** contains what is, in essence, an outline of what the program does. The outline is composed of function calls. Although **main( )** is technically not part of the C language, treat it as if it were. Don't try to use **main( )** as the name of a variable because you will probably confuse the compiler.

The general form of a C program is illustrated in Figure 1-1, where **f1( )** through **fN( )** represent user-defined functions.

The Library and Linking

Technically speaking, you can create a useful, functional C program that consists solely of the statements that you actually created. However, this is quite rare because C does not, within the actual definition of the language, provide any method of performing input/output (I/O) operations. As a result, most programs include calls to various functions contained in C's standard library.

All C compilers come with a standard C library of functions that perform most commonly needed tasks. The ANSI C standard specifies a minimal set of functions that will be contained in the library. However, your compiler will probably contain many other functions. For example, the ANSI C standard does not define any graphics functions, but your compiler will probably include some.

In some implementations of C, the library actually exists in one large file; in others it is contained in many smaller files, a setup that increases efficiency and practicality. However, for the sake of simplicity, this book uses the singular form in reference to the library.

The implementors of your C compiler have already written most of the general-purpose functions that you will use. When you call a function that is not part of your program, the C compiler "remembers" its name. Later, the *linker* combines the code you wrote with the object code already found in the standard library. This process is called *linking*. Some C compilers have their own linker while others use the standard linker supplied by your operating system.

The functions in the library are in *relocatable* format. This means that the memory addresses for the various machine-code instructions have not been absolutely defined — only offset information has been kept. When your program links with the functions in the standard library, these memory offsets are used to create the actual addresses used.

```
global declarations

return-type main(parameter list)
{
   statement sequence
}

return-type f1(parameter list)
{
   statement sequence
}

return-type f2(parameter list)
{
   statement sequence
}

     .
     .
     .

return-type fN(parameter list)
{
   statement sequence
}
```

Figure 1-1.   The general form of a C program

There are several technical manuals and books that explain this process in more detail. However, you do not need any further explanation of the actual relocation process to program in C.

Many of the functions that you will need as you write programs are in the standard library. They act as building blocks that you combine. If you write a function that you will use again and again, you can place it into a library too. Some compilers allow you to place your function in the standard library; others make you create an additional library. Either way, the code will be there for you to use repeatedly.

Remember that the ANSI standard only specifies a *minimum* standard library. Most compilers supply libraries that contain far more functions than those defined by ANSI. Moreover, some functions found in the original UNIX version of C are not defined by ANSI because they are redundant. This book covers all functions defined by ANSI as well as the most important and widely used functions defined by the old UNIX C standard. It also examines several widely used functions not defined by ANSI or the old UNIX standard. (Non-ANSI functions will be marked to avoid any confusion.)

Separate Compilation

Most short C programs are completely contained within one source file. However, as a program's length grows, so does its compile time (and long compile times make for short tempers). Hence, C allows a program to be contained in many files and lets you compile each file separately. Once you have compiled all files, they are linked, along with any library routines, to form the complete object code. The advantage of separate compilation is that if you change the code of one file, you do not need to recompile the entire program. On all but the most simple projects, this saves a substantial amount of time. (Strategies for separate compilation are covered in detail in Part Four.)

Compiling a C Program

Compiling a C program consists of these three steps:

1. Creating your program

2. Compiling your program

3. Linking your program with whatever functions are needed from the library

Some C compilers supply integrated programming environments that include an editor. With others, you must have a separate editor to create your program. Compilers only accept standard text files for input. For example, your compiler will not accept files created by certain word processors because they have control codes and nonprinting characters.

The exact method you use to compile your program will depend upon what C compiler you are using. Also, how linking is accomplished will vary between compilers and environments. Consult your users manual for details.

C's Memory Map

A compiled C program creates and uses four logically distinct regions of memory that serve specific functions. The first region is the memory that actually holds your program code. The next region is memory where global variables are stored. The remaining two regions are the stack and the heap. The *stack* is used for a great many things while your program executes. It holds the return address of function calls, arguments to functions, and local variables. It will also save the current state of the CPU. The *heap* is a region of free memory that your program can use via C's dynamic allocation functions for things like linked lists and trees.

The exact layout of your program may vary from compiler to compiler and environment to environment. For example, most C compilers for the 8086 family of processors have six different ways to organize memory because of the segmented memory architecture of the 8086. The memory models of the 8086 family of processors are discussed later in this book.

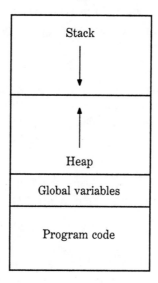

Figure 1-2.   A conceptual memory map of a C program

Although the exact physical layout of each of the four regions of memory differs among CPU types and C implementations, the diagram in Figure 1-2 shows conceptually how your C programs appear in memory.

A Review of Terms

The terms that follow will be used frequently throughout the remainder of this reference. You should be completely familiar with them.

Source Code
The text of a program that a user can read; commonly thought of as the program. The source code is input into the C compiler.

Object Code
Translation of the source code of a program into machine code, which the computer can read and execute directly. Object code is the input to the linker.

Linker
A program that links separately-compiled functions into one program. It combines the functions in the standard C library with the code that you wrote. The output of the linker is an executable program.

Library
The file containing the standard functions that your program may use. These functions include all I/O operations as well as other useful routines.

Compile Time
The events that occur while your program is being compiled. A common occurrence during compile time is a syntax error.

Run Time
The events that occur while your program is executing.

C Expressions

**T
W
O**

This chapter examines the most fundamental element of the C language: the expression. As you will see, expressions in C are substantially more general and more powerful than in most other computer languages. Expressions are formed from the atomic elements of C: data and operators. Data may be represented either by variables or by constants. C, like most other computer languages, supports a number of different types of data.

The Five Basic Data Types

There are five atomic data types in C: character, integer, floating-point, double floating-point, and valueless (**char**, **int**, **float**, **double**, and **void**, respectively). As you will see, all other data types in C are based upon one of these types. The size and range of these data types vary with each processor type and with the implementation of the C compiler. A character is generally 1 byte and an integer is often 2 bytes, but you cannot make this assumption if you want your programs to be portable to the widest range of computers. The ANSI standard only stipulates the minimal *range* of each data type, not its size in bytes.

The exact format of floating-point values will depend upon how they are implemented. Integers will generally correspond to the natural size of a word on the host computer. Values of type **char** are generally used to hold values defined by the ASCII character set. Values outside that range may be handled differently between C implementations.

The range of **float** and **double** types is given in digits of precision. The **float** and **double** magnitudes will depend upon the method used to represent the floating-point numbers. Whatever the method, the number is quite large. The ANSI standard specifies that the minimum range for a floating-point value is $1e-37$ to $1e+37$.

The type **void** either explicitly declares a function as returning no value or creates generic pointers. Both of these uses are discussed in subsequent chapters.

Type	Approximate Size in Bits	Minimal Range
char	8	−127 to 127
unsigned char	8	0 to 255
signed char	8	−127 to 127
int	16	−32,767 to 32,767
unsigned int	16	0 to 65,535
signed int	16	Same as **int**
short int	16	Same as **int**
unsigned short int	8	0 to 65,535
signed short int	8	Same as **short int**
long int	32	−2,147,483,647 to 2,147,483,647
signed long int	32	
unsigned long int	32	0 to 4,294,967,295
float	32	Six digits of precision
double	64	Ten digits of precision
long double	128	Ten digits of precision

Table 2-1.   All Data Types Defined by the ANSI Standard

Modifying the Basic Types

Except type **void**, the basic data types may have various modifiers preceding them. You use a *modifier* to alter the meaning of the base type to fit various situations more precisely. The list of modifiers is shown here:

    signed
    unsigned
    long
    short

You can apply the modifiers **signed**, **short**, **long**, and **unsigned** to character and integer base types. However, you may also apply **long** to **double**. (Note that the ANSI standard eliminates **long float** because it has the same meaning as **double**.)

Table 2-1 shows all data type combinations that adhere to the ANSI standard, along with their minimal ranges and approximate bit widths.

The use of **signed** on integers is redundant. However, it is allowed because the default integer declaration assumes a signed number. The most important use of **signed** is to modify **char** in implementations in which **char** is unsigned by default.

Some implementations may allow you to apply **unsigned** to the floating-point types (as in **unsigned double**). However, this reduces the portability of your code and is generally not recommended. Any additional or expanded types not defined by the ANSI standard will probably not be supported on every C implementation.

The difference between signed and unsigned integers is in the way that the high-order bit of the integer is interpreted. If you specify a signed integer, the C compiler generates code that assumes that the high-order bit of an integer is to be used as a *sign flag*. If the sign flag is 0, the number is positive; if it is 1, the number is negative.

In general, negative numbers are represented using the *two's complement* approach, which reverses all bits in the number (except the sign flag), adds 1 to this number, and sets the sign flag to 1.

Signed integers are important for a great many algorithms, but they only have half the absolute magnitude of their unsigned brothers.

For example, here is 32,767:

0 1 1 1 1 1 1 1   1 1 1 1 1 1 1 1

If the high-order bit were set to 1, the number would be interpreted as −1. However, if you declare this to be an **unsigned int**, the number becomes 65,535 when the high-order bit is set to 1.

Identifier Names

The ANSI C standard calls the names of variables, functions, labels, and various other user-defined objects *identifiers*. These identifiers can vary from one to several characters. The first character must be a letter or an underscore and subsequent characters must be either letters, numbers or underscores. Here are some correct and incorrect identifier names:

Correct	Incorrect
count	1count
test23	hi!there
high_balance	high...balance

The ANSI standard states that identifiers may be of any length, but at least the first six characters must be significant if the identifier will be involved in an external link process. These identifiers, called *external names*, include function names and global variables that are shared between files. If the identifier is not used in an external link process, the first 31 characters will be significant. This type of identifier is called an *internal name*. Consult the user manual to see exactly how many significant characters are allowed for the compiler that you are using.

An identifier name may be longer than the number of significant characters recognized by the compiler. However, characters past the limit will be ignored. For example, if your compiler recognizes 31 significant digits, the following identifiers will appear the same to it:

```
overly_long_identifiers_are_cumbersome
overly_long_identifiers_are_cumbersome_to_use
```

In C, upper- and lowercase are treated as distinct. Hence, **count**, **Count**, and **COUNT** are three separate identifiers. In some environments, the case of function names and global variables may be ignored if the linker is not case sensitive (but most contemporary environments support case-sensitive linking).

An identifier cannot be the same as a C keyword, and should not have the same name as functions that either you wrote or that are in the C library.

Variables

As you probably know, a *variable* is a named location in memory that is used to hold a value that may be modified by the program. All C variables must be declared before they can be used. The general form of a declaration is

type variable _ list;

Here, *type* must be a valid C data type plus any modifiers and *variable _ list* may consist of one or more identifier names with comma separators. Here are some declarations:

```
int i,j,l;

short int si;

unsigned int ui;

double balance, profit, loss;
```

Remember, in C the name of a variable has nothing to do with its type.

Where Variables Are Declared

Variables will be declared in three basic places: inside functions, in the definition of function parameters, and outside of all functions. These are local variables, formal parameters, and global variables.

Local Variables

Variables that are declared inside a function are called *local variables*. In some C literature, these variables are referred to as *automatic* variables, because in C you can use the keyword **auto** to declare them. This book uses the more common term local variable. Local variables may be referenced only by statements that are inside the block in which the variables are declared. In other words, local variables are not known outside their own code block. Remember, a block of code begins with an opening curly brace and terminates with a closing curly brace.

Local variables exist only while the block of code in which they are declared is executing. That is, a local variable is created upon entry into its block and destroyed upon exit.

The most common code block in which local variables are declared is the function. For example, consider the following two functions:

```
void func1(void)
{
  int x;

  x = 10;
}
void func2(void)
{
  int x;

  x = -199;
}
```

The integer variable **x** is declared twice, once in **func1( )** and once in **func2( )**. The **x** in **func1( )** has no bearing on or relationship to the **x** in **func2( )**. This is because each **x** is only known to the code within the same block as the variable declaration.

The C language contains the keyword **auto**, which you can use to declare local variables. However, since all nonglobal variables are, by default, assumed to be **auto**, this keyword is virtually never used. Hence, the examples in this book will not use it. (It has been said that **auto** was included in C to provide for source-level compatibility with its predecessor B.)

Most programmers declare all the variables used by a function immediately after the function's opening curly brace and before any other statements. However, you may declare local variables within any code block. The block defined by a function is simply a special case. For example,

```
void f(void)
{
  int t;

  scanf("%d",&t);

  if(t==1) {
    char s[80];   /* this is created only upon
                      entry into this block */
    printf("enter name:");
    gets(s);
    /* do something ... */
  }
}
```

Here, the local variable **s** is created upon entry into the **if** code block and destroyed upon exit. Furthermore, **s** is known only within the **if** block and may not be referenced elsewhere—even in other parts of the function that contains it.

One advantage to declaring a local variable within a conditional block is that memory for the variable will only be allocated if needed. This is because local variables do not come into existence until the block in which they are declared is entered. You might need to worry about this when producing code for dedicated controllers (like a garage door opener that responds to a digital security code) in which RAM is in short supply, for example.

Declaring variables within the block of code that uses them also helps prevent unwanted side effects. Since the variable does not exist outside the block in which it is declared, it cannot be accidentally altered. However, when each function performs one well-defined, logical task, you may not need to "protect" variables inside a function from the code that makes up the function. This is why the variables used by a function are generally declared at the start of the function.

Remember that you must declare all local variables at the start of the block in which they are defined, prior to any program statements. For example, the following function is technically incorrect and will not compile on most compilers.

```
/* this function is in error */
void f(void)
{
  int i;

  i = 10;

  int j;   /* this line will cause an error */

  j = 20;
}
```

However, if you had declared **j** within its own block of code or before the **i = 10** statement, the function would have been accepted. For example, either version shown here is syntactically correct:

```
/* defined j inside its own code block */
void f(void)
{
  int i;

  i = 10;

  {   /* define j in its own block */
    int j;

    j = 20;
  }
}
/* define j at start of function block */
void f(void)
{
  int i;
  int j;

  i = 10;
  j = 20;
}
```

Because local variables are created and destroyed with each entry and exit from the block in which they are declared, their content is lost once the block is left. This is especially important to remember when calling a function. When a function is called, its local variables are created, and upon its return they are destroyed. This means that local variables cannot retain their values between calls. (However, you can direct the compiler to retain their values by using the **static** modifier.)

Unless otherwise specified, local variables are stored on the stack. The fact that the stack is a dynamic and changing region of memory explains why local variables cannot, in general, hold their values between function calls.

You can initialize a local variable to some known value. This value will be assigned to the variable each time the block of code in which it is declared is entered. For example, the following program prints the number 10 ten times:

```c
#include "stdio.h"

void f(void);

void main(void)
{
  int i;

  for(i=0; i<10; i++)  f();
}

void f(void)
{
  int j = 10;

  printf("%d ", j);

  j++;  /* this line has no lasting effect */
}
```

Formal Parameters

If a function is to use arguments, it must declare variables that will accept the values of the arguments. These variables are called the *formal parameters* of the function. They behave like any other local variables inside the function. As shown in the following program fragment, their declarations occur after the function name and inside parentheses:

```c
/* Return 1 if c is part of string s; 0 otherwise */
is_in(char *s, char c)
{
  while(*s)
    if(*s==c) return 1;
    else s++;

  return 0;
}
```

The function **is_in( )** has two parameters: **s** and **c**. This function returns 1 if the character specified in **c** is contained within the string **s**; 0 if it is not.

You must tell C what type of variables the formal parameters are by declaring them as just shown. Then you may use them inside the function as normal local variables. Keep in mind that, as local variables, they are also dynamic and are destroyed upon exit from the function.

Make sure that the formal parameters you declare are the same type as the arguments you use to call the function. If there is a type mismatch, unexpected results can occur. Unlike many other languages, C will generally do something even in unusual circumstances, even if it is not what you want. There are few run-time errors and no bounds checking. As the programmer, you have to make sure that type mismatch errors do not occur.

The ANSI standard provides for *function prototypes,* which you can use to help verify that the arguments used to call a function are compatible with the parameters. However, you must still explicitly include function prototypes in your program to receive this added benefit. (Function prototyping is discussed in depth in Chapter 6.)

As with local variables, you may make assignments to a function's formal parameters or use them in any allowable C expression. Even though these variables receive the value of the arguments passed to the function, you can use them like any other local variable.

Global Variables

Unlike local variables, *global variables* are known throughout the program and may be used by any piece of code. Also, they will hold their value throughout the program execution. You create global variables by declaring them outside of any function. Any expression may access them, regardless of what block of code that expression is in.

In the following program, the variable **count** has been declared outside of all functions. Although its declaration occurs before the **main( )** function, you could have placed it anywhere before its first use as long as it was not in a function. However, it is best to declare global variables at the top of the program.

```
#include "stdio.h"

int count;   /* count is global  */

void func1(void);
void func2(void);

void main(void)
{
  count = 100;
  func1();
}

void func1(void)
{
  int temp;

  temp = count;
  func2();
  printf("count is %d", count); /* will print 100 */
}

void func2(void)
{
  int count;

  for(count=1; count<10; count++)
    putchar('.');
}
```

Look closely at this program. Notice that although neither **main( )** nor **func1( )** has declared the variable **count**, both may use it. **func2( )**, however, has declared a local variable called **count**. When **func2( )** references **count**, it references only its local variable, not the global one. If a global variable and a local variable have the same name, all references to that variable name inside the code block where the local variable is declared will refer to that local variable and have no effect on the global variable. This can be convenient, but forgetting this can cause your program to act strangely, even though it looks correct.

Storage for global variables is in a fixed region of memory set aside for this purpose by the C compiler. Global variables are helpful when many functions in your program use the same data. You should avoid using unnecessary global variables, however. They take up memory the entire time your program is executing, not just when they are needed. In addition, using a global where a local variable would do makes a function less general because it relies on something that must be defined outside itself. Finally, using a large number of global variables can lead to program errors because of unknown and unwanted side effects. This is evidenced in standard BASIC, where all variables are global. A major problem in developing large programs is the accidental changing of a variable's value because it was used elsewhere in the program. This can happen in C if you use too many global variables in your programs.

One of the principal reasons for a structured language is to compartmentalize code and data. In C, compartmentalization is achieved through the use of local variables and functions. For example, Figure 2-1 shows two ways to write **mul( )** — a simple function that computes the product of two integers.

Both functions return the product of the variables **x** and **y**. However, you can use the generalized, or *parameterized,* version to return the product of *any* two numbers, while you can use the specific version to find only the product of the global variables **x** and **y**.

Access Type Modifiers

The ANSI standard introduced two new type modifiers that control how variables may be accessed or modified. These modifiers are **const** and

```
General                  Specific
                         int x, y;
mul(int x, int y)        mul(void)
{                        {
    return(x*y);             return(x*y);
}                        }
```

Figure 2-1.   Two ways to write **mul( )**

volatile. They must precede the type modifiers and the type names that they modify.

const

Variables of type **const** may not be changed by your program. (A **const** variable can be given an initial value, however.) The compiler can place variables of this type into read-only memory (ROM). For example,

```
const int a=10;
```

creates an integer variable called **a** with an initial value of 10 that your program may not modify. However, you can use the variable **a** in other types of expressions. A **const** variable will receive its value either from an explicit initialization or by some hardware-dependent means.

Variables of type **const** can protect the objects pointed to by the arguments to a function from being modified by that function. That is, when a pointer is passed to a function, that function can modify the actual variable pointed to by the pointer. However, if the pointer is specified as **const** in the parameter declaration, the function code won't be able to modify what it points to. For example, the **sp＿to＿dash( )** function in the following program prints a dash for each space in its string argument. That is, the string "this is a test" will be printed as "this-is-a-test". The use of **const** in the parameter declaration ensures that the code inside the function cannot modify the object pointed to by the parameter.

```
#include "stdio.h"

void sp_to_dash(const char *str);

void main(void)
{
  sp_to_dash("this is a test");
}

void sp_to_dash(const char *str)
{
```

```
  while(*str) {
    if(*str==' ') printf("%c", '-');
    else printf("%c", *str);
    str++;
  }
}
```

If you had written **sp_to_dash( )** in such a way that the string would be modified, it will not compile. For example, if you had coded **sp_to_dash( )** as follows, you will get an error:

```
/* this is wrong */
void sp_to_dash(const char *str)
{
  while(*str) {
    if(*str==' ') *str = '-'; /* can't do this */
    printf("%c", *str);
    str++;
  }
}
```

Many functions in the C standard library use **const** in their parameter declarations. For example, the **strlen( )** function has this prototype:

int strlen(const char *str);

Specifying **str** as **const** ensures that **strlen( )** will not modify the string pointed to by **str**. In general, when a standard library function has no need to modify an object pointed to by a calling argument, it is declared as **const**.

You can also use **const** to verify that your program does not modify a variable. Remember, a variable of type **const** can be modified by something outside your program. For example, a hardware device may set its value. However, by declaring a variable as **const**, you can prove that any changes to that variable occur because of external events.

Volatile

The modifier **volatile** tells the compiler that a variable's value may be changed in ways not explicitly specified by the program. For example, a global variable's address may be passed to the operating system's clock routine and used to hold the real time of the system. In this situation, the contents of the variable are altered without any explicit assignment statements in the program. This is important because most C compilers automatically optimize certain expressions by assuming that a variable's content is unchanging if it does not occur on the left side of an assignment statement; thus, it may not be reexamined each time it is referenced. Also, some compilers change the order of evaluation of an expression during the compilation process. The **volatile** modifier prevents these changes.

You can use **const** and **volatile** together. For example, if 0x30 is assumed to be the value of a port that is changed by external conditions only, the following declaration would prevent any possibility of accidental side effects:

```
const volatile unsigned char *port=0x30;
```

Storage Class Type Specifiers

There are four storage class specifiers supported by C:

> extern
> static
> register
> auto

These specifiers tell the compiler how to store the subsequent variable. The storage specifier precedes the rest of the variable declaration. Its general form is

> *storage_specifier type var_name;*

extern

Because C allows separately compiled modules of a large program to be linked to speed up compilation and help manage large projects, there must be some way of telling all the files about the global variables required by the program. Remember, you can declare a global variable only once. If you declared two global variables with the same name inside the same file, your C compiler might print an error message like "duplicate variable name" or might simply choose one variable. The same problem occurs if you simply declare all the global variables needed by your program in each file. Although the compiler does not issue any error messages at compile time, you are actually trying to create two (or more) copies of each variable. The trouble starts when you attempt to link your modules. The linker displays an error message such as "duplicate label" because it does not know which variable to use. The solution is to declare all of your global variables in one file and use **extern** declarations in the other, as in Figure 2-2.

In File 2, the global variable list was copied from File 1 and the **extern** specifier was added to the declarations. The **extern** specifier tells the compiler that the variable types and names that follow it have been declared elsewhere. In other words, **extern** lets the compiler know what the types and names are for these global variables without actually

```
File 1                  File 2
int x, y;               extern int x, y;
char ch;                extern char ch;
main(void)              func22(void)
{                       {
    .                       x = y/10;
    .                   }
    .
}                       func23( )
                        {
func1( )                    y = 10
{                       }
   x = 123;
}
```

Figure 2-2.   Using global variables in separately compiled modules creating storage for them again. When the linker links the two modules, all references to the external variables are resolved.

When you use a global variable inside a function that is in the same file as the declaration for the global variable, you can use **extern**, as shown here:

```
int first, last;  /* global definition of first
                      and last */

void main(void)
{
  extern int first;  /* optional use of the
                        extern declaration */
    .
    .
    .
}
```

Although **extern** variable declarations can occur inside the same file as the global declaration, they are not necessary. If the C compiler finds a variable that has not been declared, the compiler checks if it matches any of the global variables. If it does, the compiler assumes that the global variable is being referenced.

static Variables

static variables are permanent variables within their own function or file. Unlike global variables, they are not known outside their function or file, but they maintain their values between calls. This feature makes them useful when you write generalized functions and function libraries that other programmers may use. **static** has different effects upon local variables than upon global ones.

static Local Variables

When you apply the **static** modifier to a local variable, the compiler creates permanent storage for it, much as it creates storage for a global variable. The key difference between a **static** local variable and a global variable is that the **static** local variable remains known only to the block in which it is declared. In simple terms, a **static** local variable is a local variable that retains its value between function calls.

static local variables are very important to the creation of standalone functions because several types of routines must preserve a value between calls. If **static** variables were not allowed, globals would have to be used, opening the door to possible side effects. A function that requires a **static** local variable is a number-series generator that produces a new number based on the last one. You could declare a global variable for this value. However, each time the function is used in a program, you would have to declare that global variable and make sure that it did not conflict with any other global variables already declared. Also, using a global variable would make this function difficult to place in a function library. The better solution is to declare the variable that holds the generated number to be **static**, as in this program fragment:

```
series(void)
{
  static int series_num;

  series_num = series_num+23;
  return(series_num);
}
```

In this example, the variable **series_num** stays in existence between function calls, instead of coming and going the way a normal local variable would. This means that each call to **series( )** can produce a new member of the series based on the preceding number without declaring that variable globally.

You can give a **static** local variable an initialization value. This value is assigned only once—not each time the block of code is entered, as with normal local variables. For example, this version of **series( )** initializes **series_num** to 100:

```
series(void)
{
  static int series_num = 100;

  series_num = series_num+23;
  return(series_num);
}
```

As the function now stands, the series will always begin with the value 123. While this is acceptable for some applications, most series generators need to let the user specify the starting point. One way to give **series_num** a user-specified value is to make **series_num** a global variable and then set its value as specified. However, not defining **series_num** as global was the point of making it **static**. This leads to the second use of **static**.

static Global Variables

Applying the specifier **static** to a global variable instructs the compiler to create a global variable that is known only to the file in which you declared the **static** global variable. This means that even though the variable is global, routines in other files may have no knowledge of it or alter its contents directly, keeping it free from side effects. For the few situations where a local **static** cannot do the job, you can create a small file that contains only the functions that need the global **static** variable, separately compile that file, and use it without fear of side effects.

To illustrate a global **static**, the series generator example from the previous section is recoded so that a seed value initializes the series through a call to a second function called **series_start( )**. The entire file containing **series( )**, **series_start( )**, and **series_num** is shown here:

```
/* this must all be in one file - preferably by itself */

static int series_num;
void series_start(int seed);
int series(void);

series(void)
{
  series_num = series_num+23;
  return(series_num);
}

/* initialize series_num */
void series_start(int seed)
{
  series_num = seed;
}
```

Calling **series_start( )** with some known integer value initializes the series generator. After that, calls to **series( )** generate the next element in the series.

To review: The names of local **static** variables are known only to the function or block of code in which they are declared. The names of global **static** variables are known only to the file in which they reside. If you place the **series( )** and **series_start( )** functions in a library, you can use the functions but cannot reference the variable **series_num**, which is hidden from the rest of the code in your program. In fact, you can even declare and use another variable called **series_num** in your program (in another file, of course). In essence, the **static** modifier permits variables that are known to the functions that need them, without confusing other functions.

static variables enable you to hide portions of your program from other portions. This can be a tremendous advantage when you are trying to manage a very large and complex program. The **static** storage specifier lets you create very general functions that can go into libraries for later use.

register Variables

The **register** storage specifier traditionally applied only to variables of type **int** and **char**. However, the ANSI standard has broadened its definition so that you can apply **register** to any variable.

Originally, the **register** specifier requested that the C compiler keep the value of a variable declared with this specifier in the register of the CPU rather than in memory, where normal variables are stored. This meant that operations on a **register** variable could occur much faster than on a variable stored in memory because the value of the variable was actually held in the CPU and did not require a memory access to determine or modify its value.

However, since the ANSI standard now allows you to modify any type of variable with **register**, it has changed the definition of what **register** does. The ANSI standard simply states "that access to the object be as fast as possible." In practice, characters and integers are still stored in registers in the CPU. Larger objects like arrays obviously cannot be stored in a register, but they may still receive preferential treatment by the compiler. Depending upon the implementation of the C compiler and its operating environment, **register** variables may be handled in any way deemed fit by the compiler's implementor. The ANSI standard also allows a compiler to ignore the **register** specifier and treat variables modified by it as if they weren't, but this is seldom done in practice.

You can only apply the **register** specifier to local variables and to the formal parameters in a function. Hence, global **register** variables are not allowed. Here is an example of how to declare a **register** variable of type **int** and use it to control a loop. This function computes the result of M^e for integers:

```
int_pwr(int m,  register int e)
{
  register int temp;

  temp = 1;

  for(; e; e--) temp = temp * m;
  return temp;
}
```

In this example, both **e** and **temp** are declared as **register** variables because both are used within the loop. The fact that **register** variables are optimized for speed makes them ideal for loop control. Generally, **register** variables are used where they will do the most good, that is, in places where many references will be made to the same variable. This is important because you can declare any number of variables as being of type **register**, but not all will receive the same access speed optimization.

The number of register variables optimized for speed allowed within any one code block is determined by both the environment and the specific implementation of C. You don't have to worry about declaring too many **register** variables because the C compiler automatically transforms **register** variables into nonregister variables when the limit is reached. (This ensures portability of C code across a broad line of processors.)

Throughout this book, most loop control variables will be of type **register**. Usually at least two **register** variables of type **char** or **int** can actually be held in the registers of the CPU. Because environments vary widely, consult your compiler's user manual to determine if you can apply any other types of optimization options.

Because a **register** variable may be stored in a register of the CPU, **register** variables do not have addresses. That is, you may not find the address of a **register** variable using the **&** operator (discussed later in this chapter).

Although the ANSI standard has broadened the description of **register**, in practice, it still generally has a meaningful effect only with integer and character types. Thus, you should probably not count on substantial speed improvements for other variable types.

Variable Initializations

You can give most variables in C a value as you declare them by placing an equal sign and a constant after the variable name. The general form of initialization is

type variable_name = constant;

Some examples are

```
char ch = 'a';
int first = 0;
float balance = 123.23
```

Global and **static** global variables are initialized only at the start of the program. Local variables (including **static** local variables) are initialized each time the block in which they are declared is entered. Local and **register** variables that are not initialized have unknown values before the first assignment is made to them.

Constants

In C, *constants* refer to fixed values that the program may not alter. C constants can be of any of the basic data types. The way each constant is represented depends upon its type. Character constants are enclosed between single quotes. For example 'a' and '%' are both character constants. The ANSI standard also defines multi-byte characters (used mostly in foreign language environments).

Integer constants are specified as numbers without fractional components. For example, 10 and −100 are integer constants. Floating-point constants require the decimal point followed by the number's fractional component. For example, 11.123 is a floating-point constant. C also allows you to use scientific notation for floating-point numbers.

There are two floating-point types: **float** and **double**. There are also several variations of the basic types that you can generate using the type modifiers. By default, the C compiler fits a numeric constant into the smallest compatible data type that will hold it. Therefore, 10 is **int** by default, but 60,000 is **unsigned** and 100,000 is **long**. Even though the value 10 could fit into a character type, the compiler will not cross type boundaries. The only exception to the smallest type rule are floating-point constants, which are assumed to be **double**s.

For most programs you will write, the compiler defaults are adequate. However, you can specify precisely the type of numeric constant you want by using a suffix. For floating-point types, if you follow the number with an F, the number is treated as a **float**. If you follow it with an L, the number becomes a **long double**. For integer types, the U suffix stands for **unsigned** and the L for **long**. Here are some examples:

Data type	Constant examples
int	1 123 21000 −234
long int	35000L −34L
short int	10 −12 90
unsigned int	10000U 987U 40000
float	123.23F 4.34e−3F
double	123.23 12312333 −0.9876324
long double	1001.2L

Hexadecimal and Octal Constants

It is sometimes easier to use a number system based on 8 or 16 rather than 10 (our standard decimal system). The number system based on 8 is called *octal* and uses the digits 0 through 7. In octal, the number 10 is the same as 8 in decimal. The base 16 number system is called *hexadecimal* and uses the digits 0 through 9 plus the letters A through F, which stand for 10, 11, 12, 13, 14, and 15, respectively. For example, the hexadecimal number 10 is 16 in decimal. Because these two number systems are used frequently, C allows you to specify integer constants in hexadecimal or octal instead of decimal. A hexadecimal constant must consist of a 0x followed by the constant in hexadecimal form. An octal constant begins with a 0. Here are some examples:

```
int hex = 0x80;    /* 128 in decimal */
int oct = 012;     /* 10 in decimal */
```

String Constants

C supports one other type of constant: the string. A *string* is a set of characters enclosed in double quotes. For example, "this is a test" is a string. You have seen examples of strings in some of the **printf( )** statements in the sample programs. Although C allows you to define string constants, it does not formally have a string data type.

You must not confuse strings with characters. A single character constant is enclosed in single quotes, as 'a'. However, "a" is a string containing only one letter.

Backslash Character Constants

Enclosing character constants in single quotes works for most printing characters. A few, however, such as the carriage return, are impossible to enter into a string from the keyboard. For this reason, C includes the special backslash character constants.

C supports several special backslash codes (listed in Table 2-2) so that you may easily enter these special characters as constants. You should use the backslash codes instead of their ASCII equivalents to help ensure portability.

For example, the following program outputs a new line and a tab and then prints the string **this is a test.**

```
#include "stdio.h"

main()
{
  printf("\n\tThis is a test");
}
```

Operators

C is very rich in built-in operators. (In fact, C places more significance on operators than do most other computer languages.) C defines four classes of operators: arithmetic, relational, logical, and bitwise. In addition, C has some special operators for particular tasks.

The Assignment Operator

In C, you can use the assignment operator within any valid C expression. This is not the case with most computer languages (including

Code	Meaning
\b	Backspace
\f	Form feed
\n	New line
\r	Carriage return
\t	Horizontal tab
\"	Double quote
\'	Single quote
\0	Null
\\	Backslash
\v	Vertical tab
\a	Alert
\N	Octal constant (where N is an octal constant)
\xN	Hexadecimal constant (where N is a hexadecimal constant)

Table 2-2.   Backslash Codes

Pascal, BASIC, and FORTRAN), which treat the assignment operator as a special case statement. The general form of the assignment operator is

variable_name = expression;

where an expression may be as simple as a single constant or as complex as you require. Like BASIC and FORTRAN, C uses a single equal sign to indicate assignment (unlike Pascal or Modula-2, which use the := construct). The *target,* or left part, of the assignment must be a variable or a pointer, not a function or a constant.

Frequently in literature on C and in compiler error messages you will see these two terms: lvalue and rvalue. Simply put, an *lvalue* is any object that can occur on the left side of an assignment statement. For all practical purposes, "lvalue" means "variable." The term *rvalue* refers to expressions on the right side of an assignment, and simply means the value of an expression.

Type Conversion in Assignments

When variables of one type are mixed with variables of another type, a *type conversion* will occur. In an assignment statement, the *type conversion rule* is easy: The value of the right side (expression side) of the assignment is converted to the type of the left side (target variable), as illustrated here:

```
int x;
char ch;
float  f;

void func(void)
{
  ch = x;    /* line 1 */
  x = f;     /* line 2 */
  f = ch;    /* line 3 */
  f = x;     /* line 4 */
}
```

In line 1, the left high-order bits of the integer variable **x** are lopped off, leaving **ch** with the lower 8 bits. If **x** were between 256 and 0, **ch** and **x** would have identical values. Otherwise, the value of **ch** would reflect only the lower-order bits of **x**. In line 2, **x** will receive the nonfractional part of **f**. In line 3, **f** will convert the 8-bit integer value stored in **ch** to the same value in the floating-point format. This also happens in line 4, except that **f** will convert a 16-bit integer value into floating-point format.

When converting from integers to characters and long integers to integers, the appropriate amount of high-order bits will be removed. In many environments, this means that 8 bits will be lost when going from an integer to a character and 16 bits will be lost when going from a long integer to an integer.

Table 2-3 summarizes these assignment type conversions. Remember that the conversion of an **int** to a **float**, or a **float** to a **double**, and so on, does not add any precision or accuracy. These kinds of conversions only change the form in which the value is represented. In addition, some C compilers (and processors) always treat a **char** variable as positive, no matter what value it has, when converting it to an **int** or **float**. Other compilers treat **char** variable values greater than 127 as negative numbers when converting. Generally speaking, you should use **char** variables for characters, and use **int**s, **short int**s, or **signed char**s when needed to avoid possible portability problems.

To use Table 2-3 to make a conversion not shown, simply convert one type at a time until you finish. For example, to convert from **double** to **int**, first convert from **double** to **float** and then from **float** to **int**.

Computer languages such as Pascal prohibit automatic type conversions. However, C was designed to simplify the life of the programmer by allowing work to be done in C rather than assembler. To replace assembler, C has to allow such type conversions.

Target Type	Expression Type	Possible Info Loss
signed char	char	If value > 127, target is negative
char	short int	High-order 8 bits
char	int	High-order 8 bits
char	long int	High-order 24 bits
int	long int	High-order 16 bits
int	float	Fractional part and possibly more
float	double	Precision, result rounded
double	long double	Precision, result rounded

Table 2-3.   Common Type Conversions (assuming a 16-bit word)

Operator	Action
−	Subtraction, also unary minus
+	Addition
*	Multiplication
/	Division
%	Modulus division
− −	Decrement
+ +	Increment

Table 2-4.   Arithmetic Operators

Multiple Assignments

C allows you to assign many variables the same value by using multiple assignments in a single statement. For example, this program fragment assigns **x**, **y**, and **z** the value 0:

```
x = y = z = 0;
```

In professional programs, variables are frequently assigned common values using this method.

Arithmetic Operators

Table 2-4 lists C's arithmetic operators. In C, the operators +, −, *, and / work as they do in most other computer languages. You can apply them to almost any built-in data type allowed by C. When you apply / to an integer or character, any remainder will be truncated. For example, 5/2 will equal 2 in integer division.

The modulus operator % also works in C as it does in other languages, yielding the remainder of an integer division. However, you cannot use it on floating-point types. The following code fragment illustrates %:

```
int x, y;

x = 5;
y = 2;
```

```
printf("%d", x/y);    /* will display 2 */
printf("%d", x%y);    /* will display 1, the remainder of
                         the integer division */

x = 1;
y = 2;

printf("%d %d", x/y, x%y); /*  will display 0 1 */
```

The last line prints a 0 and a 1 because 1/2 in integer division is 0 with a remainder of 1.

The unary minus multiplies its single operand by -1. That is, any number preceded by a minus sign switches its sign.

Increment and Decrement

C includes two useful operators not generally found in other computer languages. These are the increment and decrement operators, $+ +$ and $- -$. The operator $+ +$ adds 1 to its operand, and $- -$ subtracts one. In other words:

```
x = x+1;
```

is the same as

```
++x;
```

and

```
x = x-1;
```

is the same as

```
x--;
```

Both the increment and decrement operators may either precede or follow the operand. For example,

```
x = x+1;
```

can be written

```
++x;
```

or

```
x++;
```

There is, however, a difference when you use these operators in an expression. When an increment or decrement operator precedes its operand, C performs the increment or decrement operation before using the value of the operand. If the operator follows its operand, C uses the value of the operand before incrementing or decrementing it. For instance,

```
x = 10;
y = ++x;
```

sets **y** to 11. However, if you write the code as

```
x = 10;
y = x++;
```

y is set to 10. Either way, **x** is set to 11; the difference is in when it happens.

Most C compilers produce very fast, efficient object code for increment and decrement operations—code that is better than that generated by using the equivalent assignment statement. For this reason, you should use the increment and decrement operators when you can.

Here is the precedence of the arithmetic operators:

highest	+ + − −
	−
	* / %
lowest	+ −

Relational Operators

Operator	Action
>	Greater than
> =	Greater than or equal
<	Less than
< =	Less than or equal
= =	Equal
! =	Not equal

Logical Operators

Operator	Action
&&	AND
‖	OR
!	NOT

Table 2-5.   Relational and Logical Operators

Operators on the same level of precedence are evaluated by the compiler from left to right. Of course, you can use parentheses to alter the order of evaluation. C treats parentheses as do virtually all other computer languages. Parentheses force an operation, or set of operations, to have a higher level of precedence.

Relational and Logical Operators

In the term *relational operator*, relational refers to the relationships that values can have with one another. In the term *logical operator*, logical refers to the ways these relationships can be connected. Because the relational and logical operators often work together, they are discussed together here.

The idea of **true** and **false** underlies the concepts of relational and logical operators. In C, **true** is any value other than zero. **False** is zero. Expressions that use relational or logical operators return zero for **false** and 1 for **true**.

Table 2-5 shows the relational and logical operators. The truth table for the logical operators is shown here using 1's and 0's.

p	q	p && q	p ‖ q	!p
0	0	0	0	1
0	1	0	1	1
1	1	1	1	0
1	0	0	1	0

Both the relational and logical operators are lower in precedence than the arithmetic operators. That is, an expression like 10 > 1+12 is evaluated as if it were written 10 > (1+12). Of course, the result is false.

You can combine several operations together into one expression, as shown here:

$$10>5 \;\&\&\; !(10<9) \;\|\; 3<=4$$

In this case, the result is true.

Although C does not contain an exclusive OR (XOR) logical operator, you can easily create a function that performs this task using the other logical operators. The outcome of an XOR operation is true if and only if one operand (but not both) is true. The following program contains the function **xor( )**, which returns the outcome of an exclusive OR operation performed on the two arguments:

```
#include "stdio.h"

int xor(int a, int b);

void main(void)
{
  printf("%d", xor(1, 0));
  printf("%d", xor(1, 1));
  printf("%d", xor(0, 1));
  printf("%d", xor(0, 0));
}

/* Perform a logical XOR operation using the
   two arguments. */
xor(int a, int b)
{
  return (a ¦¦ b) && !(a && b);
}
```

The following table shows the relative precedence of the relational and logical operators:

highest   !

> > = < < =

= = ! =

&&

lowest ||

As with arithmetic expressions, you can use parentheses to alter the natural order of evaluation in a relational and/or logical expression. For example,

!0 && 0 || 0

is false. However, when you add parentheses to the same expression, as shown here, the result is true.

!(0 && 0) || 0

Remember, all relational and logical expressions produce a result of either 0 or 1. Therefore, the following program fragment is not only correct, but will print the number 1 on the display:

```
int x;

x = 100;
printf("%d", x>10);
```

Bitwise Operators

Unlike many other languages, C supports a full complement of bitwise operators. Since C was designed to take the place of assembly language for most programming tasks, it needed to be able to support many operations that can be done in assembler. *Bitwise operation* refers to testing, setting, or shifting the actual bits in a byte or word, which correspond to C's standard **char** and **int** data types and variants. You cannot use bitwise operations on **float, double, long double, void,** or other more complex types. Table 2-6 lists the operators that apply to bitwise operations. These operations are applied to the individual bits of the operands.

The bitwise AND, OR, and NOT (one's complement) are governed by the same truth table as their logical equivalents, except that they work bit by bit. The exclusive OR (^) has the truth table shown here:

p	q	p ^ q
0	0	0
1	0	1
1	1	0
0	1	1

As the table indicates, the outcome of an XOR is **true** only if exactly one of the operands is **true**; otherwise, it is **false**.

Bitwise operations most often find application in device drivers— such as modem programs, disk file routines, and printer routines— because the bitwise operations mask off certain bits, such as parity. (The parity bit confirms that the rest of the bits in the byte are unchanged. It is usually the high-order bit in each byte.)

Think of the bitwise AND as a way to clear a bit. That is, any bit that is 0 in either operand causes the corresponding bit in the outcome

Operator	Action
&	AND
¦	OR
^	Exclusive OR (XOR)
~	One's complement
> >	Shift right
< <	Shift left

Table 2-6.   Bitwise Operators

to be set to 0. For example, the following function reads a character from the modem port using the function **read_modem( )** and resets the parity bit to 0:

```
char get_char_from_modem(void)
{
  char ch;

  ch = read_modem(); /* get a character from the
                        modem port */
  return(ch & 127);
}
```

Parity is often indicated by the eighth bit, which is set to 0 by ANDing it with a byte that has bits 1 through 7 set to 1 and bit 8 set to 0. The expression **ch & 127** means to AND together the bits in **ch** with the bits that make up the number 127. The net result is that the eighth bit of **ch** is set to 0. In the following example, assume that **ch** had received the character "A" and had the parity bit set:

Parity bit

```
1 1 0 0 0 0 0 1        ch containing an "A" with parity set
0 1 1 1 1 1 1 1        127 in binary
& _____          do bitwise AND
0 1 0 0 0 0 0 1        "A" without parity
```

The bitwise OR, as the reverse of AND, can be used to set a bit. Any bit that is set to 1 in either operand causes the corresponding bit in the outcome to be set to 1. For example, the following is 128 | 3:

```
1 0 0 0 0 0 0 0    128 in binary
0 0 0 0 0 0 1 1    3 in binary
| _____      bitwise OR
1 0 0 0 0 0 1 1    result
```

An exclusive OR, usually abbreviated XOR, will set a bit on if and only if the bits being compared are different. For example, 127 ˆ 120 is

```
0 1 1 1 1 1 1 1      127 in binary
0 1 1 1 1 0 0 0      120 in binary
ˆ_____         bitwise XOR
0 0 0 0 0 1 1 1      result
```

Remember, relational and logical operators always produce a result that is either 0 or 1, whereas the similar bitwise operations may produce any arbitrary value in accordance with the specific operation. In other words, bitwise operations may produce values other than 0 or 1, while logical operators will always evaluate to 0 or 1.

The shift operators, < < and < <, move all bits in a variable to the right or left as specified. The general form of the shift right statement is

variable > > number of bit positions

The general form of the shift left statement is

variable < < number of bit positions

As bits are shifted off one end, zeroes are brought in the other end. Remember, a shift is *not* a rotate. That is, the bits shifted off one end do not come back around to the other. The bits shifted off are lost, and zeroes are brought in.

Bit-shift operations can be very useful when you are decoding input from an external device, like a D/A converter, and reading status information. The bitwise shift operators can also quickly multiply and divide integers. A shift right effectively divides a number by 2 and a shift left multiplies it by 2, as shown in Table 2-7. The following program illustrates the shift operators:

```c
/* A bit shift example. */

#include "stdio.h"

void main(void)
{
  unsigned int i;
  int j;
```

```
i = 1;

/* left shifts */
for(j=0; j<4; j++) {
  i = i << 1;   /* left shift i by 1,
                which is same as a multiply by 2 */
  printf("left shift %d: %d\n", j, i);
}

/* right shifts */
for(j=0; j<4; j++) {
  i = i >> 1;   /* right shift i by 1,
                which is same as a division by 2 */
  printf("right shift %d: %d\n", j, i);
}
}
```

The one's complement operator, ~, reverses the state of each bit in the specified variable. That is, all 1's are set to 0, and all 0's are set to 1.

The bitwise operators are often used in cipher routines. If you want to make a disk file appear unreadable, perform some bitwise manipulations on it. One of the simplest methods is to complement each byte by

---

char x;	x as each statement executes	value of x
x=7;	0 0 0 0 0 1 1 1	7
x<<1;	0 0 0 0 1 1 1 0	14
x<<3;	0 1 1 1 0 0 0 0	112
x<<2;	1 1 0 0 0 0 0 0	192
x>>1;	0 1 1 0 0 0 0 0	96
x>>2;	0 0 0 1 1 0 0 0	24

Each left shift multiplies by 2. Notice that information has been lost after x<<2 because a bit was shifted off the end.

Each right shift divides by 2. Notice that subsequent divisions do not bring back any lost bits.

Table 2-7.   Multiplication and Division with Shift Operators using the one's complement to reverse each bit in the byte, as is shown here :

Original byte	0 0 1 0 1 1 0 0
After 1st complement	1 1 0 1 0 0 1 1
After 2nd complement	0 0 1 0 1 1 0 0

Same

Notice that a sequence of two complements in a row always produces the original number. Hence, the first complement represents the coded version of that byte. The second complement decodes the byte to its original value.

You could use the **encode( )** function shown here to encode a character.

```
/* A simple cipher function. */
char encode(char ch)
{
   return(~ch); /* complement it */
}
```

The ? Operator

C contains a very powerful and convenient operator that replaces certain statements of the if-then-else form. The ternary operator **?** takes the general form

$Exp1 ? Exp2 : Exp3;$

where $Exp1$, $Exp2$, and $Exp3$ are expressions. Notice the use and placement of the colon.

The **?** operator works like this: $Exp1$ is evaluated. If it is **true**, $Exp2$ is evaluated and becomes the value of the expression. If $Exp1$ is **false**, $Exp3$ is evaluated and its value becomes the value of the expression. For example, in

```
x = 10;

y = x>9 ? 100 : 200;
```

y is assigned the value 100. If **x** had been less than 9, **y** would have received the value 200. The same code written using the **if-else** statement is

```
x = 10;

if(x>9) y = 100;
else y = 200;
```

The **?** operator will be discussed more fully in Chapter 3 in relationship to C's other conditional statements.

The & and * Pointer Operators

A *pointer* is the memory address of a variable. A *pointer variable* is a variable that is specifically declared to hold a pointer to its specified type. Knowing a variable's address can be of great help in certain types of routines. However, pointers have three main functions in C. They can provide a fast means of referencing array elements. They also allow C functions to modify their calling parameters. Lastly, they support linked lists and other dynamic data structures. Chapter 5 is devoted exclusively to pointers. However, this chapter briefly covers the two operators that are used to manipulate pointers.

The first pointer operator is **&**, a unary operator that returns the memory address of its operand. (Remember, a unary operator only requires one operand.) For example,

```
m = &count;
```

places into **m** the memory address of the variable **count**. This address is the computer's internal location of the variable. It has nothing to do with the value of **count**. You can think of **&** as meaning "the address of." Therefore, the preceding assignment statement means "**m** receives the address of **count**."

To better understand this assignment, assume that the variable **count** uses memory location 2000 to store its value. Also assume that **count** has a value of 100. Then, after the previous assignment, **m** will have the value 2000.

The second pointer operator is *, which is the complement of **&**. * is a unary operator that returns the value of the variable located at the address that follows it. For example, if **m** contains the memory address of the variable **count**,

```
q = *m;
```

places the value of **count** into **q**. Now **q** has the value 100 because 100 is stored at location 2000, the memory address that was stored in **m**. Think of * as meaning "at address." In this case, you could read the statement as "q receives the value at address m."

Unfortunately, the multiplication symbol and the "at address" symbol are the same, and the symbol for the bitwise AND and the "address of" symbol are the same. These operators have no relationship to each other. Both **&** and * have a higher precedence than all other arithmetic operators except the unary minus, with which they share equal precedence.

Variables that will hold pointers must be declared as such. Variables that will hold memory addresses, or pointers as they are called in C, must be declared by putting * in front of the variable name. This indicates to the compiler that it will hold a pointer to that type of variable. For example, to declare a pointer type variable for a **char ch**, write

```
char *ch;
```

Here, **ch** is not a character but a pointer to a character—there is a big difference. The type of data that a pointer points to, in this case **char**, is called the *base type* of the pointer. However, the pointer variable itself is a variable that holds the address to an object of the base type. Hence, a character pointer (or any pointer) is of sufficient size to hold an address as defined by the architecture of the computer that it is running on. However, remember that a pointer should only point to data that is of that pointer's base type.

You can mix both pointer and nonpointer directives in the same declaration statement. For example,

```
int x, *y, count;
```

declares **x** and **count** as integer types and **y** as a pointer to an integer type.

The following * and & operators put the value 10 into a variable called **target**. As expected, this program displays the value 10 on the screen.

```
#include "stdio.h"

void main(void)
{
  int target, source;
  int *m;

  source = 10;
  m = &source;
  target = *m;

  printf("%d", target);
}
```

The Compile-Time Operator sizeof

sizeof is a unary compile-time operator that returns the length, in bytes, of the variable or parenthesized, type-specifier that it precedes. For example, assuming that integers are 2 bytes and **float**s are 8 bytes,

```
float f;

printf("%f ", sizeof f);
printf("%d", sizeof(int));
```

will display 8 2.

Remember, to compute the size of a type, you must enclose the type name in parentheses. This is not necessary for variable names, although there is no harm done if you do so.

The ANSI standard defines a special type called **size_t**, which corresponds loosely to an unsigned integer. Technically, the value returned by **sizeof** is of type **size_t**. For all practical purposes, however, you can think of it (and use it) as if it were an unsigned value.

sizeof primarily helps to generate portable code that depends upon the size of the C built-in data types. For example, imagine a database program that needs to store six integer values per record. If you want to port the database program to a variety of computers, you must not assume the size of an integer, but must determine its actual length using **sizeof**. This being the case, you could use the following routine to write a record to a disk file:

```
/* write 6 integers to a disk file */
void put_rec(int rec[6], FILE *fp)
{
  int len;

  len = fwrite(rec, sizeof rec, 1, fp);
  if(len<>1) printf("write error");
}
```

Coded as shown, **put_rec( )** compiles and runs correctly on any computer, no matter how many bytes are in an integer.

The Comma Operator

You use the comma operator to string together several expressions. The left side of the comma operator is always evaluated as **void**. This means that the expression on the right side becomes the value of the total comma-separated expression. For example,

```
x = (y=3, y+1);
```

first assigns **y** the value 3 and then assigns **x** the value 4. The parentheses are necessary because the comma operator has a lower precedence than the assignment operator.

Essentially, the comma causes a sequence of operations. When you use it on the right side of an assignment statement, the value assigned is the value of the last expression of the comma-separated list.

The comma operator has somewhat the same meaning as the word "and" in normal English in the phrase "do this and this and this."

The Dot (.) and Arrow (—>) Operators

The . (dot) and the —> (arrow) operators reference individual elements of structures and unions. *Structures* and *unions* are compound data types that may be referenced under a single name (see Chapter 7).

The dot operator is used when working with the actual structure or union. The arrow operator is used when a pointer to a structure or union is used. For example, given the global structure,

```
struct employee {
  char name[80];
  int age;
  float wage;
} emp;

struct employee *p = &emp; /* address of emp into p */
```

You would write the following code to assign the value 123.23 to element **wage** of structure **emp**:

```
emp.wage = 123.23;
```

However, the same assignment using a pointer to structure **emp** would be

```
emp->wage = 123.23;
```

Parentheses and Square Brackets as Operators

In C, parentheses are operators that increase the precedence of the operations inside them.

Square brackets perform array indexing (they will be discussed fully in Chapter 4). Given an array, the expression within square brackets provides an index into that array. For example,

```
#include "stdio.h"

char s[80];

void main(void)
{
  s[3] = 'X';
  printf("%c", s[3]);
}
```

first assigns the value 'X' to the fourth element (remember all arrays in C begin at 0) of array s, and then prints that element.

Precedence Summary

Table 2-8 lists the precedence of all C operators. Note that all operators, except the unary operators and **?**, associate from left to right. The unary operators (*****, **&**, **−**) and **?** associate from right to left.

Expressions

Operators, constants, and variables are the constituents of expressions. An *expression* in C is any valid combination of these elements. Because most expressions tend to follow the general rules of algebra, they are often taken for granted. However, a few aspects of expressions relate specifically to C.

Order of Evaluation

The ANSI standard stipulates that the subexpressions of an expression are evaluated in an unspecified order. This leaves the C compiler free to rearrange an expression to produce the most optimal code. However, it

Highest	( ) [ ] − >.
	! ~ ++ −− − (type) * & sizeof
	* / %
	+ −
	≪ ≫
	≪= ≫=
	== !=
	&
	^
	¦
	&&
	¦¦
	?
	= += −= *= /=
Lowest	,

Table 2-8.   The Precedence of C Operators

also means that your code should never rely upon the order in which subexpressions are evaluated. For example, the expression

```
x = f1() + f2();
```

does not ensure that **f1( )** will be called before **f2( )**.

Type Conversion in Expressions

When constants and variables of different types are mixed in an expression, they are converted to the same type. The C compiler converts all operands up to the type of the largest operand, which is called *type promotion*. This is done operation by operation, as described in the following type conversion algorithm:

IF an operand is a **long double**
THEN the second is converted to **long double**
ELSE IF an operand is a **double**
THEN the second is converted to **double**
ELSE IF an operand is a **float**
THEN the second is converted to **float**
ELSE IF an operand is an **unsigned long**
THEN the second is converted to **unsigned long**
ELSE IF an operand is **long**
THEN the second is converted to **long**
ELSE IF an operand is **unsigned**
THEN the second is converted to **unsigned**

There is one additional special case: If one operand is **long** and the other is **unsigned**, and if the value of the **unsigned** cannot be represented by a **long**, both operands are converted to **unsigned long**.

Once these conversion rules have been applied, each pair of operands is of the same type and the result of each operation is the same as the type of both operands.

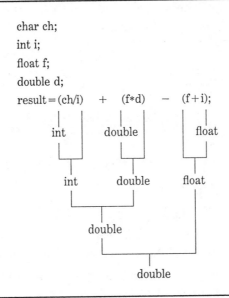

Figure 2-3.   A type conversion example

For example, consider the type conversions that occur in Figure 2-3.

First, the character **ch** is converted to an integer and **float f** is converted to **double**. Then the outcome of **ch/i** is converted to a **double** because **f*d** is **double**. The final result is **double** because, by this time, both operands are **double**.

Casts

You can force an expression to be of a specific type by using a *cast*. The general form of a cast is

(type) expression

where *type* is a valid C data type. For example, to make sure that the expression x/2 evaluates to type **float**, write

```
(float) x/2
```

Casts are often considered operators. As an operator, a cast is unary and has the same precedence as any other unary operator.

Although casts are not usually used a great deal in programming, they can be very useful when needed. For example, suppose you wish to use an integer for loop control, yet to perform computation on it requires a fractional part, as in the following program:

```
#include "stdio.h"

void main(void) /* print i and i/2 with fractions */
{
  int i;

  for(i=1; i<=100; ++i)
    printf("%d / 2 is: %f\n", i, (float) i /2);
}
```

Without the cast (**float**), only an integer division would have been performed. The cast ensures that the fractional part of the answer is displayed.

Spacing and Parentheses

You can add tabs and spaces to C expressions to make them easier to read. For example, the following two expressions are the same:

```
x=10/y~(127/x);

x = 10 / y ~(127/x);
```

Redundant or additional parentheses do not cause errors or slow down the execution of the expression. You should use parentheses to clarify the exact order of evaluation, both for yourself and for others. For example, which of the following two expressions is easier to read?

```
x=y/2-34*temp&127;

x = (y/3) - ((34*temp) & 127);
```

C Shorthand

C has a special shorthand that simplifies the coding of a certain type of assigment statement. For example,

```
x = x+10;
```

can be written as

```
x += 10;
```

The operator pair **+ =** tells the compiler to assign to **x** the value of **x** plus 10.

This shorthand works for all the binary operators in C (those that require two operands). The general form of C shorthand is

var = var operator expression

is the same as

var operator = expression

For another example,

```
x = x-100;
```

is the same as

```
x -= 100;
```

Shorthand notation is widely used in professionally written C programs; you should become familiar with it.

Program Control Statements

True and False in C
Selection Statements
Iteration Statements
Jump Statements
Expression Statements
Block Statements

This chapter discusses C's rich and varied program statements. The ANSI standard categorizes C's statements into these groups:

- selection

- iteration

- jump

- label

- expression

- block

Included in the selection statements are **if** and **switch**. (The term "conditional statement" is often used in place of "selection statement." However, the ANSI standard uses "selection" as will this book.) The iteration statements are **while, for,** and **do-while**. These are also commonly called loop statements. The jump statements are **break, continue, goto,** and **return**. The label statements include **case** and **default** statements (discussed along with the **switch** statement) and the **label** statement (discussed with **goto**). Expression statements are statements composed of a valid C expression. Block statements are simply blocks of code. (Remember, a block begins with a { and ends with a }.)

Since many C statements rely upon the outcome of some conditional test, let's begin by reviewing the concepts of true and false in C.

True and False in C

Many C statements rely upon a conditional expression that determines what course of action is to be taken. A conditional expression evaluates to either a true or false value. In C, unlike many other computer languages, a true value is any nonzero value, including negative numbers. A false value is 0. This approach to true and false allows a wide range of routines to be coded extremely efficiently, as you will see shortly.

Selection Statements

C supports two types of selection statements: **if** and **switch**. In addition, the **?** operator is an alternative to **if** in certain circumstances.

if

The general form of the **if** statement is

if (*expression*) *statement*;
else *statement*;

where a *statement* may consist of a single statement, a block of statements, or nothing (in the case of empty statements). The **else** clause is optional.

If the **if** *expression* evaluates to true (anything other than 0), the statement or block that forms the target of **if** is executed; otherwise, the statement or block that is the target of **else** will be executed, if it exists. Remember, only the code associated with **if** or the code associated with **else** executes, never both.

The conditional statement controlling **if** must produce a scalar result. A *scalar* is either an integer, character, or floating-point type. However, it is rare to use a floating-point number to control a conditional statement because this slows execution time considerably. (It takes the CPU several instructions to perform a floating-point operation. It takes relatively few instructions to perform an integer or character operation.)

For example, consider the following program which plays a very simple version of the "guess the magic number" game. It prints the message "** Right **" when the player guesses the magic number. It generates the magic number using C's random number generator **rand( )**, which returns an arbitrary number between 0 and 32,767.

```
/* Magic number program #1. */

#include "stdio.h"
#include "stdlib.h"

void main(void)
{
  int magic; /* magic number */
  int guess; /* user's guess */

  magic = rand();  /* generate the magic number */

  printf("guess the magic number: ");
  scanf("%d", &guess);

  if(guess == magic) printf("** Right **");
}
```

Taking the magic-number program further, the next version illustrates the use of the **else** statement to print a message in response to the wrong number.

```
/* Magic number program #2. */

#include "stdio.h"
#include "stdlib.h"

void main(void)
{
  int magic; /* magic number */
  int guess; /* user's guess */

  magic = rand();  /* generate the magic number */

  printf("guess the magic number: ");
  scanf("%d", &guess);

  if(guess == magic) printf("** Right **");
  else printf("Wrong");
}
```

Nested ifs

A *nested* **if** is an **if** that is the target of another **if** or **else**. Nested **ifs** are very common in programming. In C, an **else** statement always refers to the nearest **if** statement that is within the same block as the **else** and is not already associated with an **if**. For example,

```
if(i) {
  if(j) statement 1;
  if(k) statement 2; /* this if */
  else  statement 3; /* is associated with this else */
}
else statement 4; /* associated with if(i) */
```

As noted, the final **else** is not associated with **if(j)** because it is not in the same block. Rather, the final **else** is associated with **if(i)**. Also, the inner **else** is associated with **if(k)**, which is the nearest **if**.

The ANSI standard specifies that at least 15 levels of nesting must be supported. In practice, most compilers allow substantially more.

You can use a nested **if** to further improve the magic-number program by providing the player with feedback about a wrong guess.

```
/* Magic number program #3. */

#include "stdio.h"
#include "stdlib.h"

void main(void)
{
  int magic;   /* magic number */
  int guess;   /* user's guess */

  magic = rand(); /* get a random number */

  printf("guess the magic number: ");
  scanf("%d", &guess);

  if (guess == magic) {
    printf("** Right **");
    printf(" %d is the magic number\n", magic);
  }
  else {
    printf("Wrong, ");
    if(guess > magic) printf("too high\n");
    else printf("too low\n");
  }
}
```

The if-else-if Ladder

A common programming construct is the *if-else-if ladder*, sometimes called the *if-else-if staircase* because of its appearance. Its general form is

```
if (expression) statement;
else
  if (expression) statement;
  else
    if (expression) statement;
    .
    .
    .
        else statement;
```

The conditions are evaluated from the top downward. As soon as a true condition is found, the statement associated with it is executed and the rest of the ladder is bypassed. If none of the conditions are true, the final **else** is executed. That is, if all other conditional tests fail, the last **else** statement is performed. If the final **else** is not present, no action takes place if all other conditions are false.

Although the indentation of the preceding if-else-if ladder is technically correct, it can lead to overly deep indentation. For this reason, the if-else-if ladder is generally indented like this:

```
if(expression)
  statement;
else if(expression)
  statement;
else if(expression)
  statement;
  .
  .
  .
else
  statement;
```

Using an if-else-if ladder, the magic number program becomes

```
/* Magic number program #4. */

#include "stdio.h"
#include "stdlib.h"

void main(void)
{
  int magic; /* magic number */
  int guess; /* user's guess */

  magic = rand(); /* generate the magic number */

  printf("guess the magic number: ");
  scanf("%d", &guess);

  if(guess == magic) {
    printf("** Right ** ");
    printf("%d is the magic number", magic);
  }
  else if(guess > magic)
    printf("Wrong, too high");
  else printf("Wrong, too low");
}
```

The ? Alternative

You can use the **?** operator to replace **if-else** statements of the general form:

> if(*condition*)
>   *expression*
> else
>   *expression*

However, the target of both **if** and **else** must be a single expression — not another C statement.

The **?** is called a *ternary operator* because it requires three operands. It takes the general form

> *Exp1* ? *Exp2* : *Exp3*

where *Exp1*, *Exp2*, and *Exp3* are expressions. Notice the use and placement of the colon.

The value of a **?** expression is determined as follows: *Exp1* is evaluated. If it is true, *Exp2* is evaluated and becomes the value of the entire **?** expression. If *Exp1* is false, then *Exp3* is evaluated and its value becomes the value of the expression. For example, consider

```
x = 10;

y = x>9 ? 100 : 200;
```

In this example, **y** is assigned the value 100. If **x** had been less than 9, **y** would have received the value 200. The same code written with the **if-else** statement would be

```
x = 10;

if(x>9) y = 100;
else y = 200;
```

The following program uses the **?** operator to square an integer value entered by the user. However, this program preserves the sign (10 squared is 100 and -10 squared is -100).

```
#include "stdio.h"

void main(void)
{
  int isqrd, i;

  printf("enter a number: ");
  scanf("%d", &i);

  isqrd = i>0 ? i*i : -(i*i);

  printf("%d squared is %d", i, isqrd);
}
```

The use of the **?** operator to replace **if-else** statements is not restricted to assignments only. Remember, all functions (except those declared as void) may return a value. Hence, you can use one or more function calls in a C expression. When the function's name is encountered, the function is executed so that its return value may be determined. Therefore, you can execute one or more function calls using the **?** operator by placing the calls in the expressions that form the operands, as in

```
#include "stdio.h"

int f1(int n);
int f2(void);

void main(void)
{
  int t;

  printf("enter a number: ");
  scanf("%d", &t);

  /* print proper message */
  t ? f1(t) + f2() : printf("zero entered");
}

f1(int n)
{
  printf("%d ",n);
  return 0;
}

f2(void)
{
  printf("entered");
  return 0;
}
```

Entering a 0 in this example calls the **printf( )** function and displays the message **zero entered**. If you enter any other number, both **f1( )** and **f2( )** execute. Note that the value of the ? expression is discarded in this example. You don't need to assign it to anything.

A word of warning: Some C compilers rearrange the order of evaluation of an expression in an attempt to optimize the object code. This could cause functions that form the operands of the ? operator to execute in an unintended sequence.

Using the ? operator, you can rewrite the magic-number program yet again.

```
/* Magic number program #5. */

#include "stdio.h"
#include "stdlib.h"

void main(void)
{
  int magic;
  int guess;

  magic = rand(); /* generate the magic number */
```

```
  printf("guess the magic number: ");
  scanf("%d", &guess);

  if(guess == magic) {
    printf("** Right ** ");
    printf("%d is the magic number", magic);
  }
  else
    guess > magic ? printf("High") : printf("Low");
}
```

Here, the **?** operator displays the proper message based on the outcome of the test **guess > magic**.

The Conditional Expression

Sometimes newcomers to C are confused by the fact that you can use any valid C expression to control the **if** or the **?** operator. That is, you are not restricted to expressions involving the relational and logical operators (as is the case in languages like BASIC or Pascal). The program must simply evaluate to either a zero or nonzero value. For example, the following program reads two integers from the keyboard and displays the quotient. It uses an **if** statement, controlled by the second number, to avoid a divide-by-zero error.

```
/* Divide the first number by the second. */

#include "stdio.h"

void main(void)
{
  int a, b;

  printf("enter two numbers: ");
  scanf("%d%d", &a, &b);

  if(b) printf("%d\n", a/b);
  else printf("cannot divide by zero\n");
}
```

This approach works because if **b** is 0, the condition controlling **if** is false and the **else** executes. Otherwise, the condition is true (nonzero) and the division takes place. However, writing the **if** statement like this:

```
if(b != 0) printf("%d\n", a/b);
```

is redundant and potentially inefficient and is considered bad style.

switch

C has a built-in multiple-branch selection statement, **switch**, which successively tests the value of an expression against a list of integer or character constants. When a match is found, the statements associated with that constant are executed. The general form of the **switch** statement is

> switch (*expression*) {
>   case *constant1*:
>   *statement sequence*
>   break;
>   case *constant2*:
>   *statement sequence*
>   break;
>   case *constant3*:
>   *statement sequence*
>   break;
>
>   .
>   .
>   .
>
>   default:
>   *statement sequence*
> }

The value of *expression* is tested, in order, against the values of the constants specified in the **case** statements. When a match is found, the statement sequence associated with that **case** is executed until the **break** statement or the end of the **switch** statement is reached. The **default** statement is executed if no matches are found. The **default** is optional and, if it is not present, no action takes place if all matches fail.

The ANSI standard specifies that a **switch** can have at least 257 **case** statements. In practice, you will want to limit the number of **case** statements to a smaller amount for efficiency. Although **case** is a label statement, it cannot exist by itself, outside of a **switch**.

The **break** statement is one of C's jump statements. You can use it in loops as well as in the **switch** statement (see the section "Iteration Statements"). When **break** is encountered in a **switch**, program execution "jumps" to the line of code following the **switch** statement.

There are three important things to know about the **switch** statement:

• The **switch** statement differs from the **if** statement in that **switch** can only test for equality whereas **if** can evaluate a relational or logical expression.

• No two **case** constants in the same **switch** can have identical values. Of course, a **switch** statement enclosed by an outer switch may have **case** constants that are the same.

• If character constants are used in the **switch** statement, they are automatically converted to their integers.

The **switch** statement is often used to process keyboard commands, such as menu selection. As shown here, the function **menu( )** displays a menu for a spelling-checker program and calls the proper procedures:

```
menu()
{
  char ch;

  printf("1. Check Spelling\n");
  printf("2. Correct Spelling Errors\n");
  printf("3. Display Spelling Errors\n");
  printf("Strike Any Other Key to Skip\n");
  printf("     Enter your choice: ");

  ch=getchar();  /* read the selection from
                    the keyboard */

  switch(ch) {
    case '1':
      check_spelling();
      break;
    case '2':
      correct_errors();
      break;
    case '3':
```

```
      display_errors();
      break;
    default :
      printf("No option selected");
  }
}
```

Technically, the **break** statements inside the **switch** statement are optional. They terminate the statement sequence associated with each constant. If the **break** statement is omitted, execution will continue on into the next **case**'s statements until either a **break** or the end of the **switch** is reached. For example, the following function uses the "drop through" nature of the **case**s to simplify the code for a device-driver input handler:

```
/* Process a value */
void inp_handler(int i)
{
  int flag;

  flag = -1;

  switch(i) {
    case 1:  /* these cases have common statement */
    case 2:  /* sequences */
    case 3:
      flag = 0;
      break;
    case 4:
      flag = 1;
    case 5:
      error(flag);
      break;
    default:
      process(ch);
  }
}
```

This routine illustrates two aspects of **switch**. First, you can have empty conditions. In this case, the first three **case**s all execute the same statements.

```
flag = 0;
break;
```

Second, execution continues into the next **case** if no **break** statement is present. If **i** matches 4, **flag** is set to 1 and, because there is no

break statement at the end of that **case**, execution continues and the statement **error(flag)** is executed. If **i** had matched 5, **error(flag)** would have been called with a **flag** value of −1.

The fact that **case**s can run together when no **break** is present prevents the unwarranted duplication of code, resulting in very efficient code.

Note that the statements associated with each **case** are not code blocks but are statement sequences. (Of course, the entire **switch** statement does define a block). This technical distinction is only important in certain situations. For example, the following code fragment is in error and will not compile because you cannot declare a local variable in a statement sequence:

```
/* this is incorrect */
switch(c) {
  case 1:
    int t;
    .
    .
    .
```

However, you could add a local variable as shown here:

```
/* this is correct */
switch(c) {
  int t;
  case 1:
    .
    .
    .
```

Of course, you can create a block of code as one of the statements in a sequence and declare a local variable within it, as shown here:

```
/* this is correct */
switch(c) {
  case 1:
    if(1) { /* always true, used to create block */
      int t;
      .
      .
      .
    }
    .
    .
    .
```

Nested switch Statements

You can have a **switch** as part of the statement sequence of an outer **switch**. Even if the **case** constants of the inner and outer **switch** contain common values, no conflicts arise. For example, the following code fragment is perfectly acceptable:

```
switch(x) {
  case 1:
    switch(y) {
      case 0: printf("divide by zero error");
              break;
      case 1: process(x,y);
    }
    break;
  case 2:
    .
    .
    .
```

Iteration Statements

In C, and all other modern programming languages, iteration statements (also called loops) allow a set of instructions to be performed until a certain condition is reached. This condition may be predefined (as in the **for** loop), or open ended (as in the **while** and **do-while** loops).

The for Loop

The general format of C's **for** loop is found in some form or another in all procedural programming languages. However, in C, it provides unexpected flexibility and power.

The general form of the **for** statement is

for(*initialization; condition; increment) statement;*

The **for** loop allows many variations. However, the *initialization* is generally an assignment statement that is used to set the loop control variable. The *condition* is a relational expression that determines when the loop exits. The *increment* defines how the loop control variable changes each time the loop is repeated. You must separate these three major sections by semicolons. The **for** loop continues to execute as long as the condition is true. Once the condition becomes false, program execution resumes on the statement following **for**.

For example, the following program prints the numbers 1 through 100 on the screen:

```
#include "stdio.h"

main()
{
  int x;

  for(x=1; x<=100; x++) printf("%d ", x);
}
```

In the program, **x** is initially set to 1. Since **x** is less than 100, **printf( )** is called and **x** is increased by 1 and tested to see if it is still less than or equal to 100. This process repeats until **x** is greater than 100, at which point the loop terminates. In this example, **x** is the *loop control variable,* which is changed and checked each time the loop repeats.

The following example is a **for** loop that contains multiple statements:

```
for(x=100; x!=65; x-=5) {
  z = x*x;
  printf("The square of %d, %f",x,z);
}
```

Both the squaring of **x** and the call to **printf( )** are executed until **x** equals 65. Note that the loop is *negative running:* **x** is initialized to 100 and 5 is subtracted from it each time the loop repeats.

In **for** loops, the conditional test is always performed at the top of the loop. This means that the code inside the loop may not be executed at all if the condition is false to begin with. For example, in

```
x = 10;

for(y=10; y!=x; ++y) printf("%d", y);

printf("%d", y);
```

the loop will never execute because **x** and **y** are equal when the loop is entered. Because this causes the conditional expression to evaluate to false, neither the body of the loop nor the increment portion of the loop executes. Hence, **y** still has the value 10, and the output is the number 10 printed once on the screen.

for Loop Variations

The previous discussion described the most common form of the **for** loop. However, C offers several variations that increase the flexibility and applicability of the **for** loop.

One of the most common variations uses the comma operator to allow two or more variables to control the loop. (Remember, you use the comma operator to string together a number of expressions in a "do this and this" fashion. See Chapter 2.) For example, the variables **x** and **y** control the following loop, and both are initialized inside the **for** statement:

```
for(x=0, y=0; x+y<10; ++x) {
  y = getchar();
  y = y-'0';       /* subtract the ASCII code for 0
                      from y */
    .
    .
    .
}
```

Commas separate the two initialization statements. Each time **x** is incremented, the loop repeats and **y**'s value is set by keyboard input. Both **x** and **y** must be at the correct value for the loop to terminate. **y** must be initialized to 0 so that its value is defined before the first evaluation of the conditional expression. If **y** were not defined, it could contain a 10, making the conditional test false and preventing the loop from executing.

The **converge( )** function shown here demonstrates multiple loop control variables. The **converge( )** function displays a string by printing characters from both ends, converging in the middle at the specified line. This requires positioning the cursor at various, disconnected points on the screen. Because C runs under a wide variety of environments, the

ANSI C standard does not define a cursor positioning function. However, virtually all C compilers supply one, although its name may vary. This program uses Turbo C's **gotoxy( )** function to position the cursor. (It requires the header CONIO.H.)

```
/* Turbo C version. */

#include "stdio.h"
#include "conio.h" /* non-standard header file */
#include "string.h"

void converge(int line, char *message);

main()
{
  converge(10, "This is a test of converge().");
}

/* This function displays a string starting at the left
   side of the specified line.  It writes characters
   from both the ends converging at the middle.  It
   uses Turbo C's gotoxy() function to position the
   cursor.  This function is not defined by
   ANSI, but is a very common extension.
*/
void converge(int line, char *message)
{
  int i, j;

  for(i=1, j=strlen(message); i<j; i++, j--) {
    gotoxy(i, line); printf("%c", message[i-1]);
    gotoxy(j, line); printf("%c", message[j-1]);
  }
}
```

In Microsoft C, the equivalent of **gotoxy( )** is **_settextposition( )** which uses the header file GRAPH.H. The previous program, recoded for Microsoft C, is shown here:

```
/* Microsoft C version. */

#include "stdio.h"
#include "graph.h" /* non-standard header file */
#include "string.h"

void converge(int line, char *message);

main()
{
  converge(10, "This is a test of converge().");
}
```

```
/* This function displays a string starting at the left
   side of the specified line.  It writes characters
   from both the ends converging at the middle.  It
   uses Microsoft C's _settextposition() function to
   position the cursor.  This function is not defined
   by ANSI, but is a very common extension.
*/
void converge(int line, char *message)
{
  int i, j;

  for(i=1, j=strlen(message); i<j; i++, j--) {
    _settextposition(line, i);
    printf("%c", message[i-1]);
    _settextposition(line, j);
    printf("%c", message[j-1]);
  }
}
```

If you use a different C compiler, you will need to check your user manuals for the name of your cursor positioning function.

In both versions of **converge( )**, the **for** loop uses two loop control variables, **i** and **j**, to index the string from opposite ends. As the loop iterates, **i** is increased and **j** is decreased. The loop stops when **i** is equal to **j**, thus ensuring that all characters are written.

The conditional expression does not have to involve testing the loop control variable against some target value. In fact, the condition may be any relational or logical statement. This means that you can test for several possible terminating conditions.

For example, you could use the following function to log a user onto a remote system. The user has three tries to enter the password. The loop terminates when the three tries are used up or the user enters the correct password.

```
void sign_on(void)
{
  char str[20];
  int x;

  for(x=0; x<3 && strcmp(str, "password"); ++x) {
    printf("enter password please:");
    gets(str);
  }
  if(x==3) return;
  /* else log user in ... */
}
```

This function uses **strcmp( )**, the standard library function that compares two strings and returns 0 if they match.

Remember, each of the three sections of the **for** loop may consist of any valid C expression. The expressions need not actually have anything to do with what the sections are generally used for. With this in mind, consider the following example:

```
#include "stdio.h"

int sqrnum(int num);
int readnum(void);
int prompt(void);

main()
{
  int t;

  for(prompt(); t=readnum(); prompt())
    sqrnum(t);
}

prompt(void)
{
  printf("enter a number: ");
  return 0;
}

readnum(void)
{
  int t;

  scanf("%d", &t);
  return t;
}

sqrnum(int num)
{
  printf("%d\n", num*num);
  return num*num;
}
```

Look closely at the **for** loop in **main( )**. Notice that each part of the **for** loop is composed of function calls that prompt the user and read a number entered from the keyboard. If the number entered is 0, the loop terminates because the conditional expression will be false. Otherwise, the number is squared. Thus, this **for** loop uses the initialization and increment portions in a nontraditional but completely valid sense.

Another interesting trait of the **for** loop is that pieces of the loop definition need not be there. In fact, there need not be an expression present for any of the sections — the expressions are optional. For example, this loop will run until the user enters **123**:

```
for(x=0; x!=123; ) scanf("%d", &x);
```

Notice that the increment portion of the **for** definition is blank. This means that each time the loop repeats, **x** is tested to see if it equals 123, but no further action takes place. If you type **123** at the keyboard, however, the loop condition becomes false and the loop terminates.

The initialization often occurs outside the **for** statement. This most frequently happens when the initial condition of the loop control variable must be computed by some complex means as in this example:

```
gets(s);  /* read a string into s */
if(*s) x = strlen(s); /* get the string's length */

for( ;x<10; ) {
  printf("%d",x);
  ++x;
}
```

The initialization section has been left blank and **x** is initialized before the loop is entered.

The Infinite Loop

Although you can use any loop statement to create an infinite loop, **for** is traditionally used for this purpose. Since none of the three expressions that form the **for** loop are required, you can make an endless loop by leaving the conditional expression empty, as here:

```
for(;;) printf(" this loop will run forever.\n");
```

You may have an initialization and increment expression, but C programmers more commonly use the **for(;;)** construct to signify an infinite loop.

Actually, the **for(;;)** construct does not guarantee an infinite loop because C's **break** statement, encountered anywhere inside the body of a loop, causes immediate termination (**break** is discussed later in this chapter). Program control then resumes at the code following the loop, as shown here:

```
ch='\0';

for(;;) {
  ch = getchar();   /* get a character */
  if(ch=='A') break;   /* exit the loop */
}

printf("you typed an A");
```

This loop will run until the user types an **A** at the keyboard.

for Loops with No Bodies

As defined by the C syntax, a statement may be empty. This means that the body of the **for** loop (or any other loop) may also be empty. You can use this fact to improve the efficiency of certain algorithms and to create time delay loops.

Removing spaces from an input stream is a common programming task. For example, a database program may allow a query such as "show all balances less than 400." The database needs to have each word fed to it separately, without spaces. That is, the database input processor recognizes **"show"** but not **" show"**. The following loop removes leading spaces from the stream pointed to by **str**.

```
for( ; *str==' '; str++) ;
```

As you can see, this loop has no body—and no need for one either.

Time delay loops are often used in programs. The following code shows how to create one by using **for**:

```
for(t=0; t<SOME_VALUE; t++) ;
```

The while Loop

The second loop available in C is the **while** loop. Its general form is

while(*condition*) *statement*;

where *statement* is either an empty statement, a single statement or a block of statements that repeats. The *condition* may be any expression, and true is any nonzero value. The loop iterates while the condition is true. When the condition becomes false, program control passes to the line after the loop code.

The following example shows a keyboard input routine that simply loops until the user types **A**:

```
wait_for_char(void)
{
  char ch;

  ch = '\0';  /* initialize ch */
  while(ch != 'A')  ch = getchar();
  return ch;
}
```

First, **ch** is initialized to null. As a local variable, its value is not known when **wait _ for _ char( )** is executed. The **while** loop then checks to see if **ch** is not equal to **A**. Because **ch** was initialized to null, the test is true and the loop begins. Each time the user presses a key the test runs again. Once you enter an **A**, the condition becomes false because **ch** equals **A**, and the loop terminates.

Like **for** loops, **while** loops check the test condition at the top of the loop, which means that the loop code may not execute. This eliminates having to perform a separate conditional test before the loop. The **pad( )** function provides a good illustration of this. Its add spaces to the end of a string to fill the string to a predefined length. If the string is already at the desired length, no spaces are added.

```
#include "stdio.h"
#include "string.h"

void pad(char *s, int length);

void main(void)
{
```

```
    char str[80];

    strcpy(str, "this is a test");
    pad(str, 40);
    printf("%d", strlen(str));
}

/* add spaces to the end of a string */
void pad(char *s, int length)
{
  int l;

  l = strlen(s);  /* find out how long it is */

  while(l<length) {
    s[l] = ' ';    /* insert a space */
    l++;
  }
  s[l]='\0';  /* strings need to be
                  terminated in a null */
}
```

The two arguments of **pad( )** are **s**, a pointer to the string to lengthen, and **length**, the number of characters that **s** should have. If the string **s** is already equal to or greater than **length**, the code inside the **while** loop does not execute. If **s** is less than **length**, **pad( )** adds the required number of spaces. The **strlen( )** function, part of the standard library, returns the length of the string.

If several separate conditions need to terminate a **while** loop, a single variable commonly forms the conditional expression. The value of this variable is set at various points throughout the loop. In this example

```
func1(void)
{
  int working;

  working = 1;    /* i.e., true */

  while(working) {
    working = process1();
    if(working)
      working = process2();
    if(working)
      working = process3();
  }
}
```

any of the three routines may return false and cause the loop to exit.

There need not be any statements in the body of the **while** loop. For example,

```
while((ch=getchar()) != 'A') ;
```

will simply loop until the user types **A**. If you feel uncomfortable putting the assignment inside the **while** conditional expression, remember that the equal sign is just an operator that evaluates to the value of the right-hand operand.

The do-while Loop

Unlike **for** and **while** loops, which test the loop condition at the top of the loop, the **do-while** loop checks its condition at the bottom of the loop. This means that a **do-while** loop always executes at least once. The general form of the **do-while** loop is

> do {
>   *statement*;
> } while(*condition*);

Although the curly braces are not necessary when only one statement is present, they are usually used to avoid confusion (to you, not the compiler) with the **while**. The **do-while** loop iterates until *condition* becomes false.

The following **do-while** loop will read numbers from the keyboard until it finds a number less than or equal to 100.

```
do {
  scanf("%d", &num);
} while(num > 100);
```

Perhaps the most common use of the **do-while** loop is in a menu selection routine. When the user enters a valid response, it is returned as the value of the function. Invalid responses cause a reprompt. The following code shows an improved version of the spelling-checker menu developed earlier in this chapter:

```
void menu(void)
{
  char ch;

  printf("1. Check Spelling\n");
  printf("2. Correct Spelling Errors\n");
  printf("3. Display Spelling Errors\n");
  printf("      Enter your choice: ");

  do {
    ch = getchar();  /* read the selection from
                        the keyboard */
    switch(ch) {
      case '1':
        check_spelling();
        break;
      case '2':
        correct_errors();
        break;
      case '3':
        display_errors();
        break;
    }
  } while(ch!='1' && ch!='2' && ch!='3');
}
```

The **do-while** loop is a good choice because you will always want a menu
function to execute at least once. After the options have been displayed,
the program will loop until a valid option is selected.

Jump Statements

C has four statements that perform an unconditional branch: **return,
goto, break,** and **continue.** Of these, you may use **return** and **goto**
anywhere in your program. You may use the **break** and **continue**
statements in conjuction with any of the loop statements. As discussed
earlier in this chapter, you can also use the **break** with **switch.**

The Return Statement

The **return** statement is used to return from a function. It is a jump
statement because it causes execution to return (jump back) to the point
at which the call to the function was made. If **return** has a value

associated with it, that value is the return value of the function. If no return value is specified, assume that a garbage value is returned. (Some C compilers will automatically return 0 if no value is specified, but do not count on this.)

The general form of the **return** statement is

return *expression*;

Remember, the *expression* is optional.

You can use as many **return** statements as you like within a function. However, the function will stop executing as soon as it encounters the first **return**. The } that ends a function also causes the function to return. It is the same as a **return** without any specified value.

A function declared as **void** may not contain a **return** statement that specifies a value.

See Chapter 6 for more information on **return**.

The goto Statement

Since C has a rich set of control structures and allows additional control using **break** and **continue**, there is little need for **goto**. Most programmers' chief concern about **goto** is its tendency to render programs unreadable. Nevertheless, although the **goto** statement fell out of favor some years ago, it has managed to polish its tarnished image somewhat. There are no programming situations that require **goto**. Rather, it is a convenience, which, if used wisely, can be a benefit in certain programming situations. As such, **goto** is not used outside of this section.

The **goto** statement requires a label for operation. (A *label* is a valid C identifier followed by a colon.) The ANSI standard refers to this type of construct as a *label statement*. Furthermore, the label must be in the same function as the **goto** that uses it—you cannot jump between functions. The general form of the **goto** statement is

goto *label*;
.
.
.
label:

where *label* is any valid label either before or after **goto**. For example, you could create a loop from 1 to 100 using **goto** and a label, as shown here:

```
x = 1;
loop1:
  x++;
  if(x<100) goto loop1;
```

The break Statement

The **break** statement has two uses. You can use it to terminate a **case** in the **switch** statement (covered in the section on **switch** earlier in this chapter). You can also use it to force immediate termination of a loop, bypassing the normal loop conditional test.

When the **break** statement is encountered inside a loop, the loop is immediately terminated and program control resumes at the next statement following the loop. For example,

```
#include "stdio.h"

void main(void)
{
  int t;

  for(t=0; t<100; t++) {
    printf("%d ", t);
    if(t==10) break;
  }
}
```

prints the numbers 0 through 10 on the screen. Then the loop terminates because **break** causes immediate exit from the loop, overriding the conditional test **t < 100**.

Programmers often use the **break** statement in loops in which a special condition can cause immediate termination. For example, here a keypress can stop the execution of the **look _ up( )** routine:

```
look_up(char *name)
{
  do {
    /* look up names ... */
    if(kbhit()) break;
  } while(!found);
  /* process match */
}
```

If the file is very long and you are tired of waiting, you can strike a key to return from the function. The **kbhit( )** function returns 0 if you do not press a key. Otherwise, it returns a nonzero value. Because of the wide differences between computing environments, the ANSI standard does not define **kbhit( )**, but you will almost certainly have it (or one with a slightly different name) supplied with your compiler.

A **break** causes an exit from only the innermost loop. For example,

```
for(t=0; t<100; ++t) {
  count = 1;
  for(;;) {
    printf("%d ", count);
    count++;
    if(count==10) break;
  }
}
```

prints the numbers 1 through 10 on the screen 100 times. Each time the compilier encounters **break**, control is passed back to the outer **for** loop.

A **break** used in a **switch** statement will affect only that **switch**. It does not affect any loop the **switch** happens to be in.

The exit( ) Function

Just as you can break out of a loop, you can break out of a program by using the standard library function **exit( )**. This function causes immediate termination of the entire program, forcing a return to the operating system. In effect, the **exit( )** function acts as if it were breaking out of the entire program.

The general form of the **exit( )** function is

void exit(int *return_code*);

The value of *return_code* is returned to the calling process, which is usually the operating system. Zero is generally used as a return code to indicate normal program termination. Other arguments are used to indicate some sort of error.

Programmers frequently use **exit( )** when a mandatory condition for program execution is not satisfied. For example, imagine a computer game that requires a color graphics card. The **main( )** function of this game might look like this:

```
main()
{
  if(!color_card()) exit(1);
  play();
}
```

where **color_card( )** is a user-defined function that returns true if the color card is present. If the card is not in the system, **color_card( )** returns **false** and the program terminates.

As another example, this version of **menu( )** uses **exit( )** to quit the program and return to the operating system:

```
menu(void)
{

  char ch;

  printf("1. Check Spelling\n");
  printf("2. Correct Spelling Errors\n");
  printf("3. Display Spelling Errors\n");
  printf("4. Quit\n");
  printf("      Enter your choice: ");

  do {
    ch=getchar();  /* read the selection from
                      the keyboard */
      switch(ch) {
        case '1':
          check_spelling();
          break;
        case '2':
          correct_errors();
          break;
        case '3':
          display_errors();
          break;
        case '4':
          exit(0);  /* return to OS */
      }
  } while(ch!='1' && ch!='2' && ch!='3');
}
```

The continue Statement

The **continue** statement works somewhat like the **break** statement. Instead of forcing termination, however, **continue** forces the next iteration of the loop to take place, skipping any code in between. For the **for** loop, **continue** causes the conditional test and then the increment portions of the loop to execute. For the **while** and **do-while** loops, program control passes to the conditional tests. For example, the following program counts the number of spaces contained in the string entered by the user:

```
/* Count spaces */

#include "stdio.h"

main()
{
  char s[80], *str;
  int space;

  printf("enter a string: ");
  gets(s);
  str = s;

  for(space=0; *str; str++) {
    if(*str!=' ') continue;
    space++;
  }
  printf("%d spaces\n", space);
}
```

Each character is tested to see if it is a space. If it is not, the **continue** statement forces the **for** to iterate again. If the character *is* a space, **space** is incremented.

The following example shows that you can use **continue** to expedite the exit from a loop by forcing the conditional test to be performed sooner:

```
void code(void)
{
  char done, ch;

  done = 0;
  while(!done) {
    ch = getchar();
    if(ch=='$') {
      done = 1;
```

```
    continue;
  }
  putchar(ch+1);   /* shift the alphabet one
                      position */
 }
}
```

You could use this function to code a message by shifting all characters one letter higher. For example, an "a" would become a "b." The function will terminate when a $ is read. No further output will occur because the conditional test, brought into effect by **continue**, will find **done** to be true and will cause the loop to exit.

Expression Statements

Chapter 2 covers C expressions thoroughly. However, a few special points are mentioned here. Remember, an expression statement is simply a valid C expression followed by a semicolon, as in

```
func();   /* a function call */

a = b+c;  /* an assignment statement */

b+f();    /* a valid, but do-nothing statement */

;         /* an empty statement */
```

The first expression statement executes a function call. The second is an assignment. The third expression is strange but is evaluated by the C compiler because the function **f( )** may need to perform some necessary task. The final example shows that C allows a statement to be empty (sometimes called a *null statement*).

Block Statements

Block statements are simply groups of related statements that are treated as a unit. The statements that make up a block are logically bound together. A block is begun with a { and terminated by its matching }. Programmers use block statements most commonly to create a multi-statement target for some other statement, such as **if**. However, you may place a block statement anywhere you would put any other statement. For example, this is perfectly valid (although unusual) C code:

```
#include "stdio.h"

void main(void)
{
  int i;

  {  /* a block statement */
     i = 120;
     printf("%d", i);
  }
}
```

Arrays and Strings

F
O
U
R

An *array* is a collection of variables of the same type that are referenced by a common name. A specific element in an array is accessed by an index. In C, all arrays consist of contiguous memory locations. The lowest address corresponds to the first element and the highest address to the last element. Arrays may have from one to several dimensions. The most common array in C is the string, which is simply an array of characters terminated by a null. This approach to strings gives C greater power and efficiency than other languages.

Note: In C, arrays and pointers are closely related; a discussion of one usually refers to the other. This chapter focuses on arrays while Chapter 5 looks closely at pointers. You should read both to understand fully these important C constructs.

Single-Dimension Arrays

The general form for declaring a single-dimensioned array is

type var_name[size];

97

Like other variables, arrays must be explicitly declared so that the compiler may allocate space for them in memory. Here, *type* declares the base type of the array, which is the type of each element in the array. *size* defines how many elements the array will hold. For example, to declare a 100-element array called **balance**, and of type **double**, use this statement:

double balance[100];

In C, all arrays have 0 as the index of their first element. Therefore, when you write

```
char p[10];
```

you are declaring a character array that has ten elements, p[0] through [9]. For example, the following program loads an integer array with the numbers 0 through 99:

```
void main(void)
{
  int x[100];  /* this reserves 100 integer elements */
  int t;

  for(t=0; t<100; ++t) x[t] = t;
}
```

The amount of storage required to hold an array is directly related to its type and size. For a single-dimension array, the total size in bytes is computed as shown here:

total bytes = sizeof(type) * size of array

C has no bounds checking on arrays. You could overwrite either end of an array and write into some other variable's data or even into the program's code. As the programmer, it is your job to provide bounds checking where needed. For example, this code will compile without error, but is incorrect because the **for** loop will cause the array **count** to be overrun.

```
int count[10], i;

/* this causes count to be overrun */
for(i=0; i<100; i++) count[i] = i;
```

Single-dimension arrays are essentially lists of information of the same type that are stored in contiguous memory locations in index order. For example, Figure 4-1 shows how array **a** appears in memory if it starts at memory location 1000 and is declared as shown here:

```
char a[7];
```

Generating a Pointer to an Array

You can generate a pointer to the first element of an array by simply specifying the array name, without any index. For example, given

```
int sample[10];
```

you can generate a pointer to the first element by simply using the name **sample**. For example, the following program fragment assigns **p** the address of the first element of **sample**:

```
int *p;
int sample[10];

p = sample;
```

You can also specify the address of the first element of an array using the **&** operator. For example, **sample** and **&sample[0]** both produce the same results. However, in professionally written C code, you will almost never see something like **&sample[0]**.

Element	a[0]	a[1]	a[2]	a[3]	a[4]	a[5]	a[6]
Address	1000	1001	1002	1003	1004	1005	1006

Figure 4-1.   A seven-element character array beginning at location 1000

Passing Single-Dimension Arrays to Functions

In C, you cannot pass an entire array as an argument to a function. You can, however, pass a pointer to an array to a function by specifying the array's name without an index. For example, the following program fragment passes the address of **i** to **func1( )**:

```
void main(void)
{
  int i[10];

  func1(i);
  .
  .
  .
}
```

If a function receives a single-dimension array, you may declare the formal parameter in one of three ways: as a pointer, as a sized array, or as an unsized array. For example, to receive **i**, a function called **func1( )** can be declared as

```
func1(int *x) /* pointer */
{
  .
  .
  .
}
```

or

```
func1(int x[10]) /* sized array */
{
  .
  .
  .
}
```

or finally as

```
func1(int x[]) /* unsized array */
{
  .
  .
  .
}
```

All three declaration methods produce identical results because each tells the compiler that an integer pointer is going to be received. The first declaration actually uses a pointer. The second employs the standard array declaration. In the final version, a modified version of an array declaration simply specifies that an array of type **int** of some length is to be received. As you can see, the length of the array doesn't matter as far as the function is concerned because C performs no bounds checking. In fact, as far as the compiler is concerned,

```
func1(int x[32])
{
    .
    .
    .
}
```

also works because the C compiler generates code that instructs **func1( )** to receive a pointer—it does not actually create a 32-element array.

Strings

By far the most common use of one-dimensional arrays is as character strings. Remember, in C, a string is defined as a character array that is terminated by a null. A null is specified as '\0' and is generally zero. For this reason, you need to declare character arrays to be one character longer than the largest string that they are to hold. For example, to declare an array **s** that holds a 10-character string, you would write

```
char s[11];
```

This makes room for the null at the end of the string.

Although C does not have a string data type, it allows string constants. A *string constant* is a list of characters enclosed in double quotes. For example,

"hello there"

You do not need to add the null to the end of string constants manually—the C compiler does this for you automatically.

C supports a wide range of string manipulation functions. The most common are

Name	Function
strcpy(s1, s2)	Copies s2 into s1
strcat(s1, s2)	Concatenates s2 onto the end of s1
strlen(s1)	Returns the length of s1
strcmp(s1, s2)	Returns 0 if s1 and s2 are the same; less than 0 if s1 < s2; greater than 0 if s1 > s2
strchr(s1, ch)	Returns a pointer to the first occurrence of ch in s1
strstr(s1, s2)	Returns a pointer to the first occurrence of s2 in s1

These functions use the standard header file STRING.H. (These and other string functions are discussed in detail in Part Two.) The following program illustrates the use of these string functions:

```
#include "STDIO.H"
#include "STRING.H"

void main(void)
{
  char s1[80],s2[80];

  gets(s1); gets(s2);

  printf("lengths: %d %d\n", strlen(s1), strlen(s2));

  if(!strcmp(s1, s2)) printf("The strings are equal\n");

  strcat(s1, s2);
  printf("%s\n",s1);

  strcpy(s1, "This is a test.\n");
  printf(s1);
  if(strchr("hello", 'e')) printf("e is in hello\n");
  if(strstr("hi there", "hi")) printf("found hi");
}
```

If you run this program and enter the strings **"hello"** and **"hello"**, the output is

```
lengths: 6 6
The strings are equal
hellohello
This is a test.
e is in hello
found hi
```

Remember, **strcmp( )** returns **false** if the strings are equal. Be sure to use the logical operator **!** to reverse the condition, as just shown, if you are testing for equality.

Two-Dimensional Arrays

C supports multidimensional arrays. The simplest form of the multidimensional array is the two-dimensional array—an array of single-dimension arrays. To declare a two-dimensional integer array **d** of size 10,20, you would write

```
int d[10][20];
```

Pay careful attention to the declaration. Most other computer languages use commas to separate the array dimensions; C, in contrast, places each dimension in its own set of brackets.

Similarly, to access point 1,2 of array **d**, you would use

```
d[1][2]
```

The following example loads a two-dimensional array with the numbers 1 through 12 and prints them row by row.

```
#include "stdio.h"

void main(void)
{
  int t, i, num[3][4];

  for(t=0; t<3; ++t)
    for(i=0; i<4; ++i)
      num[t][i] = (t*4)+i+1;

  /* now print them out */
```

```
for(t=0; t<3; ++t) {
  for(i=0; i<4; ++i)
    printf("%3d ", num[t][i]);
  printf("\n");
}
}
```

In this example, **num[0][0]** has the value 1, **num[0][1]** the value 2, **num[0][2]** the value 3, and so on. The value of **num[2][3]** will be 12. You can visualize the **num** array as shown here:

	0	1	2	3
0	1	2	3	4
1	5	6	7	8
2	9	10	11	12

Two-dimensional arrays are stored in a row-column matrix, where the first index indicates the row and the second indicates the column. This means that the rightmost index changes faster than the leftmost when accessing the elements in the array in the order in which they are actually stored in memory. See Figure 4-2 for a graphic representation of a two-dimensional array in memory. You can think of the first index as a "pointer" to the correct row.

In the case of a two-dimensional array, the following formula yields the number of bytes of memory needed to hold it:

bytes = size of 1st index * size of 2nd index *
       sizeof(base type)

Therefore, assuming 2-byte integers, an integer array with dimensions 10,5 would have

10 * 5 * 2

or 100 bytes allocated.

When a two-dimensional array is used as an argument to a function, only a pointer to the first element is actually passed. However, a function receiving a two-dimensional array as a parameter must define at least the length of the second dimension. This is because the C compiler needs to know the length of each row if it is to index the array correctly. For example, a function that receives a two-dimensional integer array with dimensions 10,10 is declared like this:

```
func1(int x[][10])
{
        .
        .
        .
}
```

You can specify the first dimension if you like, but it is not necessary.

The C compiler needs to know the second dimension in order to work on statements such as

```
x[2][4]
```

inside the function. If the length of the rows is not known, the compiler cannot determine where the third row begins.

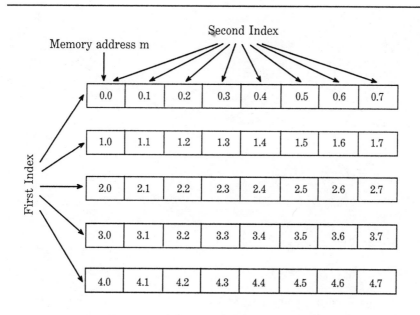

Figure 4-2.   A two-dimensional array in memory

The following short program uses a two-dimensional array to store the numeric grade for each student in a teacher's classes. The program assumes that the teacher has three classes and a maximum of 30 students per class. Notice the way the array **grade** is accessed by each of the functions.

```c
#include "stdio.h"
#include "ctype.h"
#include "stdlib.h"

/* A simple student grades database. */

#define CLASSES  3
#define GRADES   30

int grade[CLASSES][GRADES];

void enter_grades(void);
int get_grade(int num);
void disp_grades(int g[][GRADES]);

void main(void)
{
  char ch, str[80];

  for(;;) {
    do {
      printf("(E)nter grades\n");
      printf("(R)eport grades\n");
      printf("(Q)uit\n");
      gets(str);
      ch = toupper(*str);
    } while(ch!='E' && ch!='R' && ch!='Q');

    switch(ch) {
      case 'E':
        enter_grades();
        break;
      case 'R':
        disp_grades(grade);
        break;
      case 'Q':
        exit(0);
    }
  }
}

/* Enter the student's grades. */
void enter_grades(void)
{
  int t, i;
```

```
  for(t=0; t<CLASSES; t++) {
    printf("Class # %d:\n", t+1);
    for(i=0; i<GRADES; ++i)
      grade[t][i] = get_grade(i);
  }
}

/* Read a grade. */
get_grade(int num)
{
  char s[80];

  printf("enter grade for student # %d:\n",num+1);
  gets(s);
  return(atoi(s));
}

/* Display grades. */
void disp_grades(int g[][GRADES])
{
  int t, i;

  for(t=0; t<CLASSES; ++t) {
    printf("Class # %d:\n", t+1);
    for(i=0; i<GRADES; ++i)
      printf("student #%d is %d\n", i+1, g[t][i]);
  }
}
```

Arrays of Strings

It is not uncommon in programming to use an array of strings. For example, the input processor to a database may verify user commands against an array of valid commands. To create an array of strings, use a two-dimensional character array. The size of the left index determines the number of strings and the size of the right index specifies the maximum length of each string. The following code declares an array of 30 strings, each with a maximum length of 80 characters:

```
char str_array[30][80];
```

It is easy to access an individual string: You simply specify only the left index. For example, the following statement calls **gets( )** with the third string in **str_array**.

```
gets(str_array[2]);
```

The preceding statement is functionally equivalent to

```
gets(&str_array[2][0]);
```

but the first of the two forms is much more common in professionally written C code.

To understand better how string arrays work, study the following short program, which uses a string array as the basis for a very simple text editor:

```
#include "stdio.h"

#define MAX 100
#define LEN 80

char text[MAX][LEN];

/* A very simple text editor */
void main(void)
{
  register int t, i, j;

  printf("Enter an empty line to quit.\n");

  for(t=0; t<MAX; t++) {
    printf("%d: ", t);
    gets(text[t]);
    if(!*text[t]) break; /* quit on blank line */
  }

  for(i=0; i<t; i++) {
    for(j=0; text[i][j]; j++) putchar(text[i][j]);
    putchar('\n');
  }
}
```

This program inputs lines of text until a blank line is entered. Then it redisplays each line one character at a time.

Multidimensional Arrays

C allows arrays of more than two dimensions. The exact limit, if any, is determined by your compiler. The general form of a multidimensional array declaration is *type name*[*a*][*b*][*c*]. . .[*z*];

Arrays of three or more dimensions are not often used because of the amount of memory they require. For example, a four-dimensional character array with dimensions 10,6,9,4 requires

    10 * 6 * 9 * 4

or 2,160 bytes. If the array held 2-byte integers, 4,320 bytes would be needed. If the array held **double** (assuming 8 bytes per **double**), 17,280 bytes would be required. The storage required increases exponentially with the number of dimensions. Large multidimensional arrays are often dynamically allocated a piece at a time with C's dynamic allocation functions and pointers. This approach is called a *sparse array* and is covered in Chapter 21.

In multidimensional arrays, it takes the computer time to compute each index. This means that accessing an element in a multidimensional array is slower than accessing an element in a single-dimension array.

When passing multidimensional arrays into functions, you must declare all but the first dimension. For example, if you declare array **m** as

```
int m[4][3][6][5];
```

a function, **func1( )**, that receives **m**, would look like this:

```
func1(int d[][3][6][5])
{
    .
    .
    .
```

Of course, you can include the first dimension if you like.

Indexing Pointers

In C, pointers and arrays are closely related. As you know, an array name without an index is a pointer to the first element in the array. For example, consider the following array.

```
char p[l0];
```

The following statements are identical:

```
p
```
```
&p[0]
```

Put another way,

```
p==&p[0]
```

evaluates to **true** because the address of the first element of an array is the same as the address of the array.

Conversely, any pointer variable can be indexed as if it were declared to be an array. For example, consider this program fragment:

```
int *p, i[l0];
p = i;
p[5] = 100;   /* assign using index */
(p+5) = 100; /* assign using pointer arithmetic */
```

Both assigment statements place the value 100 in the sixth element of **i**. The first statement indexes **p**; the second uses pointer arithmetic. Either way, the result is the same. (Chapter 5 discusses pointers and pointer arithmetic.)

This process can also be applied to arrays of two or more dimensions. For example, assuming that **a** is a 10-by-10 integer array, these two statments are equivalent:

```
a
```
```
&a[0][0]
```

Furthermore, the 0,4 element of **a** may be referenced two ways: either by array indexing, a[0][4], or by the pointer, *(a+4). Similarly, element 1,2 is either a[1][2] or *(a+12). In general, for any two-dimensional array a[j][k] is equivalent to *(a+(j*row length)+k)

Pointers are sometimes used to access arrays because pointer arithmetic is often faster than array indexing.

In a sense, a two-dimensional array is like an array of pointers that point to arrays of rows. Therefore, using a separate pointer variable is one easy way to use pointers to access elements of a two-dimensional array. The following function will print the contents of the specified row for the global integer array **num**:

```
int num[10][10];
  .
  .
  .
void  pr_row(int j)
{
  int *p, t;

  p = &num[j][0]; /* get address of first
                        element in row j */
  for(t=0; t<10; ++t) printf("%d ", *(p+t));
}
```

You can generalize this routine by making the calling arguments be the row, the row length, and a pointer to the first array element, as shown here:

```
void pr_row(int j, int row_dimension, int *p)
{
  int t;

  p = p + (j * row_dimension);
  for(t=0; t<row_dimension; ++t)
    printf("%d ", *(p+t));
}
```

Arrays of greater than two dimensions may be reduced in a similar way. For example, a three-dimensional array can be reduced to a pointer to a two-dimensional array, which can be reduced to a pointer to a single-dimension array. Generally, an n-dimensional array can be reduced to a pointer and an $(n-1)$-dimensional array. This new array can be reduced again with the same method. The process ends when a single-dimension array is produced.

Array Initialization

C allows the initialization of arrays at the time of declaration. The general form of array initialization is similar to that of other variables, as shown here:

$type\_specifier\ array\_name[size1]...[sizeN] = \{\ value\_list\ \};$

The *value_list* is a comma-separated list of constants whose type is compatible with *type_specifier*. The first constant is placed in the first position of the array, the second constant in the second position, and so on. Note that a semicolon follows the }.

In the following example, a 10-element integer array is initialized with the numbers 1 through 10:

```
int i[10] = {1, 2, 3, 4, 5, 6, 7, 8, 9, 10};
```

This means that **i[0]** will have the value 1 and **i[9]** will have the value 10.

Character arrays that hold strings allow a shorthand initialization that takes the form:

$char\ array\_name[size] = "string";$

For example, this code fragment initializes **str** to the phrase "I like C".

```
char str[9] = "I like C";
```

This is the same as writing

```
char str[9] = {'I', ' ', 'l', 'i', 'k', 'e', ' ', 'C', '\0'};
```

Because all strings in C end with a null, you must make sure that the array you declare is long enough to include the null. This is why **str** is nine characters long even though "I like C" is only eight. When you use the string constant, the compiler automatically supplies the null terminator.

Multidimensional arrays are initialized the same as single-dimension ones. For example, the following initializes **sqrs** with the numbers 1 through 10 and their squares.

```
int sqrs[10][2] = {
  1,1,
  2,4,
  3,9,
  4,16,
  5,25,
  6,36,
  7,49,
  8,64,
  9,81,
  10,100
};
```

Unsized Array Initializations

Imagine that you are using array initialization to build a table of error messages, as shown here:

```
char e1[12] = "read error\n";
char e2[13] = "write error\n";
char e3[18] = "cannot open file\n";
```

As you might guess, it is tedious to count the characters in each message manually to determine the correct array dimension. You can let C automatically calculate the dimensions of the arrays by using unsized arrays. If, in an array initialization statement, the size of the array is not specified, the C compiler automatically creates an array big enough to hold all the initializers present. This is called an *unsized array*. Using this approach, the message table becomes

```
char e1[] = "read error\n";
char e2[] = "write error\n";
char e3[] = "cannot open file\n";
```

Given these initializations, this statement

```
printf("%s has length %d\n", e2, sizeof e2);
```

will print

```
write error has length 13
```

Besides being less tedious, unsized array initialization allows you to change any of the messages without fear of using incorrect array dimensions.

Unsized array initializations are not restricted to one-dimensional arrays. For multidimensional arrays, you must specify all but the left-most dimensions to allow the C compiler to index the array properly. In this way, you may build tables of varying lengths and the compiler automatically allocates enough storage for them. For example, the declaration of **sqrs** as an unsized array is shown here:

```
int sqrs[][2] = {
  1,1,
  2,4,
  3,9,
  4,16,
  5,25,
  6,36,
  7,49,
  8,64,
  9,81,
  10,100
};
```

The advantage of this declaration over the sized version is that you may lengthen or shorten the table without changing the array dimensions.

A Tic-Tac-Toe Example

The longer example that follows illustrates many of the ways that you can manipulate arrays with C. Two-dimensional arrays are commonly used to simulate board game matrices. This section develops a simple tic-tac-toe program.

The computer plays a very simple game. When it is the computer's turn, it uses **get_computer_move( )** to scan the matrix, looking for an unoccupied cell. When it finds one, it puts an "O" there. If it cannot find an empty location, it reports a draw game and exits. The

get_player_move( ) function asks you where you want to place an "X." The upper-left corner is location 1,1; the lower-right corner is 3,3.

The matrix array is initialized to contain spaces. This makes it easy to display the matrix on the screen.

Each time a move has been made, the program calls the **check( )** function. This function returns a space if there is no winner yet, an X if you have won, or an O if the computer has won. It scans the rows, the columns, and then the diagonals, looking for one that contains either all X's or all O's.

The **disp_matrix( )** function displays the current state of the game. Notice how initializing the matrix with spaces simplified this function.

The routines in this example all access the **matrix** array differently. Study them to make sure that you understand each array operation.

```c
/* A simple Tic Tac Toe game. */
#include "stdio.h"
#include "stdlib.h"

char matrix[3][3];   /* the tic tac toe matrix */

char check(void);
void init_matrix(void);
void get_player_move(void);
void get_computer_move(void);
void disp_matrix(void);

void main(void)
{

  char done;

  printf("This is the game of Tic Tac Toe.\n");
  printf("You will be playing against the computer.\n");

  done = ' ';

  init_matrix();

  do {
    disp_matrix();
    get_player_move();
    done = check(); /* see if winner */
    if(done!=' ') break; /* winner!*/
    get_computer_move();
    done = check(); /* see if winner */
  } while(done==' ');

  if(done=='X') printf("You won!\n");
```

```
    else printf("I won!!!!\n");

    disp_matrix(); /* show final positions */
}

/* Initialize the matrix. */
void init_matrix(void)
{
    int i, j;

    for(i=0; i<3; i++)
        for(j=0; j<3; j++) matrix[i][j] = ' ';
}

/* Get a player's move. */
void get_player_move(void)
{
    int x, y;

    printf("Enter coordinates for your X: ");
    scanf("%d%d",&x,&y);

    x--; y--;

    if(matrix[x][y]!=' ') {
        printf("Invalid move, try again.\n");
        get_player_move();
    }
    else matrix[x][y] = 'X';
}

/* Get a move from the computer. */
void get_computer_move(void)
{
    int i, j;

    for(i=0; i<3; i++) {
        for(j=0; j<3; j++)
            if(matrix[i][j]==' ') break;
        if(matrix[i][j]==' ') break;
    }

    if(i*j==9) {
        printf("draw\n");
        exit(0);
    }
    else
        matrix[i][j] = 'O';
}

/* Display the matrix on the screen. */
void disp_matrix(void)
{
    int t;

    for(t=0; t<3; t++) {
```

```
    printf(" %c | %c | %c ",matrix[t][0],
          matrix[t][1], matrix [t][2]);
    if(t!=2) printf("\n---|---|---\n");
  }
  printf("\n");
}

/* See if there is a winner. */
char check(void)
{
  int i;

  for(i=0; i<3; i++)  /* check rows */
    if(matrix[i][0]==matrix[i][1] &&
       matrix[i][0]==matrix[i][2]) return matrix[i][0];

  for(i=0; i<3; i++)  /* check columns */
    if(matrix[0][i]==matrix[1][i] &&
       matrix[0][i]==matrix[2][i]) return matrix[0][i];

  /* test diagonals */
  if(matrix[0][0]==matrix[1][1] && matrix[1][1]==matrix[2][2])
    return matrix[0][0];

  if(matrix[0][2]==matrix[1][1] && matrix[1][1]==matrix[2][0])
    return matrix[0][2];

  return ' ';
}
```

Pointers

The correct understanding and use of pointers is critical to successful C programming. There are three reasons for this: First, pointers provide the means by which functions can modify their calling arguments. Second, pointers support C's dynamic allocation routines. Third, pointers can improve the efficiency of certain routines.

Pointers are one of C's strongest but also one of its most dangerous features. For example, uninitialized, or *wild pointers*, can cause your system to crash. Perhaps worse, it is easy to use pointers incorrectly, causing bugs that are very difficult to find.

What are Pointers?

A *pointer* is a variable that holds a memory address. This address is usually the location of another variable in memory. If one variable contains the address of another variable, the first variable is said to *point* to the second. Figure 5-1 illustrates this situation.

Pointer Variables

If a variable is going to hold a pointer, it must be declared as such. A pointer declaration consists of a base type, an *, and the variable name. The general form for declaring a pointer variable is

   *type *name*;

where *type* is any valid C type and *name* is the name of the pointer variable.

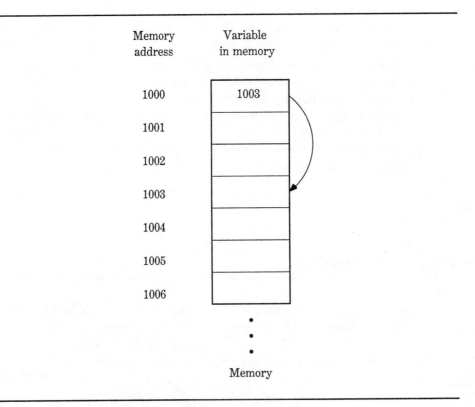

Memory address   Variable in memory

1000	1003
1001	
1002	
1003	
1004	
1005	
1006	

Memory

Figure 5-1.   One variable points to another

The base type of the pointer defines what type of variables the pointer can point to. Technically, any type of pointer can point anywhere in memory. However, all pointer arithmetic is done relative to its base type, so it is important to declare the pointer correctly. (Pointer arithmetic is discussed later in this chapter.)

The Pointer Operators

There are two special pointer operators: * and &. The & is a unary operator that returns the memory address of its operand. (Remember, a unary operator only requires one operand.) For example,

```
m = &count;
```

places into **m** the memory address of the variable **count**. This address is the computer's internal location of the variable. It has nothing to do with the value of **count**. You can think of **&** as returning "the address of." Therefore, the preceding assignment statement means "**m** receives the address of **count**."

To understand the above assignment better, assume that the variable **count** uses memory location 2000 to store its value. Also assume that **count** has a value of 100. Then, after the preceding assignment, **m** will have the value 2000.

The second pointer operator, *, is the complement of **&**. It is a unary operator that returns the value of the variable located at the address that follows. For example, if **m** contains the memory address of the variable **count**,

```
q = *m;
```

places the value of **count** into **q**. **q** will have the value 100 because 100 is stored at location 2000, which is the memory address that was stored in **m**. You can think of * as "at address." In this case, the preceding statement means "**q** receives the value at address **m**."

It is sometimes confusing to beginners that the multiplication sign and the "at address" sign are the same, and the bitwise AND and the "address of" sign are the same. These operators have no relationship to each other. Both **&** and * have a higher precedence than all other arithmetic operators except the unary minus, with which they are equal.

Your pointer variables must always point to the correct type of data. For example, when you declare a pointer to be of type **int**, the compiler assumes that any address that it holds points to an integer variable. Because C allows you to assign any address to a pointer variable, the following code fragment compiles with no error messages (or only warnings, depending upon your compiler) but does not produce the desired result:

```
void main(void)
{
  float x, y;
  int  *p;

  p = &x;
  y = *p;
}
```

This will not assign the value of **x** to **y**. Because **p** is declared as an integer pointer, only 2 bytes of information will be transferred to **y**, not the 8 bytes that normally make up a floating-point number.

Pointer Expressions

In general, expressions involving pointers conform to the same rules as other C expressions. This section examines a few special aspects of pointer expressions.

Pointer Assignments

As with any variable, you may use a pointer in the right-hand side of assignment statements to assign its value to another pointer. For example,

```
#include "stdio.h"

void main(void)
{
  int x;
  int *p1, *p2;

  p1 = &x;
  p2 = p1;
```

```
printf(" %p", p2); /* print the address of x,
                    not x's value!*/
}
```

Both **p1** and **p2** now point to **x**. The address of **x** is displayed by using the **%p printf( )** format modifier, which causes **printf( )** to display an address in the format used by the host computer.

Pointer Arithmetic

There are only two arithmetic operations that you may use on pointers: addition and subtraction. To understand what occurs in pointer arithmetic, let **p1** be an integer pointer with a current value of 2000. Also, assume integers are 2 bytes long. After the expression

```
p1++;
```

p1 contains 2002, not 2001. Each time **p1** is incremented, it will point to the next integer. The same is true of decrements. For example, assuming that **p1** has the value 2000, the expression

```
p1--;
```

causes **p1** to have the value 1998.

Each time a pointer is incremented, it points to the memory location of the next element of its base type. Each time it is decremented, it points to the location of the previous element. With pointers to characters, this will often appear as "normal" arithmetic. However, all other pointers will increase or decrease by the length of the data type they point to. For example, assuming 1-byte characters and 2-byte integers, when a character pointer is incremented, its value increases by one. However, when an integer pointer is incremented, its value increases by two. This is because pointers are incremented or decremented relative to the length of their base type so that they will always point to the next element. More generally, all pointer arithmetic is done relative to the base type of the pointer so that the pointer is always pointing to the appropriate element of the base type. Figure 5-2 illustrates this concept.

```
char *ch = 3000;
int *i = 3000;
```

Figure 5-2. All pointer arithmetic is relative to its base type

You are not limited to the increment and decrement operators. You may add or subtract integers to or from pointers. The expression

```
p1 = p1 + 12;
```

makes **p1** point to the twelfth element of **p1**'s type beyond the one it currently points to.

Besides addition and subtraction of a pointer and an integer, you may not perform other arithmetic operations on pointers. Specifically, you may not multiply or divide pointers; you may not add two pointers; you may not apply the bitwise shift and mask operators to them; and you may not add or subtract type **float** or **double** to pointers.

Pointer Comparisons

You can compare two pointers in a relational expression. For instance, given two pointers **p** and **q**, the following statment is perfectly valid:

```
if(p<q) printf("p points to lower memory than q\n");
```

Generally, pointer comparisons are used when two or more pointers point to a common object. As an example, a pair of stack routines are developed that store and retrieve integer values. A stack is a list that uses first-in, last-out accessing. It is often compared to a stack of plates on a table—the first one set down is the last one to be used. Stacks are used frequently in compilers, interpreters, spreadsheets, and other system-related software. To create a stack, you need two routines: **push( )** and **pop( )**. The **push( )** function places values on the stack and **pop( )** takes them off. These routines are shown here with a simple **main( )** function to drive them. The program puts the values you enter into the stack. If you enter **0**, a value is popped from the stack. To stop the program, enter **−1**.

```
#include "stdio.h"
#include "stdlib.h"

void push(int i);
int pop(void);

int  *tos, *pl, stack[50];

void main(void)
{
  int value;

  tos = stack;  /* let tos hold top of stack */
  pl = stack; /* initialize pl */

  do {
    printf("Enter value: ");
    scanf("%d", &value);
    if(value!=0) push(value);
    else printf("value on top is %d\n", pop());
  } while(value!=-1);
}

void push(int i)
{
  pl++;
  if(pl==(tos+50)) {
    printf("stack overflow");
    exit(1);
  }
  *pl = i;
}

pop(void)
{
  if(pl==tos) {
```

```
    printf("stack underflow");
    exit(1);
  }
  p1--;
  return *(p1+1);
}
```

You can see that memory for the stack is provided by the array **stack**. The pointer **p1** is set to point to the first byte in **stack**. The **p1** variable actually accesses the stack. The variable **tos** holds the memory address of the top of the stack. The value of **tos** prevents stack underflows. Once the stack has been initialized, **push( )** and **pop( )** may be used as a stack for integers. Both the **push( )** and **pop( )** functions perform a relational test on the pointer **p1** to detect limit errors. In **push( )**, **p1** is tested against the end of stack by adding 50 (the size of the stack) to **tos**. In **pop( )**, **p1** is checked against **tos** to be sure that a stack underflow has not occurred.

In **pop( )**, the parentheses are necessary in the **return** statement. Without them, the statement would look like this:

```
return *p1 +1;
```

which would return the value at location **p1** plus one, not the value of the location **p1+1**. You must use parentheses to ensure the correct order of evaluation when using pointers.

Pointers and Arrays

There is a close relationship between pointers and arrays. Consider this program fragment:

```
char str[80], *p1;

p1 = str;
```

Here, **p1** has been set to the address of the first array element in **str**. To access the fifth element in **str**, you could write

```
str[4]
```

or

```
*(p1+4)
```

Both statements will return the fifth element. Remember, arrays start at 0, so you use a 4 to index **str**. You also add 4 to the pointer **p1** to access the fifth element because **p1** currently points to the first element of **str**. (Recall that an array name without an index returns the starting address of the array, which is the first element.)

C provides two methods of accessing array elements: pointer arithmetic and array indexing. Pointer arithmetic can be faster than array indexing. Since speed is often a consideration in programming, C programmers commonly use pointers to access array elements.

These two versions of **puts( )**—one with array indexing and one with pointers—illustrate how you can use pointers in place of array indexing. You can use the **puts( )** function to write a string to the standard output device.

```
/* Index s as an array. */
void puts(char *s)
{
  register int t;

  for(t=0; s[t]; ++t) putchar(s[t]);

}

/* Access s as a pointer */
void puts(char *s)
{
  while(*s) putchar(*s++);
}
```

Most professional C programmers would find the second version easier to read and understand. In fact, the pointer version is the way routines of this sort are commonly written in C.

Arrays of Pointers

Pointers may be arrayed like any other data type. The declaration for an **int** pointer array of size 10 is

```
int *x[10];
```

To assign the address of an integer variable called **var** to the third element of the pointer array, write

```
x[2] = &var;
```

To find the value of **var**, write

```
*x[2]
```

If you want to pass an array of pointers into a function, you can use the same method that you use to pass other arrays—simply call the function with the array name without any indexes. For example, a function that receives array **x** looks like this:

```
void display_array(int *q[])
{
  int t;

  for(t=0; t<10; t++)
    printf("%d ", *q[t]);

}
```

Remember, **q** is not a pointer to integers, but rather a pointer to an array of pointers to integers. Therefore you need to declare the parameter **q** as an array of integer pointers, as just shown. You cannot declare **q** simply as an integer pointer because that is not what it is.

Pointer arrays are often used to hold pointers to strings. You can create a function that outputs an error message given its code number, as shown here:

```
void syntax_error(int num)
{
  static char *err[] = {
    "cannot open file\n",
    "read error\n",
    "write error\n",
    "media failure\n"
  };

  printf("%s", err[num]);
}
```

The array **err** holds pointers to each string. As you can see, **printf( )** inside **syntax_error( )** is called with a character pointer that points to one of the various error messages indexed by the error number passed to the function. For example, if **num** is passed a 2, the message "write error" is displayed.

Note that the command line argument **argv** is an array of character pointers.

Multiple Indirection

You can have a pointer point to another pointer that points to the target value. This situation is called *multiple indirection,* or *pointers to pointers.* The concept of arrays of pointers is straightforward because the indexes keep the meaning clear. However, pointers to pointers can be confusing. Figure 5-3 illustrates the concept of multiple indirection. As you can see, the value of a normal pointer is the address of the variable that contains the value desired. In the case of a pointer to a pointer, the first pointer contains the address of the second pointer, which points to the variable that contains the value desired.

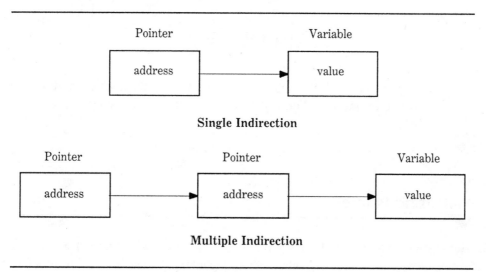

Figure 5-3. Single and multiple indirection

Multiple indirection can be carried on to whatever extent desired, but more than a pointer to a pointer is rarely needed. In fact, excessive indirection is difficult to follow and prone to conceptual errors. (Do not confuse multiple indirection with linked lists.)

A variable that is a pointer to a pointer must be declared as such. You do this by placing an additional asterisk in front of the variable name. For example, the following declaration tells the compiler that **newbalance** is a pointer to a pointer of type **float**:

```
float **newbalance;
```

You should understand that **newbalance** is not a pointer to a floating-point number but rather a pointer to a **float** pointer.

To access the target value indirectly pointed to by a pointer to a pointer, you must apply the asterisk operator twice, as in this example:

```
#include "stdio.h"

void main(void)
{
  int x, *p, **q;

  x = 10;
  p = &x;
  q = &p;

  printf("%d", **q); /* print the value of x */
}
```

Here, **p** is declared as a pointer to an integer and **q** as a pointer to a pointer to an integer. The call to **printf( )** prints the number **10** on the screen.

Initializing Pointers

After a pointer is declared but before it has been assigned a value, it contains an unknown value. Should you try to use the pointer before giving it a value, you will probably crash not only your program, but your computer's operating system—a very nasty type of error!

By convention, you should assign the value null to a pointer that is pointing nowhere to signify that it points to nothing. However, just because a pointer has a null value does not make it "safe." If you use a null pointer on the left side of an assignment statement, you still run the risk of crashing your program or operating system.

Because a null pointer is assumed to be unused, you can use the null pointer to make many of your pointer routines easier to code and more efficient. For example, you could use a null pointer to mark the end of a pointer array. A routine that accesses that array knows that it has reached the end when it encounters the null value. The **search( )** function shown here illustrates this type of approach.

```
/* look up a name */
search(char *p[], char *name)
{
  register int t;

  for(t=0; p[t]; ++t)
    if(!strcmp(p[t], name)) return t;

    return -1; /* not found */
}
```

The **for** loop inside **search( )** runs until either a match is found or a null pointer is encountered. Because the end of the array is marked with a null, the condition controlling the loop fails when it is reached.

C programmers commonly initialize strings. You saw an example of this in the **syntax _ error( )** function in the section "Arrays of Pointers." Another variation on the initialization theme is the following type of string declaration:

```
char *p="hello world\n";
```

As you can see, the pointer **p** is not an array. The reason this sort of initialization works is because of the way the compiler operates. All C compilers create what is called a *string table,* which is used internally by the compiler to store the string constants used by the program. There-fore, the preceding declaration statement places the address of "**hello**

world", as stored in the string table, into the pointer **p**. Throughout the program, **p** can be used like any other string. For example, the following program is perfectly valid:

```
#include "stdio.h"
#include "string.h"

char *p="hello world";

void main(void)
{
  register int t;

  /* print the string forward and backwards */
  printf(p);
  for(t=strlen(p)-1; t>-1; t--) printf("%c", p[t]);
}
```

Pointers to Functions

A confusing yet powerful feature of C is the *function pointer*. Even though a function is not a variable, it has a physical location in memory that can be assigned to a pointer. A function's address is the entry point of the function. Because of this, a function pointer can be used to call a function.

To understand how function pointers work, you must know a little about how a function is compiled and called in C. First, as each function is compiled, source code is transformed into object code and an entry point is established. When a call is made to a function while your program is running, a machine-language call is made to this entry point. Therefore, if a pointer contains the address of a function's entry point, it can be used to call that function.

You obtain the address of a function by using the function's name without any parentheses or arguments. (This is similar to the way an array's address is obtained when only the array name, without indexes, is used.) To see how this is done, study the following program, paying close attention to the declarations:

```
#include "stdio.h"
#include "string.h"
```

```
void check(char *a, char *b, int (*cmp)());

void main(void)
{
  char s1[80],s2[80];
  int (*p)();

  p = strcmp;

  gets(s1);
  gets(s2);

  check(s1, s2, p);
}

void check(char *a, char *b, int (*cmp) ())
{
  printf("testing for equality\n");
  if(!(*cmp)(a, b)) printf("equal");
  else printf("not equal");
}
```

When the **check( )** function is called, two character pointers and one function pointer are passed as parameters. Inside the function **check( )**, the arguments are declared as character pointers and a function pointer. Notice how the function pointer is declared. You must use a similar form when declaring other function pointers, although the return type of the function may differ. The parentheses around the ***cmp** are necessary for the compiler to interpret this statement correctly.

Inside **check( )**, the statement

```
(*cmp)(a, b)
```

calls **strcmp( )**, which is pointed to by **cmp** with the arguments **a** and **b**. Again, the parentheses around ***cmp** are necessary. This example also illustrates the general method for using a function pointer to call the function it points to.

Note that you can call **check( )** by using **strcmp( )** directly, as shown here:

```
check(s1, s2, strcmp);
```

This eliminates the need for an additional pointer variable.

You may wonder why anyone would write a program in this way. Obviously, nothing is gained and significant confusion is introduced in the previous example. However, at times it is advantageous to pass arbitrary functions into procedures or to keep an array of functions. For example, when a compiler is written, the parser (that part that evaluates expressions) often also performs function calls to various support routines—for example, the sine, cosine and tangent functions. Instead of having a large **switch** statement with all of these functions listed in it, an array of function pointers can be used with the proper function selected by its index. You can get the flavor of this type of usage by studying the expanded version of the previous example. In this program, **check( )** can be made to check for either alphabetical equality or numeric equality by simply calling it with a different comparison function.

```c
#include "stdio.h"
#include "ctype.h"
#include "stdlib.h"
#include "string.h"
void check(char *a, char *b, int (*cmp) ());
int numcmp(char *a, char *b);

void main(void)
{
  char s1[80],s2[80];

  gets(s1);
  gets(s2);

  if(isalpha(*s1))
        check(s1, s2, strcmp);
  else
        check(s1, s2, numcmp);

}

void check(char *a, char *b, int (*cmp) ())
{
  printf("testing for equality\n");
  if(!(*cmp)(a, b)) printf("equal");
  else printf("not equal");
}

numcmp(char *a, char *b)
{
  if(atoi(a)==atoi(b)) return 0;
  else return 1;
}
```

C's Dynamic Allocation Functions

Pointers provide necessary support for C's powerful dynamic allocation system. *Dynamic allocation* is the means by which a program can obtain memory while it is running. As you know, global variables are allocated storage at compile time. Local variables use the stack. However, neither global nor local variables can be added during program execution. Yet there will be times when a program needs to use variable amounts of storage. For example, a word processor or a database should take advantage of all the RAM in a system. However, because the amount of available RAM varies between computers, word processors and databases will not be able to do so using normal variables. Instead, these and other programs allocate memory as they need it using C's dynamic allocation system.

Memory allocated by C's dynamic allocation functions is obtained from the heap—the region of free memory that lies between your program and its permanent storage area and the stack. Although the size of the heap is unknown, it generally contains a fairly large amount of free memory.

The core of C's allocation system consists of the functions **malloc( )** and **free( )**. (Actually, C has several other dynamic allocation functions, but these two are the most important.) These functions work together using the free memory region to establish and maintain a list of available storage. The **malloc( )** function allocates memory and the **free( )** function releases it. That is, each time a **malloc( )** memory request is made, a portion of the remaining free memory is allocated. Each time a **free( )** memory release call is made, memory is returned to the system. Any program that uses these functions should include the header file STDLIB.H.

The **malloc( )** function has this prototype:

void *malloc(size_t *number_of_bytes*);

Here, *number_of_bytes* is the number of bytes of memory you wish to allocate. (The type **size_t** is defined in STDLIB.H as (more or less) an **unsigned** integer.) The **malloc( )** function returns a pointer of type **void**, which means that you can assign it to any type of pointer. After a successful call, **malloc( )** returns a pointer to the first byte of the region of memory allocated from the heap. If there is not enough available memory to satisfy the **malloc( )** request, an allocation failure occurs and **malloc( )** returns a null.

The code fragment shown here allocates 1000 bytes of memory:

```
char *p;

p = malloc(1000); /* get 1000 bytes */
```

After the assignment, **p** points to the first of 1000 bytes of free memory.

The next example allocates space for 50 integers. Notice the use of **sizeof** to ensure portabilty.

```
int *p;

p = malloc(50*sizeof(int));
```

Since the heap is not infinite, whenever you allocate memory, you must check the value returned by **malloc( )** to make sure that it is not null before using the pointer. Using a null pointer will almost certainly crash the computer. The proper way to allocate memory and test for a valid pointer is illustrated in this code fragment:

```
if(!(p=malloc(100)) {
  printf("Out of memory.\n");
  exit(1);
}
```

Of course, you can substitute some other sort of error handler in place of the call to **exit( )**. Just make sure that you do not use the pointer **p** if it is null.

The **free( )** function is the opposite of **malloc( )** in that it returns previously allocated memory to the system. Once the memory has been freed, it may be reused by a subsequent call to **malloc( )**. The function **free( )** has this prototype:

```
void free(void *p);
```

It is critical that you *never* call **free( )** with an invalid argument; this will destroy the free list.

C's dynamic allocation subsystem is used in conjuction with pointers to support a variety of important programming constructs, such as linked lists and binary trees. You will see several examples of these in Part Three. Another important use of dynamic allocation is the dynamic array.

Dynamically Allocated Arrays

Sometimes you will want to allocate memory using **malloc( )**, but operate on that memory as if it were an array, using array indexing. In essence, you may want to create a dynamically allocated array. Since any pointer may be indexed as if it were a single-dimension array, this presents no trouble. For example, the following program shows how you can use a dynamically allocated array:

```
/* Allocate space for a string dynamically, request user
   input, and then print the string backwards.
*/

#include "stdlib.h"
#include "stdio.h"
#include "string.h"

void main(void)
{
  char *s;
  register int t;

  s = malloc(80);

  if(!s) {
    printf("memory request failed\n");
    exit(1);
  }

  gets(s);
  for(t=strlen(s)-1; t>=0; t--) putchar(s[t]);
  free(s);
}
```

As the program shows, before its first use, **s** is tested to ensure that the allocation request succeeded and a valid pointer was returned by **malloc( )**. This is absolutely necessary to prevent accidental use of a null pointer, which, as stated earlier, will almost certainly cause a problem. Notice how the pointer **s** is used in the call to **gets( )** and then indexed as an array to print the string backwards.

Accessing allocated memory as if it were a single-dimension array is straightforward. However, multidimensional dynamic arrays pose some problems. Since the dimensions of the array have not been defined in your program, you cannot directly index a pointer as if it were a multidimensional array. To allow a dynamically allocated array, you must use this trick: Pass the pointer as a parameter to a function. This way, the function can define the dimensions of the parameter receiving the pointer, thus allowing normal array indexing. To see how this works, study the following example, which builds a table of the numbers 1 through 10 raised to their first, second, third, and fourth powers:

```
/* Display powers of the numbers 1 through 10.
   Note: even though this is a correct program,
   some compilers will issue a warning message
   concerning the argument to the functions
   table() and show(). If this happens, just
   ignore it.
*/

#include "stdio.h"
#include "stdlib.h"

int pwr(int a, int b);
void table(int p[4][10]);
void show(int p[4][10]);

void main(void)
{
  int *p;

  p = malloc(40*sizeof(int));

  if(!p) {
    printf("memory request failed\n");
    exit(1);
  }

  /* here, p is simply a pointer */
  table(p);
  show(p);
}

/* Build the table of powers. */
void table(int p[4][10]) /* now the compiler has an array
                            to work with */
{
  register int i,j;
```

```
   for(j=1; j<11; j++)
     for(i=1; i<5; i++) p[i][j] = pwr(j, i);
}

/* Display the table of integer powers. */
void show(int p[4][10]) /* now the compiler has an array
                           to work with */
{
  register int i,j;

  printf("%10s %10s %10s %10s\n",
         "N", "N^2", "N^3", "N^4");
  for(j=1; j<11; j++) {
    for(i=1; i<5; i++) printf("%10d ", p[i][j]);
    printf("\n");
  }
}

/* Raise an integer to the specified power. */
pwr(int a, int b)
{
  register int t=1;

  for(; b; b--) t = t*a;
  return t;
}
```

The output produced by this program is shown in Table 5-1.

As this program illustrates, by defining a function parameter to the desired array dimensions, you can trick the C compiler into handling

N	N^2	N^3	N^4
1	1	1	1
2	4	8	16
3	9	27	81
4	16	64	256
5	25	125	625
6	36	216	1296
7	49	343	2401
8	64	512	4096
9	81	729	6561
10	100	1000	10000

Table 5-1.   Output of the Powers Program

multidimensional dynamic arrays. Actually, as far as the C compiler is concerned, you do have a 4,10 integer array inside the functions **show( )** and **table( )**. The difference is that the storage for the array is allocated manually using the **malloc( )** statement, rather than automatically using the normal array declaration statement. Also, note the use of **sizeof** to compute the number of bytes needed for a 4,10 integer array. This guarantees the portability of this program to computers with integers of a different size.

Problems with Pointers

Nothing will get you into more trouble than a wild pointer! Pointers are a mixed blessing. They give you tremendous power and are necessary for many programs. At the same time, when a pointer accidentally contains a wrong value, it can be the most difficult bug to find.

An erroneous pointer bug is difficult to find because the pointer itself is not the problem. The problem is that each time you perform an operation using the pointer, you are reading or writing to some unknown piece of memory. If you read from it, the worst that can happen is that you get garbage. However, if you write to it, you might be writing over other pieces of your code or data. This may not show up until later in the execution of your program, and may lead you to look for the bug in the wrong place. There may be little or no evidence to suggest that the pointer is the problem. This type of bug causes programmers to lose sleep time and time again.

Because pointer errors are such nightmares, you should do your best never to generate one. To help you avoid them, a few of the more common errors are discussed here. The classic example of a pointer error is the *uninitialized pointer*. Consider this program.

```
void main(void)   /* this program is wrong */
{
  int x, *p;

  x = 10;
  *p = x;
}
```

This program assigns the value 10 to some unknown memory location. Since the pointer **p** has never been given a value, it contains a garbage value. This type of problem often goes unnoticed when your program is small because the odds are in favor of **p** containing a "safe" address — one that is not in your code, data area, or operating system. However, as your program grows, the probability increases of **p** pointing to something vital. Eventually, your program stops working. The solution is to always make sure that a pointer is pointing at something valid before it is used.

A second common error is caused by a simple misunderstanding of how to use a pointer. Consider

```
void main(void)  /* this program is wrong */
{
  int x, *p;

  x = 10;
  p = x;
  printf("%d", *p);
}
```

The call to **printf( )** does not print the value of **x**, which is 10, on the screen. It prints some unknown value because the assignment

```
p = x;
```

is wrong. That statement assigns the value 10 to the pointer **p**, which is supposed to contain an address, not a value. To correct the program, write

```
p = &x;
```

Another error that sometimes occurs is caused by incorrect assumptions about the placement of variables in memory. You can never know where your data will be placed in memory, or if it will be placed there the same way again, or whether each compiler will treat it in the same way. For these reasons, making any comparisons between pointers that do not point to a common object yields unexpected results. For example,

```
char s[80], y[80];
char *p1, *p2;
```

```
p1 = s;
p2 = y;

if(p1 < p2) . . .
```

is generally an invalid concept. (In very unusual situations, you might use something like this to determine the relative position of the variables.)

A related error results when you assume that two adjacent arrays may be indexed as one by simply incrementing a pointer across the array boundaries. For example,

```
int first[10], second[10];
int *p,t;

p = first;
for(t=0; t<20; ++t)  *p++ = t;
```

This is not a good way to initialize arrays **first** and **second** with the numbers 0 through 19. Even though it may work on some compilers under certain circumstances, it assumes that both arrays will be placed back to back in memory with **first** first. This may not always be the case.

The next program illustrates a very dangerous type of bug. See if you can find it.

```
#include "string.h"
#include "stdio.h"

void main(void)  /* this program has a bug */
{
  char *p1;
  char s[80];

  p1 = s;
  do {
    gets(s); /* read a string */

    /* print the decimal equivalent of each
       character */
    while(*p1) printf(" %d",*p1++);

  } while(strcmp(s, "done"));
}
```

This program uses **p1** to print the ASCII values associated with the characters contained in **s**. The problem is that **p1** is assigned the address of **s** only once. The first time through the loop, **p1** points to the first character in **s**. However, the second time through, it continues where it left off because it is not reset to the start of **s**. This next character may be part of the second string, another variable, or a piece of the program! The proper way to write this program is

```
#include "string.h"
#include "stdio.h"

void main(void)  /* this program is correct */
{
  char *p1;
  char s[80];

  do {
    p1 = s;
    gets(s);  /* read a string */

    /* print the decimal equivalent of each
       character */
    while(*p1) printf(" %d",*p1++);

  } while(strcmp(s, "done"));
}
```

Here, each time the loop iterates, **p1** is set to the start of the string. In general, you should remember to reinitialize a pointer if it is to be reused.

The fact that handling pointers incorrectly can cause tricky bugs is no reason to avoid using them. Just be careful, and make sure that you know where each pointer is pointing before you use it.

Functions

Functions are the building blocks of C and the place where all program activity occurs. They are one of C's most important features.

The General Form of a Function

The general form of a function is

> *type_specifier function_name(parameter list)*
> *{*
>   *body of the function*
> *}*

The *type_specifier* specifies the type of value that the **return** statement of the function returns. It may be any valid type. If no type is specified, the compiler assumes that the function returns an integer result. The *parameter list* is a comma-separated list of variable names and their associated types that receive the values of the arguments when the function is called. A function may be without parameters, in which case the parameter list is empty. However, even if there are no parameters, the parentheses are still required.

In variable declarations, you can declare many variables to be of a common type by using a comma-separated list of variable names. In contrast all function parameters must include both the type and variable name. That is, the parameter declaration list for a function takes this general form:

f(type varname1, type varname2, . . . , type varnameN)

Scope Rules of Functions

The *scope rules* of a language are the rules that govern whether a piece of code knows about or has access to another piece of code or data.

In C, each function is a discrete block of code. A function's code is private to that function and cannot be accessed by any statement in any other function except through a call to that function. (For instance, you cannot use **goto** to jump into the middle of another function.) The code that constitutes the body of a function is hidden from the rest of the program and, unless it uses global variables or data, it can neither affect nor be affected by other parts of the program. Stated another way, the code and data that are defined within one function cannot interact with the code or data defined in another function because the two functions have a different scope.

Variables that are defined within a function are called local variables. A local variable comes into existence when the function is entered and is destroyed upon exit. That is, local variables cannot hold their value between function calls. The only exception to this rule is when the variable is declared with the **static** storage class specifier. This causes the compiler to treat the variable as if it were a global variable for storage purposes, but still to limit its scope to within the function. (Chapter 2 covers global and local variables in depth.)

In C, all functions are at the same scope level. That is, you cannot define a function within a function. This is why C is not technically a block-structured language.

Function Arguments

If a function is to use arguments, it must declare variables that accept the values of the arguments. That these variables are called the formal parameters of the function. They behave like other local variables inside the function and are created upon entry into the function and destroyed upon exit. As shown in the following function, the parameter declaration occurs after the function name:

```
/* return 1 if c is part of string s; 0 otherwise */
is_in(char *s,  char c)
{
  while(*s)
    if(*s==c) return 1;
    else s++;

  return 0;
}
```

The function **is_in( )** has two parameters: **s** and **c**. This function returns 1 if the character **c** is part of the string **s**; otherwise, it returns 0.

You must make sure that the arguments used to call a function are compatible with the type of its parameters. If the types are incompatible, the compiler does not issue an error message, but unexpected results may occur. Unlike many other languages, C is robust and generally does something with any syntactically correct program, even if that program contains questionable type mismatches. For example, if a function expects a pointer but is called with a value, unanticipated results can occur. The use of function prototypes (discussed shortly) can help catch these types of errors.

As with local variables, you may make assignments to a function's formal parameters or use them in any allowable C expression. Even though these variables perform the special task of receiving the value of the arguments passed to the function, you can use them as you do any other local variable.

Call by Value, Call by Reference

In general, subroutines can be passed arguments in one of two ways. The first is called *call by value*. This method copies the value of an argument into the formal parameter of the subroutine. Therefore, changes made to the parameters of the subroutine have no effect on the variables used to call it.

Call by reference is the second way of passing arguments to a subroutine. In this method, the address of an argument is copied into the parameter. Inside the subroutine, the address is used to access the actual argument used in the call. This means that changes made to the parameter affect the variable used to call the routine.

With a few exceptions, C uses call by value to pass arguments. In general, this means that you cannot alter the variables used to call the function. (You learn later in this chapter how to force a call by reference by using a pointer to allow changes to the calling variables.) Consider the following program:

```
#include "stdio.h"

int sqr(int x);

void main(void)
{
  int t=10;

  printf("%d %d", sqr(t), t);
}

sqr(int x)
{
  x = x*x;
  return(x);
}
```

In this example, the value of the argument to **sqr( )**, 10, is copied into the parameter **x**. When the assignment **x = x*x** takes place, only the local variable **x** is modified. The variable **t**, used to call **sqr( )**, still has the value 10. Hence, the output is **100 10**.

Remember that it is a copy of the value of the argument that is passed into that function. What occurs inside the function has no effect on the variable used in the call.

Creating a Call by Reference

Even though C's parameter-passing convention is call by value, you can create a call by reference by passing a pointer to the argument. Since this causes the address of the argument to be passed to the function, you can then change the value of the argument outside the function.

Pointers are passed to functions just like any other value. Of course, you need to declare the parameters as pointer types. For example, the function **swap( )**, which exchanges the value of its two integer arguments, shows how.

```
void swap(int *x, int *y)
{
  int temp;

  temp = *x;   /* save the value at address x */
  *x = *y;     /* put y into x */
  *y = temp;   /* put x into y */
}
```

The * operator accesses the variable pointed to by its operand. (See Chapter 2 for a complete discussion of *. Also, Chapter 5 deals exclusively with pointers.) Hence, the contents of the variables used to call the function are swapped.

Remember that **swap( )** (or any other function that uses pointer parameters) must be called with the addresses of the arguments. The following program shows the correct way to call **swap( )**:

```
void swap(int *x, int *y);

void main(void)
{
  int x, y;

  x = 10;
  y = 20;
  swap(&x, &y);
}
```

In this example, the variable **x** is assigned the value 10 and **y** is assigned the value 20. Then **swap( )** is called with the addresses of **x** and **y**. The unary operator **&** is used to produce the address of the variables. Therefore, the addresses of **x** and **y**, not their values, are passed into the function **swap( )**. (See Chapter 2 for a complete discussion of the **&** operator.)

Calling Functions with Arrays

Arrays are covered in detail in Chapter 4. However, this section discusses passing arrays as arguments to functions because it is an exception to the standard call-by-value parameter passing.

When an array is used as an argument to a function, only the address of the array is passed, not a copy of the entire array. When you call a function with an array name, a pointer to the first element in the array is passed into the function. (Don't forget, in C an array name without any index is a pointer to the first element in the array.) This means that the parameter declaration must be of a compatible pointer type. There are three ways to declare a parameter that is to receive an array pointer. First, it may be declared as an array, as shown here:

```
#include "stdio.h"

void display(int num[10]);

void main(void)  /* print some numbers */
{
  int t[10], i;

  for(i=0; i<10; ++i) t[i]=i;
  display(t);
}

void display(int num[10])
{
  int i;

  for(i=0; i<10; i++) printf("%d ", num[i]);
}
```

Even though the parameter **num** is declared as an integer array of ten elements, the C compiler automatically converts it to an integer pointer. This is necessary because no parameter can actually receive an entire array. Therefore, only a pointer to an array is passed, so a pointer parameter must be there to receive it.

The second way to declare an array parameter is to specify it as an unsized array, as shown here:

```
void display(int num[])
{
  int i;
```

```
    for(i=0; i<10; i++) printf("%d ", num[i]);
}
```

Here, **num** is declared as an integer array of unknown size. Since C provides no array-boundary checks, the actual size of the array is irrelevant to the parameter (but not to the program, of course). This method of declaration also actually defines **num** as an integer pointer.

The final way that **num** can be declared—the most common form in professionally written C programs—is as a pointer, as shown here:

```
void display(int *num)
{
    int i;

    for(i=0; i<10; i++) printf("%d ", num[i]);
}
```

This is allowed because any pointer may be indexed using [] as if it were an array. (Actually, arrays and pointers are very closely linked.)

On the other hand, an array element used as an argument is treated like any other simple variable. For example, the preceding program could have been written without passing the entire array:

```
#include "stdio.h"

void display(int num);

void main(void) /* print some numbers */
{
    int t[10], i;

    for(i=0; i<10; ++i) t[i]=i;
    for(i=0; i<10; i++) display(t[i]);
}

void display(int num)
{
    printf("%d ", num);
}
```

As you can see, the parameter to **display( )** is of type **int**. It is not relevant that **display( )** is called using an array element, because only that one value of the array is used.

You should realize that when an array is used as a function argument, its address is passed to a function. This is an exception to C's call-by-value parameter passing convention. In this case, the code inside the function is operating on, and potentially altering, the actual contents of the array used to call the function. For example, consider the function **print_upper( )**, which prints its string argument in uppercase:

```c
#include "stdio.h"
#include "ctype.h"

void print_upper(char *string);

void main(void)
{
  char s[80];

  gets(s);
  print_upper(s);
}

/* Print a string in uppercase. */
void print_upper(char *string)
{
  register int t;

  for(t=0; string[t]; ++t)  {
    string[t] = toupper(string[t]);
    putchar(string[t]);
  }
}
```

After the call to **print_upper( )**, the contents of array **s** in **main( )** will change to uppercase. If this is not what you want, you could write the program like this:

```c
#include "stdio.h"
#include "ctype.h"

void print_upper(char *string);

void main(void)
{
  char s[80];

  gets(s);
  print_upper(s);
}

void print_upper(char *string)
{
  register int t;

  for(t=0; string[t]; ++t)
```

```
      putchar(toupper(string[t]));
}
```

In this version, the contents of array **s** remain unchanged because its values are not altered.

The standard library function **gets( )** is a classic example of passing arrays into functions. The **gets( )** in your standard library is more sophisticated and complex. However, the following simpler function, **xgets( )**, will give you an idea of how it works.

```
/* A very simple version of the standard
   gets() library function */
char *xgets(char *s)
{
  char ch, *p;
  int t;

  p = s;  /* gets returns a pointer to s */

  for(t=0; t<80; ++t) {
    ch = getchar();
    switch(ch) {
      case '\n':
        s[t] = '\0'; /* terminate
                        the string */
        return p;
      case '\b':
        if(t>0) t--;
        break;
      default:
        s[t] = ch;
    }
  }
  s[80] = '\0';
  return p;
}
```

The **xgets( )** function must be called with a character pointer, which can be either a variable declared as a character pointer, or the name of a character array, which by definition is a character pointer. Upon entry, **xgets( )** establishes a **for** loop from 0 to 80. This prevents larger strings from being entered at the keyboard. If more than 80 characters are entered, the function returns. (The real **gets( )** function does not have this restriction.) Because C has no built-in bounds checking, you should make sure that any variable used to call **xgets( )** can accept at least 80 characters. As you type characters on the keyboard, they are placed in the string. If you type a backspace, the counter **t** is reduced by

1. When you press ENTER, a null is placed at the end of the string, signaling its termination. Because the actual array used to call **xgets( )** is modified, upon return it contains the characters typed.

argc and argv—Arguments to main( )

Sometimes it is useful to pass information into a program when you run it. Generally, you pass information into the **main( )** function via command line arguments. A *command line argument* is the information that follows the program's name on the command line of the operating system. For example, when you compile C programs, you type something like the following after the screen prompt:

cc *program_name*

where *program_name* is the program you wish to compile. The name of the program is passed into the C compiler as an argument.

There are two special built-in arguments, **argv** and **argc**, that are used to receive command line arguments. The **argc** parameter holds the number of arguments on the command line and is an integer. It is always at least 1 because the name of the program qualifies as the first argument. The **argv** parameter is a pointer to an array of character pointers. Each element in this array points to a command line argument. All command line arguments are strings—any numbers will have to be converted by the program into the proper internal format. For example, this simple program prints **Hello** and your name on the screen if you type it directly after the program name.

```
#include "stdio.h"
#include "stdlib.h"

void main(int argc, char *argv[])
{
  if(argc!=2) {
    printf("You forgot to type your name\n");
    exit(1);
  }
  printf("Hello %s", argv[1]);
}
```

If you called this program **name** and your name was Tom, you would type **name Tom** to run the program. The output from the program would be **Hello Tom**.

In many environments, each command line argument must be separated by a space or a tab. Commas, semicolons, and the like are not considered separators. For example,

```
run Spot, run
```

is made up of three strings, while

```
Herb,Rick,Fred
```

is a single string since commas are not legal separators.

Some environments allow you to enclose within double quotes a string containing spaces. This causes the entire string to be treated as a single argument. Check your operating system manual for details on the definition of command line parameters for your system.

You must declare **argv** properly. The most common method is

```
char *argv[];
```

The empty brackets indicate that the array is of undetermined length. You can now access the individual arguments by indexing **argv**. For example, **argv[0]** points to the first string, which is always the program's name; **argv[1]** points to the first argument, and so on.

Another short example using command line arguments is the program called **countdown**, shown here. It counts down from a value specified on the command line and beeps when it reaches 0. Notice that the first argument containing the number is converted into an integer by the standard function **atoi( )**. If the string "display" is the second command line argument, the countdown will also be displayed on the screen.

```
/* Countdown program. */

#include "stdio.h"
#include "stdlib.h"
#include "ctype.h"
#include "string.h"
```

```
void main(int argc, char *argv[])
{
  int disp, count;

  if(argc<2) {
    printf("you must enter the length of the count\n");
    printf("on the command line.  Try again.\n");
    exit(1);
  }

  if(argc==3 && !strcmp(argv[2],"display")) disp = 1;
  else disp = 0;

  for(count=atoi(argv[1]); count; --count)
    if(disp) printf("%d\n", count);

  putchar(7);  /* this will ring the bell on most
                  computers */
  printf("done");
}
```

Notice that if no arguments have been specified, an error message is printed. A program with command line arguments often issues instructions if the user attempts to run the program without entering the proper information.

To access an individual character in one of the command strings, add a second index to **argv**. For example, the next program displays all of the arguments with which it was called, one character at a time:

```
#include "stdio.h"

void main(int argc, char *argv[])
{
  int t, i;

  for(t=0; t<argc; ++t) {
    i = 0;
    while(argv[t][i]) {
      putchar(argv[t][i]);
      ++i;
    }
  }
}
```

Remember, the first index accesses the string and the second index accesses the individual characters of the string.

Usually, you use **argc** and **argv** to get initial commands into your program. In theory, you can have up to 32,767 arguments, but most operating systems do not allow more than a few. You normally use these arguments to indicate a file name or an option. Using command line arguments gives your program a professional appearance and facilitates its use in batch files.

It is common practice to declare **main( )** as having no parameters using the **void** keyword when its command line parameters are not being used. However, if you like you may simply specify nothing between the parentheses.

Note: The names **argc** and **argv** are traditional but arbitrary. You may name these two parameters to **main( )** anything you like. Also, some compilers may support additional arguments to **main( )**, so be sure to check your user's manual.

The return Statement

The **return** statement has two important uses. First, it causes an immediate exit from the function that it is in. That is, it causes program execution to return to the calling code. Second, it may be used to return a value.

Returning from a Function

There are two ways that a function terminates execution and returns to the caller. The first occurs when the last statement in the function has executed and, conceptually, the function's ending curly brace (}) is encountered. (Of course, the curly brace isn't actually present in the object code, but you can think of it in this way.) For example, the **pr_reverse( )** function in this program simply prints the string "I like C" backwards on the screen.

```
#include "string.h"
#include "stdio.h"

void pr_reverse(char *s);

void main(void)
```

```
{
  pr_reverse("I like C");
}

void pr_reverse(char *s)
{
  register int t;

  for(t=strlen(s)-1; t>=0; t--) putchar(s[t]);
}
```

Once the string has been displayed, there is nothing left for **pr_reverse( )** to do, so it returns to the place it was called from.

Actually, not many functions use this default method of terminating their execution. Most functions rely on the **return** statement to stop execution either because a value must be returned or to make a function's code simpler and more efficient.

Remember, a function may contain several **return** statements. For example, the **find_substr( )** function in the following program returns the starting position of a substring within a string, or returns −1 if no match is found.

```
#include "stdio.h"

int find_substr(char *s1, char *s2);

void main(void)
{
  if(find_substr("C is fun", "is")!=-1)
    printf("substring is found");
}

/* Return index of first match of s2 in s1. */
find_substr(char *s1, char *s2)
{
  register int t;
  char *p, *p2;

  for(t=0; s1[t]; t++) {
    p = &s1[t];
    p2 = s2;
    while(*p2 && *p2==*p) {
      p++;
      p2++;
    }
    if(!*p2) return t;
  }
  return -1;
}
```

Returning Values

All functions, except those of type **void**, return a value. This value is explicitly specified by the **return** statement. If no **return** statement is present, then the return value of the function is technically undefined. (Generally, C compiler implementers return 0 when no explicit return value is specified, but you should not count on this if portability is a concern.) In other words, as long as a function is not declared as **void**, you may use it as an operand in any valid C expression. Therefore, each of the following expressions is valid in C:

```
x = power(y);

if(max(x,y) > 100) printf("greater");

for(ch=getchar(); isdigit(ch); ) ... ;
```

However, a function cannot be the target of an assignment. A statement such as

```
swap(x,y) = 100; /* incorrect statement */
```

is wrong. The C compiler will flag it as an error and will not compile a program that contains it.

When you write programs, your functions generally will be of three types. The first type is simply computational. These functions are specifically designed to perform operations on their arguments and return a value based on that operation. A computational function is a "pure" function. Examples are the standard library functions **sqrt( )** and **sin( )**, which compute the square root and sine of their arguments.

The second type of function manipulates information and returns a value that simply indicates the success or failure of that manipulation. An example is the library function **fclose( )**, which is used to close a file. If the close operation is successful, the function returns 0; if the operation is unsuccessful, it returns an error code.

The last type of function has no explicit return value. In essence, the function is strictly procedural and produces no value. An example is **exit( )**, which terminates a program. All functions that do not return values should be declared as returning type **void**. By declaring a function as **void**, you keep it from being used in an expression, thus preventing accidental misuse.

Sometimes, functions that really don't produce an interesting result return something anyway. For example, **printf( )** returns the number of characters written. Yet, it would be unusual to find a program that actually checked this. In other words, although all functions, except those of type **void**, return values, you don't have to use the return value for anything. A common question concerning function return values is, "Don't I have to assign this value to some variable since a value is being returned?" The answer is no. If there is no assignment specified, the return value is simply discarded. Consider the following programming, which uses the function **mul( )**:

```
#include "stdio.h"

int mul(int a, int b);

void main(void)
{
  int x, y, z;

  x = 10;    y = 20;
  z = mul(x, y);         /* 1 */
  printf("%d", mul(x,y));  /* 2 */
  mul(x, y);             /* 3 */
}

mul(int a, int b)
{
  return a*b;
}
```

In line 1, the return value of **mul( )** is assigned to **z**. In line 2, the return value is not actually assigned, but it is used by the **printf( )** function. Finally, in line 3, the return value is lost because it is neither assigned to another variable nor used as part of an expression.

Functions That Return Noninteger Values

When the type of a function is not explicitly declared, it automatically defaults to **int**. For many C functions, this default will work. However, when a different data type is required, the process involves two steps. First, the function must be given an explicit type specifier. Second, the type of the function must be identified before the first call made to it. Only in this way can C generate correct code for functions returning noninteger values.

Functions may be declared to return any valid C data type. Declaring functions is similar to declaring variables: the type specifier precedes the function name. The type specifier tells the compiler what type of data the function is to return. This information is critical if the program is going to run correctly because different data types have different sizes and internal representations.

Before you can use a function returning a noninteger type, its type must be made known to the rest of the program. This is because, unless directed to the contrary, C assumes that a function will return an integer value. If your program calls a function that returns a different type prior to that function's declaration, the compiler mistakenly generates the wrong code for the function call. To prevent this, you must use a special form of declaration statement near the top of your program to tell the compiler what value that function is really returning.

There are two ways to declare a function before it is used: the traditional way and the new prototype method added and strongly recommended by the ANSI C standard. Let's begin by examining the traditional approach. Even though it is outdated, many thousands of existing programs still use it, so you should be familiar with it. Moreover, the prototype method is basically an extension of the traditional concept.

Note: The traditional approach is allowed by the ANSI standard in order to provide compatibility with older code, but new uses of it are discouraged.

With the traditional approach, you specify the function's type and name near the start of your program to inform the compiler that a function will return some type of value other than an integer, as illustrated here:

```
#include "stdio.h"

float sum();  /* identify the function */
```

```
float first, second;

void main(void)
{
  first = 123.23;
  second = 99.09;
  printf("%f", sum());
}

float sum()
{
 return first + second;
}
```

The first function type declaration tells the compiler that **sum( )** returns a floating-point data type. This allows the compiler to correctly generate code for calls to **sum( )**. Without the declaration, the compiler will flag a type mismatch error.

The traditional function type declaration statement has the general form

type _ specifier function _ name( );

Even if the function takes arguments, none are listed in its type declaration.

Without the type declaration statement, a mismatch occurs between the type of data the function returns and the type of data the calling routine expects. The results will be bizarre and unpredictable. If both functions are in the same file, the compiler catches the type mismatch and does not compile the program. However, if the functions are in different files, the compiler does not detect the error. Type checking is not done at link time or run time, only at compile time. For this reason, you must make sure that both types are compatible.

Note: When a character is returned from a function declared to be of type **int**, the character value is converted into an integer. Because C cleanly handles the conversion from character to integer and back again, a function that returns a character value is often not declared as returning a character value. The programmer instead relies upon the default type conversion of characters into integers and back again. This sort of thing is found frequently in older C code and is not technically considered an error.

Function Prototypes

The ANSI C standard expanded the traditional function declaration by allowing the number and types of the function's arguments to be declared. This expanded definition is called a function prototype. Function prototypes were not part of the original C language. They are, however, one of the most important ANSI additions to C. In this book, all examples include full function prototypes. Prototypes enable C to provide stronger type checking, somewhat like that provided by languages such as Pascal. When you use prototypes, C can find and report any illegal type conversions between the type of arguments used to call a function and the type definition of its parameters. C will also catch differences between the number of arguments used to call a function and the number of parameters in the function.

The general form of a function prototype definition is

type func_name(type parm_name1, type parm_name2,...,
type parm_nameN);

The use of parameter names is optional. However, they enable the compiler to identify any type mismatches by name when an error occurs, so it is a good idea to include them.

For example, the following program produces an error message because it contains an attempt to call **sqr_it( )** with an integer argument instead of the integer pointer required. (You cannot transform an integer into a pointer.)

```
/* This program uses a function prototype to
   enforce strong type checking.
*/

void sqr_it(int *i); /* prototype */

void main(void)
{
  int x;

  x = 10;
  sqr_it(x);  /* type mismatch */
}

void sqr_it(int *i)
{
  *i = *i * *i;
}
```

Because of the need for compatibility with the original version of C, some special rules apply to function prototypes. First, when a function's return type is declared with no prototype information, the compiler simply assumes that no information about the parameters is given. As far as the compiler is concerned, the function could have several parameters or no parameters. Therefore, how does one prototype a function that does not have any parameters? The answer is this: When a function has no parameters, its prototype uses **void** inside the parentheses. For example, if a function called f( ) returns a **float** and has no parameters, its prototype looks like this:

```
float f(void);
```

This tells the compiler that the function has no parameters, and any call to that function that has parameters is an error.

Prototyping affects C's automatic type promotions. When a nonprototyped function is called, all characters are converted to integers and all **float**s into **double**s. These somewhat odd type promotions have to do with the characteristics of the original environment in which C was developed. However, if you prototype a function, the types specified in the prototype are maintained and no type promotions will occur.

Function prototypes help you trap bugs before they occur. In addition, they help verify that your program is working correctly by not allowing functions to be called with mismatched arguments.

Keep one fact firmly in mind: the ANSI standard strongly recommends the use of function prototypes, even though it is not an error if there is no prototype for a function. This is necessary to support preprototype C code. Nevertheless, your code should, in general, include full prototyping information.

Returning Pointers

Although functions that return pointers are handled just like any other type of function, a few important concepts need to be discussed.

Pointers to variables are neither integers nor unsigned integers. They are the memory addresses of a certain type of data. The reason for this distinction is because pointer arithmetic is relative to the base type. For example, if an integer pointer is incremented, it will contain a value that is 2 greater than its previous value (assuming 2-byte words). In general, each time a pointer is incremented, it points to the next data item of its type. Since each data type may be of different length, the compiler must know what type of data the pointer is pointing to in order to make it point to the next data item.

For example, this function returns a pointer to the first occurrence of the character **c** in string **s**:

```
/* Return pointer of first occurence of c in s. */
char *match(char c, char *s)
{
  while(c!=*s && *s) s++;
  return(s);
}
```

If no match is found, a pointer to the null terminator is returned. This function would not work if **s** had been declared a **float** pointer, for example. Here is a short program that uses **match( )**:

```
#include "stdio.h"

char *match(char c, char *s);  /* prototype */

void main(void)
{
  char s[80], *p;

  gets(s);
  ch = getchar();
  p = match(ch, s);
  if(p)  /* there is a match */
    printf("%s ", p);
  else
    printf("no match found");
}
```

This program reads a string and then a character. If the character is in the string, the program prints the string from the point of match. Otherwise, it prints **no match found.**

Functions of Type void

One of **void**'s uses is to declare explicitly functions that do not return values. This prevents their use in any expression and helps avert accidental misuse. For example, the function **print_vertical( )** prints its string argument vertically down the side of the screen. Since it returns no value it is declared as **void**.

```
void print_vertical(char *str)
{
  while(*str)
    printf("%c\n", *str++);
}
```

Before you can use any **void** function, you must declare its prototype. If you don't, C assumes that it is returning an integer and when the compiler actually reaches the function, it declares a type mismatch. The following program shows a proper example that prints a single command line argument vertically on the screen:

```
#include "stdio.h"

void print_vertical(char *str);   /* prototype */

void main(int argc, char *argv[])
{
  if(argc) print_vertical(argv[1]);
}

void print_vertical(char *str)
{
  while(*str)
    printf("%c\n", *str++);
}
```

Before the ANSI C standard defined **void**, functions that did not return values simply defaulted to type **int**. Therefore, don't be surprised to see many examples of this in older code.

What Does main( ) Return?

According to the ANSI standard, the **main( )** function returns an integer to the calling process, which is generally the operating system.

Returning a value from **main( )** is the equivalent of calling **exit( )** with the same value. If **main( )** does not explicitly return a value, the value passed to the calling process is technically undefined. In practice, most C compilers automatically return 0, but do not rely on this if portability is a concern.

You may also declare **main( )** as **void** if it does not return a value. Some compilers issue a warning message if a function is not declared as **void** and also does not return a value.

Recursion

In C, functions can call themselves. A function is *recursive* if a statement in the body of the function calls itself. Recursion is the process of defining something in terms of itself, and is sometimes called *circular definition*.

Examples of recursion abound. For instance, a recursive way to define an integer is as the digits 0, 1, 2, 3, 4, 5, 6, 7, 8, 9 plus or minus an integer. For example, the number 15 is the number 7 plus the number 8; 21 is 9 plus 12; and 12 is 9 plus 3.

For a computer language to be recursive, a function must be able to call itself. A simple example is the function **factr( )**, which computes the factorial of an integer. The factorial of a number N is the product of all the whole numbers between 1 and N. For example, 3 factorial is $1 \times 2 \times 3$, or 6. Both **factr( )** and its iterative equivalent are shown here:

```
factr(int n)  /* recursive */
{
  int answer;

  if(n==1) return(1);
  answer = factr(n-1)*n;
  return(answer);
}

fact(int n)     /* non-recursive */
{
  int t, answer;

  answer = 1;
  for(t=1; t<=n; t++)
    answer=answer*(t);
```

```
  return(answer);
}
```

The nonrecursive version of **fact( )** should be clear. It uses a loop that runs from 1 to **n** and progressively multiplies each number by the moving product.

The operation of the recursive **factr( )** is a little more complex. When **factr( )** is called with an argument of 1, the function returns 1. Otherwise, it returns the product of **factr(n−1)*n**. To evaluate this expression, **factr( )** is called with **n−1**. This happens until **n** equals 1 and the calls to the function begin returning.

Computing the factorial of 2, the first call to **factr( )** causes a second call with the argument of 1. This call returns 1, which is then multiplied by 2 (the original **n** value). The answer is then 2. (You might want to insert **printf( )** statements into **factr( )** to see the level of each call and what the intermediate answers are.)

When a function calls itself, new local variables and parameters are allocated storage on the stack and the function code is executed with these new variables from the start. A recursive call does not make a new copy of the function. Only the arguments are new. As each recursive call returns, the old local variables and parameters are removed from the stack and execution resumes at the point of the function call inside the function. Recursive functions could be said to "telescope" out and back.

Most recursive routines do not significantly reduce code size or improve memory utilization. Also, the recursive versions of most routines may execute a bit slower than their iterative equivalent because of the repeated function calls. In fact, many recursive calls to a function could cause a stack overrun. Because storage for function parameters and local variables is on the stack and each new call creates a new copy of these variables, the stack could possibly overwrite some other data or program memory. However, you probably will not have to worry about this unless a recursive function runs wild.

The main advantage to recursive functions is that you can use them to create clearer and simpler versions of several algorithms. For example, the QuickSort in Part Three is quite difficult to implement in an iterative way. Also, some problems, especially ones related to artificial intelligence, lend themselves to recursive solutions. Finally, some people seem to think recursively more easily than iteratively.

When writing recursive functions, you must have an **if** statement somewhere to force the function to return without the recursive call being executed. If you don't, the function will never return once you call it. Omitting the **if** is a common error when writing recursive functions. Use **printf( )** and **getchar( )** liberally during program development so that you can watch what is going on and abort execution if you see a mistake.

Declaring Variable Length and Type Parameter Lists

In C, you can specify a function that has a variable number and type of parameters. The most common example is **printf( )**. To tell the compiler that an unknown number and type of parameters may be passed to a function, you must end the declaration of its parameters using three periods. For example, this declaration specifies that **func( )** will have at least two integer parameters and an unknown number (including 0) of parameters after that.

```
func(int a, int b, ...);
```

This form of declaration is also used by a function's prototype.

Any function that uses a variable number of arguments must have at least one actual argument. For example, this is incorrect:

```
func(...);
```

For more on variable number and type parameters, see Part Two, under the standard library function **va_arg( )**.

Classic Versus Modern Function Parameter Declarations

C originally used a different parameter declaration method, sometimes called the *classic* form. This book uses a declaration approach called the *modern* form. The ANSI standard for C supports both forms, but strongly recommends the modern form. However, you should know the classic form because literally millions of lines of existing C code use it! Also, many programs use this form because it works with all compilers — even old ones.

The classic function parameter declaration consists of two parts: a parameter list, which goes inside the parentheses that follow the function name, and the actual parameter declarations, which go between the closing parentheses and the function's opening curly brace. The general form of the classic parameter definition is

```
type func _ name(parm1, parm2,. . .parmN)
type parm1;
type parm2;
     .

     .

     .
type parmN;
{
   function code
}
```

For example, this modern declaration:

```
float f(int a, int b, char ch)
{
   .

   .

   .
}
```

will look like this in its classic form:

```
float f(a, b, ch)
int a, b;
char ch;
{
   .

   .

   .
}
```

Notice that classic form can support more than one parameter in a list after the type name.

There are some subtle reasons that the modern form is a little better than the classic form. However, remember that your compiler can compile a program that uses the classic form with no trouble.

Implementation Issues

There are a few important things to remember when you create C functions that affect their efficiency and usability. These issues are the subject of this section.

Parameters and General-Purpose Functions

A general-purpose function is one that will be used in a variety of situations, perhaps by many different programmers. Typically, you should not base general-purpose functions on global data. All of the information a function needs should be passed to it by its parameters. When this is not possible, you should use static variables.

Besides making your functions general-purpose, parameters keep your code readable and less susceptible to bugs resulting from side effects.

Efficiency

Functions are the building blocks of C and are crucial to all but the simplest programs. However, in certain specialized applications, you may need to eliminate a function and replace it with *in-line code*. In-line code is the equivalent of a function's statements used without a call to that function. Use in-line code instead of function calls only when execution time is critical.

In-line code is faster than a function call for two reasons. First, a CALL instruction takes time to execute. Second, if there are arguments to pass, these have to be placed on the stack, which also takes time. For most applications, this very slight increase in execution time is of no significance. But if it is, remember that each function call uses time that would be saved if the function code were placed in line. For example, the following are two versions of a program that prints the square of the numbers from 1 to 10. The in-line version runs faster than the other because the function call takes time.

```
in line                    function call

main(void)                 main(void)
{                          {
  int x;                     int x;

  for(x=1; x<11; ++x)        for(x=1; x<11; ++x)
  printf("%d", x*x);         printf("%d", sqr(x));
}                          }

                           sqr(int a)
                           {
                             return a*a;
                           }
```

Libraries and Files

Once you have written a function, you can do three things with it: You can just leave it in the same file as the **main( )** function; you can put it in a separate file with other functions that you have written; or you can place it into a library.

Separate Files

While working on a large program, one of the most frustrating yet common tasks is searching each file to find where you put some function. A little preliminary organization will help you to avoid this problem.

First, group all functions that are conceptually related into one file. For example, if you are writing a text editor, you can put all functions for deleting text in one file, all for searching text in another, and so on.

Second, put all general-purpose functions together. For example, in database programs the input/output formatting functions are used by various other functions and belong in a separate file.

Third, group top-level functions in either a separate file or, if there is room, in the **main( )** file. Top-level functions initiate the general activity of the program, essentially defining the operation of the program.

Libraries

Technically, a library of functions differs from a separately compiled file of functions. When routines in a library are linked with the rest of your program, only the functions that your program actually uses are loaded and linked with your program. In a separately compiled file, all of the functions are loaded and linked with your program whether used or not. For most files that you create, you will probably want all of the functions in the file anyway. In the case of the C standard library, you would never want *all* of the functions linked into your program because your object code would be huge!

At times, you may want to create a library. For example, suppose you had written a special set of statistical functions. You would not want to load all these functions if your program only needed to find the mean of some set of values. In this case, a library would be useful.

Most C compilers include instructions for creating a library. Since this process varies from compiler to compiler, study your user's manual to determine what procedure you should follow.

How Big Should a Program File Be?

Because C allows separate compilation, the question of optimum file size naturally arises. This is important because compilation time is directly related to the size of the file that is being compiled. Generally, the linking process is much shorter than compiling and eliminates the need to constantly recompile working code. On the other hand, having to keep track of multiple files can be troublesome.

How large a file should be is different for every user, every compiler, and every operating environment. However, as a rule of thumb, no source file should be longer than 10,000 to 15,000 bytes.

Structures, Unions, Enumerations, and User-Defined Types

Structures
Arrays of Structures
Passing Structures to Functions
Structure Pointers
Arrays and Structures Within Structures
Bit-fields
Unions
Enumerations
Using sizeof to Ensure Portability
typedef

The C language allows you to create custom data types five different ways. The first is the *structure*, which is a grouping of variables under one name and is sometimes called a *conglomerate* data type. The second user-defined type is the *bit-field*, which is a variation on the structure and allows easy access to the bits within a word. The third is the *union*, which enables the same piece of memory to be defined as two or more different types of variables. A fourth custom data type is the *enumeration*, which is a list of symbols. The final user-defined type is created through the use of **typedef** and defines a new name for an existing type.

Structures

In C, a structure is a collection of variables referenced under one name, providing a convenient means of keeping related information together. A *structure definition* forms a template that may be used to create structure variables. The variables that make up the structure are called *structure elements*.

Generally, all of the elements in the structure are logically related. For example, the name and address information in a mailing list would normally be represented in a structure. The following code fragment shows how to create a structure template that defines the name and address fields. The keyword **struct** tells the compiler that a structure template is being defined.

```
struct addr {
  char name[30];
  char street[40];
  char city[20];
  char state[3];
  unsigned long int zip;
};
```

Notice that the definition is terminated by a semicolon. This is because a structure definition is a statement. Also, the structure tag **addr** identifies this particular data structure and is its type specifier.

At this point in the code, *no variable has actually been declared.* Only the form of the data has been defined. To declare a variable with this structure, write

```
struct addr addr_info;
```

This declares a structure variable of type **addr** called **addr _ info**. When you define a structure, you are essentially defining a complex variable type, not a variable. Not until you declare a variable of that type does one actually exist.

The C compiler automatically allocates sufficient memory to accommodate all of the variables that make up a structure variable. Figure 7-1 shows how **addr _ info** appears in memory assuming 1-byte characters and 2-byte integers.

You may also declare one or more variables as you define a structure. For example,

```
struct addr {
  char name[30];
  char street[40];
  char city[20];
```

```
  char state[3];
  unsigned long int zip;
} addr_info, binfo, cinfo;
```

defines a structure type called **addr** and declares variables **addr _ info**, **binfo**, and **cinfo** of that type.

If you only need one structure variable, the structure tag is not needed. That means that

```
struct  {
  char name[30];
  char street[40];
  char city[20];
  char state[3];
  unsigned long int zip;
} addr_info;
```

declares one variable named **addr _ info** as defined by the structure preceding it.

The general form of a structure definition is

> struct *tag* {
>   *type variable _ name*;
>   *type variable _ name*;
>   *type variable _ name*;
>
>   .
>   .
>   .
>
> } *structure _ variables*;

Name	30 bytes	
Street	40 bytes	
City	20 bytes	addr _ info
State	3 bytes	
ZIP	4 bytes	

Figure 7-1.   The **addr _ info** structure in memory

where either *tag_name* or *structure_variables* may be omitted, but not both.

Referencing Structure Elements

Individual structure elements are referenced through the use of the . operator (sometimes called the dot operator). For example, the following code assigns the ZIP code 12345 to the **zip** field of the structure variable **addr_info** declared earlier:

```
addr_info.zip = 12345;
```

The structure variable name followed by a period and the element name references that individual structure element. The general form for accessing a structure element is

structure_name.element_name

Therefore, to print the ZIP code on the screen, write

```
printf("%d", addr_info.zip);
```

This prints the ZIP code contained in the **zip** variable of the structure variable **addr_info**.

In the same fashion, the character array **addr_info.name** can be used to call **gets( )**, as shown here:

```
gets(addr_info.name);
```

This passes a character pointer to the start of the element **name**.

To access the individual elements of **addr_info.name**, you can index **name**. For example, you can print the contents of **addr_info.name** one character at a time by using the following code:

```
register int t;

for(t=0; addr_info.name[t]; ++t)
  putchar(addr_info.name[t]);
```

Structure Assignments

If your C compiler complies with the ANSI C standard, the information contained in one structure may be assigned to another structure of the same type. That is, instead of having to assign the values of all elements separately, you can employ a single assignment statement. The following program illustrates structure assignments:

```
#include "stdio.h"

void main(void)
{
  struct {
    int a;
    int b;
  } x, y;

  x.a = 10;

  y = x;  /* assign one structure to another */

  printf("%d", y.a);
}
```

After the assignment, **y.a** will contain the value 10.

Structure assignments were not allowed in the original version of C. You may not be able to use them if you are using an old-style compiler.

Arrays of Structures

Perhaps the most common usage of structures is in arrays of structures. To declare an array of structures, you must first define a structure and then declare an array variable of that type. For example, to declare a 100-element array of structures of type **addr** that had been defined earlier, write

```
struct addr addr_info[100];
```

This creates 100 sets of variables that are organized as defined in the structure **addr**.

To access a specific structure, index the structure name. For example, to print the ZIP code of structure 3, write

```
printf("%d", addr_info[2].zip);
```

Like all array variables, arrays of structures begin indexing at 0.

A Mailing-List Example

To illustrate how structures and arrays of structures are used, this section develops a simple mailing-list program that uses an array of structures to hold the address information. In this example, the stored information includes name, street, city, state, and ZIP code.

To define the basic data structure, **addr**, that will hold this information, write

```
struct addr {
  char name[30];
  char street[40];
  char city[20];
  char state[3];
  unsigned long int zip;
} addr_info[MAX];
```

Notice that the ZIP code field is an unsigned long integer. This is because some ZIP codes greater than 64,000—such as 94564—cannot be represented in a 2-byte integer. In this example, an integer holds the ZIP code to illustrate a numeric structure element. However, it is more common to use a character string that accommodates postal codes with letters as well as numbers (as used by Canada and other countries). The value of **MAX** may be defined to suit the specific need.

The first function needed for the program is **main( )**.

```
/* A simple mailing list example using an
   array of structures. */

#include "stdio.h"
#include "stdlib.h"

#define MAX 100

struct addr {
```

```
    char name[30];
    char street[40];
    char city[20];
    char state[3];
    unsigned long int zip;
} addr_info[MAX];

void init_list(void), enter(void);
void delete(void), list(void);
int menu_select(void), find_free(void);

void main(void)
{
    char choice;

    init_list(); /* initialize the structure array */
    for(;;) {
        choice=menu_select();
      switch(choice) {
        case 1: enter();
          break;
        case 2: delete();
          break;
        case 3: list();
          break;
        case 4: exit(0);
      }
    }
}
```

First, the function **init _ list( )** prepares the structure array for use by putting a null character into the first byte of the name field. The program assumes that an array element is not in use if the name field is empty. The **init _ list( )** function is shown here:

```
/* Initialize the list. */
void init_list(void)
{
    register int t;

    for(t=0; t<MAX; ++t) addr_info[t].name[0] = '\0';
}
```

The **menu _ select( )** function displays the option messages and returns the user's selection.

```
/* Get a menu selection. */
menu_select(void)
{
    char s[80];
    int c;
```

```
printf("1. Enter a name\n");
printf("2. Delete a name\n");
printf("3. List the file\n");
printf("4. Quit\n");
do {
  printf("\nEnter your choice: ");
  gets(s);
  c = atoi(s);
} while(c<0 || c>4);
return c;
}
```

The **enter( )** function prompts the user for input and places the information entered into the next free structure. If the array is full, the message **list full** is printed on the screen. **find_free( )** searches the structure array for an unused element.

```
/* Input addresses into the list. */
void enter(void)
{
  int slot;
  char s[80];

  slot = find_free();
  if(slot==-1) {
    printf("\nlist full");
    return;
  }

  printf("enter name: ");
  gets(addr_info[slot].name);

  printf("enter street: ");
  gets(addr_info[slot].street);

  printf("enter city: ");
  gets(addr_info[slot].city);

  printf("enter state: ");
  gets(addr_info[slot].state);

  printf("enter zip: ");
  gets(s);
  addr_info[slot].zip = strtoul(s, '\0', 10);
}

/* Find an unused structure. */
find_free(void)
{
  register int t;

  for(t=0; addr_info[t].name[0] && t<MAX; ++t) ;
```

```
  if(t==MAX) return -1; /* no slots free */
  return t;
}
```

Notice that **find _ free**( ) returns a −1 if every structure array variable is in use. This is a safe number because there cannot be a −1 element in an array.

The **delete**( ) function simply requires the user to specify the number of the address that needs to be deleted. The function then puts a null character in the first character position of the **name** field.

```
/* Delete an address. */
void delete(void)
{
  register int slot;
  char s[80];

  printf("enter record #: ");
  gets(s);
  slot = atoi(s);
  if(slot>=0 && slot < MAX) addr_info[slot].name[0] = '\0';
}
```

The final function the program needs is **list**( ), which prints the entire mailing list on the screen. (The ANSI C standard does not define a function that sends output to the printer because of the wide variation between environments. However, you might want to add this capability to the mailing-list program on your own.)

```
/* Display the list on the screen. */
void list(void)
{
  register int t;

  for(t=0; t<MAX; ++t) {
    if(addr_info[t].name[0]) {
      printf("%s\n", addr_info[t].name);
      printf("%s\n", addr_info[t].street);
      printf("%s\n", addr_info[t].city);
      printf("%s\n", addr_info[t].state);
      printf("%lu\n", addr_info[t].zip);
    }
  }
  printf("\n\n");
}
```

The complete mailing-list program is shown here. If you have any remaining doubts about structures, enter this program into your computer and study its execution, making changes and watching their effects.

```
/* A simple mailing list example using an
   array of structures. */

#include "stdio.h"
#include "stdlib.h"

#define MAX 100

struct addr {
  char name[30];
  char street[40];
  char city[20];
  char state[3];
  unsigned long int zip;
} addr_info[MAX];

void init_list(void), enter(void);
void delete(void), list(void);
int menu_select(void), find_free(void);

main(void)
{
  char choice;

  init_list(); /* initialize the structure array */
  for(;;) {
      choice=menu_select();
    switch(choice) {
      case 1: enter();
        break;
      case 2: delete();
        break;
      case 3: list();
        break;
      case 4: exit(0);
    }
  }
}

/* Initialize the list. */
void init_list(void)
{
  register int t;

  for(t=0; t<MAX; ++t) addr_info[t].name[0] = '\0';
}

/* Get a menu selection. */
menu_select(void)
```

```
{
  char s[80];
  int c;

  printf("1. Enter a name\n");
  printf("2. Delete a name\n");
  printf("3. List the file\n");
  printf("4. Quit\n");
  do {
    printf("\nEnter your choice: ");
    gets(s);
    c = atoi(s);
  } while(c<0 || c>4);
  return c;
}

/* Input addresses into the list. */
void enter(void)
{
  int slot;
  char s[80];

  slot = find_free();
  if(slot==-1) {
    printf("\nlist full");
    return;
  }

  printf("enter name: ");
  gets(addr_info[slot].name);

  printf("enter street: ");
  gets(addr_info[slot].street);

  printf("enter city: ");
  gets(addr_info[slot].city);

  printf("enter state: ");
  gets(addr_info[slot].state);

  printf("enter zip: ");
  gets(s);
  addr_info[slot].zip = strtoul(s, '\0', 10);
}

/* Find an unused structure. */
find_free(void)
{
  register int t;

  for(t=0; addr_info[t].name[0] && t<MAX; ++t) ;
  if(t==MAX) return -1; /* no slots free */
  return t;
}

/* Delete an address. */
```

```
void delete(void)
{
  register int slot;
  char s[80];

  printf("enter record #: ");
  gets(s);
  slot = atoi(s);
  if(slot>=0 && slot < MAX) addr_info[slot].name[0] = '\0';
}

/* Display the list on the screen. */
void list(void)
{
  register int t;

  for(t=0; t<MAX; ++t) {
    if(addr_info[t].name[0]) {
      printf("%s\n", addr_info[t].name);
      printf("%s\n", addr_info[t].street);
      printf("%s\n", addr_info[t].city);
      printf("%s\n", addr_info[t].state);
      printf("%lu\n", addr_info[t].zip);
    }
  }
  printf("\n\n");
}
```

Passing Structures to Functions

So far, all structures and arrays of structures used in the preceding examples have been global. This section gives special consideration to passing structures and their elements to functions.

Passing Structure Elements to Functions

When you pass an element of a structure variable to a function, you are actually passing the value of that element to the function. Therefore, you are passing a simple variable (unless, of course, that element is complex, such as an array of characters). For example, consider this structure:

```
struct fred {
  char x;
  int y;
```

```
    float z;
    char s[10];
} mike;
```

Here are examples of each element being passed to a function:

```
func(mike.x);   /* passes character value of x */

func2(mike.y);  /* passes integer value of y */

func3(mike.z);  /* passes float value of z */

func4(mike.s);  /* passes address of string s */

func(mike.s[2]); /* passes character value of s[2] */
```

However, if you wish to pass the address of individual structure elements, place the **&** operator before the structure name. For example, to pass the address of the elements in the structure **mike**, write

```
func(&mike.x);   /* passes address of character x */

func2(&mike.y);  /* passes address of integer y */

func3(&mike.z);  /* passes address of float z */

func4(mike.s);   /* passes address of string s */

func(&mike.s[2]); /* passes address of character s[2] */
```

Remember that the **&** operator precedes the structure name, not the individual element name. Note also that the string element **s** already signifies an address, so no **&** is required.

Passing Entire Structures to Functions

When a structure is used as an argument to a function, the entire structure is passed using the standard call-by-value method. Of course, this means that any changes made to the contents of the structure inside the function to which it is passed do not affect the structure used as an argument.

Historical note: In some early versions of C, structures could *not* be passed to functions. Instead, they were treated like arrays, and only a pointer to the structure was passed. Keep this in mind if you ever use an old C compiler.

When using a structure as a parameter, remember that the type of the argument must match the type of the parameter. For example, in this program both the argument **arg** and the parameter **parm** are declared as the same type of structure.

```
#include "stdio.h"

void main(void)
{
  struct {
    int a, b;
    char ch;
  } arg;

  arg.a = 1000;

  f1(arg);
}

f1(
  struct {
    int x, y;
    char ch;
  } parm
)
{
  printf("%d", parm.x);
}
```

This program prints the number **1000** on the screen. Although parallel structure declarations of this type are perfectly valid, a more common approach—and one that requires less work—is to define a structure globally and then use its name to declare structure variables and parameters as needed. Using this method, the same program becomes

```
#include "stdio.h"

/* define a structure type */
struct struct_type {
  int a, b;
  char ch;
} ;
```

```
void main(void)
{
  struct struct_type arg;  /* declare arg */

  arg.a = 1000;

  f1(arg);
}

f1(struct struct_type parm)
{
  printf("%d", parm.a);
}
```

This method saves some programming effort. More important, it helps ensure that the arguments and the parameters match.

Structure Pointers

C allows pointers to structures just as it allows pointers to any other type of variable. However, there are some special aspects to structure pointers that you should know.

Declaring a Structure Pointer

Like other pointers, you declare structure pointers by placing * in front of a structure variable's name. For example, assuming the previously defined structure **addr**, the following declares **addr_pointer** as a pointer to data of that type:

```
struct addr *addr_pointer;
```

Using Structure Pointers

There are two primary uses for structure pointers: to generate a call by reference call to a function, and to create linked lists and other dynamic data structures using C's allocation system. This chapter covers the first use. The second use is covered thoroughly in Part Three.

There is one major drawback to passing all but the simplest structures to functions: the overhead needed to push (and pop) all the structure elements onto the stack. In simple structures with few elements, this overhead is not too great. If several elements are used, however, or if some of the elements are arrays, run-time performance may degrade to unacceptable levels. The solution to this problem is to pass only a pointer to a function.

When a pointer to a structure is passed to a function, only the address of the structure is pushed (and popped) on the stack. This makes for very fast function calls. A second advantage, in some cases, is when a function needs to reference the actual structure argument instead of a copy. By passing a pointer, it can modify the contents of the actual elements of the structure used in the call.

To find the address of a structure variable, place the **&** operator before the structure's name. For example, given the following fragment:

```
struct bal {
  float balance;
  char name[80];
} person;

struct bal *p;  /* declare a structure pointer */
```

then

```
p = &person;
```

places the address of the structure **person** into the pointer **p**.

To access the elements of a structure using a pointer to that structure, you must use the −> operator. For example, this references the **balance** field:

```
p->balance
```

The −> is usually called the *arrow* operator, and consists of the minus sign followed by a greater than sign. The arrow is used in place of the dot operator when you are accessing a structure element using a pointer to the structure variable.

To see how a structure pointer can be used, examine this simple program, which prints the hours, minutes, and seconds on your screen using a software-delay timer.

```c
/* Display a software timer. */

#include "stdio.h"

struct my_time {
  int hours;
  int minutes;
  int seconds;
} ;

void display(struct my_time *t);
void update(struct my_time *t);
void delay(void);

void main(void)
{
  struct my_time systime;

  systime.hours = 0;
  systime.minutes = 0;
  systime.seconds = 0;

  for(;;) {
    update(&systime);
    display(&systime);
  }
}

void update(struct my_time *t)
{
  t->seconds++;
  if(t->seconds==60) {
    t->seconds = 0;
    t->minutes++;
  }
  if(t->minutes==60) {
    t->minutes = 0;
    t->hours++;
  }
  if(t->hours==24) t->hours = 0;
  delay();
}

void display(struct my_time *t)
{
  printf("%02d:", t->hours);
  printf("%02d:", t->minutes);
  printf("%02d\n", t->seconds);
}
```

```
void delay(void)
{
  long int t;
  for(t=1; t<128000; ++t) ;
}
```

The timing of this program is adjusted by varying the loop count in **delay( )**.

As you can see, a global structure called **my_time** was defined but no variable was declared. Inside **main( )**, the structure **time** was declared and initialized to 00:00:00. This means that **systime** is known directly only to the **main( )** function.

The two functions **update( )** (which changes the time) and **display( )** (which prints the time) are passed the address of **time**. In both functions, the argument is declared as a pointer to a **my_time** structure, which enables the compiler to know how to reference the structure elements.

Each structure element is actually referenced via a pointer. For example, to set the hours back to 0 when 24:00:00 is reached, write

```
if(t->hours==24) t->hours = 0;
```

This line of code tells the compiler to take the address of **t** (which is **time** in **main( )**) and assign zero to its element **hours**.

Remember, use the dot operator to access structure elements when operating on the structure itself. When you have a pointer to a structure, use the arrow operator.

Arrays and Structures Within Structures

A structure element may be either simple or complex. A simple element is any of the built-in data types, such as integer or character. You have already seen one complex element: the character array used in **addr_info**. Other complex data types are one-dimensional and multidimensional arrays of the other data types and structures.

A structure element that is an array is treated as you might expect from the earlier examples. For example, consider this structure:

```
struct x {
  int a[10][10]; /* 10 x 10 array of ints */
  float b;
} y;
```

To reference integer 3,7 in **a** of structure **y**, write

```
y.a[3][7]
```

When a structure is an element of another structure, it is called a *nested* structure. For example, the structure **address** is nested inside **emp** in this example:

```
struct emp {
  struct addr address;
  float wage;
} worker;
```

Here, a structure **emp** has been defined as having two elements. The first element is the structure of type **addr**, which contains an employee's address. The other is **wage**, which holds the employee's wage. The following code fragment assigns 93456 to the **zip** element of **address**.

```
worker.address.zip = 93456;
```

As you can see, the elements of each structure are referenced from outermost to innermost. The ANSI C standard specifies that structures may be nested to at least 15 levels.

Bit-Fields

Unlike most other computer languages, C has a built-in method for accessing a single bit within a byte. This can be useful for a number of reasons:

- If storage is limited you can store several *Boolean* (true/false) variables in one byte.

- Certain devices transmit information encoded into bits within one byte.

- Certain encryption routines need to access the bits within a byte.

Although these tasks can be performed using bytes and the bitwise operators, a bit-field can add more structure (and possibly efficiency) to your code.

To access bits, C uses a method based on the structure. A bit-field is really just a special type of structure element that defines how long, in bits, the field is to be. The general form of a bit-field definition is

```
struct tag {
  type name1 : length;
  type name2 : length;
    .
    .
    .
  type name3 : length;
} variable-list;
```

A bit-field must be declared as either **int, unsigned,** or **signed.** Bit-fields of length 1 should be declared as **unsigned** because a single bit cannot have a sign. (Some compilers may only allow **unsigned** bit-fields.)

Bit-fields are frequently used when analyzing input from a hardware device. For example, the status port of a serial communications adapter might return a status byte organized like this:

Bit	Meaning When Set
0	change in clear-to-send line
1	change in data-set-ready
2	trailing edge detected
3	change in receive line
4	clear-to-send
5	data-set-ready
6	telephone ringing
7	received signal

You can represent the information in a status byte using the following bit-field:

```
struct status_type {
  unsigned delta_cts: 1;
  unsigned delta_dsr: 1;
  unsigned tr_edge:   1;
  unsigned delta_rec: 1;
  unsigned cts:       1;
  unsigned dsr:       1;
  unsigned ring:      1;
  unsigned rec_line:  1;
} status;
```

You might use a routine similar to that shown here to enable a program to determine when it can send or receive data.

```
status = get_port_status();

if(status.cts) printf("clear to send");
if(status.dsr) printf("data ready");
```

To assign a value to a bit-field, simply use the form you would use for any other type of structure element. For example, this code fragment clears the **ring** field:

```
status.ring = 0;
```

As you can see from these examples, each bit-field is accessed with the dot operator. However, if the structure is referenced through a pointer, you must use the —> operator.

You do not have to name each bit-field. This makes it easy to reach the bit you want, bypassing unused ones. For example, if you only care about the **cts** and **dsr** bits, you could declare the **status_type** structure like this:

```
struct status_type {
  unsigned :     4;
  unsigned cts:  1;
  unsigned dsr:  1;
} status;
```

Also, notice that the bits after **dsr** do not need to be specified if they are not used.

Bit-field variables have certain restrictions. You cannot take the address of a bit-field variable. Bit-field variables cannot be arrayed. You cannot overlap integer boundaries. You cannot know, from machine to machine, whether the fields will run from right to left or from left to right. In other words, any code that uses bit-fields may have some machine dependencies.

Finally, it is valid to mix normal structure elements with bit-field elements. For example,

```
struct emp {
  struct addr address;
  float pay;
  unsigned lay_off:1;   /* lay off or active */
  unsigned hourly:1;    /* hourly pay or wage */
  unsigned deductions:3; /* IRS deductions */
};
```

defines an employee record that uses only 1 byte to hold three pieces of information: the employee's status, whether the employee is salaried, and the number of deductions. Without the bit-field, this information would have taken 3 bytes.

Unions

In C, a **union** is a memory location that is shared by two or more different variables, generally of different types, at different times. Defining a **union** is similar to defining a structure. Its general form is

```
union tag {
    type variable_name;
    type variable_name;
    type variable_name;
    .
    .
    .
} union_variables;
```

For example,

```
union u_type {
  int i;
  char ch;
} ;
```

This definition does not declare any variables. You may declare a variable either by placing its name at the end of the definition or by using a separate declaration statement. To declare a **union** variable **cnvt** of type **u_type** using the definition just given, write

```
union u_type cnvt;
```

In **union cnvt**, both integer **i** and character **ch** share the same memory location. (Of course, **i** occupies 2 bytes and **ch** uses only 1.) Figure 7-2 shows how **i** and **ch** share the same address.

At any point, you can refer to the data stored in a **cnvt** as either an integer or a character.

When a **union** is declared, the compiler automatically creates a variable large enough to hold the largest variable type in the **union**.

To access a **union** element, use the same syntax that you would use for structures: the dot and arrow operators. If you are operating on the **union** directly, use the dot operator. If the **union** variable is accessed through a pointer, use the arrow operator. For example, to assign the integer 10 to element **i** of **cnvt**, write

```
cnvt.i = 10;
```

In the next example, a pointer to **cnvt** is passed to a function:

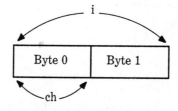

Figure 7-2.   How **i** and **ch** utilize the **union cnvt**

```
void func1(union u_type *un)
{
  un->i = 10; /* assign 10 to cnvt using
                 function */
}
```

Using a **union** can aid in the production of machine-independent (portable) code. Because the compiler keeps track of the actual sizes of the variables that make up the **union**, no machine dependencies are produced. You need not worry about the size of an **int, char, float,** or whatever.

Unions are used frequently when type conversions are needed because you can refer to the data held in the **union** in different ways. For example, you can use a **union** to create a function called **putw( )**, which writes the binary representation of an integer to a disk file. First, create a **union** of one integer and a 2-byte character array:

```
union pw {
  int i;
  char ch[2];
};
```

Now, **putw( )** can be written like this:

```
putw(union pw word, FILE *fp)
{
  putc(word->ch[0], fp); /* write first half */
  putc(word->ch[1], fp); /* write second half */
}
```

Although called with an integer, **putw( )** can still use the standard function **putc( )** to write an integer to a disk file one byte at a time. To write a word to a disk file, call **putw( )** with the integer value you want to write. Because the function is receiving a **union**, it receives the 2-byte integer value. Inside **putw( )**, however, it can refer to the data as 2 separate bytes using the **ch** array.

Enumerations

An extension to the C language added by the ANSI C standard is the enumeration. An *enumeration* is a set of named integer constants that specifiy all the legal values a variable of that type may have. Enumerations are common in everyday life. For example, an enumeration of the coins used in the United States is

penny, nickel, dime, quarter, half-dollar, dollar

Enumerations are defined much like structures; the keyword **enum** signals the start of an enumeration type. The general form for enumerations is

enum *tag* { *enumeration list* } *variable_list*;

Here, both the enumeration tag and the variable list are optional. As with structures, the enumeration tag name is used to declare variables of its type. The following code fragment defines an enumeration called **coin** and declares **money** to be of that type:

```
enum coin { penny, nickel, dime, quarter,
        half_dollar, dollar};

enum coin money;
```

Given this definition and declaration, the following types of statements are perfectly valid:

```
money = dime;

if(money==quarter) printf("is a quarter\n");
```

The key point to understand about an enumeration is that each of the symbols stands for an integer value. As such, they may be used anywhere that an integer may be used. Each symbol is given a value one greater than the symbol it precedes. The value of the first enumeration symbol is 0. Therefore,

```
printf("%d %d", penny, dime);
```

displays **0 2** on the screen.

You can specify the value of one or more of the symbols by using an initializer. Do this by following the symbol with an equal sign and an integer value. Symbols that appear after initializers are assigned values greater than the previous initialization value. For example, the following code assigns the value of 100 to **quarter**:

```
enum coin { penny, nickel, dime, quarter=100,
            half_dollar, dollar};
```

Now, the values of these symbols are

penny	0
nickel	1
dime	2
quarter	100
half_dollar	101
dollar	102

One common but erroneous assumption about enumerations is that the symbols can be input and output directly. This is not the case. For example, the following code fragment will not perform as desired:

```
/* this will not work */

money = dollar;

printf("%s", money);
```

Remember, **dollar** is simply a name for an integer; it is not a string. For the same reason, you cannot use this code to achieve the desired results:

```
/* this code is wrong */

gets(s);

strcpy(money, s);
```

That is, a string that contains the name of a symbol is not automatically converted to that symbol.

Actually, creating code to input and output enumeration symbols is quite tedious (unless you are willing to settle for their integer values). For example, you need the following code to display, in words, the kind of coin that **money** contains:

```
switch(money) {
  case penny: printf("penny");
    break;
  case nickel: printf("nickel");
    break;
  case dime: printf("dime");
    break;
  case quarter: printf("quarter");
    break;
  case half_dollar: printf("half_dollar");
    break;
  case dollar: printf("dollar");
}
```

Sometimes, you can declare an array of strings and use the enumeration value as an index to translate an enumeration value into its corresponding string. For example, this code also outputs the proper string:

```
char name[]={
  "penny",
  "nickel",
  "dime",
  "quarter",
  "half_dollar",
  "dollar"
};
printf("%s", name[money]);
```

Of course, this only works if no symbol is initialized because the string array must be indexed starting at 0.

Since enumeration values must be converted manually to their human-readable string values for console I/O, they are most useful in routines that do not make such conversions. An enumeration is often used to define a compiler's symbol table, for example. Enumerations are also used to help prove the validity of a program by providing a compile-time redundancy check confirming that a variable is assigned only valid values.

Using sizeof to Ensure Portability

You have seen that structures, unions, and enumerations can be used to create variables of different sizes, and that the actual size of these variables may change from machine to machine. The **sizeof** unary operator computes the size of any variable or type and can help eliminate machine-dependent code from your programs.

For example, assume a C implementation common to many microcomputer C compilers, which has the sizes for data types shown here:

Type	Size in Bytes
char	1
int	2
long	4
float	4
double	8

Therefore, the following code will print the numbers **1**, **2**, and **4** on the screen:

```
char ch;
int i;
float f;

printf("%d",sizeof(ch));

printf("%d",sizeof(i));

printf("%d",sizeof(f));
```

sizeof is a *compile-time operator*: all the information necessary to compute the size of any variable is known at compile time. For example, consider

```
union x {
  char ch;
  int i;
  float f;
} u_var;
```

The **sizeof(u_var)** is 4. At run time, it does not matter what the **union u_var** is actually holding. All that matters is the size of the largest variable it can hold because the **union** must be as large as its largest element.

typedef

C allows you to define explicitly new data type names by using the keyword **typedef**. You are not actually *creating* a new data class, but rather defining a new name for an existing type. This process can help make machine-dependent programs more portable — only the **typedef** statements would have to be changed. It also can aid in self-documenting your code by allowing descriptive names for the standard data types. The general form of the **typedef** statement is

typedef *type name*;

where *type* is any allowable data type and *name* is the new name for this type. The new name you define is in addition to, not a replacement for, the existing type name.

For example, you could create a new name for **float** by using

```
typedef float balance;
```

This statement tells the compiler to recognize **balance** as another name for **float**. Next, you could create a **float** variable using **balance**:

```
balance over_due;
```

Here, **over_due** is a floating-point variable of type **balance**, which is another word for **float**.

Now that **balance** has been defined, it can be used on the right side of another **typedef**. For example,

```
typedef overdraft balance;
```

tells the compiler to recognize **overdraft** as another name for **balance**, which is another name for **float**.

Using **typedef** can make your code easier to read and easier to port to a new machine. But remember, you are *not* creating any new data types.

Console I/O

E
I
G
H
T

C is practically unique in its approach to input/output operations. This is because the C language does not define any keywords that perform I/O. Instead, input and output are accomplished through library functions. C's I/O system is an elegant piece of engineering that offers a flexible yet cohesive mechanism for transferring data between devices. However, C's I/O system is quite large and involves several different functions.

In C, there are both console and file I/O. Technically, C makes little distinction between console I/O and file I/O. However, they are conceptually very different worlds. This chapter examines in detail the console I/O functions. The next chapter presents the file I/O system and describes how the two systems relate.

With one exception, this chapter covers only console I/O functions defined by the ANSI C standard. Neither the ANSI C standard nor the traditional C standard define any functions that perform "fancy" screen control or graphics because these operations vary widely between machines. Instead, the standard C console I/O functions perform only TTY-based output. However, most compilers include in their libraries screen control and graphics functions that apply to the specific environment the compiler is designed to run under. Part Two covers a representative sample of these functions.

Note: This chapter refers to the console I/O functions as performing input from the keyboard and output to the screen. However, these functions actually have the standard input and standard output of the system as the target and/or source of their I/O operations. Furthermore, standard input and standard output may be redirected to other devices. These concepts are covered in Chapter 9.

Reading and Writing Characters

The simplest of the console I/O functions are **getchar( )**, which reads a character from the keyboard, and **putchar( )**, which prints a character to the screen. The **getchar( )** function waits until a key is pressed and then returns its value. The key pressed is also automatically echoed to the screen. The **putchar( )** function writes its character argument to the screen at the current cursor position. The prototypes for **getchar( )** and **putchar( )** are shown here:

    int getchar(void);
    int putchar(int c);

The **getchar( )** function returns an integer, but the low-order byte contains the character. Also, you can call **putchar( )** with a character argument. Even though **putchar( )** is declared as using an integer parameter, only the low-order byte is actually output to the screen. The **putchar( )** function returns the character written, or **EOF** if an error occurs. (The **EOF** macro is defined in STDIO.H and is generally equal to −1.) Integers are used for compatibility with the original version of C. The header file for these functions is in STDIO.H.

The following program inputs characters from the keyboard and reverses their case. That is, it prints uppercase as lowercase and lowercase as uppercase. To stop the program, enter a period.

```
#include "stdio.h"
#include "ctype.h"

void main(void)
{
  char ch;

  printf("Enter some text (type a period to quit).\n");
  do {
    ch = getchar();
```

```
    if(islower(ch)) ch = toupper(ch);
    else ch = tolower(ch);
    putchar(ch);
  } while (ch!='.');
}
```

When using **getchar( )**, remember that any key represents a valid return value. That is, keys like the carriage return, TAB, and ESC may be returned by **getchar( )**.

A Problem with getchar( )

There are some potential problems with **getchar( )**. ANSI has defined **getchar( )** to be compatible with the original, UNIX-based version of C. Unfortunately, in its original form, **getchar( )** buffers input until ENTER is pressed. This is because the original UNIX systems line-buffered terminal input—that is, you had to press ENTER for input to be sent to the computer. This leaves one or more characters waiting in the input queue after **getchar( )** returns, which is annoying in interactive environments. Even though the ANSI standard specifies that **getchar( )** can be implemented as an interactive function, it seldom is. Therefore, if the preceding program did not behave as you expected, you now know why.

Alternatives to getchar( )

getchar( ) may not be implemented by your compiler so as to make it useful in an interactive environment. If this is the case, you will probably want to use a different function to read characters from the keyboard. The ANSI standard does not define any function that is guaranteed to provide interactive input, but many C compilers include alternative keyboard input functions. Although these functions are not defined by ANSI, they are recommended since **getchar( )** does not fill the needs of most programmers.

Two of the most common alternative functions, **getch( )** and **getche( )**, have these prototypes:

```
int getch(void);
int getche(void);
```

For most compilers, the prototypes for these functions are found in CONIO.H. The **getch( )** function waits for a keypress after which it returns immediately. It does not echo the character to the screen. The **getche( )** function is the same as **getch( )**, but the key is echoed. This book often uses **getche( )** or **getch( )** instead of **getchar( )** when a character needs to be read from the keyboard in an interactive program. However, if your compiler does not support these alternative functions, or if **getchar( )** is implemented as an interactive function by your compiler, you should substitute **getchar( )** when necessary.

For example, the previous program is shown here using **getch( )** instead of **getchar( )**:

```
#include "stdio.h"
#include "conio.h"
#include "ctype.h"

void main(void)
{
  char ch;

  printf("Enter some text (type a period to quit).\n");
  do {
    ch = getch();
    if(islower(ch)) ch = toupper(ch);
    else ch = tolower(ch);
    putchar(ch);
  } while (ch!='.');
}
```

Reading and Writing Strings

The next step up in console I/O, in terms of complexity and power, are the functions **gets( )** and **puts( )**. They enable you to read and write strings of characters at the console.

The **gets( )** function reads a string of characters entered at the keyboard and places them at the address pointed to by its character pointer argument. You may type characters at the keyboard until you strike a carriage return. The carriage return does not become part of the string; instead, a null terminator is placed at the end and **gets( )** returns. In fact, you cannot use **gets( )** to return a carriage return (although **getchar( )** can do so). You can correct typing mistakes by using the BACKSPACE key before pressing ENTER. The prototype for **gets( )** is

char *gets(char *str);

where *str* is a character array that receives the characters input by the user. **gets( )** also returns a pointer to *str*. The **gets( )** function prototype is found in STDIO.H. The following program reads a string into the array **str** and prints its length:

```
#include "stdio.h"
#include "string.h"

void main(void)
{
  char str[80];

  gets(str);
  printf("length is %d", strlen(str));
}
```

The **puts( )** function writes its string argument to the screen followed by a newline. Its prototype is:

int puts(char *s);

puts( ) recognizes the same backslash codes as **printf( )**, such as '\t' for tab. A call to **puts( )** requires far less overhead than the same call to **printf( )** because **puts( )** can only output a string of characters—it cannot output numbers or do format conversions. Therefore, **puts( )** takes up less space and runs faster than **printf( )**. For this reason, the **puts( )** function is often used when it is important to have highly optimized code. The **puts( )** function returns **EOF** if an error occurs. Otherwise, it returns a nonzero value. However, when writing to the console, you can usually assume that no error will occur, so the return value of **puts( )** is seldom monitored. The following statement displays **hello**:

```
puts("hello");
```

Function	Operation
getchar( )	Reads a character from the keyboard; waits for carriage return
getche( )	Reads a character with echo; does not wait for carriage return; not defined by ANSI, but a common extension
getch( )	Reads a character without echo; does not wait for carriage return; not defined by ANSI, but a common extension
putchar( )	Writes a character to the screen
gets( )	Reads a string from the keyboard
puts( )	Writes a string to the screen

Table 8-1. Simple I/O Functions

Table 8-1 summarizes the simplest functions that perform console I/O operations.

The following program, a simple computerized dictionary, demonstrates several of the basic console I/O functions. It prompts the user to enter a word and then checks to see if the word matches one in its built-in database. If a match is found, the program prints the word's meaning. Pay special attention to the indirection used in this program. If you have any trouble understanding it, remember that the **dic** array is an array of pointers to strings. Notice that the list must be terminated by two nulls.

```
/* A simple dictionary. */

#include "stdio.h"
#include "conio.h"
#include "string.h"
#include "ctype.h"

/* list of words and meanings */
char  *dic[][40] = {
  "atlas", "a volume of maps",
  "car", "a motorized vehicle",
  "telephone", "a communication device",
  "airplane", "a flying machine",
  "", ""   /* null terminate the list */
};

void main(void)
{
  char word[80], ch;
  char **p;
```

```
do {
  puts("\nEnter word: ");
  gets(word);

  p = (char **)dic;

  /* find matching word and print its meaning */
  do {
    if(!strcmp(*p, word)) {
      puts("meaning:");
      puts(*(p+1));
      break;
    }
    if(!strcmp(*p, word)) break;
    p = p + 2;   /* advance through the list */
  } while(*p);
  if(!*p) puts("word not in dictionary");
  printf("another? (y/n): ");
  ch = getche();
} while(toupper(ch) != 'N');
}
```

Formatted Console I/O

The functions **printf( )** and **scanf( )** perform formatted output and input—that is, they can read and write data in various formats that are under your control. The **printf( )** function writes data to the console. The **scanf( )** function, its complement, reads data from the keyboard. Both functions can operate on any of the built-in data types, including characters, strings, and numbers.

printf( )

The prototype for **printf( )** is

    int printf(char *control_string, argument_list);

The prototype for **printf( )** is in STDIO.H. The **printf( )** function returns the number of characters written or a negative value if an error occurs.

The *control_string* consists of two types of items. The first type is characters that will be printed on the screen. The second type contains format specifiers that define the way the subsequent arguments are displayed. A format specifier begins with a percent sign and is followed by the format code. There must be exactly the same number of arguments as there are format specifiers, and the format specifiers and the arguments are matched in order from left to right. For example, this **printf( )** call

```
printf("I like %c %s", 'C', "very much!");
```

displays

```
I like C very much!
```

The **printf( )** function accepts a wide variety of format specifiers, as shown in Table 8-2.

Code	Format
%c	Character
%d	Signed decimal integers
%i	Signed decimal integers
%e	Scientific notation (lowercase e)
%E	Scientific notation (uppercase E)
%f	Decimal floating point
%g	Uses %e or %f, whichever is shorter
%G	Uses %E or %F, whichever is shorter
%o	Unsigned octal
%s	String of characters
%u	Unsigned decimal integers
%x	Unsigned hexadecimal (lowercase letters)
%X	Unsigned hexadecimal (uppercase letters)
%p	Displays a pointer
%n	The associated argument is an integer pointer into which the number of characters written so far is placed
%%	Prints a % sign

Table 8-2.   printf( ) Format Specifiers

Printing Characters

To print an individual character, use **%c**. This causes its matching argument to be output, unmodified, to the screen.

To print a string, use **%s**.

Printing Numbers

You may use either **%d** or **%i** to indicate a signed decimal number. These format specifiers are equivalent; both are supported for historical reasons.

To output an unsigned value, use **%u**.

The **%f** format specifier displays numbers in floating point.

The **%e** and **%E** specifiers tell **printf( )** to display a **double** argument in scientific notation. Numbers represented in scientific notation take this general form:

$$x.dddddE+/-yy$$

If you want to display the letter "E" in uppercase, use the **%E** format; otherwise use **%e**.

You can tell **printf( )** to use either **%f** or **%e** by using the **%g** or **%G** format specifiers. This causes **printf( )** to select the format specifier that produces the shortest output. Where applicable, use **%G** if you want "E" shown in uppercase; otherwise, use **%g**. The following program demonstrates the effect of the **%g** format specifier:

```
#include "stdio.h"

void main(void)
{
  double f;

  for(f=1.0; f<1.0e+10; f=f*10)
    printf("%g ", f);
}
```

It produces the following output.

```
1 10 100 1000 10000 100000 1000000 1e+007 1e+008 1e+009
```

You can display unsigned integers in octal or hexadecimal format using **%o** and **%x**, respectively. Since the hexadecimal number system uses the letters "A" through "F" to represent the numbers 10 through 15, you can display these letters in either upper- or lowercase. For uppercase, use the **%X** format specifier and for lowercase, use **%x**, as shown here:

```
#include "stdio.h"

void main(void)
{
  unsigned num;

  for(num=0; num<255; num++) {
    printf("%o ", num);
    printf("%x ", num);
    printf("%X\n", num);
  }
}
```

Displaying an Address

If you wish to display an address, use **%p**. This format specifier causes **printf( )** to display a machine address in a format compatible with the type of addressing used by the computer. The next program displays the address of **sample**:

```
#include "stdio.h"

int sample;

void main(void)
{
  printf("%p", &sample);
}
```

The %n Specifier

The **%n** format specifier is different from the others. Instead of telling **printf( )** to display something, it causes **printf( )** to load the variable pointed to by its corresponding argument with a value equal to the number of characters that have been output. In other words, the value that corresponds to the **%n** format specifier must be a pointer to a variable. After the call to **printf( )** has returned, this variable will hold the number of characters output, up to the point at which the %n was encountered. Examine this program to understand this somewhat unusual format code.

```
#include "stdio.h"

void main(void)
{
  int count;

  printf("this%nis a test\n", &count);
  printf("%d", count);
}
```

This program displays **this is a test** followed by the number 4. The %n format specifier is used primarily to enable your program to perform dynamic formatting.

Format Modifiers

Many format specifiers may take modifiers that alter their meaning slightly. For example, you can specify a minimum field width, the number of decimal places, and left justification. The format modifier goes between the percent sign and the actual code.

The Minimum Field Width Specifier

An integer placed between the % sign and the format code acts as a *minimum field width specifier*. This pads the output with spaces to ensure that it reaches a certain minimum length. If the string or number is longer than that minimum, it will still be printed in full. The default padding is done with spaces. If you wish to pad with 0's, place a 0 before the field width specifier. For example, %05d will pad a number of less than five digits with 0's so that its total length is five. The following program demonstrates the minimum field width specifier:

```
#include "stdio.h"

void main(void)
```

```
{
  double item;

  item = 10.12304;

  printf("%f\n", item);
  printf("%10f\n", item);
  printf("%012f\n", item);
}
```

This program produces the following output:

```
10.123040
 10.123040
00010.123040
```

The minimum field width modifier is most commonly used to produce tables in which the columns line up. For example, the next program produces a table of squares and cubes for the numbers between 1 and 19:

```
#include "stdio.h"

void main(void)
{
  int i;

  /* display a table of squares and cubes */
  for(i=1; i<20; i++)
    printf("%8d %8d %8d\n", i, i*i, i*i*i);
}
```

A sample of its output is shown here:

```
 1       1       1
 2       4       8
 3       9      27
 4      16      64
 5      25     125
 6      36     216
 7      49     343
 8      64     512
 9      81     729
10     100    1000
11     121    1331
12     144    1728
13     169    2197
14     196    2744
15     225    3375
```

```
16      256     4096
17      289     4913
18      324     5832
19      361     6859
```

The Precision Specifier

The *precision specifier* follows the minimum field width specifier (if there is one). It consists of a period followed by an integer. Its exact meaning depends upon the type of data it is applied to.

When you apply the precision specifier to floating-point data, it determines the number of decimal places displayed. For example, **%10.4f** displays a number at least ten characters wide with four decimal places.

Applied to strings, the precision specifier specifies the maximum field length. For example, **%5.7s** displays a string at least five and not exceeding seven characters long. If the string is longer than the maximum field width, the end characters will be truncated.

When applied to integer types, the precision specifier determines the minimum number of digits that will appear for each number. Leading zeros are added to achieve the required number of digits.

The following program illustrates the precision specifier:

```
#include "stdio.h"

void main(void)
{
  printf("%.4f\n", 123.1234567);
  printf("%3.8d\n", 1000);
  printf("%10.15s\n", "This is a simple test.");
}
```

It produces the following output:

```
123.1235
00001000
This is a simpl
```

Justifying Output

By default, all output is right-justified. That is, if the field width is larger than the data printed, the data will be placed on the right edge of the field. You can force output to be left-justified by placing a minus sign directly after the %. For example, %−10.2f left-justifies a floating-point number with two decimal places in a 10-character field.

The following program illustrates left justification:

```
#include "stdio.h"

void main(void)
{
  printf("right-justified:%8d\n", 100);
  printf(" left-justified:%-8d\n", 100);
}
```

Handling Other Data Types

There are two format command modifiers that allow **printf( )** to display **short** and **long** integers. These modifiers may be applied to the **d, i, o, u,** and **x** type specifiers. The **1** modifier tells **printf( )** that a **long** data type follows. For example, %**ld** means that a **long int** is to be displayed. The **h** modifier instructs **printf( )** to display a **short int**. For instance, %**hu** indicates that the data is of type **short unsigned int**.

The **L** modifier may also prefix the floating-point specifiers **e, f,** and **g** and indicates that a **long double** follows.

The * and # Modifiers

The **printf( )** function supports two additional modifiers to some of its format specifiers: * and #.

Preceding **g, f,** or **e** specifiers with a # ensures that there will be a decimal point even if there are not decimal digits. If you precede the **x** format specifier with a #, the hexadecimal number will be printed with a 0x prefix. You cannot apply # to any other format specifiers.

Instead of constants, the minimum field width and precision specifiers may be provided by arguments to **printf( )**. To accomplish this, use an * as a placeholder. When the format string is scanned, **printf( )** will match the * to an argument in the order in which they occur. For example, in Figure 8-1, the minimum field width is 10, the precision is 4, and the value to be displayed is 123.3.

The following program illustrates both # and *:

```
#include "stdio.h"

void main(void)
{
  printf("%x %#x\n", 10, 10);
  printf("%*.*f", 10, 4, 1234.34);
}
```

scanf( )

scanf( ) is the general-purpose console input routine. It can read all the built-in data types and automatically convert numbers into the proper internal format. It is much like the reverse of **printf( )**. The prototype for **scanf( )** is

> int scanf(char *control_string, argument_list);

The prototype for **scanf( )** is in STDIO.H. The **scanf( )** function returns the number of data items successfully assigned a value. If an error occurs, **scanf( )** returns **EOF**. The control_string determines how values are read into the variables pointed to in the argument_list.

The control string consists of three classifications of characters.

- Format specifiers
- White-space characters
- Non-white-space characters

Let's take a look at each of these now.

```
printf("%*.*f", 10, 4, 123.3);
```

Figure 8-1.   How the * is matched to its value

Code	Meaning
%c	Read a single character
%d	Read a decimal integer
%i	Read a decimal integer
%e	Read a floating-point number
%f	Read a floating-point number
%g	Read-floating-point number
%o	Read an octal number
%s	Read a string
%x	Read a hexadecimal number
%p	Read a pointer
%n	Receives an integer value equal to the number of characters read so far
%u	Read an unsigned integer
%[]	Scan for a set of characters

Table 8-3. scanf( ) Format Specifiers

Format Specifiers

The input format specifiers are preceded by a % sign and tell **scanf( )** what type of data is to be read next. These codes are listed in Table 8-3. The format specifiers are matched, in order from left to right, with the arguments in the argument list. Let's look at some examples.

Inputting Numbers

To read a decimal number, use the **%d** or **%i** specifiers. (These specifiers, which do precisely the same thing, are both included for compatibility with older versions of C.)

To read a floating-point number represented in either standard or scientific notation, use **%e**, **%f**, or **%g**. (Again, these specifiers, which do precisely the same thing, are included for compatibility with older versions of C.)

You can use **scanf( )** to read integers in either octal or hexadecimal form by using the **%o** and **%x** format commands, respectively. The **%x** may be in either upper- or lowercase. Either way, you may enter the letters "A" through "F" in either case when entering hexadecimal numbers. The following program reads an octal and hexadecimal number:

```
#include "stdio.h"

void main(void)
{
  int i, j;

  scanf("%o%x", &i, &j);
  printf("%o %x", i, j);
}
```

The **scanf( )** function stops reading a number when the first non-numeric character is encountered.

Inputting Unsigned Integers

To input an unsigned integer, use the **%u** format specifier. For example,

```
unsigned num;
```

```
scanf("%u", &num);
```

reads an unsigned number and puts its value into **num**.

Reading Individual Characters Using scanf( )

As you learned earlier in this chapter, you can read individual characters using **getchar( )** or a derivative function. You can also use **scanf( )** for this purpose if you use the **%c** format specifier. However, like most implementations of **getchar( )**, **scanf( )** line buffers input when the **%c** specifier is used. This makes it somewhat troublesome in an interactive environment.

Although spaces, tabs, and newlines are used as field separators when reading other types of data, when reading a single character, white-space characters are read like any other character. For example, with an input stream of "**x y**", this code fragment

```
scanf("%c%c%c", &a, &b, &c);
```

returns with the character **x** in **a**, a space in **b**, and the character **y** in **c**.

Reading Strings

The **scanf( )** function can be used to read a string from the input stream using the **%s** format specifier. Using **%s** causes **scanf( )** to read characters until it encounters a white-space character. The characters that are read are put into the character array pointed to by the corresponding argument and the result is null terminated. As it applies to **scanf( )**, a white-space character is either a space, a carriage return, or a tab. Unlike **gets( )**, which reads a string until a carriage return is typed, **scanf( )** reads a string until the first white space. This means that you cannot use **scanf( )** to read a string like "this is a test" because the first space terminates the reading process. To see the effect of the %s specifier, try this program using the string "hello there".

```
#include "stdio.h"

void main(void)
{
  char str[80];

  printf("enter a string: ");
  scanf("%s", str);
  printf("here's your string: %s", str);
}
```

The program responds with only the "hello" portion of the string.

Inputting an Address

To input a memory address (pointer), use the %p format specifier. Do not attempt to use an unsigned integer or any other format specifier to input an address because %p makes **scanf( )** read the address in the format used by the CPU. For example, this program inputs a pointer and then displays what is at that memory address:

```
#include "stdio.h"

void main(void)
{
  char *p;

  printf("enter an address: ");
  scanf("%p", &p);
  printf("at location %p is %c\n", p, *p);
}
```

The %n Specifier

The %n specifier instructs **scanf( )** to assign the number of characters read from the input stream at the point at which the %n was encountered to the variable pointed to by the corresponding argument.

Using a Scanset

The ANSI C standard has added to **scanf( )** a new feature called a *scanset*. A scanset defines a set of characters that may be read by **scanf( )** and assigned to the corresponding character array. You define a scanset by putting a string of the characters to scan for inside square brackets. The beginning square bracket must be prefixed by a percent sign. For example, the following scanset tells **scanf( )** to read only the characters "X," "Y," and "Z."

```
%["XYZ"]
```

When you use a scanset, **scanf( )** continues to read characters and put them into the corresponding character array until it encounters a character that is not in the scanset. The corresponding variable must be a pointer to a character array. Upon return from **scanf( )**, this array will contain a null-terminated string that consists of the characters that have been read. To see how this works, try this program:

```
#include "stdio.h"

void main(void)
{

  int i;
  char str[80], str2[80];

  scanf("%d%[abcdefg]%s", &i, str, str2);
  printf("%d %s %s", i, str, str2);
}
```

Enter **123abcdtye** followed by ENTER. The program will then display **123 abcd tye**. Because the "t" is not part of the scanset, **scanf( )** stops reading characters into **str** when it encounters the "t." The remaining characters are put into **str2**.

You can specify an inverted set if the first character in the set is a ^. The ^ instructs **scanf( )** to accept any character that is *not* defined by the scanset.

You can specify a range using a hyphen. For example, this tells **scanf( )** to accept the characters "A" through "Z":

```
%["A-Z"]
```

One important point to remember is that the scanset is case sensitive. If you want scan for both upper- and lowercase letters, you must specify them individually.

Discarding Unwanted White Space

A white-space character in the control string causes **scanf( )** to skip over one or more white-space characters in the input stream. A white-space character is either a space, a tab, or a newline. In essence, one white-space character in the control string causes **scanf( )** to read, but not store, any number (including zero) of white-space characters up to the first non-white-space character.

Non-White-Space Characters in the Control String

A non-white-space character in the control string causes **scanf( )** to read and discard matching characters in the input stream. For example, "%d,%d" causes **scanf( )** to read an integer, read and discard a comma, and then read another integer. If the specified character is not found, **scanf( )** terminates. If you wish to read and discard a percent sign, use %% in the control string.

You Must Pass scanf( ) Addresses

All the variables used to receive values through **scanf( )** must be passed by their addresses. This means that all arguments must be pointers to the variables used as arguments. Recall that this is C's way of creating a call by reference, and it allows a function to alter the contents of an argument. For example, to read an integer into the variable **count**, you would use the following **scanf( )** call:

```
scanf("%d", &count);
```

Strings will be read into character arrays, and the array name, without any index, is the address of the first element of the array. So, to read a string into the character array **str**, you would use

```
scanf("%s", str);
```

In this case, **str** is already a pointer and need not be preceded by the **&** operator.

Format Modifiers

As with **printf( )**, **scanf( )** allows a number of its format specifiers to be modified.

The format specifiers can specify a maximum field length modifier. This is an integer, placed between the % and the format, that limits the number of characters read for that field. For example, to read no more than 20 characters into **str**, write

```
scanf("%20s", str);
```

If the input stream is greater than 20 characters, a subsequent call to input begins where this call leaves off. For example, if you enter

ABCDEFGHIJKLMNOPQRSTUVWXYZ

as the response to the **scanf( )** call in this example, only the first 20 characters, or up to the "T," are placed into **str** because of the maximum size specifier. This means that the remaining characters, "UVWXYZ" have not yet been used. If another **scanf( )** call is made, such as

```
scanf("%s", str);
```

the letters "UVWXYZ" are placed into **str**. Input for a field may terminate before the maximum field length is reached if a white space is encountered. In this case, **scanf( )** moves on to the next field.

To read a long integer, put an "l" in front of the format specifier. To read a short integer, put an "h" in front of the format specifier. These modifiers can be used with the **d**, **i**, **o**, and **x** formats.

By default, the %**f**, %**e**, and %**g** specifiers instruct **scanf( )** to assign data to a **float**. If you put an "l" in front of one of these specifiers, **scanf( )** assigns the data to a **double**. Using an "L" tells **scanf( )** that the variable receiving the data is a **long double**.

Suppressing Input

You can tell **scanf( )** to read a field but not assign it to any variable by preceding that field's format code with an *. For example, given

```
scanf("%d%*c%d", &x, &y);
```

you could enter the coordinate pair **10,10**. The comma would be correctly read, but not assigned to anything. Assignment suppression is especially useful when you need to process only a part of what is being entered.

File I/O

N
I
N
E

As you probably know, the C language does not contain any I/O statements. Instead, all I/O operations take place through calls to functions in the C standard library. This approach makes C's file system extremely powerful and flexible. C's I/O system is also unique because data may be transferred in either its internal binary representation or in a human-readable text format. This makes it easy to create files to fit any need.

ANSI C I/O Versus UNIX I/O

The ANSI standard defines a complete set of I/O functions that can be used to read and write any type of data. In contrast, the old UNIX C standard contains two distinct systems of routines that handle I/O operations. The first method loosely parallels the one defined by the ANSI standard and is called the *buffered file system* (sometimes the terms *formatted* or *high-level* are used instead). The second is the *UNIX-like* file system (sometimes called either *unformatted* or *unbuffered*) and is defined under only the old UNIX standard. The

ANSI standard does not define the unbuffered file system because, among other things, the two file systems are largely redundant and the UNIX-like file system may not be relevant to certain environments that could otherwise support C. This chapter emphasizes the ANSI C file system. The fact that ANSI has failed to define the UNIX-like I/O system suggests that its use will decline. In fact, it would be very hard to justify its use on any new project. However, because UNIX-like routines have been used in thousands of existing C programs, they are discussed briefly at the end of this chapter.

Streams and Files

Before beginning our discussion of ANSI C's file system it is important to understand the difference between the terms *streams* and *files*. The C I/O system supplies a consistent interface to the C programmer independent of the actual device being accessed. That is, the C I/O system provides a level of abstraction between the programmer and the device being used. This abstraction is called a stream and the actual device is called a file. It is important to understand how streams and files interact.

Streams

The C file system is designed to work with a wide variety of devices, including terminals, disk drives, and tape drives. Even though each device is very different, the buffered file system transforms each into a logical device called a *stream*. All streams behave similarly. Because streams are largely device independent, the same function can write to a disk file or to another device, such as the console. There are two types of streams: text and binary.

Text Streams

A *text stream* is a sequence of characters. The ANSI standard allows (but does not require) a text stream to be organized into lines terminated by a newline character. However, the newline character is optional on the last line and is determined by the implementation (actually, most C compilers do not terminate text streams with newline characters). In a text stream, certain character translations may occur as required by the host environment. For example, a newline may be converted to a carriage return/linefeed pair. Therefore, there may not be a one-to-one relationship between the characters that are written (or read) and those in the external device. Also, because of possible translations, the number of characters written (or read) may not be the same as those in the external device.

Binary Streams

A *binary stream* is a sequence of bytes with a one-to-one correspondence to those in the external device—that is, no character translations occur. Also, the number of bytes written (or read) is the same as the number on the external device. However, an implementation-defined number of null bytes may be appended to a binary stream. These null bytes might be used to pad the information so that it fills a sector on a disk, for example.

Files

In C, a *file* may be anything from a disk file to a terminal or printer. You associate a stream with a specific file by performing an open operation. Once a file is open, information may be exchanged between it and your program.

Not all files have the same capabilities. For example, a disk file can support random access while a keyboard cannot. This brings up an important point about the C I/O system: All streams are the same but all files are not.

If the file can support random access (sometimes referred to as *position requests)*, opening that file also initializes the *file position indicator* to the start of the file. As each character is read from or written to the file, the position indicator is incremented, ensuring progression through the file.

You disassociate a file from a specific stream with a close operation. If you close a file opened for output, the contents, if any, of its associated stream are written to the external device. This process is generally referred to as *flushing* the stream, and guarantees that no information is accidentally left in the disk buffer. All files are closed automatically when your program terminates, normally by **main( )** returning to the operating system or by a call to **exit( )**. Files are not closed when a program crashes.

Each stream that is associated with a file has a file control structure of type **FILE**. This structure is defined in the header STDIO.H. Never modify this file control block.

C's separation of streams and files may seem unnecessary or strange, but its main purpose is consistency of interface. In C, you need only think in terms of streams and use only one file system to accomplish all I/O operations. The C compiler converts the raw input or output into an easily managed stream.

File System Basics

The ANSI file system is composed of several interrelated functions. The most common of these are shown in Table 9-1. These functions require that the header file STDIO.H be included in any program in which they are used. Notice that most of the functions begin with the letter "f." This is a holdover from the UNIX C standard, which defined two file systems. The UNIX I/O functions did not begin with a prefix and most of the formatted I/O system functions were prefixed with the "f." The ANSI committee elected to maintain this naming convention in the interest of continuity.

The header file STDIO.H provides the prototypes for the I/O functions and defines these three types: **size_t**, **fpos_t**, and **FILE**. The **size_t** type is essentially the same as **unsigned**, as is the **fpos_t**. The **FILE** type is discussed in the next section.

STDIO.H also defines several macros. The ones relevant to this chapter are **EOF**, **SEEK_SET**, **SEEK_CUR**, and **SEEK_END**. The **EOF** macro is generally defined as −1 and is the value returned when an input function tries to read past the end of the file. The other macros are used with **fseek( )**, which is the function that performs random access on a file.

The File Pointer

The file pointer is the common thread that unites the buffered I/O system. A *file pointer* is a pointer to information that defines various things about the file, including its name, status, and the current position of the file. In essence, the file pointer identifies a specific disk file and is used by the associated stream to direct the operation of the buffered I/O functions. A file pointer is a pointer variable of type **FILE** that is defined in STDIO.H. In order to read or write files, your program needs to use file pointers. To obtain a file pointer variable, use a statement like this:

```
FILE *fp;
```

Name	Function
fopen( )	Opens a file
fclose( )	Closes a file
putc( )	Writes a character to a file
fputc( )	Same as putc( )
getc( )	Reads a character from a file
fgetc( )	Same as getc( )
fseek( )	Seeks to a specified byte in a file
fprintf( )	Is to a file what **printf( )** is to the console
fscanf( )	Is to a file what **scanf( )** is to the console
feof( )	Returns **true** if end-of-file is reached
ferror( )	Returns **true** if an error has occurred
rewind( )	Resets the file position locator to the beginning of the file
remove( )	Erases a file
fflush( )	Flushes a file

Table 9-1.   The Most Common Buffered File-System Functions

Opening a File

The **fopen( )** function opens a stream for use and links a file with that stream. Then it returns the file pointer associated with that file. Most often (and for the rest of this discussion) the file is a disk file. The **fopen( )** function has this prototype:

FILE *fopen(const char *_filename_, const char *_mode_);

where _filename_ is a pointer to a string of characters that make up a valid file name and may include a path specification. The string pointed to by _mode_ determines how the file will be opened. Table 9-2 shows the legal values for _mode_. Strings like "r + b" may also be represented as "rb + ."

As stated, the **fopen( )** function returns a file pointer. Your program should never alter the value of this pointer. If an error occurs when it is trying to open the file, **fopen( )** returns a null pointer.

As Table 9-2 shows, a file may be opened in either text or binary mode. In most implementations, in text mode, carriage return/linefeed sequences are translated to newline characters on input. On output, the reverse occurs: Newlines are translated to carriage return/linefeeds. No such translations occur on binary files.

Mode	Meaning
r	Open a text file for reading
w	Create a text file for writing
a	Append to a text file
rb	Open a binary file for reading
wb	Create a binary file for writing
ab	Append to a binary file
r +	Open a text file for read/write
w +	Create a text file for read/write
a +	Append or create a text file for read/write
r + b	Open a binary file for read/write
w + b	Create a binary file for read/write
a + b	Append a binary file for read/write

Table 9-2. The Legal Values for Mode

If you wished to open a file named TEST for writing, you could enter

```
FILE *fp;

fp = fopen("test", "w");
```

However, you will usually see the preceding code written like this:

```
FILE *fp;
if ((fp = fopen("test","w"))==NULL) {
  printf("cannot open file\n");
  exit(1);
}
```

The macro **NULL** is defined in STDIO.H as '\0'. If you open a file using this method, **fopen( )** detects any error in opening a file, such as a write-protected or a full disk, before attempting to write to it. A null is used to indicate failure because no file pointer will ever have that value.

If you use **fopen( )** to open a file for writing, any preexisting file by that name will be erased and a new file started. If no file by that name exists, one will be created. If you want to add to the end of the file, you must use mode "a". You can only open existing files for read operations. If the file does not exist, an error is returned. Finally, if a file is opened for read/write operations, it will not be erased if it exists. However, if it does not exist it will be created.

The ANSI standard specifies that at least eight files may be open at any one time. However, most C compilers and environments allow more than this.

Closing a File

The **fclose( )** function closes a stream that was opened by a call to **fopen( )**. It writes any data still remaining in the disk buffer to the file and does a formal operating-system-level close on the file. Failure to close a stream invites all kinds of trouble, including lost data, destroyed files, and possible intermittent errors in your program. An **fclose( )** also frees the file control block associated with the stream, making it available for reuse. In most cases, there is an operating system limit to the number of open files you may have at any one time, so you may have to close one file before opening another.

The **fclose( )** function has this prototype

int fclose(FILE *fp*);

where *fp* is the file pointer returned by the call to **fopen( )**. A return value of zero signifies a successful close operation. Any other value indicates an error. You can use the standard function **ferror( )** (discussed shortly) to determine and report any problems. Generally, **fclose( )** will only fail when a disk has been prematurely removed from the drive or there is no more space on the disk.

Writing a Character

The ANSI standard defines two equivalent functions that output a character: **putc( )** and **fputc( )**. (Technically, **putc( )** is implemented as a macro.) There are two identical functions simply to preserve compatibility with older versions of C. This book uses **putc( )**, but you can use **fputc( )** if you like.

The **putc( )** function writes characters to a file that was previously opened for writing using the **fopen( )** function. The prototype of this function is

int putc(int *ch*, FILE *fp*);

where *fp* is the file pointer returned by **fopen( )** and *ch* is the character to be output. The file pointer tells **putc( )** which disk file to write to. For historical reasons, *ch* is defined as an **int** but only the low-order byte is used.

If a **putc( )** operation is successful, it returns the character written. Otherwise, it returns **EOF**.

Reading a Character

The ANSI standard defines two equivalent functions that input a character—**getc( )** and **fgetc( )**—to preserve compatibility with older versions of C. This book uses **getc( )** (which is implemented as a macro), but you can use **fgetc( )** if you like.

The **getc( )** function reads characters from a file opened in read mode by **fopen( )**. The prototype of **getc( )** is

    int getc(FILE *fp);

where *fp* is a file pointer of type **FILE** returned by **fopen( )**. For historical reasons, **getc( )** returns an integer, but the high-order byte is zero.

The **getc( )** function returns an **EOF** mark when the end of the file has been reached. Therefore, to read a text file until the end-of-file mark is read, you could use the following code:

```
do {
  ch = getc(fp);
} while(ch!=EOF);
```

Using fopen( ), getc( ), putc( ), and fclose( )

The functions **fopen( )**, **getc( )**, **putc( )**, and **fclose( )** constitute the minimal set of file routines. The following program, KTOD, is a simple example of using **putc( )**, **fopen( )**, and **fclose( )**. It simply reads characters from the keyboard and writes them to a disk file until the user types a dollar sign. The file name is specified from the command line. For example, if you call this program KTOD, typing **KTOD TEST** allows you to enter lines of text into the file called TEST.

```
/* KTOD: A key to disk program. */

#include "stdio.h"
#include "stdlib.h"

void main(int argc, char *argv[])
{
  FILE *fp;
  char ch;

  if(argc!=2) {
    printf("You forgot to enter the filename\n");
    exit(1);
  }

  if((fp=fopen(argv[1], "w"))==NULL) {
    printf("cannot open file\n");
    exit(1);
```

```
  }

  do {
    ch = getchar();
    putc(ch, fp);
  } while (ch!='$');

  fclose(fp);
}
```

The complementary program DTOS reads any ASCII file and displays the contents on the screen.

```
/* DTOS: A program that reads files and displays them
        on the screen.
*/

#include "stdio.h"
#include "stdlib.h"

void main(int argc, char *argv[])
{
  FILE *fp;
  char ch;

  if(argc!=2) {
    printf("You forgot to enter the filename\n");
    exit(1);
  }

  if((fp=fopen(argv[1], "r"))==NULL) {
    printf("cannot open file\n");
    exit(1);
  }

  ch = getc(fp);    /* read one character */

  while (ch!=EOF) {
    putchar(ch);  /* print on screen */
    ch = getc(fp);
  }

  fclose(fp);
}
```

Try these two programs. First use KTOD to create a text file. Then read its contents using DTOS.

Using feof( )

As stated earlier, the buffered file system can also operate on binary data. When a file is opened for binary input, an integer value equal to the **EOF** mark may be read. This would cause the input routine to indicate an end-of-file condition even though the physical end of the file had not been reached. To solve this problem, C includes the function **feof( )**, which determines when the end of the file is reached when reading binary data. The **feof( )** function has this prototype:

    int feof(FILE *fp);

Its prototype is in STDIO.H. It returns true if the end of the file has been reached; otherwise, it returns 0. Therefore, the following routine reads a binary file until the end of the file is encountered:

```
while(!feof(fp)) ch = getc(fp);
```

Of course, you can apply this method to text files as well as binary files.

The following program, which copies text or binary files, contains an example of **feof( )**. The files are opened in binary mode and the **feof( )** checks for the end of the file.

```
/* Copy a file. */
#include "stdio.h"
#include "stdlib.h"

void main(int argc, char *argv[])
{
  FILE *in, *out;
  char ch;

  if(argc!=3) {
    printf("You forgot to enter a filename\n");
    exit(1);
  }

  if((in=fopen(argv[1], "rb"))==NULL) {
    printf("cannot open source file\n");
    exit(1);
  }
  if((out=fopen(argv[2], "wb")) == NULL) {
    printf("cannot open destination file\n");
    exit(1);
  }

  /* this code acutally copies the file */
  while(!feof(in)) {
    ch = getc(in);
    if(!feof(in)) putc(ch, out);
```

```
    }

    fclose(in);
    fclose(out);
}
```

Working with Strings: fputs( ) and fgets( )

In addition to **getc( )** and **putc( )**, C supports the related functions **fputs( )** and **fgets( )**, which read and write character strings to and from a disk file. These functions work just like **putc( )** and **getc( )**, but instead of reading or writing a single character, they read or write strings. They have the following prototypes:

> int fputs(const char *str*, FILE **fp*);
> char *fgets(char *str*, int *length*, FILE **fp*);

The prototypes for **fgets( )** and **fputs( )** are in STDIO.H.

The function **fputs( )** works like **puts( )**, but it writes the string to the specified stream. It returns **EOF** if an error occurs.

The **fgets( )** function reads a string from the specified stream until either a newline character is read or *length* −1 characters have been read. If a newline is read, it will be part of the string (unlike **gets( )**). The resultant string will be null terminated. The function returns a pointer to **str** if successful and a null pointer if an error occurs.

In the following program, the **fputs( )** function reads strings from the keyboard and writes them to the file called TEST. To terminate the program, enter a blank line. Since **gets( )** does not store the newline character, one is added before the string is written to the file so that the file can be read more easily.

```
#include "stdio.h"
#include "stdlib.h"
#include "string.h"

void main(void)
{
  char str[80];
  FILE *fp;

  if((fp = fopen("TEST", "w"))==NULL) {
    printf("cannot open file\n");
    exit(1);
```

```
  }
  do {
    printf("enter a string (CR to quit):\n");
    gets(str);
    strcat(str, "\n");   /* add a newline */
    fputs(str, fp);
  } while(*str!='\n');
}
```

rewind( )

The **rewind( )** function resets the file position indicator to the beginning of the file specified as its argument. That is, it "rewinds" the file. Its prototype is

   void rewind(FILE *fp)

where fp is a valid file pointer. The prototype for **rewind( )** is in STDIO.H.

   To see an example of **rewind( )**, you can modify the program from the previous section so that it displays the contents of the file just created. To accomplish this, the program rewinds the file after input is complete and then uses **fgets( )** to read back the file. Notice that the file must now be opened in read/write mode using "w+" for the mode parameter.

```
#include "stdio.h"
#include "stdlib.h"
#include "string.h"

void main(void)
{
  char str[80];
  FILE *fp;

  if((fp = fopen("TEST", "w+"))==NULL) {
    printf("cannot open file\n");
    exit(1);
  }
  do {
    printf("enter a string (CR to quit):\n");
    gets(str);
    strcat(str, "\n");   /* add a newline */
    fputs(str, fp);
  } while(*str!='\n');
```

```
/* now, read and display the file */
rewind(fp);  /* reset file position indicator to
                start of the file. */
while(!feof(fp)) {
  fgets(str, 79, fp);
  printf(str);
}
}
```

ferror( )

The **ferror( )** function determines whether a file operation has produced an error. The **ferror( )** function has this prototype:

   int ferror(FILE *fp)

where fp is a valid file pointer. It returns **true** if an error has occurred during the last file operation; otherwise, it returns false. Because each file operation sets the error condition, **ferror( )** should be called immediately after each file operation; otherwise, an error may be lost. The prototype for **ferror( )** is in STDIO.H.

The following program illustrates **ferror( )** by removing tabs from a text file and substituting the appropriate number of spaces. The tab size is defined by **TAB_SIZE**. Notice how **ferror( )** is called after each disk operation. To use the program, execute it after specifying the names of the input and output files on the command line.

```
/* The program substitutes spaces for tabs
   in a text file and supplies error checking.
*/

#include "stdio.h"
#include "stdlib.h"

#define TAB_SIZE 8
#define IN 0
#define OUT 1

void err(int e);

void main(int argc, char *argv[])
{
  FILE *in, *out;
  int tab, i;
  char ch;
```

```
if(argc!=3) {
  printf("usage: detab <in> <out>\n");
  exit(1);
}

if((in = fopen(argv[1], "rb"))==NULL) {
  printf("cannot open %s\n", argv[1]);
  exit(1);
}

if((out = fopen(argv[2], "wb"))==NULL) {
  printf("cannot open %s\n", argv[1]);
  exit(1);
}

tab = 0;
do {
  ch = getc(in);
  if(ferror(in)) err(IN);

  if(ch=='\t') { /* If tab found, then */
    /* output appropriate number of spaces. */
    for(i=tab; i<8; i++) {
      putc(' ', out);
      if(ferror(out)) err(OUT);
    }
    tab = 0;
  }
  else {
    putc(ch, out);
    if(ferror(out)) err(OUT);
    tab++;
    if(tab==TAB_SIZE) tab = 0;
    if(ch=='\n' || ch=='\r') tab = 0;
  }
} while(!feof(in));
fclose(in);
fclose(out);
}

void err(int e)
{
  if(e==IN) printf("error on input\n");
  else printf("error on output\n");
  exit(1);
}
```

Erasing Files

The **remove( )** function erases the specified file. Its prototype is

int remove(char *filename);

It returns zero if successful. Otherwise, it returns a nonzero value.

The following program erases the file specified on the command line. However, it first gives you a chance to change your mind. A utility like this might be useful to new computer users.

```c
/* Double check before erasing. */

#include "stdio.h"
#include "stdlib.h"
#include "ctype.h"

main(int argc, char *argv[])
{
  char str[80];

  if(argc!=2) {
    printf("usage: xerase <filename>\n");
    exit(1);
  }

  printf("erase %s? (Y/N): ", argv[1]);
  gets(str);

  if(toupper(*str)=='Y')
    if(remove(argv[1])) {
      printf("cannot erase file\n");
      exit(1);
    }

  return 0;  /* return success to OS */
}
```

Flushing a Stream

If you wish to flush the contents of an output stream, use the **fflush( )** function, whose prototype is shown here:

int fflush(FILE *fp);

This function writes the contents of any buffered data to the file associated with *fp*. If you call **fflush( )** with a null, all files opened for output are flushed.

The **fflush( )** function returns 0 if successful; otherwise, it returns **EOF**.

fread( ) and fwrite( )

To read and write data types that are longer than one byte, the ANSI C file system provides two functions: **fread( )** and **fwrite( )**. These functions allow the reading and writing of blocks of any type of data. Their prototypes are

size _ t fread(void *buffer, size _ t num _ bytes,
      size _ t count, FILE *fp);
size _ t fwrite(const void *buffer, size _ t num _ bytes,
      size _ t count, FILE *fp);

For **fread( )**, *buffer* is a pointer to a region of memory that will receive the data from the file. For **fwrite( )**, *buffer* is a pointer to the information that will be written to the file. The number of bytes to be read or written is specified by *num _ bytes*. The argument *count* determines how many items (each *num _ bytes* in length) are read or written. (Remember, the type **size _ t** is defined in STDIO.H and is more or less the same as **unsigned**.) Finally, *fp* is a file pointer to a previously opened stream. The prototypes of both of the functions are defined in STDIO.H.

The **fread( )** function returns the number of items read. This value may be less than *count* if the end of the file is reached or an error occurs. The **fwrite( )** function returns the number of items written. This value will equal *count* unless an error occurs.

Using fread( ) and fwrite( )

As long as the file has been opened for binary data, **fread( )** and **fwrite( )** can read and write any type of information. For example, the following program writes and then reads back a **double**, an **int**, and a **long** to and from a disk file. Notice how it uses **sizeof** to determine the length of each data type.

```
/* Write some non-character data to a disk file
   and read it back.
 */
#include "stdio.h"
#include "stdlib.h"
```

```
void main(void)
{
  FILE *fp;
  double d = 12.23;
  int i = 101;
  long l = 123023L;

  if((fp=fopen("test","wb+"))==NULL) {
    printf("cannot open file\n");
    exit(1);
  }

  fwrite(&d, sizeof(double), 1, fp);
  fwrite(&i, sizeof(int), 1, fp);
  fwrite(&l, sizeof(long), 1, fp);

  rewind(fp);

  fread(&d, sizeof(double), 1, fp);
  fread(&i, sizeof(int), 1, fp);
  fread(&l, sizeof(long), 1, fp);

  printf("%f %d %ld", d, i, l);
  fclose(fp);
}
```

As this program illustrates, the buffer can be (and often is) simply the memory used to hold a variable. In this simple program, the return values of **fread( )** and **fwrite( )** are ignored. In the real world, however, you should check their return values for errors.

One of the most useful applications of **fread( )** and **fwrite( )** involves reading and writing user-defined data types, especially structures. For example, given this structure:

```
struct struct_type {
  float balance;
  char name[80];
} cust;
```

the following statement writes the contents of **cust** to the file pointed to by *fp*.

```
fwrite(&cust, sizeof(struct struc_type), 1, fp);
```

To illustrate just how easy it is to write large amounts of data using **fread( )** and **fwrite( )**, a simple mailing list program is delevoped. The list will be stored in an array of structures of this type:

```
struct list_type {
  char name[40];
  char street[40];
  char city[30];
  char state[3];
  char zip[10];
} list[SIZE];
```

The value of **SIZE** determines how many addresses the list can hold.

When the program executes, the **name** field of each structure is initialized with a null in the first position. By convention, the program assumes that that structure is unused if the name is of 0 length.

The routines **save( )** and **load( )**, shown next, are used to save and load the mailing-list database. Note how little code is contained in each routine because of the power of **fread( )** and **fwrite( )**. Notice also how these functions check the return values of **fread( )** and **fwrite( )** for errors.

```
/* Save the list. */
void save(void)
{
  FILE  *fp;
  register int i;

  if((fp=fopen("maillist","wb"))==NULL) {
    printf("cannot open file\n");
    return;
  }

  for(i=0; i<SIZE; i++)
    if(*list[i].name)
      if(fwrite(&list[i],
          sizeof(struct list_type), 1, fp)!=1)
            printf("file write error\n");
}

/* load the file */
void load(void)
{
  FILE  *fp;
  register int i;

  if((fp=fopen("maillist", "rb"))==NULL) {
    printf("cannot open file\n");
    return;
  }

  init_list();
  for(i=0; i<SIZE; i++)
    if(fread(&list[i],
        sizeof(struct list_type), 1, fp)!=1) {
```

```
        if(feof(fp)) return;
        printf("file read error\n");
    }
}
```

Both routines confirm a successful file operation by checking the return value of **fread( )** or **fwrite( )**. Also, **load( )** must explicitly check for end-of-file via **feof( )** because **fread( )** returns the same value whether end-of-file has been reached or an error has occurred.

The entire mailing-list program is shown next. You may wish to use this as a core for further enhancements, including the ability to delete names and search for addresses.

```
/* A very simple mailing list database */

#include "stdio.h"
#include "ctype.h"
#include "stdlib.h"
#include "string.h"

#define SIZE 100

struct list_type {
  char name[40];
  char street[40];
  char city[30];
  char state[3];
  char zip[10];
} list[SIZE];

int menu(void);
void init_list(void), enter(void);
void display(void), save(void);
void load(void);

void main(void)
{
  char choice;

  init_list();

  for(;;) {
    choice = menu();
    switch(choice) {
      case 'e': enter();
        break;
      case 'd': display();
        break;
      case 's': save();
        break;
      case 'l': load();
```

```
        break;
      case 'q': exit(0);
    }
  }
}

/* Initialize the list. */
void init_list(void)
{
  register int t;

  for(t=0; t<SIZE; t++) *list[t].name = '\0';
  /* a zero length name signifies empty */
}

/* Put names into list. */
void enter(void)
{
  register int i;

  for(i=0; i<SIZE; i++)
    if(!*list[i].name) break;

  if(i==SIZE) {
    printf("list full\n");
    return;
  }
  printf("name: ");
  gets(list[i].name);

  printf("street: ");
  gets(list[i].street);

  printf("city: ");
  gets(list[i].city);

  printf("state: ");
  gets(list[i].state);

  printf("zip: ");
  gets(list[i].zip);
}

/* display the list */
void display(void)
{
  register int t;

  for(t=0; t<SIZE; t++) {
    if(*list[t].name) {
      printf("%s\n", list[t].name);
      printf("%s\n", list[t].street);
      printf("%s\n", list[t].city);
      printf("%s\n", list[t].state);
      printf("%s\n\n", list[t].zip);
    }
```

```
  }
}

/* Save the list. */
void save(void)
{
  FILE  *fp;
  register int i;

  if((fp=fopen("maillist","wb"))==NULL) {
    printf("cannot open file\n");
    return;
  }

  for(i=0; i<SIZE; i++)
    if(*list[i].name)
      if(fwrite(&list[i],
          sizeof(struct list_type), 1, fp)!=1)
            printf("file write error\n");
}

/* load the file */
void load(void)
{
  FILE  *fp;
  register int i;

  if((fp=fopen("maillist", "rb"))==NULL) {
    printf("cannot open file\n");
    return;
  }

  init_list();
  for(i=0; i<SIZE; i++)
    if(fread(&list[i],
        sizeof(struct list_type), 1, fp)!=1) {
          if(feof(fp)) return;
          printf("file read error\n");
    }
}

/* get a menu selection */
menu(void)
{
  char s[80];

  do {
    printf("(E)nter\n");
    printf("(D)isplay\n");
    printf("(L)oad\n");
    printf("(S)ave\n");
    printf("(Q)uit\n\n");
    printf("choose one: ");
    gets(s);
  } while(!strchr("edlsq", tolower(*s)));
```

```
    return tolower(*s);
}
```

fseek( ) and Random-Access I/O

You can perform random read and write operations using the buffered I/O system with the help of **fseek( )**, which sets the file position locator. Its prototype type is shown here:

    int fseek(FILE *fp, long numbytes, int origin);

Here, fp is a file pointer returned by a call to **fopen( )**. numbytes, a long integer, is the number of bytes from origin which will become the new current position, and origin is one of the following macros defined in STDIO.H:

Origin	Macro Name
Beginning of file	SEEK _ SET
Current position	SEEK _ CUR
End-of-file	SEEK _ END

Therefore, to seek numbytes from the start of the file, origin should be **SEEK_SET**. To seek from the current position use **SEEK_CUR**, and to seek from the end of the file use **SEEK_END**. The **fseek( )** function returns 0 when successful and a nonzero value if an error occurs. Remember, numbytes must be a **long**.

The following fragment illustrates **fseek( )**. It seeks to and displays the specified byte in the specified file. Specify the file name and then the byte to seek to on the command line.

```
#include "stdio.h"
#include "stdlib.h"

void main(int argc, char *argv[])
{
    FILE *fp;
```

```
if(argc!=3) {
  printf("Usage: SEEK filename byte\n");
  exit(1);
}

if((fp = fopen(argv[1], "r"))==NULL) {
  printf("cannot open file\n");
  exit(1);
}

if(fseek(fp, atol(argv[2]), SEEK_SET)) {
  printf("seek error\n");
  exit(1);
}
printf("Byte at %ld is %c\n", atol(argv[2]), getc(fp));
fclose(fp);
}
```

You can use **fseek( )** to seek in multiples of any type of data by simply multiplying the size of the data by the number of the item you want to reach. For example, if you have a mailing-list file produced by the example in the previous section, the following code fragment seeks to the tenth address.

```
fseek(fp, 9*sizeof(struct list_type), SEEK_SET);
```

fprintf( ) and fscanf( )

In addition to the basic I/O functions already discussed, the buffered I/O system includes **fprintf( )** and **fscanf( )**. These functions behave exactly like **printf( )** and **scanf( )** except that they operate with files. The prototypes of **fprintf( )** and **fscanf( )** are

> int fprintf(FILE *fp*, const char *control_string*,...);
> int fscanf(FILE *fp*, const char *control_string*,...);

where *fp* is a file pointer returned by a call to **fopen( )**. **fprintf( )** and **fscanf( )** direct their I/O operations to the file pointed to by *fp*.

As an example, the following program reads a string and an integer from the keyboard, writes them to a disk file, and then reads and displays the information on the screen.

```
/* fscanf() - fprintf() example */

#include "stdio.h"
#include "io.h"
#include "stdlib.h"

void main(void)
{
  FILE *fp;
  char s[80];
  int t;

  if((fp=fopen("test", "w")) == NULL) {
    printf("cannot open file\n");
    exit(1);
  }

  printf("enter a string and a number: ");
  fscanf(stdin, "%s%d", s, &t); /* read from
                                      keyboard */
  fprintf(fp, "%s %d", s, t); /* write to file */
  fclose(fp);

  if((fp=fopen("test","r")) == NULL) {
    printf("cannot open file\n");
    exit(1);
  }

  fscanf(fp, "%s%d", s, &t); /* read from file */
  fprintf(stdout, "%s %d", s, t); /* print on
                                       screen */
}
```

A word of warning: Although **fprintf( )** and **fscanf( )** often are the easiest way to write and read assorted data to disk files, they are not always the most efficient. Because formatted ASCII data is being written as it would appear on the screen (instead of in binary), extra overhead is incurred with each call. So, if speed or file size is a concern, you should probably use **fread( )** and **fwrite( )**.

The Standard Streams

Whenever a C program starts execution, three streams are opened automatically. They are standard input (**stdin**), standard output (**stdout**), and standard error (**stderr**). Normally, these streams refer to the console, but they may be redirected by the operating system to some other device in environments that support redirectable I/O. (Redirectable I/O is supported by UNIX, OS/2, and DOS, for example.)

Because the standard streams are file pointers, they may be used by the buffered I/O system to perform I/O operations on the console. For example, **putchar( )** could be defined like this:

```
putchar(char c)
{
  putc(c, stdout);
}
```

In general, **stdin** is used to read from the console, and **stdout** and **stderr** are used to write to the console. You may use **stdin**, **stdout**, and **stderr** as file pointers in any function that uses a variable of type **FILE ***. For example, you can use **fputs( )** to output a string to the console using a call like this:

```
fputs("hello there", stdout);
```

Keep in mind that **stdin**, **stdout**, and **stderr** are not variables in the normal sense and may not be assigned a value using **fopen( )**. Also, just as these file pointers are created automatically at the start of your program, they are closed automatically at the end; you should not try to close them.

The Console I/O Connection

Recall from Chapter 8 that C makes little distinction between console I/O and file I/O. The console I/O functions described in Chapter 8 actually direct their I/O operations to either **stdin** or **stdout**. In essence, the console I/O functions are simply special versions of their parallel file functions. The reason they exist is as a convenience to you, the programmer.

As described in the previous section, you can perform console I/O using any of C's file system functions. However, what might surprise you is that you can perform disk file I/O using console I/O functions, such as **printf( )**! This is because all of the console I/O functions described in Chapter 8 operate on **stdin** and **stdout**. In environments that allow redirection of I/O, this means that **stdin** and **stdout** could refer to a device other than the keyboard and screen. For example, consider this program:

```
#include "stdio.h"

void main(void)
{
  char str[80];

  printf("enter a string: ");
  gets(str);
  printf(str);
}
```

Assume that this program is called TEST. If you execute TEST normally, it displays its prompt on the screen, reads a string from the keyboard, and displays that string on the display. However, in an environment that supports I/O redirection, either **stdin**, **stdout**, or both could be redirected to a file. For example, in a DOS or OS/2 environment, executing TEST like this:

```
TEST > OUTPUT
```

causes the output of TEST to be written to a file called OUTPUT. Executing TEST like this:

```
TEST < INPUT > OUTPUT
```

directs **stdin** to the file called INPUT and sends output to the file called OUTPUT.

When a C program terminates, any redirected streams are reset to their default status.

Using freopen( ) to Redirect the Standard Streams

You can redirect the standard streams by using the **freopen( )** function. This function associates an existing stream with a new file. Hence, you can use it to associate a standard stream with a new file. Its prototype is

FILE *freopen(const char *_filename_,
            const char *_mode_, FILE *_stream_);

where *filename* is a pointer to the file name you wish associated with the stream pointed to by *stream*. The file is opened using the value of *mode*, which may have the same values as the one used with **fopen( )**.

The following program uses **freopen( )** to redirect **stdout** to a file called OUTPUT:

```
#include "stdio.h"

void main(void)
{
  char str[80];

  freopen("OUTPUT", "w", stdout);

  printf("enter a string: ");
  gets(str);
  printf(str);
}
```

In general, redirecting the standard streams by using **freopen( )** is useful in special situations, such as debugging. However, performing disk I/O using redirected **stdin** and **stdout** is not as efficient as using functions like **fread( )** or **fwrite( )**.

The UNIX-Like File System

Because C was originally developed under the UNIX operating system, it includes a second disk file I/O system that closely mirrors the UNIX low-level disk file routines. The UNIX-like file system uses functions that are separate from the buffered file system functions. These are shown in Table 9-3.

Remember, the UNIX-like file system is sometimes called the un-buffered file system. This is because you must provide and maintain *all* disk buffers—the routines will not do it for you. Unlike the **getc( )** and **putc( )** functions, which write and read characters from or to a stream of data, the **read( )** and **write( )** functions read or write one complete buffer of information with each call. (This is similar to **fread( )** and **fwrite( )**.)

Name	Function
read( )	Reads a buffer of data
write( )	Writes a buffer of data
open( )	Opens a disk file
close( )	Closes a disk file
lseek( )	Seeks to the specified byte in a file
unlink( )	Removes a file from the directory

Table 9-3.   The UNIX-Like Unbuffered I/O Functions

Recall that the unbuffered file system is not defined by the ANSI standard and its use will probably diminish over the next few years. For this reason, it is not recommended for new projects. However, a great many existing C programs use it and it is supported by virtually all existing C compilers.

The header file used by the UNIX-like file system is called IO.H in many implementations. For some functions, you will also need to include the header file FNCTL.H.

Note: Many implementations of C do not allow you to use the ANSI file functions and the UNIX-like file functions in the same program. Just to be safe, use either one system or the other.

open( )

Unlike the high-level I/O system, the low-level system does not use file pointers of type **FILE**, but rather file descriptors of type **int**. The prototype for **open( )** is

int open(const char *filename*, int *mode*);

where *filename* is any valid file name and *mode* is one of the following macros, which are defined in the header file FCNTL.H.

Mode	Effect
O_RDONLY	Read
O_WRONLY	Write
O_RDWR	Read/Write

Many compilers have additional modes—such as text, binary, and the like—so check your user's manual. A successful call to **open( )** returns a positive integer. A return value of −1 means that the file cannot be opened.

The call to **open( )** is usually written like this:

```
int fd;

if((fd=open(filename, mode)) == -1)  {
  printf("cannot open file\n");
  exit(1);
}
```

In most implementations, the operation fails if the file specified in the **open( )** statement does not appear on the disk. (That is, it doesn't create a new file.) However, depending upon the exact implementation of your C compiler, you may be able to use **open( )** to create a file that is currently nonexistent. Check your user's manual.

close( )

The prototype for **close( )** is

> int close(int *file_descriptor*);

Here, *file_descriptor* must be a valid file descriptor previously obtained through a call to **open( )** or **creat( )**. **close( )** returns a −1 if unable to close the file. It returns 0 if successful.

The **close( )** function releases the file descriptor so that it can be reused for another file. There is always some limit to the number of open files that may exist simultaneously, so you should close a file when it is no longer needed. More important, a close operation forces any information in the internal disk buffers of the operating system to be written to disk. Failure to close a file usually leads to loss of data.

creat( )

If your compiler does not allow you to create a new file using **open( )**, or if you want to ensure portability, you must use **creat( )** to create a new file for write operations. The prototype for **creat( )** is

    int creat(const char *filename, int mode);

where *filename* is any valid file name. The *mode* argument specifies an access code for the file, such as read-only, for example. Consult your C user's manual for specific details.

read( ) and write( )

Once a file has been opened for writing, it may be accessed by **write( )**. The prototype for the **write( )** function is

    int write(int fd, const void *buf, unsigned size);

Each time a call to **write( )** is executed, *size* number of characters are written to the disk file specified by *fd* from the buffer pointed to by *buf*. The buffer may be either an allocated region of memory or a variable.

The **write( )** function returns the number of bytes written after a successful write operation. Upon failure, most implementations return an **EOF**, but check your user's manual.

The **read( )** function is the complement of **write( )**. Its prototype is

    int read(int fd, void *buf, unsigned size);

where *fd*, *buf*, and *size* are the same as for **write( )**, except that **read( )** places the data read into the buffer pointed to by *buf*. If **read( )** is successful, it returns the number of characters actually read. It returns 0 upon the physical end-of-file, and −1 if errors occur.

The following program illustrates some aspects of the unbuffered I/O system. It reads lines of text from the keyboard and writes them to a disk file. After they are written, the program reads them back.

```
/* Read and write using unbuffered I/O */

#include "stdio.h"
#include "io.h"
#include "stdlib.h"
#include "string.h"
#include "fcntl.h"

#define BUF_SIZE  128

void input(char *buf, int fd1);
void display(char *buf, int fd2);

void main(void)
{
  char buf[BUF_SIZE];
  int fd1, fd2;

  if((fd1=open("test",  O_WRONLY))==-1) { /* open for write */
    printf("cannot open file\n");
    exit(1);
  }

  input(buf, fd1);

  /* now close file and read back */
  close(fd1);

  if((fd2=open("test", O_RDONLY))==-1) { /* open for read */
    printf("cannot open file\n");
    exit(1);
  }

  display(buf, fd2);
  close(fd2);
}

/* Input text */
void input(char *buf, int fd1)
{
  register int t;
  do {
    for(t=0; t<BUF_SIZE; t++) buf[t] = '\0';
    gets(buf); /* input chars from keyboard */
    if(write(fd1, buf, BUF_SIZE)!=BUF_SIZE) {
      printf("error on write\n");
      exit(1);
    }
  } while (strcmp(buf, "quit"));
}

/* Display file. */
void display(char *buf, int fd2)
{
  for(;;) {
    if(read(fd2, buf, BUF_SIZE)==0) return;
```

```
    printf("%s\n", buf);
  }
}
```

unlink( )

If you wish to erase a file, use **unlink( )**. Its prototype is

    int unlink(const char *filename);

where *filename* is a character pointer to any valid file name. **unlink( )** returns a −1 if unable to erase the file. This could happen if the file is not on the disk to begin with or if the disk is write-protected.

Random Access Using lseek( )

The UNIX-like file system supports random access via calls to **lseek( )**. The prototype for **lseek( )** is

    long lseek(int *fd*, long *offset*, int *origin*);

where *fd* is a file descriptor returned by a **creat( )** or **open( )** call. The *offset* is generally a **long**, but check your C compiler's user's manual. *origin* may be one of these macros (defined in IO.H): **SEEK_SET**, **SEEK_CUR**, or **SEEK_END**. These are the effects of each value for *origin:*

    SEEK_SET: Seek *offset* bytes from the start of the file
    SEEK_CUR: Seek *offset* bytes from the current position
    SEEK_END: Seek *offset* from the end of the file

The **lseek( )** function returns the current file position as measured from the start of the file. Upon failure, a −1L is returned.

    The program shown here uses **lseek( )**. To run it, specify a file from the command line. You are prompted for the buffer you wish to read.

Enter a negative number to exit. You may want to change the buffer size to match the sector size of your system, although this is not necessary. Here, the buffer size is 128:

```
/* Demonstrate lseek(). */

#include "stdio.h"
#include "io.h"
#include "stdlib.h"
#include "fcntl.h"

#define BUF_SIZE  128

void main(int argc, char *argv[])
{
  char buf[BUF_SIZE+1], s[10];
  int fd, sector;

  if(argc!=2) {
    printf("usage: dump <sector>\n");
    exit(1);
  }

  buf[BUF_SIZE+1] = '\0'; /* null terminate buffer */

  if((fd=open(argv[1], O_RDONLY))==-1) {
    printf("cannot open file\n");
    exit(1);
  }

  do {
    printf("\nbuffer: ");
    gets(s);

    sector = atoi(s); /* get the sector to read */

    if(lseek(fd, (long)sector*BUF_SIZE, 0)==-1L)
      printf("seek error\n");

    if(read(fd, buf, BUF_SIZE)==0) {
      printf("sector out of range\n");
    }
    else
      printf(buf);
  } while(sector>=0);
  close(fd);
}
```

The C Preprocessor and Comments

You can include various instructions to the compiler in the source code for a C program. These are called *preprocessor directives*, and although not actually part of the C language, they expand the scope of the C programming environment. This chapter also examines comments.

The C Preprocessor

As defined by the ANSI standard, the C preprocessor contains the following directives:

    #if
    #ifdef
    #ifndef
    #else

```
#elif
#include
#define
#undef
#line
#error
#pragma
```

As you can see, all preprocessor directives begin with a **#** sign. In addition, each preprocessing directive must be on its own line. For example,

```
#include "stdio.h"  #include "stdlib.h"
```

will not work.

#define

The **#define** directive defines an identifier and a string that will be substituted for the identifier each time the identifier is encountered in the source file. The ANSI C standard refers to the identifier as a *macro name* and to the replacement process as *macro substitution*. The general form of the directive is

> #define *macro _ name string*

Notice that there is no semicolon in this statement. There may be any number of spaces between the identifier and the string, but once the string begins, it is only terminated by a newline.

For example, if you wish to use the word **TRUE** for the value 1 and the word **FALSE** for the value 0, you would declare two macro **#define**s

```
#define TRUE 1
#define FALSE 0
```

This causes the compiler to substitute a 1 or a 0 each time **TRUE** or **FALSE** is encountered in your source file. For example, the following prints **0 1 2** on the screen:

```
printf("%d %d %d", FALSE, TRUE, TRUE+1);
```

Once a macro name has been defined, it may be used as part of the definition of other macro names. For example, this code defines the values of **ONE, TWO,** and **THREE**:

```
#define ONE      1
#define TWO      ONE+ONE
#define THREE    ONE+TWO
```

Macro substitution is simply replacing an identifier with its associated string. Therefore, if you wish to define a standard error message, you might write something like this:

```
#define E_MS "standard error on input\n"

printf(E_MS);
```

The compiler will actually substitute the string "standard error on input\n" when the identifier **E_MS** is encountered. To the compiler, the **printf( )** statement will actually appear to be

```
printf("standard error on input\n");
```

No text substitutions occur if the identifier is within a quoted string. For example,

```
#define XYZ this is a test
printf("XYZ");
```

does not print **this is a test**, but rather **XYZ**.

If the string is longer than one line, you may continue it on the next by placing a backslash at the end of the line, as shown here:

```
#define LONG_STRING "this is a very long \
string that is used as an example"
```

C programmers commonly use uppercase letters for defined identifiers. This convention helps anyone reading the program know at a glance that a macro substitution will take place. Also, it is best to put all **#define**s at the start of the file or in a separate include file rather than sprinkling them throughout the program.

Macro substitution is most frequently used to define names for "magic numbers" that occur in a program. For example, you may have a program that defines an array and has several routines that access that array. Instead of "hard-coding" the array's size with a constant, you should define a size and use that name whenever the array size is needed. In this way, you only need to make one change and recompile to alter the size of the array. For example,

```
#define MAX_SIZE 100

float balance[MAX_SIZE];
```

The **#define** directive has another powerful feature: The macro name can have arguments. Each time the macro name is encountered, the arguments associated with it are replaced by the actual arguments found in the program. For example,

```
#include "stdio.h"

#define ABS(a)  (a)<0 ? -(a) : (a)

void main(void)
{
  printf("abs of -1 and 1: %d %d", ABS(-1), ABS(1));
}
```

When this program is compiled, **a** in the macro definition will be substituted with the values −1 and 1. The parentheses that enclose **a** ensure proper substitution in all cases. For example, if the parentheses around **a** were removed, this expression

```
ABS(10-20)
```

would be converted to

```
10-20<0 ?  -10-20  :  10-20
```

and would yield the wrong result.

The use of macro substitutions in place of real functions has one major benefit: It increases the speed of the code because there is no function call overhead. However, this increased speed is paid for with an increase in the size of the program because of duplicated code.

#error

The **#error** directive forces the compiler to stop compilation. It is used primarily for debugging. The general form of the **#error** directive is

#error *error_message*

The *error_message* is not between double quotes. When the **#error** directive is encountered, the error message is displayed, possibly along with other information defined by the creator of the compiler.

#include

The **#include** directive instructs the compiler to read another source file in addition to the one that contains the **#include** directive. The name of the additional source file must be enclosed between double quotes or angle brackets. For example,

```
#include "stdio.h"
#include <stdio.h>
```

both instruct the C compiler to read and compile the header for the disk-file library routines.

Include files can have **#include** directives in them. This is referred to as *nested includes*. The number of levels of nesting varies between compilers. However, the ANSI standard stipulates that at least eight nested inclusions will be available.

If the file name is enclosed in angle brackets, the file is searched for as defined by the creator of the compiler. Often, this means searching some special directory set aside for include files. If the file name is enclosed in quotes, the file is looked for in an implementation-defined manner. For many implementations, this means searching the current working directory. If the file is not found, the search is repeated as if the file name had been enclosed in angle brackets.

Conditional Compilation Directives

There are several directives that allow you to selectively compile portions of your program's source code. This process is called *conditional compilation* and is used widely by commerical software houses that provide and maintain many customized versions of one program.

#if, #else, #elif, and #endif

If the constant expression following **#if** is true, the code that is between it and **#endif** is compiled. Otherwise, the intervening code is skipped. The **#endif** directive marks the end of an **#if** block.

The general form of **#if** is

```
#if constant_expression
    statement sequence
#endif
```

If the constant expression is true, the block of code is compiled; otherwise, it is skipped. For example,

```
/* simple #if example */
#include "stdio.h"

#define MAX 100

void main(void)
{
#if MAX>99
  printf("compiled for array greater than 99\n");
#endif
}
```

This program displays the message on the screen because **MAX** is greater than 99. This example illustrates an important point. The expression that follows the **#if** is evaluated at compile time. Therefore, it must contain only previously defined identifiers and constants—no variables may be used.

The **#else** directive works much like the **else** that is part of the C language: It establishes an alternative if **#if** fails. The previous example can be expanded as shown here:

```
/* simple #if/#else example */
#include "stdio.h"

#define MAX 10
void main(void)
{
#if MAX>99
  printf("compiled for array greater than 99\n");
#else
  printf("compiled for small array\n");
#endif
}
```

In this case, **MAX** is defined to be less than 99 so the **#if** portion of the code is not compiled. The **#else** alternative is compiled, however, and the message **compiled for small array** is displayed.

Notice that **#else** is used to mark both the end of the **#if** block and the beginning of the **#else** block. This is necessary because there can only be one **#endif** associated with any **#if**.

The **#elif** directive means "else if" and establishes an if-else-if chain for multiple compilation options. **#elif** is followed by a constant expression. If the expression is true, that block of code is compiled and no other **#elif** expressions are tested. Otherwise, the next block in the series is checked. The general form for **#elif** is

```
#if expression
     statement sequence
#elif expression 1
     statement sequence
#elif expression 2
     statement sequence
#elif expression 3
     statement sequence
#elif expression 4
     .
     .
     .
#elif expression N
     statement sequence
#endif
```

For example, the following fragment uses the value of **ACTIVE_ COUNTRY** to define the currency sign:

```
#define US 0
#define ENGLAND 1
#define FRANCE 2

#define ACTIVE_COUNTRY US

#if ACTIVE_COUNTRY==US
  char currency[]="dollar";
#elif ACTIVE_COUNTRY==ENGLAND
  char currency[]="pound";
#else
  char currency[]="franc";
#endif
```

#ifs and **#elif**s may be nested up to an implementation-specific limit, with **#endif**, **#else**, or **#elif** associating with the nearest **#if** or **#elif**. For example, the following is perfectly valid:

```
#if MAX>100
   #if SERIAL_VERSION
     int port=198;
   #elif
     int port=200;
   #endif
#else
```

```
    char out_buffer[100];
#endif
```

#ifdef and #ifndef

Another method of conditional compilation uses the directives **#ifdef**
and **#ifndef**, which mean "if defined" and "if not defined," respectively.
The general form of **#ifdef** is

> #ifdef *macro__name*
> > *statement sequence*
> #endif

If *macro__name* has been previously defined in a **#define** statement,
the block of code will be compiled.
 The general form of **#ifndef** is

> #ifndef *macro__name*
> > *statement sequence*
> #endif

If *macro__name* is currently undefined by a **#define** statement, the
block of code is compiled.
 Both **#ifdef** and **#ifndef** may use an **#else** statement, but not
#elif.
 For example,

```
#include "stdio.h"

#define TED 10

void main(void)
{
#ifdef TED
  printf("Hi Ted\n");
#else
  printf("Hi anyone\n");
#endif
#ifndef RALPH
  printf("RALPH not defined\n");
#endif
}
```

will print **Hi Ted** and **RALPH not defined**. However, if **TED** were not defined, **Hi anyone** would be displayed, followed by **RALPH not defined**.

You may nest **#ifdef**s and **#ifndef**s to any level, as with **#if**s.

#undef

The **#undef** directive removes a previously defined definition of the macro name that follows it. The general form for **#undef** is

    #undef *macro_name*

For example,

```
#define LEN 100
#define WIDTH 100

char array[LEN][WIDTH];

#undef LEN
#undef WIDTH
/* at this point both LEN and WIDTH are undefined */
```

Both **LEN** and **WIDTH** are defined until the **#undef** statements are encountered.

    #undef is used principally to allow macro names to be localized to only those sections of code that need them.

#line

The **#line** directive changes the contents of __LINE__ and __FILE__, which are predefined identifiers in the compiler. The __LINE__ identifier contains the line number of the currently compiled line code. The __FILE__ identifier is a string that contains the name of the source file being compiled. The general form for **#line** is

    #line *number "filename"*

where *number* is any positive integer and becomes the new value of **_ _LINE _ _**, and the optional *filename* is any valid file identifier, which becomes the new value of the **_ _ FILE _ _**. **#line** is primarily used for debugging and special applications.

For example, the following code specifies that the line count will begin with 100 and the **printf( )** statement displays the number 102 because it is the third line in the program after the **#line 100** statement.

```
#include "stdio.h"

#line 100   /* reset the line counter */
void main(void)     /* line 100 */
{           /* line 101 */
  printf("%d\n",__LINE__);  /* line 102 */
}
```

#pragma

The **#pragma** directive is an implementation-defined directive that allows various instructions to be given to the compiler. For example, a compiler may have an option that supports program execution tracing. A trace option would then be specified by a **#pragma** statement. You must check the compiler's user's manual for details and options.

The # and ## Preprocessor Operators

ANSI C provides two preprocessor operators: **#** and **##**. These operators are used when using a macro **#define**.

The **#** operator turns the argument it precedes into a quoted string. For example, consider this program.

```
#include "stdio.h"

#define mkstr(s)  # s

void main(void)
{
```

```
   printf(mkstr(I like C));
}
```

The C preprocessor turns the line

```
printf(mkstr(I like C));
```

into

```
printf("I like C");
```

The ## operator concatenates two tokens. For example,

```
#include "stdio.h"

#define concat(a, b)   a ## b

void main(void)
{
  int xy = 10;

  printf("%d", concat(x, y));
}
```

The preprocessor transforms

```
printf("%d", concat(x, y));
```

into

```
printf("%d", xy);
```

If these operators seem strange to you, keep in mind that they are not needed or used in most C programs. They exist primarily to allow the preprocessor to handle some special cases.

Predefined Macro Names

The ANSI standard specifies five built-in predefined macro names. They are

```
_ _LINE_ _
_ _FILE_ _
_ _DATE_ _
_ _TIME_ _
_ _STDC_ _
```

If your compiler is nonstandard, some or all of these macros may be missing. Your compiler may also supply more predefined macros. The **_ _LINE_ _** and **_ _FILE_ _** macros were discussed in the section on **#line**.

The **_ _DATE_ _** macro contains a string of the form *month/day/year*. This string represents the date of the translation of the source file into object code.

The time of the translation of the source code into object code is contained as a string in **_ _TIME_ _**. The form of the string is *hour:minute:second*.

The macro **_ _STDC_ _** contains the decimal constant 1. This means that the implementation conforms to the standard. If the macro contains any other number, the implementation varies from the standard.

Comments

In C, all comments begin with the character pair **/*** and end with ***/**. There must be no spaces between the asterisk and the slash. The compiler ignores any text between the beginning and ending comment symbols. For example, this program prints only **hello** on the screen:

```c
#include "stdio.h"

void main(void)
{
  printf("hello");
  /* printf("there"); */
}
```

Comments may be placed anywhere in a program, as long as they do not appear in the middle of keyword or identifier. That is, this comment is valid:

```
x = 10+ /* add the numbers */5;
```

while

```
swi/*this will not work*/tch(c) { ...
```

is incorrect because a C keyword cannot contain a comment. However, you should not generally place comments in the middle of expressions because it obscures their meaning.

Comments may not be nested. That is, one comment may not contain another comment. For example, this code fragment causes a compile-time error:

```
/* this is an outer comment
  x = y/a;
  /* this is an inner comment - and causes an error */
*/
```

You should include comments whenever they are needed to explain the operation of the code. All but the most obvious functions should have a comment at the top that states what the function does, how it is called, and what it returns.

The C Standard Library

Linking, Libraries, and Header Files
I/O Functions
String and Character Functions
Mathematical Functions
Time, Date, and Other System-Related Functions
Dynamic Allocation
Screen and Graphics Functions
Miscellaneous Functions

**P
A
R
T

T
W
O**

Part Two of this book examines the C standard library. Chapter 11 discusses linking, libraries, and header files. Chapters 12 through 18 describe the functions in the standard library—each chapter concentrates on a specific function group.

Included are the library functions as defined by both the ANSI C standard and the de facto original UNIX standard. No standard exists for the graphics functions, but since they are commonly included, a representative sample is examined. Because many compiler implementors take great pride in the completeness of their library, your compiler's library will probably contain a few functions not discussed here. Therefore, it is always a good idea to browse through your user's manual.

Linking, Libraries, and Header Files

The Linker
The C Standard Library
Header Files
Redefinition of Library Functions

The C compiler itself is relatively easy to develop. It is the library functions that take the most time and effort. One reason for this is that many functions must interface with the operating system. In addition, the C standard library defines a large and diverse set of functions. Indeed, it is the richness and flexibility of the standard library that sets C apart from many other languages. To fully understand the nature of the executable program produced by your compiler, you should know how the linker works, how libraries differ from object files, and the role of header files.

The Linker

The linker has two functions. The first, as the name implies, is to combine (link) various pieces of object code. The second is to resolve the addresses of jump and call instructions found in the relocatable format of the object file. To understand its operation, let's look more closely at the process of separate compilation.

Separate Compilation

In *separate compilation*, parts of a program are compiled separately and then linked to form the finished executable program. The output of the compiler is a relocatable object file, and the output of the linker is an executable file. The role the linker plays is twofold. First, it physically combines the files specified in the link list into one program file. Second, it also resolves external references. An external reference is created anytime the code in one file refers to code in another file. This may be through either a function call or a reference to a global variable. For example, when the two files shown here are linked, file 2's reference to **count** must be resolved. The linker tells the code in file 2 where **count** will be found in memory.

File 1:

```
int count;
void display(void);

void main(void)
{
  count = 10;
  display();
}
```

File 2:

```
#include "stdio.h"

extern int count;

void display (void)
{
    printf("%d",count);
}
```

In a similar fashion, the linker tells file 1 where the function **display( )** is located so that it may be called.

When the compiler generates the object code for **display( )**, it substitutes a placeholder for the address of **count** because the compiler has no way of knowing where **count** is. The same sort of thing occurs when **main( )** is compiled. The address of **display( )** is unknown, so a placeholder is used. This process forms the basis for relocatable code.

Relocatable Code

Relocatable code is simply object code that may run in any available memory region that is large enough to hold it. In a relocatable object file, the address of each call, jump, or global variable is not fixed, but is relative. To understand how relocatable code is created, you need to understand *absolute code*. For this discussion it is necessary to work with the actual machine instructions that would be generated by the C compiler, using a pseudo-assembly code fragment that somewhat resembles the 8086 assembly code. (Don't worry if you don't know assembly language, this example is very simple.)

The pseudo-assembly code shown here corresponds to the C code shown after it:

```
        mov a,0
label1: out a,123   ; send it out port 123
        inc a       ; increment the a register
        cmp a,100   ; is it equal to 100?
        out 123     ; output to port 123
        jnz label1  ; jmp not zero
```

```
/* C code version */
for(x=0; x<100; x++) out(x, 123);
```

In this example, the **a** register is initialized to zero. Then the program loops 100 times, each time sending the value in register **a** out port 123. The **inc** instruction increments the **a** register, and **cmp** compares the **a** register with the value 100. If the **a** register is equal to 100, the zero flag is set. The **jnz** instruction is read "jump not zero" and means to jump to the specified address if the zero flag is not set. The function **out( )** in the C code version is assumed to translate into the corresponding **out** instruction in the pseudo-assembly code.

If an absolute assembler is used, the code is assembled to run at some specified absolute location. For example, assume the **mov** instruction requires 3 bytes. If the code were assembled to run at address 100, the label associated with the **jnz** instruction would be replaced by the address 103. This also implies that the object code for this program only runs correctly if it is placed in memory starting at 100. It cannot be loaded anywhere else.

Absolute addressing is fairly common in simple microcomputer systems. However, it is inadequate for general use because it requires that the location in memory where the program will be run is known at the time of assembly. This not only prevents the code from being linked with other code later on, but keeps the operating system from making the most efficient use of its resources. For these reasons, relocatable object code is generally used instead.

Relocatable code is created by using a *relocating assembler*. It uses no fixed address, only offsets from the beginning of the file. (An *offset* represents the number of bytes a label is from the start of the file.) The offsets are stored by the assembler in a table along with the label name. This table is sometimes called an *offset table*. The offset table is then used during the linking process to determine actual addresses. Using the previous assembly code example, and assuming that each instruction requires 3 bytes, the table entry for **label1** looks like the following illustration.

label1	3

When the linker links the code fragment containing **label1** with the rest of the code that makes up the program, the offset 3 is added to the current value of the location counter to compute the correct value to use in the **jnz** instruction. For example, if the location counter is 230 when the label is resolved, value 233 becomes the target address of the jump instruction. This discussion of the relocation process is, of course, an abstraction. Although the general principles are correct, the actual implementation will vary widely between environments.

Address relocation is needed for all types of jump instructions as well as for call instructions because both use memory addresses. In addition, all global data requires relocation.

Even though you will be working with C and not assembler, the relocation process is handled the same because the output of a C compiler is, loosely speaking, assembly code. (Some compilers actually output assembly code and use an assembler to assemble it, while others output relocatable object code directly.)

Linking with Overlays

Many C compiler manufacturers supply an overlay linker. An *overlay linker* works like a regular linker but can also create overlays. An *overlay* is a piece of object code that is stored in a disk file and loaded and executed only when needed. The place in memory into which an overlay is loaded is called the *overlay region*. Overlays allow you to create and run programs that would be larger than available memory, because only the parts of the program that are currently in use are in memory.

To understand how overlays work, imagine that you have a program consisting of seven object files called F1 through F7. Assume also that there is insufficient free memory to run the program if the object files were all linked together in the normal way—you can only link the first five files before running out of memory. To remedy this situation, instruct the linker to create overlays consisting of files F5, F6, and F7. Each time a function in one of these files is invoked, the *overlay manager* (provided by the linker) finds the proper file and places it into the overlay region, allowing execution to proceed. The code in files F1 through F4 remains resident at all times. Figure 11-1 illustrates this situation.

As you might guess, the principal advantage of overlays is that they enable you to write very large programs. The main disadvantage — and the reason that overlays are usually a last resort — is that the loading process takes time and has a significant impact on the overall speed of the program execution. For this reason, you should group related functions together if you have to use overlays, so that the number of overlay loads is minimized. For example, if the application is a mailing list, it makes sense to place all sorting routines in one overlay, printing routines in another, and so on.

Sometimes a better alternative to overlays is *chaining*. In a chaining approach, one program instructs the operating system to load and execute another program. Although not defined by the ANSI standard, many compilers contain a special chaining function. This function is often called **exec( )**, but check your user's manual.

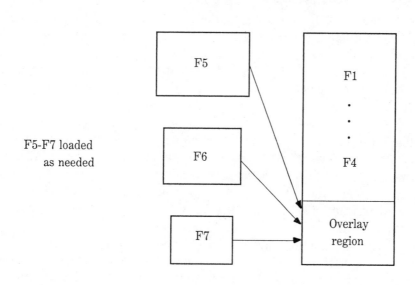

Figure 11-1.   A program with overlays in memory

The C Standard Library

The C standard library contains the object code to the functions provided with the compiler. For most C compilers, the standard library is contained in one file. However, some implementations have grouped related functions in their own libraries for efficiency or because of size restrictions.

The ANSI standard has defined both the content and the form of the C standard library. However, many compilers supply additional functions not specified by the standard. For example, it is common for a compiler to have graphics functions, mouse-handler routines, and the like. As long as you will not be porting your programs to a new environment, you can use these nonstandard functions. However, if your code must be portable, the use of these functions must be restricted.

Library Files Versus Object Files

Although libraries are similar to object files, they have one crucial difference: Not all the code in the library is added to your program. When you link a program that consists of several object files, all of the code in each object file becomes part of the finished executable program. This happens whether the code is actually used or not. In other words, all object files specified at link time are combined to form the program. However, this is not the case with library files.

A library is a collection of functions. Unlike an object file, a library file stores the name of each function, the function's object code, plus relocation information necessary to the linking process. When your program references a function contained in a library, the linker looks up that function and adds that code to your program. In this way, only functions that you actually use in your program are added to the executable file.

Because functions are selectively added to your program when a library is used, the C standard functions are contained in libraries rather than object files. (If they were in object files, every program you wrote would be several hundred thousand bytes long!)

Header Files

Many functions in the standard library work with their own specific data types, to which your program must have access. These types are defined in *header files* supplied with the compiler, and they must be included (using **#include**) in any file that uses the specific functions to which they refer. One of the most common examples is the file STDIO.H, which provides the type **FILE** that is necessary for disk file operations.

If the header files conform to the ANSI C standard, they also contain the full function prototype for the functions related to the header file. This provides a means of stronger type checking than formerly available to the C programmer. By including the header files that correspond to the standard functions used by your program, you can catch potential type-mismatch errors. For example, since it includes STRING.H (the string function's header), the following code produces a warning message when compiled:

```
#include "string.h"

char s1[]="hello ";
char s2[]="there.";

void main(void)
{
  int p;

  p = strcat(s1, s2);
}
```

Because **strcat( )** is declared as returning a character pointer, the compiler can now issue a warning that an error may have been made on the line that assigns it to the integer **p**.

Table 11-1 shows the standard header files defined by the ANSI standard.

The ANSI standard reserves identifier names beginning with an underscore and followed by either a second underscore or a capital letter for use in header files.

The remaining chapters in this book, which describe each function in the standard library, will indicate which of these header files are necessary for each function.

Header File	Purpose
ASSERT.H	Defines the **assert( )** macro
CTYPE.H	Character handling
ERRNO.H	Error reporting
FLOAT.H	Defines implementation-dependent floating-point values
LIMITS.H	Defines implementation-dependent various limits
LOCALE.H	Supports the **setlocale( )** function
MATH.H	Various definitions used by the math library
SETJMP.H	Supports nonlocal jumps
SIGNAL.H	Defines signal values
STDARG.H	Supports variable-length argument lists
STDDEF.H	Defines some commonly used constants
STDIO.H	Supports file I/O
STDLIB.H	Miscellaneous declarations
STRING.H	Supports string functions
TIME.H	Supports system time functions

Table 11-1.   The Standard Header Files

Macros in Header Files

Many of the C standard functions are actually macro definitions contained in a header file. For example, **abs( )**, which returns the absolute value of its integer argument, could be defined as a macro, as shown here:

```
#define abs(i)  (i)<0 ? -(i) : (i)
```

Generally, whether a standard function is defined as a macro or as a regular C function is of no consequence. However, in rare situations where this is unacceptable—for example, where code size is to be minimized—you have to create a real function and substitute it for the macro. Sometimes the C library itself also has a real function that you can use to replace a macro.

To force the compiler to use the real function (either from the library or written by you), you need to prevent the compiler from substituting the macro when the function name is encountered. Although there are several ways to do this, by far the best is simply to undefine the macro name using **#undef**. For example, to force the compiler to substitute the real function for the previously defined macro, you would insert this line of code near the beginning of your program:

```
#undef abs
```

Then, since **abs** is no longer defined as a macro, the function version is used.

Redefinition of Library Functions

Although linkers may vary slightly between implementations, they all operate in essentially the same way. For example, if your program consists of three files called F1, F2, and F3, the linker command line looks something like this:

    link F1 + F2 + F3,,,LIBC;

where LIBC is the name of the standard library.

Note: Some linkers automatically use the standard library and do not require that it be specified explicitly. Also, most integrated programming environments, such as Turbo C and Quick C, automatically include the appropriate library files.

As the process begins, the linker generally first attempts to resolve all external references by using only the files F1, F2, and F3. Once this is done, the library is searched if unresolved external references still exist.

Because most linkers proceed in the order just described, you can redefine a function in the standard library; your function is found first and used to resolve all references to it. Therefore, by the time the library is scanned, there are no unresolved references to the redefined function, and it is not loaded from the library.

You must be very careful when you redefine library functions because you could be creating unexpected side effects. This is because the library functions use other library functions. For example, the **fwrite( )** function might use **putc( )**. Therefore, a redefinition of **putc( )** could cause **fwrite( )** to behave unexpectedly. A better idea is simply to use a different name for the functions that you want to redefine. This averts unexpected side effects.

I/O Functions

Most C compilers support at least two different I/O systems: the buffered file system defined by the ANSI C standard and the UNIX-like unbuffered file system. DOS-based compilers generally support a third I/O system: direct console I/O. This chapter describes all functions that are part of the ANSI standard file system, the most important functions that are part of the UNIX-like file system, and several of the DOS-based direct console I/O functions.

The functions that make up the ANSI C input/output system can be grouped into two major categories: console I/O and file I/O. Strictly speaking, console I/O is made up of functions that are special-case versions of the more general functions found in the file system. However, console I/O and file I/O are different enough that they are often thought of as separate. The first part of this book treated the console I/O and file I/O as somewhat distinct systems to emphasize their differences. However this section makes no such distinction because both I/O types use a common logical interface.

The header file associated with the buffered I/O functions defined by ANSI is called STDIO.H. It defines several macros and types used by the file system. The most important type is **FILE**, which is used to declare a file pointer. Two other types are **size_t** and **fpos_t**. The **size_t** type is essentially equivalent to **unsigned**. The **fpos_t** type defines an object that can hold all the information needed to uniquely specify every position within a file.

Many of the functions defined by ANSI set the built-in global integer variable **errno** when an error occurs. Your program can check this variable when an error occurs to obtain more information about the error. The values that **errno** may take are implementation-dependent.

The UNIX-like I/O system is not defined by the ANSI C standard and is expected to decline in popularity. The most commonly used UNIX-like I/O system functions are included in this chapter because they are still widely used in existing programs. For many C compilers, the header file related to the UNIX-like file system is called IO.H. However, check your user's manual for details.

For DOS-based compilers, the direct console I/O functions generally use the CONIO.H header file. (Be sure to check your user's manual, however, because the header file might have a different name.)

For an overview of the C I/O system and a detailed discussion of the most important I/O functions, refer to Chapters 8 and 9 in Part One.

#include "conio.h"
char *cgets(char *str);

Description

The **cgets( )** function is not defined by the ANSI C standard. It is commonly included in the library of DOS-based compilers.

The **cgets( )** function reads a string entered from the keyboard into the array pointed to by *str*. Prior to the call to **cgets( )**, the first byte of *str* must be set to the maximum length of the string you want to read. Upon return, the second byte of *str* will contain the number of characters actually read. Therefore, the array pointed to by *str* must be at least 2 bytes longer than the largest string you want to read. When you have finished entering a string, enter a carriage return, which is converted into a null to terminate the string. The string will begin at the third byte of the array.

The **cgets( )** function returns a pointer to **str[2]**.

In some implementations, **cgets( )** does not allow redirection to devices other than the keyboard. Also, **cgets( )** may operate relative to a window rather than the screen. Check your user's manual for details.

Example

This program reads from the keyboard a string of up to 20 characters long:

```
#include "conio.h"

void main(void)
{
  char s[23];
```

```
  s[0] = 20;
  cputs("enter a string: ");
  cgets(s);
  cputs(&s[2]);
}
```

Related Functions

cputs( ), gets( ), fgets( ), puts( )

#include "stdio.h"
void clearerr(FILE *stream);

Description

The **clearerr( )** function resets to zero (off) the file error flag pointed to by *stream.* The end-of-file indicator is also reset.

The error flags for each stream are initially set to zero by a successful call to **fopen( )**. Once an error has occurred, the flags stay set until either an explicit call to **clearerr( )** or **rewind( )** is made.

File errors can occur for a wide variety of reasons, many of which are system dependent. You can determine the exact nature of the error by calling **perror( )**, which displays what error has occurred (see **perror( )**).

Example

This program copies one file to another. If an error is encountered, a message is printed and the error is cleared.

```
/* Copy one file to another. */
#include "stdio.h"
#include "stdlib.h"

void main(int argc, char *argv[])
{
  FILE *in, *out;
  char ch;

  if(argc!=3) {
    printf("You forgot to enter a filename\n");
    exit(1);
  }
```

```
if((in=fopen(argv[1], "rb")) == NULL) {
  printf("cannot open file\n");
  exit(1);
}
if((out=fopen(argv[2], "wb")) == NULL) {
  printf("cannot open file\n");
  exit(1);
}

while(!feof(in)) {
  ch = getc(in);
  if(ferror(in)) {
    printf("read error");
    clearerr(in);
    break;
  } else {
    putc(ch, out);
    if(ferror(out)) {
      printf("write error");
      clearerr(out);
      break;
    }
  }
}
fclose(in);
fclose(out);
}
```

Related Functions

feof( ), **ferror( )**, and **perror( )**

#include "io.h"
int close(int fd);

Description

The **close( )** function belongs to the UNIX-like file system and is not defined by the ANSI standard. When **close( )** is called with a valid file descriptor, it closes the file associated with it and flushes the write buffers if applicable. (File descriptors are created through a successful call to **open( )** or **creat( )** and do not relate to streams or file pointers).

When successful, **close( )** returns zero; otherwise, it returns −1. There are several reasons that you may not be able to close a file. The most common is the premature removal of the medium. For example, if you remove a disk from the drive before the file is closed, an error results.

Example

This program opens and closes a file by using the UNIX-like file system:

```
#include "fcntl.h"
#include "io.h"
#include "stdio.h"
#include "stdlib.h"

void main(int argc, char *argv[])
{
  int fd;

  if((fd=open(argv[1], O_RDONLY))==-1) {
    printf("cannot open file");
    exit(1);
  }

  printf("file is existent\n");

  if(close(fd)) printf("error in closing file\n");
}
```

Related Functions

open( ), creat( ), read( ), write( ), unlink( )

#include "conio.h"
int cprintf(const char *format, . . .);

Description

The **cprintf( )** function is not defined by the ANSI C standard. It is commonly included in the library of DOS-based compilers.

The **cprintf( )** function operates exactly like **printf( )**, but in many implementations its output is not redirectable to other devices. Also, in some environments **cprintf( )** operates relative to a window instead of the screen. Check your user's manual for details.

Example

This program displays the string **I like C** on the screen:

```
#include "conio.h"

void main(void)
{
  cprintf("I like C");
}
```

Related Functions

cscanf( ), **cputs( )**

#include "conio.h"
int cputs(const char *str);

Description

The **cputs( )** function is not defined by the ANSI C standard. It is commonly included in the library of DOS-based compilers.

The **cputs( )** function outputs to the screen the string pointed to by *str*. In some implementations, its output may not be redirected. Also, for some environments, **cputs( )** may output its string relative to a window rather than the screen. Refer to your user's manual for details.

cputs( ) returns the last character written if successful; it returns **EOF** if unsuccessful.

Example

This program writes **this is a test** on the screen:

```
#include "conio.h"

void main(void)
{
  cputs("this is a test");
}
```

Related Function

cprintf( )

#include ''io.h''
int creat(char *filename, int pmode);

Description

The **creat( )** function is part of the UNIX-like file system and is not defined by the ANSI C standard. Its purpose is to create a new file with the name pointed to by *filename* and to open it for writing. On success, **creat( )** returns a file descriptor that is greater than or equal to zero; on failure, it returns a −1. (File descriptors are integers and do not relate to streams or file pointers).

The value of *pmode* determines the file's access setting, sometimes called its *permission mode*. The value of *pmode* is highly dependent upon the operating system; check the user's manual for details. In general, the access modes a file may have include read-only, read/write, and a security access setting. For many compilers, the values of *pmode* are defined as macros in the header file called STAT.H (sometimes found in the SYS directory). The commonly used names and their meanings are shown here:

S_IWRITE	Allow output
S_IREAD	Allow input
S_IREAD ¦ S_IWRITE	Allow input/output

If the specified file already exists at the time of the call to **creat( )**, it is erased and all previous contents are lost.

Example

The following code fragment creates a file called TEST.

```
#include "io.h"
#include "sys\stat.h"
#include "stdio.h"
#include "stdlib.h"

void main(void)
{
  int fd;

  if(fd=creat("test", S_IWRITE))==-1) {
    printf("cannot open file\n");
    exit(1);
  }
}
```

Related Functions

open( ), **close( )**, **read( )**, **write( )**, **unlink( )**, **eof( )**

#include "conio.h"
int cscanf(const char *format, . . .);

Description

The **cscanf( )** function is not defined by the ANSI C standard. It is commonly included in the library of DOS-based compilers.

The **cscanf( )** function operates exactly like **scanf( )**, but in many implementations its input cannot be redirected to any device other than the keyboard. Also, in some environments **cscanf( )** operates relative to a window instead of the screen. Check your user's manual for details.

Example

This program reads a string entered from the keyboard:

```
#include "conio.h"

void main(void)
{
  char str[80];
```

```
  cprintf("enter a string: ");
  cscanf("%s", str);
  cprintf(str);
}
```

Related Functions

cprintf( ), cgets( )

#include "io.h"
int eof(int fd);

Description

The **eof( )** function is part of the UNIX-like file system and is not defined by the ANSI standard. When called with a valid file descriptor, **eof( )** returns 1 if the end of the file has been reached; otherwise, it returns zero. If an error has occurred, **eof( )** returns −1.

Example

The following program displays a text file on the console using **eof( )** to determine when the end of the file has been reached:

```
#include "fcntl.h"
#include "io.h"
#include "stdio.h"
#include "stdlib.h"

void main(int argc, char *argv[])
{
  int fd;
  char ch;

  if((fd=open(argv[1], O_RDONLY))==-1) {
    printf("cannot open file\n");
    exit(1);
  }

  while(!eof(fd)) {
    read(fd, &ch, 1);  /* read one char at a time */
    printf("%c", ch);
  }
```

```
    close(fd);
}
```

Related Functions

open( ), close( ), read( ), write( ), unlink( )

#include "stdio.h"
int fclose(FILE *stream);

Description

The **fclose( )** function closes the file associated with *stream* and flushes its buffer. After an **fclose( )**, *stream* is no longer connected with the file and any automatically allocated buffers are deallocated.

If **fclose( )** is successful, it returns zero; otherwise, it returns a nonzero number. Trying to close a file that has already been closed is an error. Removing the storage media before closing a file also generates an error, as does lack of sufficient free disk space.

Example

The following code opens and closes a file:

```
#include "stdio.h"
#include "stdlib.h"

void main(void)
{
  FILE *fp;

  if((fp=fopen("test", "rb"))==NULL) {
    printf("cannot open file\n");
    exit(1);
  }

  if(fclose(fp)) printf("file close error\n");
}
```

Related Functions

fopen( ), freopen( ), fflush( )

#include "stdio.h"
int feof(FILE *stream);

Description

The **feof( )** function checks the file position indicator to determine if the end of the file associated with *stream* has been reached. A nonzero value is returned if the file position indicator is at end-of-file; otherwise, the function returns zero.

Once the end of the file has been reached, subsequent read operations return **EOF** until either **rewind( )** is called or the file position indicator is moved using **fseek( )**. **EOF** is defined in STDIO.H.

The **feof( )** function is particularly useful when you are working with binary files because the end-of-file marker is also a valid binary integer. Explicit calls must be made to **feof( )** to determine when the end of a binary file has been reached.

Example

This code fragment shows the proper way to read to the end of a binary file:

```
/*
   Assume that fp has been opened as a binary file
   for read operations.
*/

while(!feof(fp)) getc(fp);
```

Related Functions

clearerr( ), **ferror( )**, **perror( )**, **putc( )**, **getc( )**

#include "stdio.h"
int ferror(FILE *stream);

Description

The **ferror( )** function checks for a file error on the given *stream*. A return value of zero indicates that no error has occurred, while a nonzero value means an error.

The error flags associated with *stream* stay set until either the file is closed or **rewind( )** or **clearerr( )** is called.

To determine the exact nature of the error, use the **perror( )** function.

Example

The following code fragment aborts program execution if a file error occurs:

```
/*
  Assume that fp points to a stream opened for write
  operations.
*/

while(!done) {
  putc(info, fp);
  if(ferror(fp)) {
    printf("file error\n");
    exit(1);
  }
}
```

Related Functions

clearerr( ), **feof( )**, **perror( )**

#include "stdio.h"
int fflush(FILE *stream);

Description

If *stream* is associated with a file opened for writing, a call to **fflush( )** physically writes to the file the contents of the output buffer. If *stream* points to an input file, the contents of the input buffer are cleared. In either case, the file remains open.

A return value of zero indicates success; **fflush( )** returns **EOF** if a write error has occurred.

All buffers are automatically flushed either upon normal program termination or when they are full. Closing a file also flushes its buffer.

Example

The following code fragment flushes the buffer after each write operation:

```
/*
  Assume that fp is associated with an output file.
*/
    .
    .
    .
fwrite(buf, sizeof(data_type), 1, fp);
fflush(fp);
    .
    .
    .
```

Related Functions

fclose( ), fopen( ), fread( ), fwrite( ), getc( ), putc( )

#include "stdio.h"
int fgetc(FILE *stream);

Description

The **fgetc( )** function returns the next character from the input stream from the current position and increments the file position indicator. The character is read as an **unsigned char** that is converted to an integer.

If the end of the file is reached, **fgetc( )** returns **EOF**. However, since **EOF** is a valid integer value, you must use **feof( )** to check for end-of-file when working with binary files. If **fgetc( )** encounters an error, **EOF** is also returned. Again, if working with binary files you must use **ferror( )** to check for file errors.

Example

The following program reads and displays the contents of a text file.

```
#include "stdio.h"
#include "stdlib.h"

void main(int argc, char *argv[])
{
  FILE *fp;
  char ch;

  if((fp=fopen(argv[1],"r"))==NULL) {
    printf("cannot open file\n");
```

```
    exit(l);
  }

  while((ch=fgetc(fp))!=EOF) {
    printf("%c", ch);
  }

  fclose(fp);
}
```

Related Functions

fputc( ), getc( ), putc( ), fopen( )

#include "stdio.h"
int fgetpos(FILE *stream, fpos _ t *position);

Description

The **fgetpos( )** function stores the current value of the file position indicator in the object pointed to by *position*. The object pointed to by *position* must be of type **fpos _ t**, a type defined in STDIO.H. The value stored there is useful only in a subsequent call to **fsetpos( )**.

If an error occurs, **fgetpos( )** returns nonzero; otherwise, it returns zero.

Example

The following fragment stores the current file location in **file _ loc**:

```
FILE *fp;
fpos_t file_loc;
 .
 .
 .
fgetpos(fp, &file_loc);
```

Related Functions

fsetpos( ), fseek( ), ftell( )

#include "stdio.h"
char *fgets(char *str, int num, FILE *stream);

Description

The **fgets( )** function reads up to **num −1** characters from *stream* and places them into the character array pointed to by *str*. Characters are read until either a newline or an **EOF** is received or until the specified limit is reached. After the characters have been read, a null is placed in the array immediately after the last character read. A newline character is retained and is part of *str*.

If successful, **fgets( )** returns *str*; a null pointer is returned upon failure. If a read error occurs, the contents of the array pointed to by *str* are indeterminate. Because a null pointer is returned either when an error has occurred or when the end of the file is reached, you should use **feof( )** or **ferror( )** to determine what has actually happened.

Example

This program uses **fgets( )** to display the contents of the text file specified in the first command line argument:

```
#include "stdio.h"
#include "stdlib.h"

void main(int argc, char *argv[])
{
  FILE *fp;
  char str[128];

  if((fp=fopen(argv[1], "r"))==NULL) {
    printf("cannot open file\n");
    exit(1);
  }

  while(!feof(fp)) {
    if(fgets(str, 126, fp)) printf("%s", str);
  }

  fclose(fp);
}
```

Related Functions

fputs( ), **fgetc( )**, **gets( )**, **puts( )**

#include "stdio.h"
FILE *fopen(const char *fname, const char *mode);

Description

The **fopen( )** function opens a file whose name is pointed to by *fname* and returns the stream that is associated with it. The type of operations that are allowed on the file are defined by the value of *mode*. The legal values for *mode* as specified by the ANSI standard are shown in Table 12-1. The file name must be a string of characters that constitutes a valid file name as defined by the operating system and may include a path specification if the environment supports it.

If **fopen( )** opens the specified file, a **FILE** pointer is returned. If the file cannot be opened, a null pointer is returned.

As Table 12-1 shows, a file may be opened in either text or binary mode. In text mode, some character translations may occur. For example, newlines may be converted into carriage return/linefeed sequences. No such translations occur on binary files.

Mode	Meaning
"r"	Open text file for reading
"w"	Create text file for writing
"a"	Append to text file
"rb"	Open binary file for reading
"wb"	Create binary file for writing
"ab"	Append to binary file
"r+"	Open text file for read/write
"w+"	Create text file for read/write
"a+"	Open text file for read/write
"rb+	Open binary file for read/write
"wb+"	Create binary file for read/write
"ab+"	Open binary file for read/write

Table 12-1. The Legal Values for Mode

This code fragment illustrates the correct way to open a file:

```
FILE *fp;

if ((fp = fopen("test", "w"))==NULL) {
  puts("cannot open file\n");
  exit(1);
}
```

This method detects any error in opening a file (such as trying to open a file on a write-protected or a full disk), before attempting to write to it. A **NULL** is returned when an error occurs because no file pointer ever has that value. **NULL** is defined in STDIO.H.

If you use **fopen( )** to open a file for write, any preexisting file by that name is erased and a new file started. If no file by that name exists, one is created. If you want to add to the end of the file, you must use mode "a". If the file does not exist, an error is returned. Opening a file for read operations requires that the file exists. If it does not, an error is returned. Finally, if a file is opened for read/write operations it is not erased if it exists; however, if it does not exist it is created.

When accessing a file opened for read/write operations, you may not follow an output operation with an input operation without an intervening call to either **fflush( )**, **fseek( )**, **fsetpos( )**, or **rewind( )**. Also, you may not follow an input operation with an output operation without an intervening call to one of the previously mentioned functions.

Example

This fragment opens a file called TEST for binary read/write operations:

```
FILE *fp;

if((fp=fopen("test", "rb+"))==NULL) {
  printf("cannot open file\n");
  exit(1);
}
```

Related Functions

fclose( ), **fread( )**, **fwrite( )**, **putc( )**, **getc( )**

#include "stdio.h"
int fprintf(FILE *stream, const char *format, . . .);

Description

The **fprintf( )** function outputs to the stream pointed to by *stream* the values of the arguments in its argument list as specified in the *format* string. The return value is the number of characters actually printed. If an error occurs, a negative number is returned.

There may be from zero to several arguments—the maximum number is system dependent.

The operations of the format control string and commands are identical to those in **printf( )**; see the **printf( )** function for a complete description.

Example

This program creates a file called TEST and writes **this is a test. 10 20.01** into the file using **fprintf( )** to format the data.

```
#include "stdio.h"
#include "stdlib.h"

void main(void)
{
  FILE *fp;

  if((fp=fopen("test", "wb"))==NULL) {
    printf("cannot open file\n");
    exit(1);
  }

  fprintf(fp, "this is a test %d %f", 10, 20.01);

  fclose(fp);
}
```

Related Functions

printf( ), fscanf( )

#include "stdio.h"
int fputc(int ch, FILE *stream);

Description

The **fputc( )** function writes the character *ch* to the specified stream at the current file position and then advances the file position indicator.

Even though *ch* is declared as an **int** for historical purposes, it is converted by **fputc( )** into an **unsigned char**. Because all character arguments are elevated to integers at the time of the call, character variables are generally used as arguments. If an integer were used, the high-order byte would simply be discarded.

The value returned by **fputc( )** is the value of the character written. If an error occurs, **EOF** is returned. For files opened for binary operations, an **EOF** may be a valid character and you must use the **ferror( )** function to determine whether an error has actually occurred.

Example

This function writes the contents of a string to the specified stream:

```
void write_string(char *str, FILE *fp)
{
  while(*str) if(!ferror(fp)) fputc(*str++, fp);
}
```

Related Functions

fgetc( ), **fopen( )**, **fprintf( )**, **fread( )**, **fwrite( )**

#include "stdio.h"
int fputchar(int ch);

Description

The **fputchar( )** function writes the character *ch* to **stdout**. This function is not defined by the ANSI C standard, but is a common addition. Even though *ch* is declared to be an **int** for historical purposes, it is converted by **fputchar( )** into an **unsigned char**. Because all character arguments are elevated to integers at the time of the call, character variables are usually used as arguments. If an integer were used, the high-order byte would simply be discarded. A call to **fputchar( )** is the functional equivalent of a call to **fputc(ch, stdout)**.

The value returned by **fputchar( )** is the value of the character written. If an error occurs, **EOF** is returned. For files opened for binary operations, **EOF** may be a valid character and you need to use the **ferror( )** function to determine whether an error has actually occurred.

Example

This function writes the contents of a string to **stdout**:

```
write_string(char *str)
{
  while(*str) if(!ferror(fp)) fputchar(*str++);
}
```

Related Functions

fgetc( ), **fopen( )**, **fprintf( )**, **fread( )**, **fwrite( )**

#include "stdio.h"
int fputs(const char *str, FILE *stream);

Description

The **fputs( )** functions writes to the specified stream the contents of the string pointed to by *str*. The null terminator is not written.

The **fputs( )** function returns nonnegative on success and **EOF** on failure.

If the stream is opened in text mode, certain character translations may take place. This means that there may not be a one-to-one mapping of the string onto the file. However, if the stream is opened in binary mode, no character translations occur and there will be a one-to-one mapping between the string and the file.

Example

This code fragment writes the string **this is a test** to the stream pointed to by **fp**.

```
fputs("this is a test", fp);
```

Related Functions

fgets( ), **gets( )**, **puts( )**, **fprintf( )**, **fscanf( )**

#include "stdio.h"
int fread(void *buf, size_t size, size_t count,
FILE *stream);

Description

The **fread( )** function reads *count* number of objects, each *size* bytes in length, from the stream pointed to by *stream* and places them in the array pointed to by *buf.* The file position indicator is advanced by the number of characters read.

The **fread( )** function returns the number of items actually read. If fewer items are read than are requested in the call, either an error has occurred or the end of the file has been reached. You must use **feof( )** or **ferror( )** to determine what has taken place.

If the stream is opened for text operations, certain character translations may occur (such as carriage return and linefeed sequences being transformed into newlines).

Example

The following program reads ten floating-point numbers from a disk file called BALANCE into the array **bal.**

```
#include "stdio.h"
#include "stdlib.h"

void main(void)
{
  FILE *fp;
  float bal[10];

  if((fp=fopen("test", "rb"))==NULL) {
    printf("cannot open file\n");
    exit(1);
  }

  if(fread(bal, sizeof(float), 10, fp)!=10) {
    if(feof(fp)) printf("premature end of file");
    else printf("file read error");
  }

  fclose(fp);
}
```

Related Functions

fwrite( ), fopen( ), fscanf( ), fgetc( ), getc( )

#include "stdio.h"
FILE *freopen(const char *fname, const char *mode,
FILE *stream);

Description

The **freopen( )** function associates an existing stream with a different file. The new file's name is pointed to by *fname*, the access mode is pointed to by *mode*, and the stream to be reassigned is pointed to by *stream*. The string *mode* uses the same format as **fopen( )**. For a complete discussion, see the description of **fopen( )**.

When called, **freopen( )** first tries to close a file that may currently be associated with *stream*. However, if the attempt to close the file fails, the **reopen( )** function still continues to open the other file.

The **freopen( )** function returns a pointer to *stream* on success; otherwise, the function returns a null pointer.

The main use of **freopen( )** is to redirect the system-defined files **stdin**, **stdout**, and **stderr** to some other file.

Example

The program shown here uses **freopen( )** to redirect the stream **stdout** to the file called OUT. Because **printf( )** writes to **stdout**, the first message is displayed on the screen and the second is written to the disk file.

```
#include "stdio.h"
#include "stdlib.h"

void main(void)
{
  FILE *fp;

  printf("This will display on the screen\n");

  if((fp=freopen("OUT", "w" ,stdout))==NULL) {
    printf("cannot open file\n");
    exit(1);
  }

  printf("this will be written to the file OUT");

  fclose(fp);
}
```

Related Functions

fopen( ), fclose( )

#include "stdio.h"
int fscanf(FILE *stream, const char *format, . . .);

Description

The **fscanf( )** function works exactly like the **scanf( )** function, but it reads the information from the stream specified by *stream* instead of **stdin**. See the **scanf( )** function for details.

The **fscanf( )** function returns the number of arguments actually assigned values. This number does not include skipped fields. A return value of **EOF** means that a failure occurred before the first assignment was made.

Example

This code fragment reads a string and a **float** from the stream **fp**.

```
char str[80];
float f;

fscanf(fp, "%s%f", str, &f);
```

Related Functions

scanf( ), fprintf( )

#include "stdio.h"
int fseek(FILE *stream, long offset, int origin);

Description

The **fseek( )** function sets the file position indicator associated with *stream* according to the values of *offset* and *origin*. It supports random I/O operations. The *offset* is the number of bytes from *origin* to seek to.

The values for *origin* must be one of these macros (defined in STDIO.H):

Name	Meaning
SEEK_SET	Seek from start of file
SEEK_CUR	Seek from current location
SEEK_END	Seek from end of file

A return value of zero means that **fseek( )** succeeded. A nonzero value indicates failure.

In most implementations, and as specified by the ANSI standard, *offset* must be a **long** in order to support files larger than 64K.

You may use **fseek( )** to move the position indicator anywhere in the file, even beyond the end. However, it is an error to set the position indicator before the beginning of the file.

The **fseek( )** function clears the end-of-file flag associated with the specified stream. Furthermore, it nullifies any prior **ungetc( )** on the same stream. (See **ungetc( )**.)

Example

The following function seeks to the specified structure of type **addr**. Notice the use of **sizeof** to obtain the size of the structure.

```
struct addr {
  char name[40];
  char street[40];
  char city[40];
  char state[3];
  char zip[10];
} info;

void find(long client_num)
{
  FILE *fp;

  if((fp=fopen("mail", "rb")) == NULL) {
    printf("cannot open file\n");
    exit(1);
  }

  /* find the proper structure */
  fseek(fp, client_num*sizeof(struct addr), SEEK_SET);
```

```
/* read the data into memory */
fread(&info, sizeof(struct addr), 1, fp);

fclose(fp);
}
```

Related Functions

ftell( ), rewind( ), fopen( ), fgetpos( ), fsetpos( )

#include "stdio.h"
int fsetpos(FILE *stream, const fpos_t *position);

Description

The **fsetpos( )** function moves the file position indicator to the point specified by the object pointed to by *position*. This value must have been previously obtained through a call to **fgetpos( )**. The type **fpos_t** is defined in STDIO.H. After **fsetpos( )** is executed, the end-of-file indicator is reset. Also, any previous call to **ungetc( )** is nullified.

    If **fsetpos( )** fails, it returns nonzero. On success, it returns zero.

Example

This code fragment resets the current file position indicator to the value stored in **file_loc.**

```
fsetpos(fp, &file_loc);
```

Related Functions

fgetpos( ), fseek( ), ftell( )

#include "stdio.h"
long ftell(FILE *stream);

Description

The **ftell( )** function returns the current value of the file position indicator for the specified stream. For binary streams, the value is the number of bytes the indicator is from the beginning of the file. For text streams, the return value may not be meaningful except as an argument to **fseek( )** because of possible character translations. For instance, carriage return/linefeeds may be substituted for newlines, which affects the apparent size of the file.

The **ftell( )** function returns −1L when an error occurs. If the stream is incapable of random seeks—if it is a terminal, for instance—the return value is undefined.

Example

This code fragment returns the current value of the file position indicator for the stream pointed to by **fp**:

```
long i;

if((i=ftell(fp))==-1L)
    printf("A file error has occurred\n");
```

Related Functions

fseek( ), fgetpos( )

#include "stdio.h"
int fwrite(const void *buf, size _ tm int size, size _ t count,
FILE *stream);

Description

The **fwrite( )** function writes *count* number of objects (each *size* bytes in length) to the stream pointed to by *stream* from the character array pointed to by *buf.* The file position indicator is advanced by the number of characters written.

The **fwrite( )** function returns the number of items actually written, which will equal the number requested if the function is successful. If fewer items are written than are requested, an error has occurred. For text streams, various character translations may take place but will not affect the return value.

Example

This program writes a **float** to the file TEST. Notice that **sizeof** is used both to determine the number of bytes in a **float** variable and to ensure portability.

```
#include "stdio.h"
#include "stdlib.h"

void main(void)
{
  FILE *fp;
  float f=12.23;

  if((fp=fopen("test", "wb"))==NULL) {
    printf("cannot open file\n");
    exit(1);
  }

  fwrite(&f, sizeof(float), 1, fp);

  fclose(fp);
}
```

Related Functions

fread( ), fscanf( ), getc( ), fgetc( )

#include "stdio.h"
int getc(FILE *stream);

Description

The **getc( )** function returns the next character from the input *stream* from the current position and increments the file position indicator. The character is read as an **unsigned char** that is converted to an integer.

If the end of the file is reached, **getc( )** returns **EOF**. However, since **EOF** is a valid integer value, you must use **feof( )** to check for end-of-file when working with binary files. If **getc( )** encounters an error, **EOF** is also returned. When working with binary files, you must use **ferror( )** to check for file errors.

The **getc( )** and **fgetc( )** functions are identical; in most implementations, **getc( )** is simply defined as the macro shown here:

```
#define getc(fp) fgetc(fp)
```

This causes the **fgetc( )** function to be substituted for the **getc( )** macro.

Example

The following program reads and displays the contents of a text file.

```
#include "stdio.h"
#include "stdlib.h"

void main(int argc, char *argv[])
{
  FILE *fp;
  char ch;

  if((fp=fopen(argv[1], "r"))==NULL) {
    printf("cannot open file\n");
    exit(1);
  }

  while((ch=getc(fp))!=EOF) {
    printf("%c", ch);
  }

  fclose(fp);
}
```

Related Functions

fputc( ), fgetc( ), putc( ), fopen( )

#include ''conio.h''
int getch(void);
int getche(void);

Description

The **getch( )** and **getche( )** functions are not defined by the ANSI C standard. However, they are commonly included with DOS-based compilers.

The **getch( )** function returns the next character read from the console but does not echo that character to the screen.

The **getche( )** function returns the next character read from the console and echos that character to the screen.

Both of these functions bypass C's standard I/O functions and work directly with the operating system. Essentially, **getch( )** and **getche( )** perform direct keyboard input.

Example

This code fragment uses **getch( )** to read the user's menu selection for a spelling checker program:

```
do {
  printf("1: check spelling\n");
  printf("2: correct spelling\n");
  printf("3: lookup a word in the dictionary\n");
  printf("4: quit\n");

  printf("\nEnter your selection: ");
  choice = getch();
} while(!strchr("1234", choice));
```

Related Functions

getc( ), getchar( ), fgetc( )

#include "stdio.h"
int getchar(void);

Description

The **getchar( )** function returns the next character from **stdin**. The character is read as an **unsigned char** that is converted to an integer.

If the end of the file is reached, **getc( )** returns **EOF**. However, since **EOF** is a valid integer value, you must use **feof( )** to check for end-of-file when working with binary files. If **getc( )** encounters an error, **EOF** is also returned. If you are working with binary files, you must use **ferror( )** to check for file errors.

The **getchar( )** function (or macro) is functionally equivalent to **getc(stdin)**.

Example

This program reads characters from **stdin** into the array **s** until the user presses ENTER. Finally, the string is displayed.

```
#include "stdio.h"

void main(void)
{
  char s[256], *p;

  p = s;

  while((*p++=getchar())!='\n') ;
```

```
  *p = '\0';   /* add null terminator */
  printf(s);
}
```

Related Functions

fputc( ), **fgetc( )**, **putc( )**, **fopen( )**

#include "stdio.h"
char *gets(char *str);

Description

The **gets( )** function reads characters from **stdin** and places them into the character array pointed to by *str*. Characters are read until a newline or an **EOF** is received. The newline character is not made part of the string; instead, it is translated into a null to terminate the string.

If successful, **gets( )** returns *str*; a null pointer is returned upon failure. If a read error occurs, the contents of the array pointed to by *str* are indeterminate. Because a null pointer is returned when either an error has occurred or when the end of the file is reached, use **feof( )** or **ferror( )** to determine what has actually happened.

There is no limit to the number of characters that **gets( )** will read. For this reason, it is your job to make sure that the array pointed to by *str* is not overrun.

Example

This program uses **gets( )** to read a file name:

```
#include "stdio.h"
#include "stdlib.h"

void main(void)
{
  FILE *fp;
  char fname[128];

  printf("Enter filename: ");
  gets(fname);

  if((fp=fopen(fname, "r"))==NULL) {
```

```
    printf("cannot open file\n");
    exit(1);
  }

  fclose(fp);
}
```

Related Functions

fputs( ), **fgetc( )**, **fgets( )**, **puts( )**

#include "stdio.h"
int getw(FILE *stream);

Description

The **getw( )** function is not defined by the ANSI C standard, but is included with many C compilers.

The **getw( )** function returns the next integer from *stream* and advances the file position indicator appropriately.

Because the integer read may have a value equal to **EOF**, you must use **feof( )** or **ferror( )** to determine when end-of-file is reached or whether an error has occurred.

Example

This program reads integers from the file INTTEST and reports their sum:

```
#include "stdio.h"
#include "stdlib.h"

void main(void)
{
  FILE *fp;
  int sum=0;

  if((fp=fopen("inttest", "rb"))==NULL) {
    printf("cannot open file\n");
    exit(1);
  }

  while(!feof(fp))
    sum = getw(fp)+sum;
```

```
      printf("the sum is %d", sum);

      fclose(fp);
}
```

Related Functions

putw( ), fread( )

#include "conio.h"
int kbhit(void);

Description

The **kbhit( )** function is not defined by the ANSI standard. However, it is found, under various names, in virtually all C implementations. It returns a nonzero value if a key has been pressed at the console. Otherwise, it returns zero. (Under no circumstances does it wait for a key to be pressed.)

Example

This **for** loop exits if a key is pressed:

```
for(;;) {
  if(kbhit()) break;
  .
  .
  .
}
```

Related Functions

fgetc( ), getc( )

#include "io.h"
long lseek(int fd, long offset, int origin);

Description

The **lseek( )** function is part of the UNIX-like I/O system and is not defined by the ANSI C standard.

The **lseek( )** function sets the file position indicator to the location specified by *offset* and *origin*. The *offset* is the number of bytes from *origin* to seek to. The values for *origin* must be one of these macros (defined in IO.H):

Name	Meaning
SEEK_SET	Seek from start of file
SEEK_CUR	Seek from current location
SEEK_END	Seek from end of file

The **lseek( )** function returns *offset* on success. Upon failure, it returns −1L.

Example

The example shown here allows you to examine a file one sector at a time by using the UNIX-like I/O system. You will want to change the buffer size to match the sector size of your system.

```
#include "io.h"
#include "fcntl.h"
#include "stdlib.h"
#include "stdio.h"

#define BUF_SIZE  128

void main(int argc, char *argv[])
{
  char buf[BUF_SIZE+1], s[10];
  int fd, sector;

  buf[BUF_SIZE+1] = '\0'; /* null terminate buffer for printf */
  if((fd=open(argv[1], O_RDONLY))==-1) { /* open for write */
    printf("cannot open file\n");
    exit(1);
  }
  do {
    printf("buffer: ");
    gets(s);

    sector = atoi(s); /* get the sector to read */

    if(lseek(fd, (long)sector*BUF_SIZE, SEEK_SET)==-1L)
      printf("seek error\n");

    if(read(fd, buf, BUF_SIZE)==0) {
```

```
      printf("sector out of range\n");
    }
    else
      printf(buf);
  } while(sector>0);
  close(fd);
}
```

Related Functions

read( ), **write( )**, **open( )**, **close( )**

#include "fcntl.h"
#include "io.h"
int open(char *fname, int mode);

Description

The **open( )** function is part of the UNIX-like I/O system and is not defined by the ANSI C standard.

Unlike the buffered I/O system, the UNIX-like system does not use file pointers of type **FILE**; instead it uses file descriptors of type **int**. The **open( )** function opens a file whose name is pointed to by *fname* and sets its access mode as specified by *mode*. The values *mode* may have are shown here (these macros are defined in FCNTL.H):

Mode	Effect
O_RDONLY	Open for reading
O_WRONLY	Open for writing
O_RDWR	Open for reading and writing

Note: Many compilers have additional modes—such as text, binary, and the like—so check your user's manual.

A successful call to **open( )** returns a positive integer that is the file descriptor associated with the file. A return value of −1 means that the file cannot be opened.

In most implementations, the operation fails if the file specified in the **open( )** statement does not appear on the disk. However, depending upon the implementation, you may be able to use **open( )** to create a file that is currently nonexistent. Check your user's manual.

Example

You will usually see the call to **open( )** like this:

```
int fd;

if((fd=open(filename, mode)) == -1)  {
  printf("cannot open file\n");
  exit(1);
}
```

Related Functions

close( ), read( ), write( )

#include "stdio.h"
void perror(const char *str);

Description

The **perror( )** function maps the value of the global **errno** onto a string and writes that string to **stderr**. If the value of *str* is not null, the string is written first, followed by a colon and the implementation-defined error message.

Example

In this fragment, an error is reported if it occurs.

```
#include "stdio.h"
  .
  .
  .
if(ferror(fp)) perror("file error: ");
```

#include "stdio.h"
int printf(const char *format, . . .);

Description

The **printf( )** function writes to **stdout** the arguments that make up the argument list under the control of the string pointed to by *format*.

The string pointed to by *format* contains two types of items. The first type consists of characters that will be printed on the screen. The second type contains format commands that define the way the arguments are displayed. A format command consists of a percent sign followed by the format code. The format commands are shown in Table 12-2. There must be exactly the same number of arguments as there are format commands, and the format commands and arguments are matched in order. For example, this **printf( )** call:

```
printf("Hi %c %d %s", 'c', 10, "there!");
```

displays **Hi c 10 there!**.

If there are insufficient arguments to match the format commands, the output is undefined. If there are more arguments than format commands, the remaining arguments are discarded.

The **printf( )** function returns the number of characters actually printed. A negative return value indicates an error.

The format commands may have modifiers that specify the field width, the number of decimal places, and a left-justification flag. An integer placed between the percent sign and the format command acts as a minimum field-width specifier, padding the output with blanks or zeros to ensure that it is a minimum length. If the string or number is greater than that minimum, it will be printed in full. The default padding is done with spaces. If you wish to pad with zeros, place a zero before the field width specifier. For example, **%05d** pads a number of less than five digits with zeros so that its total length is five digits.

To specify the number of decimal places printed for a floating-point number, place a decimal point followed by the desired number of decimal places after the field-width specifier. For example, **%10.4f** displays a number at least ten characters wide with four decimal places. When this is applied to strings or integers, the number following the period specifies the maximum field length. For example, **%5.7s** displays a string that

Code	Format
%c	Character
%d	Signed decimal integers
%i	Signed decimal integers
%e	Scientific notation (lowercase e)
%E	Scientific notation (uppercase E)
%f	Decimal floating point
%g	Uses %e or %f, whichever is shorter (if %g, uses lowercase e)
%G	Uses %E or %f, whichever is shorter (if %G, uses uppercase E)
%o	Unsigned octal
%s	String of characters
%u	Unsigned decimal integers
%x	Unsigned hexadecimal (lowercase letters)
%X	Unsigned hexadecimal (uppercase letters)
%p	Displays a pointer
%n	Associated argument is an integer pointer into which is placed the number of characters written so far
%%	Prints a % sign

Table 12-2.   **printf( )** Format Commands

is at least five characters long and does not exceed seven. If the string is longer than the maximum field width, the end characters are truncated.

By default, all output is right justified. That is, if the field width is larger than the data printed, the data will be placed on the right edge of the field. You can force the information to be left justified by placing a minus sign directly after the percent sign. For example, %−10.2f left justifies a floating-point number with two decimal places in a ten-character field.

There are two format specifiers that allow **printf( )** to display **short** and **long** integers. These specifiers may be applied to the **d, i, o, u,** and **x** type specifiers. The **l** specifier tells **printf( )** that a **long** data type follows. For example, %ld means that a **long int** is to be displayed. The **h** specifier instructs **printf( )** to display a **short int**. Therefore, %hu indicates that the data is of type **short unsigned int**.

The l modifier may also prefix the floating-point specifiers **e**, **f**, and **g** and indicates that a **double** follows.

The command **%n** places the number of characters written so far in an integer variable whose pointer is specified in the argument list. For example, this code fragment displays the number **14** after the line **this is a test.**

```
int i;

printf("this is a test %n", &i);
printf("%d", i);
```

The # has a special meaning when used with some **printf( )** format specifiers. Preceding a **g**, **f**, or **e** specifier with a # ensures that the decimal point will be present even if there are no decimal digits. If you precede the **x** format specifier with a #, the hexadecimal number will be printed with a **0x** prefix. The # cannot be applied to any other format specifiers.

The minimum field width and precision specifiers may be provided by arguments to **printf( )** instead of by constants. To accomplish this, use an * as a placeholder. When the format string is scanned, **printf( )** will match * to arguments in the order in which they occur.

See the discussion of **printf( )** in Chapter 8 for further details.

Example

This program displays the output shown in its comments:

```
#include "stdio.h"

void main(void)
{
  /* This prints "this is a test" left justified
     in 20 character field.
  */
  printf("%-20s", "this is a test");

  /* This prints a float with 3 decimal places in a 10
     character field.  The output will be "    12.234".
  */
```

```
    printf("%10.3f", 12.234657);
}
```

Related Functions

scanf( ), fprintf( )

#include ''stdio.h''
int putc(int ch, FILE *stream);

Description

The **putc( )** function writes the character contained in the least significant byte of *ch* to the output stream pointed to by *stream*. Because character arguments are elevated to integer at the time of the call, you may use character variables as arguments to **putc( )**.

The **putc( )** function returns the character written; it returns **EOF** if an error occurs. If the output stream has been opened in binary mode, **EOF** is a valid value for *ch*. This means that you must use **ferror( )** to determine if an error has occurred.

The **putc( )** function is often implemented as a macro with **fputc( )** substituted because **fputc( )** is functionally equivalent to **putc( )**.

Example

The following loop writes the characters in string **str** to the stream specified by **fp**. The null terminator is not written.

```
for(; *str; str++) putc(*str, fp);
```

Related Functions

fgetc( ), fputc( ), getchar( ), putchar( )

#include "conio.h"
int putch(int ch);

Description

The **putch( )** function is not defined by the ANSI C standard. However, it is commonly included in the standard library of DOS-based compilers.

The **putch( )** function outputs to the screen the character specified in the low-order byte of *ch*. In many implementations, its output may not be redirected. Also, in some environments it may operate relative to a window rather than the screen.

Example

This outputs the character **A** to the screen.

```
putch('A');
```

Related Functions

putc( ), **putchar( )**

#include "stdio.h"
int putchar(int ch);

Description

The **putchar( )** function writes to **stdout** the character contained in the least significant byte of *ch*. The **putchar( )** function is functionally equivalent to **putc(ch,stdout)**. Because character arguments are elevated to integer at the time of the call, you may use character variables as arguments to **putchar( )**.

On success, the **putchar( )** function returns the character written. It returns **EOF** if an error occurs. If the output stream has been opened in binary mode, **EOF** is a valid value for *ch*. This means that you must use **ferror( )** to determine if an error has occurred.

Example

The following loop writes to **stdout** the characters in string **str**. The null terminator is not written.

```
for(; *str; str++) putchar(*str);
```

Related Function

putc( )

#include "stdio.h"
int puts(char *str);

Description

The **puts( )** function writes the string pointed to by *str* to the standard output device. The null terminator is translated to a newline.

The **puts( )** function returns a nonnegative value if successful and **EOF** upon failure.

Example

The following code writes the string **this is an example** to **stdout**.

```
#include "stdio.h"
#include "string.h"

void main(void)
{
    char str[80];

    strcpy(str, "this is an example");

    puts(str);
}
```

Related Functions

putc( ), gets( ), printf( )

#include "stdio.h"
int putw(int i, FILE *stream);

Description

The **putw( )** function is not defined by the ANSI C standard, but is commonly included in the standard library.

The **putw( )** function writes the integer i to *stream* at the current file position and increments the file position pointer appropriately.

The **putw( )** function returns the value written. A return value of **EOF** means an error has occurred in the stream if it is in text mode. Because **EOF** is also a valid integer value, you must use **ferror( )** to detect an error in a binary stream.

Example

This code fragment writes the value **100** to the stream pointed to by **fp:**

```
putw(100, fp);
```

Related Functions

getw( ), **printf( )**, **fwrite( )**

#include "io.h"
int read(int fd, char *buf, unsigned int count);

Description

The **read( )** function is part of the UNIX-like I/O system and is not defined by the ANSI C standard.

The **read( )** function reads *count* number of bytes from the file described by *fd* into the buffer pointed to by *buf.* The file position indicator is increased by the number of bytes read. If the file is opened in text mode, character translations may take place.

The return value will be equal to the number of bytes actually read. This number may be smaller than *count* if either an end-of-file or an error is encountered. A value of −1 means an error; a value of zero is returned if an attempt is made to read at end-of-file.

The **read( )** function tends to be very implementation dependent and may behave differently than stated here. Please check your user's manual for details.

Example

This program reads the first 100 bytes from the file TEST into the array **buffer**.

```
#include "fcntl.h"
#include "io.h"
#include "stdlib.h"
#include "stdio.h"

void main(void)
{
  int fd;
  char buffer[100];

  if((fd=open("test", O_RDONLY))==-1) {
    printf("cannot open file\n");
    exit(1);
  }

  if(read(fd, buffer, 100)!=100) printf("read error");
}
```

Related Functions

open( ), close( ), write( ), lseek( )

#include "stdio.h"
int remove(const char *fname);

Description

The **remove( )** function erases the file specified by *fname*. It returns zero if the file is successfully deleted and nonzero if an error occurs.

Example

This program removes the file whose name is specified on the command line:

```
#include "stdio.h"

void main(int argc, char *argv[])
{
  if(remove(argv[1])==-1) printf("remove error");
}
```

Related Function

rename( )

#include "stdio.h"
int rename(const char *oldfname, const *newfname);

Description

The **rename( )** function changes the name of the file specified by *old-fname* to *newfname*. The *newfname* must not match any existing directory entry.

The **rename( )** function returns zero if successful and nonzero if an error has occurred.

Example

This program renames the file specified as the first command line argument to that specified by the second command line argument. Assuming the program is called CHANGE, a command line consisting of CHANGE THIS THAT will change the name of a file called THIS to THAT.

```
#include "stdio.h"

void main(int argc, char *argv[])
{
   if(rename(argv[1], argv[2])!=0) printf("rename error");
}
```

Related Function

remove( )

#include "stdio.h"
void rewind(FILE *stream);

Description

The **rewind( )** function moves the file position indicator to the start of the specified stream. It also clears the end-of-file and error flags associated with *stream*. It has no return value.

Example

This function reads twice the stream pointed to by **fp**, displaying the file each time.

```
void re_read(FILE *fp)
{
    /* read once */
    while(!feof(fp)) putchar(getc(fp));
    rewind(fp);

    /* read twice */
    while(!feof(fp)) putchar(getc(fp));
}
```

Related Function

fseek( )

#include "stdio.h"
int scanf(const char *format, . . .);

Description

The **scanf( )** function is a general-purpose input routine that reads the stream **stdin**. It can read all the built-in data types and automatically convert them into the proper internal format. It is the complement of **printf( )**.

The control string pointed to by *format* consists of three types of characters:

- Format specifiers
- White-space characters
- Non-white-space characters

The input format specifiers are preceded by a percent sign and tell **scanf( )** what type of data is to be read next. These codes are listed in Table 12-3. For example, %s reads a string while %d reads an integer.

The format string is read left to right and the format codes are matched, in order, with the arguments that make up the argument list.

A white-space character in the control string causes **scanf( )** to skip over one or more white-space characters in the input stream. A white-space character is either a space, a tab, or a newline. In essence, one white-space character in the control string causes **scanf( )** to read, but

Code	Meaning
%c	Read a single character
%d	Read a decimal integer
%i	Read a decimal integer
%e	Read a floating-point number
%f	Read a floating-point number
%g	Read a floating-point number
%o	Read an octal number
%s	Read a string
%x	Read a hexadecimal number
%p	Read a pointer
%n	Receives an integer value equal to the number of characters read so far
%u	Read an unsigned integer
%[ ]	Scan for a set of characters

Table 12-3. scanf( ) Format Codes

not store, any number (including zero) of white-space characters up to the first non-white-space character.

A non-white-space character causes **scanf( )** to read and discard a matching character. For example, *"%d,%d"* causes **scanf( )** to read an integer, read and discard a comma, and then read another integer. If the specified character is not found, **scanf( )** terminates.

All the variables used to receive values through **scanf( )** must be passed by their addresses. This means that all arguments must be pointers to the variables used as arguments. This is C's way of creating a call by reference, and it allows a function to alter the contents of an argument. For example, to read an integer into the variable **count,** you would use the following **scanf( )** call:

```
scanf("%d", &count);
```

Strings are read into character arrays, and the array name, without any index, is the address of the first element of the array. So, to read a string into the character array **address,** use

```
scanf("%s", address);
```

In this case, **address** is already a pointer and need not be preceded by the **&** operator.

The input data items must be separated by spaces, tabs, or newlines. Punctuation such as commas, semicolons, and the like do not count as separators. This means that

```
scanf("%d%d", &r, &c);
```

accepts an input of **10 20**, but fails with **10,20**. The **scanf( )** format codes are matched in order with the variables receiving the input in the argument list.

An * placed after the % and before the format specifier reads data of the specified type but suppresses its assignment. Thus,

```
scanf("%d%*c%d", &x, &y);
```

given the input **10/20** places the value 10 into **x**, discards the divide sign, and gives **y** the value 20.

The format commands can specify a maximum field-length modifier. This is an integer placed between the % and the format command code that limits the number of characters read for any field. For example, if you wish to read no more than 20 characters into **address**, you would write

```
scanf("%20s", address);
```

If the input stream were greater than 20 characters, a subsequent call to input would begin where this call left off. Input for a field may terminate before the maximum field length is reached if a white space is encountered. In this case, **scanf( )** moves on to the next field.

Although spaces, tabs, and newlines are used as field separators, they are read like any other character when reading a single character. For example, with an input stream of "x y",

```
scanf("%c%c%c", &a, &b, &c);
```

returns with the character **x** in **a**, a space in **b**, and the character **y** in **c**.

Be careful: Any other characters in the control string—including spaces, tabs, and newlines—are used to match and discard characters from the input stream. Any character that matches is discarded. For example, given the input stream "10t20",

```
scanf("%st%s", &x, &y);
```

places 10 into **x** and 20 into **y**. The t is discarded because of the **t** in the control string.

The ANSI C standard has added to **scanf( )** a new feature called a scanset that was not part of the original UNIX version. A scanset defines a set of characters that may be read by **scanf( )** and assigned to the corresponding character array. You define a scanset by putting inside square brackets a string of the characters you want to scan for. The beginning square bracket must be prefixed by a percent sign. For example, this scanset tells **scanf( )** to read only the characters **A**, **B**, and **C**:

```
%["ABC"]
```

When you use a scanset, **scanf( )** continues to read characters and put them into the corresponding character array until a character that is not in the scanset is encountered. The corresponding variable must be a pointer to a character array. Upon return from **scanf( )**, the array will contain a null-terminated string made up of the characters read.

You can specify an inverted set if the first character in the set is a ^. When the ^ is present, it instructs **scanf( )** to accept any character that *is not* defined by the scanset.

You can specify a range using a hyphen. For example, this tells **scanf( )** to accept the letters "A" through "Z":

```
%["A-Z"]
```

Remember that the scanset is case sensitive. Therefore, if you want to scan for both upper- and lowercase letters, you must specify them individually.

The **scanf( )** function returns a number equal to the number of fields that were successfully assigned values. This number does not include fields that were read but not assigned because the * modifier was used to suppress the assignment. **EOF** is returned if an error occurs before the first field is assigned.

Example

The operation of these **scanf( )** statements is explained in their comments:

```
char str[80];
int i;

/* read a string and an integer */
scanf("%s%d", str, &i);

/* read up to 79 chars into str */
scanf("%79s", str);

/* skip the integer between the two strings */
scanf("%s%*d%s", str, &i, str);
```

Related Functions

printf( ), **fscanf( )**

#include "stdio.h"
void setbuf(FILE *stream, char *buf);

Description

The **setbuf( )** function either specifies the buffer the specified stream will use, or, if called with *buf* set to null, turns off buffering. If a programmer-defined buffer is to be specified, it must be **BUFSIZ** characters long. **BUFSIZ** is defined in STDIO.H.

The **setbuf( )** function returns no value.

Example

The following fragment associates a programmer-defined buffer with the stream pointed to by **fp**.

```
char buffer[BUFSIZ];
   .
   .
   .
setbuf(fp, buffer);
```

Related Functions

fopen(), fclose(), setvbuf()

#include "stdio.h"
int setvbuf (FILE *stream, char *buf, int mode,
size _ t size);

Description

The **setvbuf()** function allows the programmer to specify the buffer, its size, and its mode for the specified stream. The character array pointed to by *buf* is used as *stream's* buffer for I/O operations. The size of the buffer is set by *size*, and *mode* determines how buffering will be handled. If *buf* is null, **setvbuf()** will allocate its own buffer.

The legal values of *mode* are **_IOFBF**, **_IONBF**, and **_IOLBF**. These are defined in STDIO.H. When the mode is set to **_IOFBF**, full buffering takes place. If the mode is **_IOLBF**, the stream is line buffered, which means that the buffer is flushed each time a newline character is written for output streams; for input streams, an input request reads all characters up to a newline. In either case, the buffer is also flushed when full. When the mode is set to **_IONBF**, no buffering takes place.

The value of *size* must be greater than zero.

The **setvbuf()** function returns zero on success; nonzero on failure.

Example

This code fragment sets the stream **fp** to line-buffered mode with a buffer size of 128:

```
#include "studio.h"
char buffer[128];
    .
    .
    .
setvbuf(fp, buffer, _IOLBF, 128);
```

Related Function

setbuf()

#include "stdio.h"
int sprintf(char *buf, const char *format, . . .);

Description

The **sprintf()** function is identical to **printf()**, but the output is put into the array pointed to by *buf*. See **printf()** for details.

The return value is equal to the number of characters actually placed into the array.

Example

After this code fragment executes, **str** holds **one, 2, 3**:

```
char str[80];

sprintf(str,"%s %d %c", "one", 2, '3');
```

Related Functions

printf( ), fsprintf( )

#include "stdio.h"
int sscanf(const char *buf, const char *format, . . .);

Description

The **sscanf( )** function is identical to **scanf( )**, but data is read from the array pointed to by *buf* rather than **stdin**. See **scanf( )** for details.

The return value is equal to the number of variables that were actually assigned values. This number does not include variables that were skipped through the use of the * format specifier. A value of zero means that no fields were assigned; **EOF** indicates that an error occurred before the first assignment.

Example

This program prints the message **hello 1** on the screen:

```
#include "stdio.h"

void main(void)
{
  char str[80];
  int i;

  sscanf("hello 1 2 3 4 5", "%s%d", str, &i);
  printf("%s %d", str, i);
}
```

Related Functions

scanf( ), fscanf( )

#include "io.h"
long tell(int fd);

Description

The **tell( )** function is part of the UNIX-like I/O system and is not defined by the ANSI C standard.

The **tell( )** function returns the current value of the file position indicator associated with the file descriptor *fd*. This value is the number of bytes the position indicator is from the start of the file. A return value of −1L indicates an error.

Example

This code fragment prints the current value of the position indicator for the file described by **fd**:

```
long pos;
 .
 .
 .
pos = tell(fd);
printf("Position is %ld bytes from the start", pos);
```

Related Functions

ftell( ), lseek( ), open( ), close( ) read( ), write( )

#include "stdio.h"
FILE *tmpfile(void);

Description

The **tmpfile( )** function opens a temporary file for update and returns a pointer to the stream. The function automatically uses a unique file name to avoid conflicts with existing files.

The **tmpfile( )** function returns a null pointer on failure; otherwise it returns a pointer to the stream.

The temporary file created by **tmpfile( )** is automatically removed when the file is closed or the program terminates.

Example

The following fragment creates a temporary working file.

```
FILE *temp;

if((temp=tmpfile())==NULL) {
  printf("cannot open temporary work file\n");
  exit(1);
}
```

Related Function

tmpnam( )

#include "stdio.h"
char *tmpnam(char *name);

Description

The **tmpnam( )** function generates a unique file name and stores it in the array pointed to by *name*. The main purpose of **tmpnam( )** is to generate a temporary file name that is different from any other file in the directory.

The function may be called up to **TMP_MAX** times. **TMP_MAX** is defined in STDIO.H, and the ANSI C standard states that it will be at least 25. Each time **tmpnam( )** is called, it generates a new temporary file name.

A pointer to *string* is returned on success; otherwise, a null pointer is returned.

Example

This program displays three unique temporary file names:

```
#include "stdio.h"

void main(void)
{
  char name[40];
  int i;

  for(i=0; i<3; i++) {
    tmpnam(name);
    printf("%s ", name);
  }
}
```

Related Function

tmpfile( )

#include "stdio.h"
int ungetc(int ch, FILE *stream);

Description

The **ungetc( )** function returns the character specified by the low-order byte of *ch* to the input stream *stream*. This character is then returned by the next read operation on *stream*. A call to **fflush( )** or **fseek( )** undoes an **ungetc( )** operation and discards the character.

A one-character pushback is guaranteed; however, some implementations will accept more.

You may not use **ungetc( )** on an **EOF**.

A call to **ungetc( )** clears the end-of-file flag associated with the specified stream. The value of the file position indicator for a text stream is undefined until all pushed-back characters are read, in which case it is the same as it was before the first **ungetc( )** call. For binary streams, each **ungetc( )** call decrements the file position indicator.

The return value is equal to *ch* on success and **EOF** on failure.

Example

This function reads words from the input stream pointed to by **fp**. The terminating character is returned to the stream for later use. For example, given the input **count/10**, the first call to **read_word( )** returns **count** and puts the "/" back on the input stream.

```
void read_word(FILE *fp, char *token)
{

  while(isalpha(*token=getc(fp))) token++;
  ungetc(fp, *token);
}
```

Related Function

getc( )

#include "io.h"
int unlink(const char *fname);

Description

The **unlink( )** function is part of the UNIX-like I/O system and is not defined by the ANSI standard.

The **unlink( )** function removes the specified file from the directory. It returns zero on success and −1 on failure.

Example

This program deletes the file specified as the first command line argument.

```
#include "io.h"
#include "stdio.h"

void main(int argc, char *argv[])
{
  if(unlink(argv[1])==-1) printf("cannot remove file");
}
```

Related Functions

open( ), close( )

#include "stdarg.h"
#include "stdio.h"
int vprintf(char *format, va _ list arg _ ptr);
int vfprintf (FILE *stream, const char *format,
va _ list arg _ ptr);
int vsprintf(char *buf, char *format, va _ list arg _ ptr);

Description

The functions **vprintf( )**, **vfprintf( )**, and **vsprintf( )** are functionally equivalent to **printf( )**, **fprintf( )**, and **sprintf( )**, respectively. However, the argument list has been replaced by a pointer to a list of arguments. This pointer must be of type **va _ list** and is defined in STDARG.H. See **va _ arg( )**, **va _ start( )**, and **va _ end( )** in Chapter 18 for further information on passing variable length arguments to functions.

Example

This code fragment shows how to set up a call to **vprintf( )**. The call to **va _ start( )** creates a variable-length argument pointer to the start of the argument list. This pointer must be used in the call to **vprintf( )**. The call to **va _ end( )** clears the variable-length argument pointer.

```
#include "stdio.h"
#include "stdarg.h"

void print_message(char *format, ...);

void main(void)
```

```
{
  print_message("cannot open file %s", "test");
}

void print_message(char *format, ...)
{
  va_list ptr; /* get an arg ptr */

  /* initialize ptr to point to the first argument after the
     format string
  */
  va_start(ptr, format);

  /* print out message */
  vprintf(format, ptr);
  va_end(ptr);
}
```

Related Functions

va _ list( ), va _ start( ), va _ end( )

#include ''io.h''
int write(int fd, char *buf, unsigned int buffer);

Description

The **write**( ) function is part of the UNIX-like I/O system and is not defined by the ANSI standard.

The **write**( ) function writes *count* number of bytes to the file described by *fd* from the buffer pointed to by *buf*. The file position indicator is increased by the number of bytes written. If the file is opened in text mode, character translations may take place.

The return value will be equal to the number of bytes actually written. This number may be smaller than *count* if an error is encountered. A value of −1 means an error has occurred.

The **write**( ) function tends to be implementation-dependent and may behave differently than stated here. Check your user's manual for details.

Example

This program writes the 100 bytes from **buffer** to the file TEST.

```
#include "io.h"
#include "stdlib.h"
#include "stdio.h"
#include "fcntl.h"

void main(void)
{
  int fd;
  char buffer[100];

  if((fd=open("test", O_WRONLY))==-1) {
    printf("cannot open file\n");
    exit(1);
  }

  gets(buffer);

  if(write(fd, buffer, 100)!=100) printf("write error");
  close(fd);
}
```

Related Functions

read( ), close( ), write( ), lseek( )

String and Character Functions

The C standard library has a rich and varied set of string- and character-handling functions. In C, a string is a null-terminated array of characters. In a standard implementation, the string functions require the header file STRING.H to provide their prototypes. The character functions use CTYPE.H as their header file. These files may have different names if the compiler does not follow the ANSI C standard or the old UNIX standard. Your compiler may also supply additional character and string functions, so check your user's manual.

Because C has no bounds checking on array operations, it is the programmer's responsibility to prevent an array overflow. According to the ANSI standard, if an array has overflowed, its "behavior is undefined"—a nice way of saying that your program is about to crash!

In C, a *printable character* is one that can be displayed on a terminal. These are usually the characters between a space (0x20) and tilde (0xfE). *Control characters* have values between 0 and 0x1F as well as DEL (0x7F).

The arguments to the character functions are traditionally integer. However, only the low-order byte is used; the character function automatically converts the argument to **unsigned char**. Nevertheless, you can call these functions with character arguments because characters are automatically elevated to integers at the time of the call.

The header file STRING.H defines the **size_t** type, which is essentially the same as **unsigned**.

#include "ctype.h"
int isalnum(int ch);

Description

The **isalnum( )** function returns nonzero if its argument is a letter or a digit. If the character is not an alphanumeric, **isalnum( )** returns zero.

Example

This program checks each character read from **stdin** and reports all alphanumeric characters:

```
#include "ctype.h"
#include "stdio.h"

void main(void)
{
  char ch;

  for(;;) {
    ch = getc(stdin);
    if(ch==' ') break;
    if(isalnum(ch)) printf("%c is alphanumeric\n", ch);
  }
}
```

Related Functions

isalpha( ), iscntrl( ), isdigit( ), isgraph( ), isprint( ), ispunct( ), isspace( )

#include "ctype.h"
int isalpha(int ch);

Description

The **isalpha( )** function returns nonzero if *ch* is a letter of the alphabet; otherwise, it returns zero. What constitutes a letter may vary from language to language—in English, it is upper- and lowercase letters from "A" to "Z."

Example

This program checks each character read from **stdin** and reports all letters:

```
#include "ctype.h"
#include "stdio.h"

void main(void)
{
  char ch;

  for(;;) {
    ch = getchar();
    if(ch==' ') break;
    if(isalpha(ch)) printf("%c is a letter\n", ch);
  }
}
```

Related Functions

isalnum( ), **iscntrl( )**, **isdigit( )**, **isgraph( )**, **isprint( )**, **ispunct( )**, **isspace( )**

#include "ctype.h"
int iscntrl(int ch);

Description

The **iscntrl( )** function returns nonzero if *ch* is between 0 and 0x1F or is equal to 0x7F (DEL); otherwise, it returns zero.

Example

This program checks each character read from **stdin** and reports all control characters:

```
#include "ctype.h"
#include "stdio.h"

void main(void)
{
 char ch;

 for(;;) {
  ch = getchar( );
  if(ch==' ') break;
  if(iscntrl(ch)) printf("%c is a control char\n", ch);
 }
}
```

Related Functions

isalnum( ), isalpha( ), isdigit( ), isgraph( ), isprint( ), ispunct( ),
isspace( )

#include "ctype.h"
int isdigit(int ch);

Description

The isdigit( ) function returns nonzero if *ch* is a digit (that is, zero
through 9). Otherwise, it returns zero.

Example

This program checks each character read from **stdin** and reports all
digits:

```
#include "ctype.h"
#include "stdio.h"

void main(void)
{
  char ch;

  for(;;) {
    ch = getchar();
    if(ch==' ') break;
    if(isdigit(ch)) printf("%c is a digit\n", ch);
  }
}
```

Related Functions

isalnum( ), isalpha( ), iscntrl( ), isgraph( ), isprint( ), ispunct( ),
isspace( )

#include "ctype.h"
int isgraph(int ch);

Description

The **isgraph( )** function returns nonzero if *ch* is any printable character other than a space; otherwise, it returns zero. Although implementation-dependent, printable characters are generally in the range 0x21 through 0x7E.

Example

This program checks each character read from **stdin** and reports all printable characters.

```
#include "ctype.h"
#include "stdio.h"

void main(void)
{
  char ch;

  for(;;) {
    ch = getchar();
    if(isgraph(ch)) printf("%c is printable\n", ch);
    if(ch==' ') break;
  }
}
```

Related Functions

isalnum( ), isalpha( ), iscntrl( ), isdigit( ), isprint( ), ispunct( ), isspace( )

#include "ctype.h"
int islower(int ch);

Description

The **islower( )** function returns nonzero if *ch* is a lowercase letter; otherwise, it returns zero.

Example

This program checks each character read from **stdin** and reports all lowercase letters.

```
#include "ctype.h"
#include "stdio.h"

void main(void)
{
  char ch;

  for(;;) {
    ch = getchar();
    if(ch==' ') break;
    if(islower(ch)) printf("%c is lowercase\n", ch);
  }
}
```

Related Function

isupper( )

#include ''ctype.h''
int isprint(int ch);

Description

The **isprint( )** function returns nonzero if *ch* is a printable character, including a space; otherwise, it returns zero. Although implementation-dependent, printable characters are often in the range 0x20 through 0x7E.

Example

This program checks each character read from **stdin** and reports all printable characters:

```
#include "ctype.h"
#include "stdio.h"

void main(void)
{
  char ch;

  for(;;) {
    ch = getchar();
    if(isprint(ch)) printf("%c is printable\n",ch);
    if(ch==' ') break;
  }
}
```

Related Functions

isalnum( ), isalpha( ), iscntrl( ), isdigit( ), isgraph( ), ispunct( ), isspace( )

#include "ctype.h"
int ispunct(int ch);

Description

The **ispunct( )** function returns nonzero if *ch* is a punctuation character; otherwise, it returns zero. The term *punctuation,* as defined by this function, includes all printing characters that are neither alphanumeric nor a space.

Example

This program checks each character read from **stdin** and reports all punctuation:

```
#include "ctype.h"
#include "stdio.h"

void main(void)
{
  char ch;

  for(;;) {
    ch = getchar();
    if(ch==' ') break;
    if(ispunct(ch)) printf("%c is punctuation\n", ch);
  }
}
```

Related Functions

isalnum( ), isalpha( ), iscntrl( ), isdigit( ), isgraph( ), isspace( )

#include "ctype.h"
int isspace(int ch);

Description

The **isspace( )** function returns nonzero if *ch* is either a space, horizontal tab, vertical tab, formfeed, carriage return, or newline character; otherwise, it returns zero.

Example

This program checks each character read from **stdin** and reports all white-space characters:

```
#include "ctype.h"
#include "stdio.h"

void main(void)
{
  char ch;

  for(;;) {
    ch = getchar();
    if(isspace(ch)) printf("%c is white space\n", ch);
    if(ch==' ') break;
  }
}
```

Related Functions

isalnum( ), isalpha( ), iscntrl( ), isdigit( ), isgraph( ), ispunct( )

#include "ctype.h"
int isupper(int ch);

Description

The **isupper( )** function returns nonzero if *ch* is uppercase; otherwise, it returns zero.

Example

This program checks each character read from **stdin** and reports all uppercase letters:

```
#include "ctype.h"
#include "stdio.h"

void main(void)
{
  char ch;

  for(;;) {
    ch = getchar();
    if(ch==' ') break;
    if(isupper(ch)) printf("%c is uppercase\n", ch);
  }
}
```

Related Function

islower( )

#include "ctype.h"
int isxdigit(int ch);

Description

The **isxdigit( )** function returns nonzero if *ch* is a hexadecimal digit; otherwise, it returns zero. A hexadecimal digit will be in the range "A" through "F," "a" through "f," or 0 through 9.

Example

This program checks each character read from **stdin** and reports all hexadecimal digits:

```
#include "ctype.h"
#include "stdio.h"

void main(void)
{
  char ch;

  for(;;) {
    ch = getchar();
    if(ch==' ') break;
    if(isxdigit(ch)) printf("%c is hexadecimal \n", ch);
  }
}
```

Related Functions

isalnum( ), isalpha( ), iscntrl( ), isdigit( ), isgraph( ), ispunct( ), isspace( )

#include "string.h"
void *memchr(const void *buffer, int ch, size_t count);

Description

The **memchr( )** function searches the array pointed to by *buffer* for the first occurrence of *ch* in the first *count* characters.

The **memchr( )** function returns a pointer to the first occurrence of *ch* in *buffer,* or a null pointer if *ch* is not found.

Example

This program prints **is a test** on the screen:

```
#include "stdio.h"
#include "string.h"

void main(void)
{
  char *p;

  p = memchr("this is a test", ' ', 14);
  printf(p);
}
```

Related Functions

memcpy( ), **memmove( )**

#include "string.h"
int memcmp(const void *buf1, const void *buf2,
size_t count);

Description

The **memcmp( )** function compares the first *count* characters of the arrays pointed to by *buf1* and *buf2*. The comparison is done alphabetically.

The **memcmp( )** function returns an integer that is interpreted as follows:

Value	Meaning
Less than zero	*buf1* is less than *buf2*
Zero	*buf1* is equal to *buf2*
Greater than zero	*buf1* is greater than *buf2*

Example

This program shows the outcome of a comparison of its two command line arguments:

```
#include "stdio.h"
#include "string.h"
#include "stdlib.h"

void main(int argc, char *argv[])
{
  int outcome, len, l1, l2;

  if(argc!=3) {
    printf("incorrect number of parameters");
    exit(1);
  }

  /* find the length of shortest */
  l1 = strlen(argv[1]);
  l2 = strlen(argv[2]);
  len = l1 < l2 ? l1:l2;

  outcome = memcmp(argv[1], argv[2], len);
  if(!outcome) printf("equal");
  else if(outcome<0) printf("first less than second");
  else printf("first greater than second");
}
```

Related Functions

memchr( ), **memcpy( )**, **strcmp( )**

#include "string.h"
void *memcpy(void *to, const void *from, size_t count);

Description

The **memcpy( )** function copies *count* characters from the array pointed to by *from* into the array pointed to by *to*. If the arrays overlap, the behavior of **memcpy( )** is undefined.

The **memcpy( )** function returns a pointer to *to*.

Example

This program copies the contents of **buf1** into **buf2** and displays the result:

```
#include "stdio.h"
#include "string.h"

#define SIZE 80

void main(void)
{
  char buf1[SIZE], buf2[SIZE];

  strcpy(buf1, "When, in the course of...");
  memcpy(buf2, buf1, SIZE);
  printf(buf2);
}
```

Related Function

memmove( )

#include "string.h"
void *memmove(void *to, const void *from, size_t count);

Description

The **memmove( )** function copies *count* characters from the array pointed to by *from* into the array pointed to by *to*. If the arrays overlap, the copy will take place correctly, placing the correct contents into *to* but leaving *from* modified.

The **memmove( )** function returns a pointer to *to*.

Example

This program copies the contents of **str1** into **str2** and displays the result:

```
#include "stdio.h"
#include "string.h"

#define SIZE 80

void main(void)
{
  char str1[SIZE], str2[SIZE];

  strcpy(str1, "When, in the course of...");
  memmove(str2, str1, SIZE);
  printf(str2);
}
```

Related Function

memcpy( )

#include ''string.h''
void *memset(void *buf, int ch, size_t count);

Description

The **memset( )** function copies the low-order byte of *ch* into the first *count* characters of the array pointed to by **buf**. It returns **buf**.

  memset( ) is most commonly used to initialize a region of memory to some known value.

Example

This fragment initializes to null the first 100 bytes of the array pointed to by **buf**. Then it sets the first 10 bytes to **X** and displays the string **XXXXXXXXXX**.

```
memset(buf, '\0', 100);
memset(buf, 'X', 10);
printf(buf);
```

Related Functions

memcmp( ), memcpy( ), memmove( )

#include "string.h"
char *strcat(char *str1, const char *str2);

Description

The **strcat( )** function concatenates a copy of *str2* to *str1* and terminates *str1* with a null. The null terminator that originally ended *str1* is overwritten by the first character of *str2*. The string *str2* is untouched by the operation. If the arrays overlap, the behavior of **strcat( )** is undefined.

The **strcat( )** function returns *str1*.

Remember, no bounds checking takes place. It is your responsibility to ensure that *str1* is large enough to hold both its original contents and those of *str2*.

Example

This program appends the first string read from **stdin** to the second. For example, assuming the user enters **hello** and **there**, the program prints **therehello**.

```
#include "stdio.h"
#include "string.h"

void main(void)
{
  char s1[80], s2[80];

  gets(s1);
  gets(s2);

  strcat(s2, s1);
  printf(s2);
}
```

Related Functions

strchr( ), strcmp( ), strcpy( )

#include "string.h"
char *strchr(const char *str, int ch);

Description

The **strchr( )** function returns a pointer to the first occurrence of the low-order byte of *ch* in the string pointed to by *str*. If no match is found, a null pointer is returned.

Example

This program prints the string **is a test:**

```
#include "stdio.h"
#include "string.h"

void main(void)
{
  char *p;

  p = strchr("this is a test", ' ');
  printf(p);
}
```

Related Functions

strpbrk( ), strspn( ), strstr( ), strtok( )

#include "string.h"
int strcoll(const char *str1, const char *str2);

Description

The **strcoll( )** function compares the string pointed to by *str1* with the one pointed to by *str2*. The comparison is performed in accordance with the locale specified by using the **setlocale( )** function. (See **setlocale( )** for details.)

The **strcoll( )** function returns an integer that is interpreted as follows:

Value	Meaning
Less than zero	*str1* is less than *str2*
Zero	*str1* is equal to *str2*
Greater than zero	*str1* is greater than *str2*

Example

This code fragment prints **equal** on the screen.

```
if(strcoll("hi", "hi")) printf("equal");
```

Related Functions

memcmp( ), strcmp( )

#include "string.h"
int strcmp(const char *str1, const char *str2);

Description

The **strcmp( )** function alphabetically compares two strings and returns an integer based on the outcome, as shown here:

Value	Meaning
Less than zero	*str1* is less than *str2*
Zero	*str1* is equal to *str2*
Greater than zero	*str1* is greater than *str2*

Example

You can use the following function as a password-verification routine. It returns zero on failure and 1 on success.

```
password(void)
{
  char s[80];

  printf("enter password: ");
  gets(s);

  if(strcmp(s, "pass")) {
    printf("invalid password\n");
    return 0;
  }
  return 1;
}
```

Related Functions

strchr( ), strcpy( ), strncmp( )

#include "string.h"
char *strcpy(char *str1, const char *str2);

Description

The **strcpy( )** function copies the contents of *str2* into *str1*. *Str2* must be a pointer to a null-terminated string. The **strcpy( )** function returns a pointer to *str1*.

If *str1* and *str2* overlap, the behavior of **strcpy( )** is undefined.

Example

The following code fragment copies **hello** into string **str**:

```
char str[80];

strcpy(str, "hello");
```

Related Functions

memcpy( ), strchr( ), strcmp( ), strncmp( )

#include "stdio.h"
int strcspn(const char *str1, const *str2);

Description

The **strcspn( )** function returns the length of the initial substring of the string pointed to by *str1* that is made up of only those characters not contained in the string pointed to by *str2*. Stated differently, **strcspn( )** returns the index of the first character in the string pointed to by *str1* that matches any of the characters in the string pointed to by *str2*.

Example

The following program prints the number 8.

```
#include "string.h"
#include "stdio.h"

void main(void)
{
  int len;

  len = strcspn("this is a test", "ab");
  printf("%d", len);
}
```

Related Functions

strpbrk( ), strrchr( ), strstr( ), strtok( )

#include ''string.h''
char *strerror(int errnum);

Description

The **strerror( )** function returns a pointer to an implementation-defined string that is associated with the value of *errnum*. Under no circumstances should you modify the string.

Example

This code fragment prints an implementation-defined error message on the screen:

```
printf(strerror(10));
```

#include ''string.h''
size_t strlen(char *str);

Description

The **strlen( )** function returns the length of the null-terminated string pointed to by *str*. The null is not counted.

Example

The following code fragment prints 5 on the screen:

```
printf("%d", strlen("hello"));
```

Related Functions

memcpy( ), strchr( ), strcmp( ), strncmp( )

#include "string.h"
char *strncat(char *str1, const *str2, size — t count);

Description

The **strncat( )** function concatenates not more than *count* characters of the string pointed to by *str2* to the string pointed to by *str1* and terminates *str1* with a null. The null terminator that originally ended *str1* is overwritten by the first character of *str2*. The string *str2* is untouched by the operation. If the strings overlap, the behavior of **strncat( )** is undefined.

The **strncat( )** function returns *str1*.

Remember, no bounds checking takes place, so it is your responsibility to ensure that *str1* is large enough to hold its original contents as well as those of *str2*.

Example

This program appends the first string read from **stdin** to the second and prevents an array overflow from occurring to **s1**. For example, assuming the user enters **hello** and **there**, the program prints **therehello**.

```
#include "stdio.h"
#include "string.h"

void main(void)
{
  char s1[80], s2[80];
  unsigned int len;

  gets(s1);
  gets(s2);

  /* compute how many chars will actually fit */
  len = 79-strlen(s2);

  strncat(s2, s1, len);
  printf(s2);
}
```

Related Functions

strcat( ), strnchr( ), strncmp( ), strncpy( )

#include "string.h"
int strncmp(const char *str1, const char *str2,
size_t count);

Description

The **strncmp( )** function alphabetically compares not more than *count* characters from the two null-terminated strings and returns an integer based on the outcome, as shown here:

Value	Meaning
Less than zero	*str1* is less than *str2*
Zero	*str1* is equal to *str2*
Greater than zero	*str1* is greater than *str2*

If there are fewer than *count* characters in either string, the comparison ends when the first null is encountered.

Example

The following function compares the first eight characters of two command line arguments and reports if they are equal:

```
#include "stdio.h"
#include "string.h"
#include "stdlib.h"

void main(int argc, char *argv[])
{
  if(argc!=3) {
    printf("incorrect number of parameters");
    exit(1);
  }

  if(!strncmp(argv[1], argv[2], 8))
    printf("the filenames are the same\n");

}
```

Related Functions

strcmp( ), strnchr( ), strncpy( )

#include "string.h"
char *strncpy(char *str1, const char *str2, size_t count);

Description

The **strncpy( )** function copies up to *count* characters from the string pointed to by *str2* into the string pointed to by *str1*. *Str2* must be a pointer to a null-terminated string. The **strncpy( )** function returns a pointer to *str1*.

If *str1* and *str2* overlap, the behavior of **strncpy( )** is undefined.

If the string pointed to by *str2* has fewer than *count* characters, nulls will be appended to *str1* until *count* characters have been copied.

Alternately, if the string pointed to by *str2* is longer than *count* characters, the resultant string pointed to by *str1* is not null terminated.

The **strncpy( )** function returns a pointer to *str1*.

Example

The following code fragment copies at most 79 characters of **str1** into **str2**, thus ensuring that no array boundary overflow occurs.

```
char str1[128], str2[80];

gets(str1);
strncpy(str2, str1, 79);
```

Related Functions

memcpy( ), strchr( ), strncat( ), strncmp( )

#include "string.h"
char *strpbrk(const char *str1, const char *str2);

Description

The **strpbrk( )** function returns a pointer to the first character in the string pointed to by *str1* that matches any character in the string pointed to by *str2*. Null terminators are not included. If there are no matches, a null pointer is returned.

Example

This program prints the message **s is a test** on the screen:

```
#include "stdio.h"
#include "string.h"

void main(void)
{
  char *p;

  p = strpbrk("this is a test", " absj");
  printf(p);
}
```

Related Functions

strrchr( ), strspn( ), strstr( ), strtok( )

#include ''string.h''
char *strrchr(const char *str, int ch);

Description

The **strrchr( )** function returns a pointer to the last occurrence of the low-order byte of *ch* in the string pointed to by *str*. If no match is found, a null pointer is returned.

Example

This program prints the string **is a test**.

```
#include "string.h"
#include "stdio.h"

void main(void)
{
  char *p;

  p = strrchr("this is a test", 'i');
  printf(p);
}
```

Related Functions

strpbrk( ), strspn( ), strstr( ), strtok( )

#include "stdio.h"
size_t strspn(const char *str1, const char *str2);

Description

The **strspn( )** function returns the length of the initial substring of the string pointed to by *str1* that consists only of those characters contained in the string pointed to by *str2*. Stated differently, **strspn( )** returns the index of the first character in the string pointed to by *str1* that does not match any of the characters in the string pointed to by *str2*.

Example

This program prints 8:

```
#include "string.h"
#include "stdio.h"

void main(void)
{
  int len;

  len = strspn("this is a test", "siht ");
  printf("%d", len);
}
```

Related Functions

strpbrk( ), strrchr( ), strstr( ), strtok( )

#include "stdio.h"
char *strstr(const char *str1, const char *str2);

Description

The **strstr( )** function returns a pointer to the first occurrence of the string pointed to by *str2* in the string pointed to by *str1*. It returns a null pointer if no match is found.

Example

This program displays the message **is is a test**.

```
#include "string.h"
#include "stdio.h"

void main(void)
{
  char *p;

  p = strstr("this is a test", "is");
  printf(p);
}
```

Related Functions

strchr( ), strcspn( ), strpbrk( ), strrchr( ), strspn( ), strtok( )

#include "string.h"
char *strtok(char *str1, const char *str2);

Description

The **strtok( )** function returns a pointer to the next token in the string pointed to by *str1*. The characters that make up the string pointed to by *str2* are the delimiters that terminate the token. A null pointer is returned when there is no token to return.

The first time **strtok( )** is called, *str1* is actually used in the call. Subsequent calls must use a null pointer for the first argument.

It is important to understand that the **strtok( )** function modifies the string pointed to by *str1*. Each time a token is found, a null is placed where the delimiter was found. In this way, **strtok( )** can continue to advance through the string.

You can use a different set of delimiters for each call to **strtok( )**.

Example

This program tokenizes the string "The summer soldier, the sunshine patriot", with spaces and commas being the delimiters. The output is

"The ¦ summer ¦ soldier ¦ the ¦ sunshine ¦ patriot"

```
#include "stdio.h"
#include "string.h"

void main(void)
{
  char *p;

  p = strtok("The summer soldier, the sunshine patriot"," ");
  printf(p);
  do {
    p = strtok('\0', ", ");
    if(p) printf("|%s", p);
  } while(p);
}
```

Related Functions

strchr( ), strcspn( ), strpbrk( ), strrchr( ), strspn( )

#include "string.h"
size _ t strxfrm(char *str1, const char *str2,
size _ t count);

Description

The **strxfrm( )** function transforms the first *count* characters of the string pointed to by *str2* so that it can be used by the **strcmp( )** function. **strxfrm( )** then puts the result into the string pointed to by *str1*. After the transformation, the outcome of a **strcmp( )** using *str1* and a **strcoll( )** using the original string pointed to by *str2* will be the same. The main use for the **strxfrm( )** function is in foreign language environments that do not use the ASCII collating sequence.

The **strxfrm( )** function returns the length of the transformed string.

Example

The following line transforms the first ten characters of the string pointed to by **s2** and puts the result in the string pointed to by **s1**.

```
strxfrm(s1, s2, 10);
```

Related Function

strcoll( )

#include "ctype.h"
int tolower(int ch);

Description

The **tolower( )** function returns the lowercase equivalent of *ch* if *ch* is a letter; otherwise, *ch* is returned unchanged.

Example

This code fragment displays **q**.

```
putchar(tolower('Q'));
```

Related Function

toupper( )

#include "ctype.h"
int toupper(int ch);

Description

The **toupper( )** function returns the uppercase equivalent of *ch* if *ch* is a letter; otherwise, *ch* is returned unchanged.

Example

This code displays **A**.

```
putchar(toupper('a'));
```

Related Function

tolower( )

Mathematical Functions

The ANSI C standard defines 22 mathematical functions that fall into the following categories:

- Trigonometric functions
- Hyperbolic functions
- Exponential and logarithmic functions
- Miscellaneous

Even if your compiler is not completely standard, the math functions described here are probably applicable.

All the math functions require the header MATH.H in any program that uses them. In addition to declaring the math functions, this header defines three macros called **EDOM**, **ERANGE**, and **HUGE＿VAL**. If an argument to a math function is not in the domain for which it is defined, an implementation-defined value is returned and the built-in global integer variable **errno** is set equal to **EDOM**. If a routine produces a result too large to be represented by a **double**, an overflow occurs. This causes the routine to return **HUGE＿VAL** and sets **errno** to **ERANGE**, indicating a range error. If an underflow occurs, the routine returns zero and sets **errno** to **ERANGE**. If your compiler does not comform to the ANSI standard, the exact operation of the routines in error situations may be different.

#include "math.h"
double acos(double arg);

Description

The **acos( )** function returns the arc cosine of *arg*. The argument to **acos( )** must be in the range −1 to 1; otherwise, a domain error occurs.

Example

This program prints the arc cosines of the values −1 through 1, in increments of one tenth.

```
#include "math.h"
#include "stdio.h"

void main(void)
{
  double val=-1.0;

  do {
    printf("arc cosine of %f is %f\n", val, acos(val));
    val += 0.1;
  } while(val<=1.0);
}
```

Related Functions

asin( ), atan( ), atan2( ), cos( ), cosh( ), sin( ), sinh( ), tan( ), tanh( )

#include "math.h"
double asin(double arg);

Description

The **asin( )** function returns the arc sine of *arg*. The argument to **asin( )** must be in the range −1 to 1; otherwise, a domain error occurs.

Example

This program prints the arc sines of the values −1 through 1, in increments of one tenth:

```
#include "math.h"
#include "stdio.h"

void main(void)
{
  double val=-1.0;

  do {
    printf("arc sine of %f is %f\n", val, asin(val));
    val += 0.1;
  } while(val<=1.0);
}
```

Related Functions

acos( ), atan( ), atan2( ), cos( ), cosh( ), sin( ), sinh( ), tan( ), tanh( )

#include "math.h"
double atan(double arg);

Description

The **atan( )** function returns the arc tangent of *arg*.

Example

This program prints the arc tangents of the values −1 through 1, in increments of one tenth:

```
#include "math.h"
#include "stdio.h"

void main(void)
{
  double val=-1.0;

  do {
    printf("arc tangent of %f is %f\n", val, atan(val));
    val += 0.1;
  } while(val<=1.0);
}
```

Related Functions

acos( ), asin( ), atan2( ), cos( ), cosh( ), sin( ), sinh( ), tan( ), tanh( )

#include "math.h"
double atan2(double y, double x);

Description

The **atan2( )** function returns the arc tangent of *y/x*. It uses the signs of its arguments to compute the quadrant of the return value.

Example

This program prints the arc tangents of *y*, from −1 through 1, in increments of one tenth:

```
#include "math.h"
#include "stdio.h"

void main(void)
{
  double val=-1.0;

  do {
    printf("atan2 of %f is %f\n", val, atan2(val,1.0));
    val += 0.1;
  } while(val<=1.0);
}
```

Related Functions

acos( ), asin( ), atan( ), cos( ), cosh( ), sin( ), sinh( ), tan( ), tanh( )

#include "math.h"
double ceil(double num);

Description

The **ceil( )** function returns the smallest integer represented as a **double** not less than *num*. For example, given 1.02, **ceil( )** returns **2.0**. Given −1.02, **ceil( )** returns **−1**.

Example

This code fragment prints **10** on the screen:

```
printf("%f", ceil(9.9));
```

Related Functions

floor( ), **fmod( )**

#include "math.h"
double cos(double arg);

Description

The **cos( )** function returns the cosine of *arg*. The value of *arg* must be in radians.

Example

This program prints the cosines of the values −1 through 1, in increments of one tenth:

```
#include "math.h"
#include "stdio.h"

void main(void)
{
  double val=-1.0;

  do {
    printf("cosine of %f is %f\n", val, cos(val));
    val += 0.1;
  } while(val<=1.0);
}
```

Related Functions

acos( ), asin( ), atan( ), atan2( ), cosh( ), sin( ), sinh( ), tan( ), tanh( )

#include "math.h"
double cosh(double arg);

Description

The **cosh( )** function returns the hyperbolic cosine of *arg*. The value of *arg* must be in radians.

Example

The following program prints the hyperbolic cosines of the values −1 through 1, in increments of one tenth.

```
#include "math.h"
#include "stdio.h"

void main(void)
{
  double val=-1.0;

  do {
    printf("hyperbolic cosine of %f is %f\n", val, cosh(val));
    val += 0.1;
  } while(val<=1.0);
}
```

Related Functions

acos( ), asin( ), atan( ), atan2( ), cos( ), sin( ), tan( ), tanh( ),

#include "math.h"
double exp(double arg);

Description

The **exp( )** function returns the natural logarithm **e** raised to the *arg* power.

Example

This fragment displays the value of **e** (rounded to 2.718282):

```
printf("value of e to the first: %f", exp(1.0));
```

Related Function

log( )

#include "math.h"
double fabs(double num);

Description

The **fabs( )** function returns the absolute value of *num*.

Example

This program prints **1.0 1.0** on the screen.

```
#include "math.h"
#include "stdio.h"

void main(void)
{
  printf("%1.1f %1.1f", fabs(1.0), fabs(-1.0));
}
```

Related Function

abs( )

#include "math.h"
double floor(double num);

Description

The **floor( )** function returns the largest integer (represented as a **double**) not greater than *num*. For example, given 1.02, **floor( )** returns 1.0. Given −1.02, **floor( )** returns −2.0.

Example

This code fragment prints **10** on the screen:

```
printf("%f", floor(10.9));
```

Related Functions

fceil( ), fmod( )

#include "math.h"
double fmod(double x, double y);

Description

The **fmod( )** function returns the remainder of *x/y*.

Example

The following program prints **1.0** on the screen—the remainder of 10/3.

```
#include "math.h"
#include "stdio.h"

void main(void)
{
  printf("%1.1f", fmod(10.0, 3.0));
}
```

Related Functions

ceil( ), fabs( ), floor( )

#include "math.h"
double frexp(double num, int *exp);

Description

The **frexp( )** function decomposes the number *num* into a mantissa in the range 0.5 to less than 1, and an integer exponent such that $num = mantissa * 2^{exp}$. The mantissa is returned by the function and the exponent is stored at the variable pointed to by *exp*.

Example

This code fragment prints **0.625** for the mantissa and **4** for the exponent:

```
int e;
double f;

f = frexp(10.0,&e);
printf("%f %d", f, e);
```

Related Function

ldexp( )

#include "math.h"
double ldexp(double num, int exp);

Description

The **ldexp( )** returns the value of $num * 2^{exp}$. If overflow occurs, **HUGE _ VAL** is returned.

Example

This program displays the number 4.

```
#include "math.h"
#include "stdio.h"

void main(void)
{
  printf("%f", ldexp(1,2));
}
```

Related Functions

frexp( ), **modf( )**

#include "math.h"
double log(double num);

Description

The **log( )** function returns the natural logarithm for *num*. A domain error occurs if *num* is negative and a range error occurs if the argument is zero.

Example

The following program prints the natural logarithms for the numbers 1 through 10.

```
#include "math.h"
#include "stdio.h"

void main(void)
{
  double val=1.0;

  do {
    printf("%f %f\n", val, log(val));
    val++;
  } while (val<11.0);
}
```

Related Function

log10( )

#include "math.h"
double log10(double num);

Description

The **log10( )** function returns the base 10 logarithm for *num*. A domain error occurs if *num* is negative and a range error occurs if the argument is zero.

Example

This program prints the base 10 logarithms for the numbers 1 through 10:

```
#include "math.h"
#include "stdio.h"

void main(void)
{
  double val=1.0;

  do {
    printf("%f %f\n", val, log10(val));
    val++;
  } while (val<11.0);
}
```

Related Function

log( )

#include "math.h"
double modf(double num, int *i);

Description

The **modf( )** function decomposes *num* into its integer and fractional parts. It returns the fractional portion and places the integer part in the variable pointed to by *i*.

Example

This code fragment prints **10** and **0.123** on the screen:

```
int i;
double f;

f = modf(10.123, &i);
printf("%d %f",i , f);
```

Related Functions

frexp( ), ldexp( )

#include "math.h"
double pow(double base, double exp);

Description

The **pow( )** function returns *base* raised to the *exp* power ($base^{exp}$). A domain error occurs if *base* is zero and *exp* is less than or equal to zero. This also happens if *base* is negative and *exp* is not an integer. An overflow produces a range error.

Example

The following program prints the first ten powers of 10.

```
#include "math.h"
#include "stdio.h"

void main(void)
{
  double x=10.0, y=0.0;

  do {
    printf("%f\n", pow(x, y));
    y++;
  } while(y<11.0);
}
```

Related Functions

exp( ), **log( )**, **sqrt( )**

#include "math.h"
double sin(double arg);

Description

The **sin( )** function returns the sine of *arg*. The value of *arg* must be in radians.

Example

This program prints the sines of the values −1 through 1, in increments of one tenth:

```
#include "math.h"
#include "stdio.h"

void main(void)
{
  double val=-1.0;
  do {
    printf("sine of %f is %f\n", val, sin(val));
    val += 0.1;
  } while(val<=1.0);
}
```

Related Functions

acos( ), asin( ), atan( ), atan2( ), cos( ), cosh( ), sinh( ), tan( ), tanh( )

#include "math.h"
double sinh(double arg);

Description

The **sinh( )** function returns the hyperbolic sine of *arg*. The value of *arg* must be in radians.

Example

This program prints the hyperbolic sines of the values −1 through 1, in increments of one tenth:

```
#include "math.h"
#include "stdio.h"

void main(void)
{
  double val=-1.0;

  do {
    printf("hyperbolic sine of %f is %f\n", val, sinh(val));
    val += 0.1;
  } while(val<=1.0);
}
```

Related Functions

acos( ), asin( ), atan( ), atan2( ), cos( ), cosh( ), sin( ), tan( ), tanh( )

#include "math.h"
double sqrt(double num);

Description

The **sqrt( )** function returns the square root of *num*. If it is called with a negative argument, a domain error occurs.

Example

This code fragment prints 4 on the screen:

```
printf("%f", sqrt(16.0));
```

Related Functions

exp( ), **log( )**, **pow( )**

#include "math.h"
double tan(double arg);

Description

The **tan( )** function returns the tangent of *arg*. The value of *arg* must be in radians.

Example

This program prints the tangent of the values −1 through 1, in increments of one tenth:

```
#include "math.h"
#include "stdio.h"

void main(void)
{
  double val=-1.0;

  do {
    printf("tangent of %f is %f\n", val, tan(val));
    val += 0.1;
  } while(val<=1.0);
}
```

Related Functions

acos( ), **asin( )**, **atan( )**, **atan2( )**, **cos( )**, **cosh( )**, **sin( )**, **sinh( )**, **tanh( )**

#include "math.h"
double tanh(double arg);

Description

The **tanh( )** function returns the hyperbolic tangent of *arg*. The value of *arg* must be in radians.

Example

This program prints the hyperbolic tangent of the values −1 through 1, in increments of one tenth:

```
#include "math.h"
#include "stdio.h"

void main(void)
{
  double val=-1.0;

  do {
    printf("Hyperbolic tangent of %f is %f\n", val, tanh(val));
    val += 0.1;
  } while(val<=1.0);
}
```

Related Functions

acos( ), asin( ), atan( ), atan2( ), cos( ), cosh( ), sin( ), sinh( ), tan( )

Time, Date, and Other
System-Related Functions

This chapter covers functions that are more sensitive to the operating system than others. The functions defined by the ANSI C standard include the time and date functions as well as **setlocale( )**. These functions use the operating system's time and date information or, in the case of **setlocale( )**, its geographic information.

This chapter also discusses a category of functions that allow direct operating-system interfacing. None of these functions are defined by the ANSI C standard because each operating environment is different. This chapter uses DOS because it is the most widely used operating system. However, even C compilers that operate under DOS may have slightly different approaches to the interfacing functions. This chapter uses the most generalizable functions defined by Microsoft's version 5.1 DOS C compiler and assumes that you know how DOS system calls are accessed. But you should be able to generalize to the functions provided by your own compiler. (Operating system interfacing and use of system resources is discussed in detail later in this guide.) The DOS interface functions call the related DOS function directly, bypassing any standard C function.

This chapter also discusses functions defined by Microsoft C that interface with the ROM-BIOS of the PC. The BIOS provides the lowest level support for the computer's various hardware devices and is the base upon which DOS is built. The BIOS functions are not defined by the ANSI standard but are a representative sample of the type of functions provided with most DOS and PC-based C compilers. The ones shown here are compatible with Microsoft C 5.1.

The ANSI C standard defines several functions that handle the date and time of the system as well as elapsed time. These functions require the header file TIME.H. This header defines three types: **clock _ t**,

time _ t, and **tm**. The types **clock _ t** and **time _ t** can represent the system time and date as a long integer. The ANSI C standard refers to this as *calendar time*. The structure type **tm** holds the date and time broken down into their elements. The **tm** structure is defined as shown here:

```
struct tm {
  int tm_sec;  /* seconds, 0-59 */
  int tm_min;  /* minutes, 0-59 */
  int tm_hour; /* hours, 0-23 */
  int tm_mday; /* day of the month, 1-31 */
  int tm_mon;  /* months since Jan, 0-11 */
  int tm_year; /* years from 1900 */
  int tm_wday; /* days since Sunday, 0-6 */
  int tm_yday; /* days since Jan 1, 0-365 */
  int tm_isdst /* Daylight Savings Time indicator */
}
```

The value of **tm _ isdst** is positive if daylight savings time is in effect, zero if it is not in effect, and negative if no information is available. The ANSI C standard refers to this form of the time and date as *broken-down time*.

In addition, TIME.H defines the macro **CLK _ TCK**, which is the number of system clock ticks per second.

The **setlocale( )** function requires the header file LOCALE.H.

The DOS interfacing functions defined by Microsoft C require the header DOS.H. This defines a union that corresponds to the registers of the 8086 family of CPUs and is used by some of the system-interfacing functions. This union is defined as the union of two structures to allow each register to be accessed either by word or byte. The structures and union are shown here, as defined by Microsoft:

```
/*   Copyright (c) 1985-1988, Microsoft Corporation.
     All rights reserved.
*/

/* word registers */

struct WORDREGS {
    unsigned int ax;
    unsigned int bx;
    unsigned int cx;
    unsigned int dx;
    unsigned int si;
    unsigned int di;
    unsigned int cflag;
    };
```

```
/* byte registers */

struct BYTEREGS {
    unsigned char al, ah;
    unsigned char bl, bh;
    unsigned char cl, ch;
    unsigned char dl, dh;
    };

/* general purpose registers union -
   overlays the corresponding word and byte registers.
 */

union REGS {
    struct WORDREGS x;
    struct BYTEREGS h;
    };
```

DOS.H also defines the structure type **SREGS**, which some functions use to set the segment registers. This structure is defined by Microsoft as:

```
/*   Copyright (c) 1985-1988, Microsoft Corporation.
     All rights reserved.
 */

/* segment registers */

struct SREGS {
    unsigned int es;
    unsigned int cs;
    unsigned int ss;
    unsigned int ds;
    };
```

The BIOS interface functions require the header file BIOS.H.

Several functions described in this chapter assign the built-in global integer variable **errno** an error-code value when an error occurs. Consult your user's manual for details.

#include "time.h"
char *asctime(struct tm *ptr);

Description

The **asctime( )** function returns a pointer to a string that converts the information stored in the structure pointed to by *ptr* into the following form.

day month date hours:minutes:seconds year\n\0

For example:

Wed Jun 19 12:05:34 1999

The structure pointer passed to **asctime( )** is generally obtained from either **localtime( )** or **gmtime( )**.

The buffer used by **asctime( )** to hold the formatted output string is a statically allocated character array and is overwritten each time the function is called. To save the contents of the string, you need to copy it elsewhere.

Example

This program displays the local time defined by the system:

```
#include "time.h"
#include "stdio.h"

void main(void)
{
  struct tm *ptr;
  time_t lt;

  lt = time(NULL);
  ptr = localtime(&lt);
  printf(asctime(ptr));
}
```

Related Functions

ctime( ), gmtime( ), localtime( ), time( )

#include "dos.h"
int bdos(int fnum, unsigned dx, unsigned al);

Description

The **bdos( )** function is not defined by the ANSI C standard and only applies to DOS-based C compilers. It may also have a slightly different name, so check your user's manual.

The **bdos( )** function accesses the DOS system call specified by *fnum*. It first places the values *dx* into the **DX** register and *al* into the **AL** register and then executes an INT 21H instruction.

The **bdos( )** function returns the value of the **AX** register, which is used by DOS to return information.

The **bdos( )** function can only be used to access system calls that either take no argument or require only **DX** and/or **AL** as their arguments.

Example

This program reads characters directly from the keyboard, bypassing all of C's I/O functions, until the user presses ENTER:

```
/* do raw keyboard reads */
#include "dos.h"

void main(void)
{
  while((255 & bdos(1, 0, 0))!='\r') ;
}
```

Related Functions

intdos( ), intdosx( )

#include "bios.h"
int _bios_disk(unsigned cmd, struct diskinfo_t *info);

Description

The **_bios_disk( )** function is not defined by the ANSI C standard and only applies to DOS-based C compilers. It may also have a slightly different name, so check your user's manual.

The **_bios_disk( )** function performs BIOS-level disk operations using interrupt 0x13. These operations ignore the logical structure of the disk, including files. All operations take place on sectors.

Microsoft defines the **diskinfo_t** structure as follows.

```
struct diskinfo_t {
   unsigned drive;
   unsigned head;
   unsigned track;
   unsigned sector;
   unsigned nsectors;
   void far *buffer;
};
```

The drive affected is specified in **drive**, with 0 corresponding to A, 1 to B, and so on for floppy drives. The first fixed disk is drive 0x80, the second 0x81, and so forth. The part of the disk operated upon is specified in **head**, **track**, and **sector**. The **nsectors** field specifies the number of sectors to read or write and **buffer** points to a buffer that holds information written to or read from the disk. Refer to the IBM PC *Technical Reference Manual* for details on the operation and options of the BIOS-level disk routines. Remember, direct control of the disk requires thorough and intimate knowledge of the hardware and DOS. It is best avoided except in unusual situations.

Related Functions

fread( ), **fwrite( )**

#include "bios.h"
unsigned _bios_equiplist(void);

Description

The **_bios_equiplist( )** function is not defined by the ANSI C standard and only applies to DOS-based C compilers. It may also have a slightly different name, so check your user's manual.

The **_bios_equiplist( )** function returns a value that specifies what equipment is in the computer. This value is encoded as shown here:

Bit	Equipment
0	Must boot from the floppy drive
1	80x87 math coprocessor installed

2, 3   Motherboard RAM size

           0 0: 16k

           0 1: 32k

           1 0: 48k

           1 1: 64k

4, 5   Initial video mode

           0 0: unused

           0 1: 40x25 BW, color adapter

           1 0: 80x25 BW, color adapter

           1 1: 80x25, monochrome adapter

6, 7   Number of floppy drives

           0 0: one

           0 1: two

           1 0: three

           1 1: four

8   DMA chip installed

9, 10, 11   Number of serial ports

           0 0 0: zero

           0 0 1: one

           0 1 0: two

           0 1 1: three

           1 0 0: four

           1 0 1: five

           1 1 0: six

           1 1 1: seven

12   Game adapter installed

13   Serial printer installed (PC*jr* only)

14, 15   Number of printers

           0 0: zero

           0 1: one

           1 0: two

           1 1: three

Example

This program displays the number of floppy drives installed in the computer:

```
#include "bios.h"
#include "stdio.h"

void main(void)
{
  unsigned eq;

  eq = _bios_equiplist();

  eq >>= 6; /* shift bits 6 and 7 into lowest position */

  printf("number of disk drives: %d", (eq & 3) + 1);
}
```

Related Function

_bios_serialcom( )

#include "bios.h"
int _bios_keybrd(unsigned cmd);

Description

The _bios_keybrd( ) function is not defined by the ANSI C standard and only applies to DOS-based C compilers. It may have a slightly different name, so check your user's manual.

The _bios_keybrd( ) function performs direct keyboard operations. The value of *cmd* determines what operation is executed.

If *cmd* is zero, _bios_keybrd( ) returns the next key pressed. (It waits until a key is pressed.) It returns a 16-bit quantity that consists of two different values. The low-order byte contains the ASCII character code if a normal key is pressed and contains zero if a special key is pressed. Special keys include the arrow keys and the function keys. The high-order byte contains the scan code of the key, which corresponds loosely to the key's position on the keyboard.

If *cmd* is 1, _bios_keybrd( ) checks to see if a key has been pressed. It returns nonzero if a key has been pressed; otherwise, it returns zero.

When *cmd* is 2, the shift status is returned. The status of the various keys that shift a state are encoded into the low-order part of the return value as shown here:

Bit	Meaning
0	Right SHIFT pressed
1	Left SHIFT pressed
3	CTRL key pressed
4	ALT pressed
5	SCROLL LOCK ON
6	NUM LOCK ON
7	CAPS LOCK ON
8	INSERT ON

Example

This code fragment generates random numbers until a key is pressed. It allows you to start **rand( )**, the random number generator, from a random point.

```
while(!_bios_keybrd(1)) rand();
```

Related Functions

getche( ), kbhit( )

#include "bios.h"
unsigned _bios_memsize(void);

Description

The **_bios_memsize( )** function is not defined by the ANSI C standard and only applies to DOS-based C compilers. It may also have a slightly different name, so check your user's manual.

The _bios_memsize( ) function returns the amount of memory (in units of 1K) installed in the system.

Example

This program reports the amount of memory in the system:

```
#include "bios.h"
#include "stdio.h"

void main(void)
{
  printf("%uK bytes of ram", _bios_memsize());
}
```

Related Function

_bios_equiplist( )

#include "bios.h"
int _bios_printer(unsigned cmd, unsigned port,
unsigned data);

Description

The _bios_printer( ) function is not defined by the ANSI C standard and only applies to DOS-based C compilers. It may also have a slightly different name, so check your user's manual.

The _bios_printer( ) function controls the printer port specified in *port*. If *port* is zero, LPT1 is used; if *port* is 1, LPT2 is accessed. The exact function performed is contingent upon the value of *cmd*. The legal values for *cmd* are shown here:

Value	Meaning
0	Print the data
1	Initialize the printer port
2	Return the status of the port

The printer port status is encoded into the low-order byte of the return value, as shown here:

Bit	Meaning
0	Time-out error
1	Unused
2	Unused
3	I/O error
4	Printer selected
5	Out-of-paper error
6	Acknowledge
7	Print NOT busy

Example

This fragment prints the string **hello** on the printer connected to LPT1:

```
char p[]="hello";

while(*p) _bios_printer(0, 0, *p++);
```

Related Function

_bios_serialcom( )

#include "bios.h"
int _bios_serialcom(unsigned cmd, unsigned port, unsigned data);

Description

The **_bios_serialcom( )** function is not defined by the ANSI C standard and only applies to DOS-based C compilers. It may also have a slightly different name, so check your user's manual.

The _bios_serialcom( ) function manipulates the RS232 asynchronous communication port specified in *port*. Its operation is determined by the value of *cmd*, whose values are shown here:

cmd	Meaning
0	Initialize the port
1	Send a character
2	Receive a character
3	Return the port status

For access to COM1, *port* must be zero. For access to COM2, *port* must be 1.

Before using the serial port, you will probably want to initialize it to something other than its default setting. To do this, call _bios_serialcom( ) with *cmd* set equal to zero. The way the port is set up is determined by the value of the low-order byte of *data*, which is encoded with initialization parameters, as shown here:

```
bit numbers:   7 6 5   4 3   2   1 0
baud  _____|    |    |   |
parity  _____|    |   |
stop-bits  _____|   |
data-bits  _____|
```

The baud is encoded as shown here:

Baud	Bit Pattern
9600	1 1 1
4800	1 1 0
2400	1 0 1
1200	1 0 0
600	0 1 1
300	0 1 0

150	0	0	1
110	0	0	0

The parity bits are encoded as shown here:

Parity	Bit Pattern
No parity	0 0 or 1 0
Odd	0 1
Even	1 1

The number of stop bits is determined by bit 2 of the serial port initialization byte. If it is 1, two stop bits are used; otherwise, one stop bit is used. Finally, the number of data bits is set by the code in bits 1 and 0 of the initialization byte. Of the four possible bit patterns, only two are valid. If bits 1 and 0 contain the pattern 1 0, seven data-bits are used. If they contain 1 1, eight data-bits are used.

For example, if you want to set the port to 9600 baud, even parity, one stop-bit, and eight data-bits, you would use this bit pattern:

```
           1  1  1   1  1   0   1 1
baud _____|      |    |   |
parity _____|      |   |
stop-bits _____|     |
data-bits _____|
```

In decimal, this works out to 251.

The return value of **_bios_serialcom( )** is always a 16-bit quantity. The high-order byte contains the status bits, which have these values:

Meaning When Set	Bit
Data ready	0
Overrun error	1
Parity error	2
Framing error	3
Break-detect error	4

Transfer holding register empty	5
Transfer shift register empty	6
Time-out error	7

If *cmd* is set to 0, 1, or 3, the low-order byte is encoded as shown here:

Meaning When Set	Bit
Change in clear-to-send	0
Change in data-set-ready	1
Trailing-edge ring detector	2
Change in line signal	3
Clear-to-send	4
Data-set-ready	5
Ring indicator	6
Line signal detected	7

When *cmd* has a value of 2, the lower-order byte contains the value received by the port.

Example

This initializes port 0 to 9600 baud, even parity, one stop-bit, and eight data-bits:

```
_bios_serialcom(0, 0, 251);
```

Related Function

bioskey( )

#include "bios.h"
unsigned _bios_timeofday(int cmd, long *newtime);

Description

The _bios_timeofday( ) function is not defined by the ANSI C standard and only applies to DOS-based C compilers. It may also have a slightly different name, so check your user's manual.

The **_bios_timeofday( )** function reads or sets the system clock. The system clock ticks at a rate of about 18.2 ticks per second. Its value is zero at midnight and increases until reset at midnight again or manually set to some value. If *cmd* is zero, **_bios_timeofday( )** returns the current value of the timer. If *cmd* is 1, the timer is set to the value of *newtime*.

Example

This program prints the current value of the timer:

```
#include "bios.h"
#include "stdio.h"

void main(void)
{
  long t;

  _bios_timeofday(0, &t);
  printf("timer value is %ld", t);
}
```

Related Functions

ctime( ), time( )

#include "time.h"
clock_t clock(void);

Description

The **clock( )** function returns a value that approximates the amount of time the calling program has been running. To transform this value into seconds, divide it by **CLK_TCK**. A value of −1 is returned if the time is not available.

Example

The following function displays the current execution time, in seconds, for the program calling it.

```
void elapsed_time(void)
{
  printf("elapsed time: %u secs.\n", clock());
}
```

Related Functions

asctime( ), ctime( ), time( )

#include ''time.h''
char *ctime(const time _ t *time);

Description

Given a pointer to the calendar time, the **ctime**( ) function returns a pointer to a string of the form

day month year hours:minutes:seconds year\n\0

The calendar time is generally obtained through a call to **time**( ).

The buffer used by **ctime**( ) to hold the formatted output string is a statically allocated character array and is overwritten each time the function is called. To save the contents of the string, you need to copy it elsewhere.

Example

This program displays the local time defined by the system:

```
#include "time.h"
#include "stdio.h"

void main(void)
{
  time_t lt;

  lt = time(NULL);
  printf(ctime(&lt));
}
```

Related Functions

asctime( ), gmtime( ), localtime( ), time( )

#include "time.h"
double difftime(time_t time2, time_t time1);

Description

The **difftime( )** function returns the difference, in seconds, between *time1* and *time2*. That is, it returns *time2* − *time1*.

Example

This program times the number of seconds that it takes for the empty **for** loop to go from 0 to 500,000:

```
#include "time.h"
#include "stdio.h"

void main(void)
{
  time_t start,end;
  long unsigned t;

  start = time(NULL);
  for(t=0; t<500000; t++) ;
  end = time(NULL);
  printf("loop used %f seconds\n", difftime(end, start));
}
```

Related Functions

asctime( ), gmtime( ), localtime( ), time( )

#include "dos.h"
void _disable(void);

Description

The **_disable( )** function is not defined by the ANSI C standard and only applies to DOS-based C compilers. It may also have a slightly different name, so check your user's manual.

The **_disable( )** function disables interrupts. The only interrupt that it allows is the NMI (nonmaskable interrupt). Use this function with care because many devices in the system use interrupts.

Related Function

_enable( )

#include "dos.h"
unsigned _dos_allocmem(unsigned size, unsigned *seg);

Description

The **_dos_allocmem( )** function is not defined by the ANSI C standard and only applies to DOS-based C compilers. It may also have a slightly different name, so check your user's manual.

The **_dos_allocmem( )** function allocates a paragraph aligned block of memory. It puts the segment address of the block into the unsigned integer pointed to by *seg*. The *size* argument specifies the number of paragraphs to be allocated (a paragraph is 16 bytes).

If the requested memory can be allocated, a zero is returned. If insufficient free memory exists, no assignment is made to the unsigned integer pointed to by *seg* and it returns nonzero. On error, **errno** is also set to **ENOMEM** (insufficient memory).

Example

This code fragment allocates 100 paragraphs of memory:

```
unsigned i;

i = 0;

if((i = _dos_allocmem(100, &i)==0)
   printf("allocate successful");
else
  printf("allocation failed\n");
```

Related Functions

_dos_freemem( ), _dos_setblock( )

#include ''dos.h''
unsigned _dos_close(int fd);

Description

The _dos_close( ) function is not defined by the ANSI C standard and only applies to DOS-based C compilers. It may also have a slightly different name, so check your user's manual.

The _dos_close( ) function closes the file specified by the file descriptor *fd*. It is functionally equivalent to the UNIX-like **close( )** function. Remember, file descriptors are used by the UNIX-like file system and do not relate to the ANSI C file system. The function returns zero if successful. Otherwise, it returns nonzero and sets **errno** to **EBADF** (bad file descriptor).

Example

This fragment closes the file associated with the file descriptor **fd**.

```
_dos_close(fd);
```

Related Functions

_dos_creat( ), _dos_open( )

#include ''dos.h''
unsigned _dos_creat(char *fname, unsigned attr, int *fd);
unsigned _dos_creatnew(char *fname, unsigned attr,
int *fd);

Description

The _dos_creat( ) and _dos_creatnew( ) functions are not defined by the ANSI C standard and only apply to DOS-based C compilers. They may have slightly different names, so check your user's manual.

The **_dos_creat( )** function creates a file by the name pointed to by *fname* with the attributes specified by *attr*. It returns a file descriptor to the file in the integer pointed to by *fd*. (File descriptors are used by the UNIX-like file system, not the ANSI C file system.) If the file already exists, it is erased. The **_dos_creatnew( )** function is the same as **_dos_creat( )**, but if the file already exists, it is not erased and **_dos_creatnew( )** returns an error.

The valid values for *attr* are shown here (the macros are defined in DOS.H):

Macro	Meaning
_A_NORMAL	Normal file
_A_RDONLY	Read-only file
_A_HIDDEN	Hidden file
_A_SYSTEM	System file
_A_VOLID	Volume label
_A_SUBDIR	Subdirectory
_A_ARCH	Archive byte set

Both functions return zero if successful and nonzero on failure. On failure, **errno** contains one of these values: **ENOENT** (file not found), **EMFILE** (too many open files), **EACCES** (access denied), or **EEXIST** (file already exists).

The **_dos_creat( )** and **_dos_creatnew( )** functions are similar to the UNIX-like **creat( )** function.

Example

This fragment opens a file called TEST.TST for output:

```
int fd;

if(_dos_creat("test.tst", _A_NORMAL, &fd))
  printf("cannot open file");
```

Related Function

_dos_open( )

#include ''dos.h''
int dosexterr(struct DOSERROR *err);

The **dosexterr( )** function is not defined by the ANSI C standard and only applies to DOS-based C compilers. It may also have a slightly different name, so check your user's manual.

The **dosexterr( )** function fills the structure pointed to by *err* with extended error information when a DOS call fails. The **DOSERROR** structure is defined like this:

```
struct DOSERROR {
    int exterror; /* error code */
    char class;   /* class of error */
    char action;  /* suggested action */
    char locus;   /* location of error */
};
```

For the proper interpretation of the information returned by DOS, refer to a DOS technical reference.

Related Function

ferror( )

#include ''dos.h''
int _dos_findfirst(char *fname, unsigned attr, struct
find_t *ptr);
int _dos_findnext(struct find_t *ptr);

Description

The **_dos_findfirst( )** and **_dos_findnext( )** functions are not defined by the ANSI C standard and only apply to DOS-based C compilers. They may also have slightly different names, so check your user's manual.

The **_dos_findfirst( )** function searches for the first file name that matches the one pointed to by *fname*. The file name may include both a drive specifier and a path name. Also, the file name may include the wildcard characters * and ?. If a match is found, the structure pointed to by *ptr* is filled with information about the file.

Microsoft defines the **find_t** structure as follows:

```
struct find_t {
  char reserved[21];/* used by DOS */
  char attrib;       /* attribute of file */
  unsigned wr_time; /* last time file was written to */
  unsigned wr_date; /* last date file was written to */
  long size;         /* size in bytes */
  char name[13];     /* filename */
};
```

The *attrib* parameter determines what type of files are found by **_dos_findfirst**. *attrib* can be one or more of the following macros (defined in DOS.H):

Macro	Meaning
_A_NORMAL	Normal file
_A_RDONLY	Read-only file
_A_HIDDEN	Hidden file
_A_SYSTEM	System file
_A_VOLID	Volume label
_A_SUBDIR	Subdirectory
_A_ARCH	Archive byte set

The **_dos_findnext( )** function continues a search started by **_dos_findfirst( )**. The buffer pointed to by *ptr* must be the one used in the call to **_dos_findfirst( )**.

Both the **_dos_findfirst( )** and **_dos_findnext( )** functions return zero on success and nonzero on failure or when no more matches are found. On failure, **errno** is set to **ENOENT** (file name not found).

Example

This program displays all files that have .C extension and their sizes in the current working directory:

```
#include "dos.h"
#include "stdio.h"

void main(void)
{
  struct find_t f;
  register int done;

  done = _dos_findfirst("*.c", _A_NORMAL, &f);
  while(!done) {
    printf("%s %ld\n", f.name, f.size);
    done = _dos_findnext(&f);
  }
}
```

#include ''dos.h''
unsigned _dos_freemem(unsigned seg);

Description

The _ **dos** _ **freemem**( ) function is not defined by the ANSI C standard and only applies to DOS-based C compilers. It may also have a slightly different name, so check your user's manual.

The _ **dos** _ **freemem**( ) function frees the block of memory whose segment is in *seg*. This memory must have been previously allocated using _ **dos** _ **allocmem**( ). The function returns zero on success; upon failure, it returns nonzero and sets **errno** to **ENOMEM** (insufficient memory).

Example

This code fragment illustrates how to allocate and free memory using _ **dos** _ **allocmem**( ) and _ **dos** _ **freemem**( ):

```
unsigned i;

if(_dos_allocmem(some, &i)!=0)
  printf("allocation error");
else
  _dos_freemem(i);
```

Related Functions

_ **dos** _ **allocmem**( ), _ **dos** _ **setblock**( )

#include "dos.h"
void _dos_getdate(struct dosdate_t *d);
void _dos_gettime(struct dostime_t *t);

Description

The _dos_getdate( ) and _dos_gettime( ) functions are not defined by the ANSI C standard and only apply to DOS-based C compilers. They may also have slightly different names, so check your user's manual.

The _dos_getdate( ) function fills the structure pointed to by *d* with the DOS form of the current system date. The _dos_gettime( ) function fills the structure pointed to by *t* with the DOS form of the current system time.

Microsoft defines the **dosdate_t** structure as follows:

```
struct dosdate_t {
  unsigned char day;
  unsigned char month;
  unsigned int year;
  unsigned char dayofweek;   /* Sunday is 0 */
};
```

Microsoft defines the **dostime_t** structure as shown here:

```
struct dostime_t {
  unsigned char hour;
  unsigned char minute;
  unsigned char second;
  unsigned char hsecond; /* hundredths of second */
};
```

Example

This program displays the date and time using DOS system calls:

```
#include "dos.h"
#include "stdio.h"

void main(void)
{
  struct dostime_t t;
  struct dosdate_t d;
```

```
    _dos_getdate(&d);
    _dos_gettime(&t);

    printf("date: %d/%d/%d\n", d.day, d.month, d.year);
    printf("time: %d:%d:%d\n", t.hour, t.minute,
            t.second);
}
```

Related Functions

_ dos _ setdate( ), _ dos _ settime( )

#include "dos.h"
void _ dos _ getdiskfree(unsigned drive, struct diskfree _ t *dfptr);

Description

The _ dos _ getdiskfree( ) function is not defined by the ANSI C standard and only applies to DOS-based C compilers. It may also have a slightly different name, so check your user's manual.

The _ dos _ getdiskfree( ) function returns the amount of free disk space in the structure pointed to by *dfptr* for the drive specified by *drive*. The drives are numbered from 1 beginning with A. You can specify the default drive by calling **dfree( )** with a value of zero. The **diskfree _ t** structure is defined by Microsoft as follows:

```
struct diskfree_t {
  unsigned total_clusters;
  unsigned avail_clusters;
  unsigned sectors_per_cluster;
  unsigned bytes_per_sector;
};
```

Example

The following program prints the number of free clusters available for use on drive C.

```
#include "dos.h"
#include "stdio.h"

void main(void)
{
  struct diskfree_t p;

  _dos_getdiskfree(3, &p); /* drive C */

  printf("Number of free clusters is %d.",
        p.avail_clusters);
}
```

Related Function

_dos_getftime( )

#include "dos.h"
void _dos_getdrive(unsigned *drive);

Description

The _dos_getdrive( ) function is not defined by the ANSI C standard and only applies to DOS-based C compilers. It may also have a slightly different name, so check your user's manual.

The _dos_getdrive( ) function returns the number of the current disk drive of the system in the integer pointed to by *drive*. Drive A is encoded as 1, drive B as 2, and so on.

Example

This code fragment displays the current disk drive:

```
unsigned d;

_dos_getdrive(&d);
printf("drive is %c", d+'A');
```

Related Function

_dos_setdrive( )

#include "dos.h"
unsigned _dos_getfileattr(char *fname, unsigned *attrib);

Description

The **_dos_getfileattr( )** function is not defined by the ANSI C standard and only applies to DOS-based C compilers. It may also have a slightly different name, so check your user's manual.

The **_dos_getfileattr( )** function returns the attribute of the file specified by *fname* in the unsigned integer pointed to by *attrib*, which may be one of the following values (the macros are defined by Microsoft in DOS.H.):

Macro	Meaning
_A_NORMAL	Normal file
_A_RDONLY	Read-only file
_A_HIDDEN	Hidden file
_A_SYSTEM	System file
_A_VOLID	Volume label
_A_SUBDIR	Subdirectory
_A_ARCH	Archive byte set

The **_dos_getfileattr( )** function returns zero if successful; nonzero otherwise. If failure occurs, **errno** is set to **ENOENT** (invalid file).

Example

This code fragment determines if the file TEST.TST is a normal file:

```
unsigned attr;

if(_dos_getfileattr("test.tst", &attr))
  printf("file error");

if(attr & _A_NORMAL) printf("file is normal");
```

Related Function

_dos_setfileattr( )

#include "dos.h"
unsigned _dos_getftime(int fd, unsigned *fdate,unsigned *ftime);

Description

The **_dos_getftime( )** function is not defined by the ANSI C standard and only applies to DOS-based C compilers. It may also have a slightly different name, so check your user's manual.

The function **_dos_getftime( )** returns the time and date of creation for the file associated with file descriptor *fd* in the integers pointed to by *ftime* and *fdate*.

The bits in the object pointed to by *ftime* are encoded as shown here:

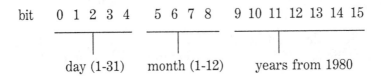

bit	0 1 2 3 4	5 6 7 8 9 10	11 12 13 14 15
	seconds/2 (0-29)	minutes (0-59)	hours (0-23)

The bits in the object pointed to by *fdate* are encoded like this:

bit	0 1 2 3 4	5 6 7 8	9 10 11 12 13 14 15
	day (1-31)	month (1-12)	years from 1980

As indicated, the year is represented as the number of years from 1980. Therefore, if the year is 2000, the value of bits 9 through 15 will be 20.

The **_dos_getftime( )** function returns zero if successful. If an error occurs, it returns nonzero and sets **errno** to **EBADF** (bad file number).

Remember that files associated with file descriptors use the UNIX-like I/O system, which is not defined by or related to the ANSI C file system.

Example

This program prints the year that the file TEST.TST was created:

```
#include "io.h"
#include "dos.h"
#include "fcntl.h"
#include "stdio.h"
#include "stdlib.h"

void main(void)
{
  struct {
    unsigned day: 5;
    unsigned month: 4;
    unsigned year: 7;
  } d;

  unsigned t;
  int fd;

  if((fd=open("TEST.TST", O_RDONLY))==-1) {
    printf("cannot open file");
    exit(1);
  }

  _dos_getftime(fd, (unsigned *) &d, &t);

  printf("date of creation: %u", d.year+1980);
}
```

Related Function

_dos_setftime( )

#include "dos.h"
void (interrupt far * _dos_getvect(unsigned intr))(void);

Description

The _dos_getvect( ) function is not defined by the ANSI C standard and only applies to DOS-based C compilers. It may also have a slightly different name, so check your user's manual.

The _dos_getvect( ) function returns the address of the interrupt service routine associated with the interrupt specified in *intr*. This value is returned as a **far** pointer.

Example

The following code fragment returns the address of the print screen function (which is associated with interrupt 5).

```
void (interrupt far *p)(void);

p = _dos_getvect(5);
```

Related Function

setvect( )

#include "dos.h"
void _dos_keep(unsigned status, unsigned size);

Description

The _dos_keep( ) function is not defined by the ANSI C standard and only applies to DOS-based C compilers. It may also have a slightly different name, so check your user's manual.

The _dos_keep( ) function executes an interrupt 0x31, which causes the current program to terminate but stay resident. The value of *status* is returned to DOS as a return code. The size of the program that is to stay resident is specified in *size*. The rest of the memory is freed for use by DOS.

Because terminate and stay resident programs are quite complex, there is no example here. However, my book, *Born to Code in C* (Berkeley, Calif.: Osborne/McGraw-Hill, 1989), covers this important topic in depth.

#include "dos.h"
unsigned _dos_open(char *fname, unsigned mode, int *fd);

Description

The _dos_open( ) function is not defined by the ANSI C standard and only applies to DOS-based C compilers. It may also have a slightly different name, so check your user's manual.

The _dos_open( ) function opens the file whose name is pointed to by *fname* in the mode specified by *mode* and returns a file descriptor to the file in the integer pointed to by *fd*. Remember, file descriptors are used by the UNIX-like file system and do not relate to the ANSI C file system.

The most common values for *mode* are

Value	Meaning
O_RDONLY	Read-only
O_WRONLY	Write-only
O_RDWR	Read/write

These macros are defined in DOS.H.

The _dos_open( ) function returns zero if successful and nonzero on failure. If an error occurs, **errno** is set to either **EINVAL** (access mode invalid) or **ENOENT** (file not found).

Example

The following code fragment opens a file called TEST.TST for read-/write operations:

```
int fd;

if(_dos_open("test.tst", O_RDWR, &fd))
    printf("error opening file");
```

Related Functions

_dos_close( ), _dos_creat( ), _dos_creatnew( )

#include "dos.h"
int _dos_read(int fd, void *buf, unsigned count, unsigned *numread);

Description

The _dos_read( ) function is not defined by the ANSI C standard and only applies to DOS-based C compilers. It may also have a slightly different name, so check your user's manual.

The **_dos_read( )** function reads up to *count* bytes from the file specified by the file descriptor *fd* into the buffer pointed to by *buf*. The number of bytes actually read is returned in *numread*.

Upon success, **_dos_read( )** returns zero; it returns nonzero on failure. The return value is determined by DOS. You will need DOS technical documentation to determine the nature of any errors that occur.

Example

This fragment reads up to 128 characters from the file described by **fd**:

```
unsigned count
char *buf[128];

if(_dos_read(fd, buf, 128, &count))
  printf("error reading file");
```

Related Function

_dos_write( )

#include "dos.h"
unsigned _dos_setblock(unsigned size,
unsigned seg, unsigned *max);

Description

The **_dos_setblock( )** function is not defined by the ANSI C standard and only applies to DOS-based C compilers. It may also have a slightly different name, so check your user's manual.

The **_dos_setblock( )** function changes the size of the block of memory whose segment address is *seg*. The new *size* is specified in paragraphs (16 bytes). The block of memory must have been previously allocated with **_dos_allocmem( )**.

If the size adjustment cannot be made, **_dos_setblock( )** returns the largest block (in paragraphs) that can be allocated in the object pointed to by *max*.

On success, **_dos_setblock( )** returns zero; on failure, it returns nonzero and sets **errno** to **ENOMEM** (insufficient memory).

Example

This code fragment attempts to resize to 100 paragraphs the block of memory whose segment address is in **seg**:

```
unsigned max;

if(_dos_setblock(seg, 100, &max)!=0)
    printf("resize error, largest block is %u", max);
```

Related Functions

_dos_allocmem( ), **_dos_freemem( )**

#include "dos.h"
void _dos_setdate(struct dosdate_t *d);
void _dos_settime(struct dostime_t *t);

Description

The **_dos_setdate( )** and **_dos_settime( )** functions are not defined by the ANSI C standard and only apply to DOS-based C compilers. They may also have slightly different names, so check your user's manual.

The **_dos_setdate( )** function sets the DOS system date as specified in the structure pointed to by *d*. The **_dos_settime( )** function sets the DOS system time as specified in the structure pointed to by *t*.

Microsoft defines the **dosdate_t** structure in the following listing.

```
struct dosdate_t {
  unsigned char day;
  unsigned char month;
  unsigned int year;
  unsigned char dayofweek;   /* Sunday is 0 */
};
```

Microsoft defines the **dostime_t** structure as shown here:

```
struct dostime_t {
  unsigned char hour;
  unsigned char minute;
  unsigned char second;
  unsigned char hsecond; /* hundredths of second */
};
```

Example

This code sets the system time to 10:10:10.0:

```
struct dostime_t t;

t.hour = 10;
t.minute  = 10;
t.second  = 10;
t.hsecond = 0;

_dos_settime(&t);
```

Related Functions

_dos_getdate( ), _dos_gettime( )

#include "dos.h"
void _dos_setdrive(unsigned drive, unsigned *num);

The _dos_setdrive( ) function is not defined by the ANSI C standard and only applies to DOS-based C compilers. It may also have a slightly different name, so check your user's manual.

The _dos_setdrive( ) function changes the current disk drive to the one specified by *drive*. Drive A corresponds to 1, drive B to 2, and so on. The number of drives in the system is returned in the integer pointed to by *num*.

Example

This fragment makes drive B the current drive:

```
unsigned num;

_dos_setdrive(2, &num);
```

Related Function

$-$ dos $-$ getdrive( )

#include "dos.h"
unsigned $-$ dos $-$ setfileattr(char *fname, unsigned *attrib);

Description

The $-$ dos $-$ setfileattr( ) function is not defined by the ANSI C standard and only applies to DOS-based C compilers. It may also have a slightly different name, so check your user's manual.

The $-$ dos $-$ setfileattr( ) function sets the attribute of the file specified by *fname* to the attribute specified by *attrib*, which must be one of the following values (the macros are defined by Microsoft in DOS.H):

Macro	Meaning
$-$ A $-$ NORMAL	Normal file
$-$ A $-$ RDONLY	Read-only file
$-$ A $-$ HIDDEN	Hidden file
$-$ A $-$ SYSTEM	System file
$-$ A $-$ VOLID	Volume label
$-$ A $-$ SUBDIR	Subdirectory
$-$ A $-$ ARCH	Archive byte set

The $-$ dos $-$ setfileattr( ) function returns zero if successful; nonzero otherwise. If failure occurs, **errno** is set to **ENOENT** (file not found) or **EACCES** (access denied).

Example

The following fragment sets the file TEST.TST to read-only.

```
unsigned attr;

attr = _A_RDONLY;

if(_dos_setfileattr("test.tst", &attr))
  printf("file error");
```

Related Function

_dos_getfileattr( )

#include "dos.h"
unsigned _dos_setftime(int fd, unsigned fdate,
unsigned ftime);

Description

The _dos_setftime( ) function is not defined by the ANSI C standard and only applies to DOS-based C compilers. It may also have a slightly different name, so check your user's manual.

The _dos_setftime( ) function sets the date and time of the file specified by *fd*, which must be a valid file descriptor.

The bits in the object pointed to by *ftime* are encoded as shown here:

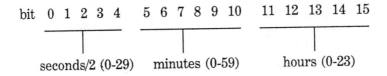

The bits in the object pointed to by *fdate* are encoded like this:

As indicated, the year is represented as the number of years from 1980. Therefore, to set the year to 2000, the value of bits 9 through 15 must be 20.

The **_dos_setftime( )** function returns zero if successful. If an error occurs, it returns nonzero and sets **errno** to **EBADF** (bad file number).

Remember that files associated with file descriptors use the UNIX-like I/O system, which is not defined by or related to the ANSI C file system.

Example

This code changes the year of the file's creation date to 2000:

```
#include "io.h"
#include "dos.h"
#include "fcntl.h"
#include "stdlib.h"

void main(void)
{
  struct {
    unsigned day: 5;
    unsigned month: 4;
    unsigned year: 7;
  } d;

  unsigned t;
  int fd;

  if((fd=open("TEST.TST", O_RDONLY))==-1) {
    printf("cannot open file");
    exit(1);
  }

  _dos_getftime(fd, (unsigned *) &d, &t);
  d.year = 20;

  _dos_setftime(fd, (unsigned *) &d, &t);
}
```

Related Function

_dos_getftime( )

#include ''dos.h''
void _dos_setvect(unsigned intr,
void (interrupt far *isr)( ));

Description

The _dos_setvect( ) function is not defined by the ANSI C standard and only applies to DOS-based C compilers. It may also have a slightly different name, so check your user's manual.

The _dos_setvect( ) function puts the address of the interrupt service routine pointed to by *isr* into the vectored interrupt table at the location specified by *intr*.

Related Function

getvect( )

#include ''dos.h''
int _dos_write(int fd, void *buf, unsigned count,unsigned
*numwritten);

Description

The _dos_write( ) function is not defined by the ANSI C standard and only applies to DOS-based C compilers. It may also have a slightly different name, so check your user's manual.

The _dos_write( ) function writes up to *count* bytes to the file specified by the file descriptor *fd* from the buffer pointed to by *buf*. The number of bytes actually written is returned in *numwritten*.

Upon success, _dos_write( ) returns zero; it returns nonzero on failure. The return value is determined by DOS; you will need DOS technical documentation to determine the nature of any errors that occur.

Example

This fragment writes 128 characters from the file described by **fd**:

```
unsigned count
char *buf[128];
    .
    .
    .
if(_dos_write(fd, buf, 128, &count))
  printf("error writing file");
```

Related Function

_dos_read( )

#include "dos.h"
void _enable(void);

Description

The _enable( ) function is not defined by the ANSI C standard and only applies to DOS-based C compilers. It may also have a slightly different name, so check your user's manual.

The _enable( ) function enables interrupts.

Related Function

_disable( )

#include "dos.h"
unsigned FP_OFF(void far *ptr)
unsigned FP_SEG (void far *ptr);

Description

The **FP_OFF( )** and **FP_SEG( )** macros are not defined by the ANSI C standard and only apply to DOS-based C compilers. They may also have slightly different names, so check your user's manual.

The **FP_OFF( )** macro returns the offset portion of the far pointer **ptr**. The **FP_SEG( )** macro returns the segment of the far pointer **ptr**.

Example

This program prints the segment and offset of the far pointer **ptr**:

```
#include "dos.h"
#include "stdlib.h"
#include "stdio.h"

void main(void)
{
  char far *ptr;

  ptr = (char far *) malloc(100);

  printf("segment:offset of ptr: %u %u", FP_SEG(ptr),
         FP_OFF(ptr));
}
```

#include "time.h"
struct tm *gmtime(time_t *time);

Description

The **gmtime( )** function returns a pointer to the broken-down form of *time* in the form of a **tm** structure. The time is represented in Greenwich mean time. The *time* value is generally obtained through a call to **time( )**.

The structure used by **gmtime( )** to hold the broken-down time is statically allocated and is overwritten each time the function is called. To save the contents of the structure, you need to copy it elsewhere.

Example

This program prints both the local time and the Greenwich mean time of the system:

```
#include "time.h"
#include "stdio.h"
```

```
/* Print local and GM time. */
void main(void)
{
  struct tm *local, *gm;
  time_t t;

  t = time(NULL);
  local = localtime(&t);
  printf("Local time and date: %s", asctime(local));
  gm = gmtime(&t);
  printf("Greenwich mean time and date: %s", asctime(gm));
}
```

Related Functions

asctime(), localtime(), time()

#include "dos.h"
void harderr(void (far *int_handler)( ));
void hardresume(int code);
void hardretn(int code);

Description

The **harderr( )**, **hardresume( )**, and **hardretn( )** functions are not defined by the ANSI C standard and only apply to DOS-based C compilers. They may have slightly different names, so check your user's manual.

The **harderr( )** function allows you to replace DOS's default hardware error handler with one of your own. The function is called with the address of the function that is to become the new error handling routine. It is executed each time an interrupt 0x24 occurs.

The error interrupt handler can exit in one of three ways: First, the **hardresume( )** function causes the handler to exit to DOS, returning the value of *code*. Second, the handler can execute a **return**, which causes an exit to DOS. Third, the handler can return to the program via a call to **hardretn( )**, with a return value of *code*.

Interrupt service functions are complex, so no example is shown. Also, the implementation of these functions varies greatly from compiler to compiler. Refer to your user's manual for details.

```
#include "dos.h"
int int86(int int_num, union REGS *in_regs,
        union REGS *out_regs);
int int86x(int int_num, union REGS *in_regs,
        union REGS *out_regs,
        struct SREGS *sregs);
```

Description

The **int86( )** and **int86x( )** functions are not defined by the ANSI C standard and only apply to DOS-based C compilers. They may also have slightly different names, so check your user's manual.

The **int86( )** function executes a software interrupt specified by *int_num*. The contents of the union *in_regs* is first copied into the register of the processor; then the proper interrupt is executed.

Upon return, the union *out_regs* contains the values of the registers that the CPU has upon return from the interrupt. The value returned by **int86( )** is the value of the **AX** register at the time of the return.

The union **REGS** is defined in the header DOS.H.

The **int86x( )** function is identical to **int86( )**, but you can set the values of the 8086 **ES** and **DS** segment registers by using the *sregs* parameter. Upon return from the call, the contents of the object pointed to by *sregs* contains the values of the current segment registers. The **DS** register is automatically restored to its value prior to the call to **int86x( )**.

Example

The **int86( )** function is often used to call ROM routines in the BIOS. For example, this function executes an INT 10H function code 0, which sets the video mode to the mode specified by the argument **mode**.

```
#include "dos.h"

set_mode(char mode)
{
  union REGS in, out;

  in.h.al = mode;
```

```
    in.h.ah = 0; /* set mode function number */

    int86(0x10, &in, &out);
}
```

Related Functions

bdos( ), intdos( )

#include "dos.h"
int intdos(union REGS *in_regs, union REGS *out_regs);
int intdosx(union REGS *in_regs, union REGS *out_regs,
struct SREGS *segregs);

Description

The **intdos( )** and **intdosx( )** functions are not defined by the ANSI C standard and only apply to DOS-based C compilers. They may also have slightly different names, so check your user's manual.

The **intdos( )** function accesses the DOS system call specified by the contents of the union pointed to by *in_regs*. It executes an INT 21H instruction and the outcome of the operation is placed in the union pointed to by *out_regs*. The **intdos( )** function returns the value of the **AX** register, which is used by DOS to return information. Upon return, an error has occurred if the carry flag is set.

The **intdos( )** function accesses system calls that either require arguments in registers other than **DX** or **AL**, or that return information in a register other than **AX**.

The union **REGS** defines the registers of the 8088/8086 family of processors and is found in the DOS.H header file.

For **intdosx( )**, the value of *segregs* specifies the **DS** and **ES** registers. This function is principally for use in programs compiled with the large data models.

Example

The following program reads the time directly from the system clock, bypassing all of C's time functions.

```
#include "dos.h"
#include "stdio.h"

void main(void)
{
  union REGS in, out;

  in.h.ah = 0x2c;   /* get time function number */
  intdos(&in, &out);
  printf("time is %.2d:%.2d:%.2d", out.h.ch, out.h.cl, out.h.dh);
}
```

Related Functions

bdos( ), int86( )

#include "time.h"
struct tm *localtime(const time_t *time);

Description

The **localtime( )** function returns a pointer to the broken-down form of *time* in the form of a **tm** structure. The time is represented in local time. The *time* value is generally obtained through a call to **time( )**.

The structure used by **localtime( )** to hold the broken-down time is statically allocated and is overwritten each time the function is called. To save the contents of the structure, you need to copy it elsewhere.

Example

This program prints both the local time and the Greenwich mean time of the system:

```
#include "time.h"
#include "stdio.h"

/* print local and Greenwich mean time */
void main(void)
{
  struct tm *local;
  time_t t;

  t = time(NULL);
  local = localtime(&t);
```

```
    printf("Local time and date: %s", asctime(local));
    local = gmtime(&t);
    printf("GMT time and date: %s", gmtime(local));
}
```

Related Functions

asctime( ), gmtime( ), time( )

#include "time.h"
time _ t mktime(struct tm *time);

Description

The **mktime( )** function returns the calendar time equivalent of the broken-down time in the structure pointed to by *time*. This function is primarily used to initialize the system time. The elements **tm _ wday** and **tm _ yday** are set by the function, so they need not be defined at the time of the call.

If **mktime( )** cannot represent the information as a valid calendar time, it returns a −1.

Example

This program tells you what day of the week January 3, 1999 is:

```
#include "time.h"
#include "stdio.h"

void main(void)
{
  struct tm t;
  time_t t_of_day;

  t.tm_year = 1999-1900;
  t.tm_mon = 0;
  t.tm_mday = 3;
  t.tm_hour = 0;   /* hour, min, sec don't matter */
  t.tm_min = 0;    /* as long as they don't cause a */
  t.tm_sec = 1;    /* new day to occur */
  t.tm_isdst = 0;

  t_of_day = mktime(&t);
```

```
  printf(ctime(&t_of_day));
}
```

Related Functions

asctime( ), ctime( ), gmtime( ), time( )

#include "dos.h"
void segread(struct SREGS *sregs);

Description

The **segread( )** function is not defined by the ANSI C standard and only applies to DOS-based C compilers. It may also have a slightly different name, so check your user's manual.

The **segread( )** function copies the current values of the 8086 segment registers into the structure of **SREGS** pointed to by *sregs*.

#include "locale.h"
char *setlocale(int type, const char *locale);

Description

The **setlocale( )** function allows you to query or set certain parameters that are sensitive to the geo-political location where a program is used. For example, in Europe, the comma is used in place of the decimal point.

If *locale* is null, **setlocale( )** returns a pointer to the current localization string. Otherwise, **setlocale( )** attempts to use the specified localization string to set the locale parameters as specified by *type*.

At the time of the call, *type* must be one of the following macros:

```
LC_ALL
LC_COLLATE
LC_CTYPE
LC_MONETARY
LC_NUMERIC
LC_TIME
```

LC_ALL refers to all localization categories. **LC_COLLATE** affects the operation of the **strcoll( )** function. **LC_CTYPE** alters the way the character functions work. **LC_MONETARY** determines the monetary format. **LC_NUMERIC** changes the decimal-point character for formatted input/output functions. Finally, **LC_TIME** determines the behavior of the **strftime( )** function.

The ANSI standard defines two possible strings for *locale*. The first is "C", which specifies a minimal environment for C compilation. The second is " ", the null string, which specifies the implementation-defined default environment. All other values for *locale* are implementation defined and affect portability.

The **setlocale( )** function returns a pointer to a string associated with the *type* parameter.

Example

This program displays the current locale setting:

```
#include "locale.h"
#include "stdio.h"

void main(void)
{
  printf(setlocale(LC_ALL,""));
}
```

Related Functions

strcoll( ), strftime( ), time( )

#include "time.h"
size_t strftime(char *str, size_t maxsize, char const *fmt, const struct tm *time);

Description

The **strftime( )** function places time and date information, along with other information, into the string pointed to by *str*. **strftime( )** uses the format commands found in the string pointed to by *fmt* and the broken-down time *time*. A maximum of *maxsize* characters is placed into *str*.

The **strftime( )** function works a little like **sprintf( )**. It recognizes a set of format commands that begin with the percent sign (%) and places its formatted output into a string. The format commands specify the exact way various time and date information is represented in *str*. Any other characters found in the format string are placed into *str* unchanged. The time and date displayed are in local time. The format commands are shown in Table 15-1. Notice that many of them are case sensitive.

Command	Replaced by
%a	Abbreviated weekday name
%A	Full weekday name
%b	Abbreviated month name
%B	Full month name
%c	Standard date and time string
%d	Day-of-month as decimal (1-31)
%H	Hour, range (0-23)
%I	Hour, range (1-12)
%j	Day-of-year as decimal (1-366)
%m	Month as decimal (1-12)
%M	Minute as decimal (0-59)
%p	Locale's equivalent of AM or PM
%S	Second as decimal (0-59)
%U	Week-of-year, Sunday being first day (0-52)
%w	Weekday as decimal (0-6, Sunday being 0)
%W	Week-of-year, Monday being first day (0-52)
%x	Standard date string
%X	Standard time string
%y	Year in decimal without century (00-99)
%Y	Year including century as decimal
%Z	Timezone name
%%	The percent sign

Table 15-1. The **strftime( )** Format Commands

The **strftime( )** function returns the number of characters placed in the string pointed to by *str*. If an error occurs, the function returns zero.

Example

Assuming that **ltime** points to a structure that contains 10:00:00 AM, Jan 2, 1994, the following fragment prints **It is now 10 AM.**

```
strftime(str, 100, "It is now %H %p", ltime)
printf(str);
```

Related Functions

gmtime( ), **localtime( )**, **time( )**

#include "time.h"
time _ t time(time _ t *time);

Description

The **time( )** function returns the current calendar time of the system. If the system has no time, **time( )** returns −1.

The **time( )** function can be called either with a null pointer or with a pointer to a variable of type **time_t**. If the latter is used, the argument is also assigned the calendar time.

Example

This program displays the local time defined by the system:

```
#include "time.h"
#include "stdio.h"

void main(void)
{
  struct tm *ptr;
  time_t lt;

  lt = time(NULL);
```

```
    ptr = localtime(&lt);
    printf(asctime(ptr));
}
```

Related Functions

ctime( ), gmtime( ), localtime( ), strftime( )

Dynamic Allocation

There are two primary ways in which a C program can store information in the main memory of the computer. The first method involves global and local variables—including arrays and structures. In the case of global and static local variables, the storage is fixed throughout your program's run time. For local variables, storage is allocated from the stack space of the computer. Although these variables are efficiently implemented in C, they require that the programmer know, in advance, the amount of storage needed for every situation.

The second way information can be stored is through C's dynamic allocation system. In this method, storage for information is allocated from free memory as needed. Traditionally, the free memory region lies between your program and its permanent storage area, and the stack. (For the 8086 family of processors, the location of the heap changes depending upon what memory model is used. 8086 memory models are discussed shortly.) Figure 16-1 shows conceptually how a C program would appear in memory. The stack grows downward as it is used, so the amount of memory it needs is determined by how your program is designed. For example, a program with many recursive functions makes much greater demands on stack memory than one that does not have recursive functions because local variables are stored on the stack. The memory required for the program and global data is fixed during program execution. Memory to satisfy an allocation request is taken from the free memory area, starting just above the global variables and growing towards the stack. As you might guess, under fairly extreme cases the stack may run into the heap.

At the core of C's dynamic allocation system are the functions **malloc( )** and **free( )**—part of the standard C library. Each time a **malloc( )** memory request is made, a portion of the remaining free memory is allocated. Each time a **free( )** memory release call is made, memory is returned to the system. The most common way to implement **malloc( )** and **free( )** is to organize the free memory into a linked list.

439

However, the memory management method is implementation dependent.

The ANSI C standard specifies that the prototypes for those dynamic allocation functions defined by the standard are in STDLIB.H.

The ANSI C standard specifies that the dynamic allocation system returns **void** pointers, which are *generic* (they may point to any object). However, some older compilers return a **char** pointer. In this case, you must use an explicit type cast when assigning to pointers of other types.

The ANSI C standard defines only four functions for the dynamic allocation system: **calloc( )**, **malloc( )**, **free( )**, and **realloc( )**. However, this book examines several others that are in wide use—especially in the 8086 family of CPU environments. The basis for the nonstandard functions is Microsoft C version 5.1, but most compilers will have similar functions but the names may differ. The nonstandard functions use the header file MALLOC.H. Some of these additional functions are necessary to support the segmented architecture of the 8086 family of proces-

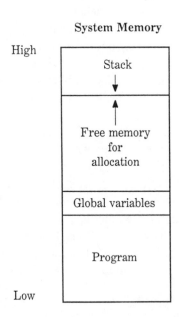

Figure 16-1.   A C program's use of memory

sors efficiently. These functions do not relate to compilers designed for other processors, such as the 68000. Because of the segmented memory of the 8086 family of processors, three new, nonstandard type modifiers are generally supported by compilers built for these processors. They are **near, far,** and **huge**, which are used to create pointers of a type other than that normally used by the memory model used to compile the program. The architecture of the 8086 family of processors allows the direct access of 1 megabyte (or more with the 80286 or 80386) of RAM, but it requires both a segment and an offset address. (If you are not working with an 8086 based computer, you can skip ahead.)

The 8086 family of processors view memory as a collection of 64K chunks, each called a segment. Each byte of memory is defined by its segment address (held in a segment register of the CPU) and its offset (held in another register) within that segment. Both the segment and offset use 16-bit values. When a memory address being accessed lies within the current segment, only the 16-bit offset need be loaded to access a specific byte of memory. However, if the memory address lies outside the current segment, both the 16-bit segment and the 16-bit offset need to be loaded. Thus, when accessing memory within the current segment, the C compiler can treat a pointer or a call or jump instruction as a 16-bit object. When accessing memory outside the current segment, the compiler must treat a pointer or call or jump instruction as a 32-bit entity.

Given the segmented nature of the 8086 family, you can organize memory into one of these six models (shown in order of increasing execution time):

Tiny	All segment registers are set to the same value and all addressing is done using 16 bits. This means that the code, data, and stack must all fit within the same 64K segment. Fastest program execution
Small	All code must fit in one 64K segment and all data must fit in a second 64K segment. All pointers are 16 bits. As fast as tiny model
Medium	All data must fit in one 64K segment, but the code may use multiple segments. All pointers to data are 16 bits, but all jumps and calls require 32-bit addresses. Quick access to data, slower code execution

Compact	All code must fit in one 64K segment, but the data may use multiple segments. However, no data item can exceed 64K. All pointers to data are 32 bits, but jumps and calls may use 16-bit addresses. Slow access to data, faster code execution
Large	Both code and data may use multiple segments. All pointers are 32 bits. However, no single data item can exceed 64K. Slower program execution
Huge	Both code and data may use multiple segments. All pointers are 32 bits. Single data items can exceed 64K. Slowest program execution

As you might guess, it is much faster to access memory via 16-bit pointers than 32-bit pointers because half as many bits need to be loaded into the CPU for each memory reference.

Occasionally, you will need to reference a pointer that is different from the default provided by your memory model. Many 8086-based C compilers allow pointers of either 16 or 32 bits to be explicitly created by the program, thus overriding the default memory model. Typically, this occurs when a program requires a lot of data for one specific operation. In this case, a **far** pointer is created and the memory is allocated with a nonstandard version of **malloc( )** that allocates memory from outside the default data segment. In this way, all other memory accesses remain fast and execution time does not suffer as much as if a larger model were used. The reverse can also happen: A program that uses a larger model may establish a **near** pointer to a piece of frequently accessed memory to enhance performance. Because the actual methods of overriding the default memory model differ from compiler to compiler, check your user's manual for details.

Many 8086-based C compilers restrict the size of a single data item to 64K—the size of one segment. However, you can use the **huge** modifier to create a pointer that can point to an object larger than 64K.

#include "malloc.h"
void *alloca(size _ t size);

Description

The **alloca( )** function is not defined by the ANSI C standard. It may also have a slightly different name, so check your user's manual.

The **alloca( )** function allocates *size* bytes of memory from the system stack (not the heap) and returns a character pointer to it. A null pointer is returned if the allocation request cannot be honored.

Memory allocated with **alloca( )** is automatically released when the function that called **alloca( )** returns. This means that you should never use a pointer generated by **alloca( )** as an argument to **free( )**.

Example

The following code allocates 80 bytes from the stack by using **alloca( )**:

```
#include "malloc.h"
#include "stdio.h"

void main(void)
{
  char *str;

  if(!(str=alloca(80))) {
    printf("allocation error - aborting");
    exit(1);
  }
  .
  .
  .
}
```

Related Functions

malloc( ), stackavail( )

#include "stdlib.h"
void *calloc(size_t num, size_t size);

Description

The **calloc( )** function allocates an amount of memory equal to *num* * *size*. That is, **calloc( )** allocates sufficient memory for an array of *num* objects of size *size*.

The **calloc( )** function returns a pointer to the first byte of the allocated region. If there is not enough memory to satisfy the request, a null pointer is returned. You should always verify that the return value is not a null pointer before using it.

Example

This function returns a pointer to a dynamically allocated array of 100 floats:

```
#include "stdlib.h"
#include "stdio.h"

float *get_mem(void)
{
  float *p;

  p = calloc(100, sizeof(float));
  if(!p) {
    printf("allocation failure - aborting");
    exit(1);
  }
  return p;
}
```

Related Functions

free( ), **malloc( )**, **realloc( )**

#include "malloc.h"
_ffree(void far *ptr);

Description

The **_ffree( )** function is not defined by the ANSI C standard and applies mostly to 8086-based compilers. It may also have a slightly different name, so check your user's manual.

The **_ffree( )** function returns to the system the memory pointed to by the **far** pointer *ptr*. This makes the memory available for future allocation. The pointer must have previously been allocated by using **_fmalloc( )**.

_ffree( ) must only be called with a pointer that was previously allocated by using _fmalloc( )—it cannot free pointers allocated by other allocation functions. Using an invalid pointer in the call usually destroys the memory management mechanism and causes a system crash.

Example

This program allocates memory from outside the default data segment and then frees it. Note the use of **far** to establish a **far** pointer. Remember that **far** is not part of standard C and relates mostly to compilers that run on the 8086 family of processors.

```
#include "malloc.h"
#include "stdio.h"
#include "stdlib.h"

void main(void)
{
  char far *str;

  if((str = _fmalloc(128))==NULL) {
      printf("allocation error - aborting");
      exit(1);
    }

  /* now free the memory */
  _ffree(str);
}
```

Related Functions

calloc( ), _fmalloc( ), realloc( )

#include "malloc.h"
void far * _fmalloc(size _t size);

Description

The _fmalloc( ) function is not defined by the ANSI C standard and applies mostly to 8086-based C compilers. It may also have a slightly different name, so check your user's manual.

The _fmalloc( ) function returns a **far** pointer to the first byte of a region of memory of size *size* that has been allocated from outside the default data segment. If there is insufficient memory outside the default data segment, the heap is tried. If both fail to satisfy the request, _fmalloc( ) returns a null pointer. You must always verify that the return value is not a null pointer before using it.

Example

This function allocates sufficient memory from outside the default data segment to hold structures of type **addr**. Note the use of **far** to establish a **far** pointer. Remember that **far** is not part of standard C and relates mostly to compilers that run on the 8086 family of processors.

```
#include "malloc.h"
#include "stdlib.h"
#include "stdio.h"

struct addr {
  char name[40];
  char street[40];
  char city[40];
  char state[3];
  char zip[10];
};
struct addr *get_struct(void)
{
  struct addr far *p;

  if((p = _fmalloc(sizeof(addr)))==NULL) {
    printf("allocation error - aborting");
    exit(1);
  }
  return p;
}
```

Related Functions

calloc( ), _ffree( ), realloc( )

#include "malloc.h"
size_t _fmsize(void far *ptr);

Description

The _fmsize( ) function is not defined by the ANSI C standard and applies mostly to 8086-based compilers. It may also have a slightly different name, so check your user's manual.

The **_fmsize( )** function returns the number of bytes in the allocated block of memory pointed to by the **far** pointer *ptr*. This memory must have been allocated with **_fmalloc( )**.

Example

This program displays the size of the block of memory required to hold the structure **addr**:

```
#include "malloc.h"
#include "stdio.h"

struct addr {
  char name[40];
  char street[40];
  char city[40];
  char state[3];
  char zip[10];
};

void main(void)
{
  struct addr far *p;

  p = _fmalloc(sizeof(struct addr));

  printf("size of block is %u", _fmsize(p));
}
```

Related Function

_fmalloc( )

#include "stdlib.h"
void free(void *);

Description

The **free( )** function returns to the heap the memory pointed to by *ptr*, making the memory available for future allocation.

free( ) must only be called with a pointer that was previously allocated with one of the dynamic allocation system's functions (either **malloc( )**, **realloc( )**, or **calloc( )**). Using an invalid pointer in the call will probably destroy the memory management mechanism and cause a system crash.

Example

This program allocates room for the strings entered by the user and then frees the memory:

```
#include "stdlib.h"
#include "stdio.h"

void main(void)
{
  char *str[100];
  int i;

  for(i=0; i<100; i++) {
    if((str[i] = malloc(128))==NULL) {
      printf("allocation error - aborting");
      exit(1);
    }
    gets(str[i]);
  }

  /* now free the memory */
  for(i=0; i<100; i++) free(str[i]);
}
```

Related Functions

calloc( ), malloc( ), realloc( )

#include ''malloc.h''
unsigned _freect(size_t size);

Description

The _freect( ) function is not defined by the ANSI C standard. It may also have a slightly different name, so check your user's manual.

The _**freect**( ) function returns the approximate number of items of size *size* that can be allocated from the free memory left in the heap.

Example

This program displays the number of floating-point values that may be stored in the heap:

```
#include "malloc.h"
#include "stdio.h"

void main(void)
{
  printf("number of floats that will fit in the heap: ");
  printf("%u\n", _freect(sizeof(float)));
}
```

Related Functions

malloc( ), _memavl( )

#include ''malloc.h''
void huge *halloc(long n, size _ t size);

Description

The **halloc**( ) function is not defined by the ANSI C standard and applies mostly to 8086-based C compilers. It may also have a slightly different name, so check your user's manual.

The **halloc**( ) function returns a **huge** pointer to the first byte of a region of memory of size *size* * *num* that has been allocated from outside the default data segment. That is, *num* objects of size *size* bytes are allocated. If the allocation request fails due to insufficient free memory, **halloc**( ) returns a null pointer. You should always verify that the return value is not a null pointer before using it.

The **halloc**( ) function allocates a block of memory larger than 64K on 8086-based computers. The value of *size* may need to be an even number.

Example

This function allocates sufficient memory from outside the default data segment to hold 128,000 bytes. Note the use of **huge** to establish a **huge** pointer. Remember that **huge** is not part of standard C and relates mostly to compilers that run on the 8086 family of processors.

```
#include "malloc.h"
#include "stdio.h"
#include "stdlib.h"

char huge *get_ram(void)
{
  char huge *p;

  if((p = halloc(1, 128000))==NULL) {
    printf("allocation error - aborting");
    exit(1);
  }
  return p;
}
```

Related Functions

calloc( ), **hfree( )**, **malloc()**, **realloc( )**

#include "malloc.h"
void hfree(void huge *ptr);

Description

The **hfree( )** function is not defined by the ANSI C standard and applies mostly to 8086-based C compilers. It may also have a slightly different name, so check your user's manual.

The **hfree( )** function returns to the system the memory pointed to by the **huge** pointer *ptr*. This makes the memory available for future allocation. The pointer must have previously been allocated with **halloc( )**.

hfree( ) must only be called with a pointer that was previously allocated by using **halloc( )**, which allocates blocks of memory greater than 64K. Using an invalid pointer in the call will probably destroy the memory management mechanism and cause a system crash.

Example

This program first allocates memory from outside the default data segment and then frees it:

```
#include "malloc.h"
#include "stdlib.h"
#include "stdio.h"

void main(void)
{
  char huge *large;

  if((large = halloc(1, 128000))==NULL) {
      printf("allocation error - aborting");
      exit(1);
    }

  /* now free the memory */
  hfree(large);
}
```

Related Functions

calloc( ), **halloc( )**, **malloc( )**, **realloc( )**

#include ''stdlib.h''
void *malloc(size _ t size);

Description

The **malloc( )** function returns a pointer to the first byte of a region of memory of size *size* that has been allocated from the heap. If there is insufficient memory in the heap to satisfy the request, **malloc( )** returns a null pointer. You must always verify that the return value is not a null pointer before using it. Attempting to use a null pointer will usually result in a system crash.

Example

This function allocates sufficient memory to hold structures of type **addr:**

```
struct addr {
  char name[40];
  char street[40];
  char city[40];
  char state[3];
  char zip[10];
```

```
};
struct addr *get_struct(void)
{
  struct addr *p;

  if((p = malloc(sizeof(addr)))==NULL) {
    printf("allocation error - aborting");
    exit(1);
  }
  return p;
}
```

Related Functions

calloc( ), free( ), realloc( )

#include "malloc.h"
size_t _memavl(void);

Description

The _memavl( ) function is not defined by the ANSI C standard. It may also have a slightly different name, so check your user's manual.

The _memavl( ) function returns the approximate number of bytes of free memory left in the heap.

Example

This program prints the number of bytes available for allocation:

```
#include "malloc.h"
#include "stdio.h"

void main(void)
{
  printf("number of bytes available for allocation: ");
  printf("%u", _memavl());
}
```

Related Functions

free( ), _freect( ), malloc( )

#include "malloc.h"
size _ t _ msize(void *ptr);

Description

The _ msize( ) function is not defined by the ANSI C standard. It may also have a slightly different name, so check your user's manual.

The _ msize( ) function returns the number of bytes in the allocated block of memory pointed to by *ptr*. This memory must have been allocated with **malloc( )**, **realloc( )**, or **calloc( )**.

Example

This program displays the size of the block of memory that is required to hold the structure **addr**:

```
#include "malloc.h"
#include "stdio.h"

struct addr {
  char name[40];
  char street[40];
  char city[40];
  char state[3];
  char zip[10];
};

void main(void)
{
  struct addr *p;

  p = malloc(sizeof(struct addr));

  printf("size of block is %u", _msize(p));
}
```

Related Functions

malloc( ), realloc( )

#include "malloc.h"
void _ nfree(char near *ptr);

Description

The _ nfree( ) function is not defined by the ANSI C standard and applies mostly to 8086-based C compilers. It may also have a slightly different name, so check your user's manual.

The _nfree( ) function returns to the system the memory pointed to by the **near** pointer *ptr*. This makes the memory available for future allocation. The pointer must have previously been allocated with _nmalloc( ).

_nfree( ) must only be called with a pointer that was previously allocated by using _nmalloc( ), which allocates blocks of memory from the default data segment. Using an invalid pointer in the call will probably destroy the memory management mechanism and cause a system crash.

Example

This program first allocates memory from inside the default data segment and then frees it. Note the use of **near** to establish a **near** pointer. Remember that **near** is not part of standard C and relates mostly to compilers that run on the 8086 family of processors.

```
#include "malloc.h"
#include "stdio.h"
#include "stdlib.h"

void main(void)
{
  char near *str;

  if((str = _nmalloc(128))==NULL) {
      printf("allocation error - aborting");
      exit(1);
    }

  /* now free the memory */
  _nfree(str);
}
```

Related Functions

calloc( ), halloc( ), malloc( ), _nmalloc( ), realloc( )

#include "malloc.h"
char near * _nmalloc(size _ t size);

Description

The _nmalloc( ) function is not defined by the ANSI C standard and applies mostly to 8086-based C compilers. It may also have a slightly different name, so check your user's manual.

The **_nmalloc( )** function returns a **near** pointer to the first byte of a region of memory of size *size* that has been allocated from inside the default data segment. This is only meaningful for programs compiled for one of the 8086 large data model addressing modes, and it allows the use of a 16-bit pointer. If the allocation request fails due to insufficient free memory, **_nmalloc( )** returns a null pointer. You must always verify that the return value is not a null pointer before using it.

Example

This function allocates sufficient memory from inside the default data segment to hold 128 bytes. Note the use of **near** to establish a **near** pointer. Remember that **near** is not part of standard C and relates mostly to compilers that run on the 8086 family of processors.

```
char near *get_near_ram(void)
{
  char near *p;

  if((p = _nmalloc(128))==NULL) {
    printf("allocation error - aborting");
    exit(1);
  }
  return p;
}
```

Related Functions

calloc( ), malloc( ), _nfree( ), realloc( )

#include "malloc.h"
unsigned _nmsize(void near *ptr);

Description

The **_nmsize( )** function is not defined by the ANSI C standard and applies mostly to 8086-based compilers. It may also have a slightly different name, so check your user's manual.

The **_nmsize( )** function returns the number of bytes in the allocated block of memory pointed to by the **near** pointer *ptr*. This memory must have been allocated with **_nmalloc( )**.

Example

This program displays the size of the block of memory that is required to hold the structure **addr**:

```
#include "malloc.h"
#include "stdio.h"

struct addr {
  char name[40];
  char street[40];
  char city[40];
  char state[3];
  char zip[10];
};

void main(void)
{
  struct addr near *p;

  p = _nmalloc(sizeof(struct addr));

  printf("size of block is %u", _nmsize(p));
}
```

Related Function

_nmalloc( )

#include "stdlib.h"
void *realloc(void *ptr, size_t size);

Description

The **realloc( )** function changes the size of the previously allocated memory pointed to by *ptr* to that specified by *size*. The value of *size* may be greater or less than the original. A pointer to the memory block is returned because **realloc( )** may need to move the block in order to increase its size. If this occurs, the contents of the old block are copied into the new block—no information is lost.

If *ptr* is null, **realloc( )** simply allocates *size* bytes of memory, and returns a pointer to it. If *size* is zero, the memory pointed to by *ptr* is freed.

If there is not enough free memory in the heap to allocate *size* bytes, a null pointer is returned and the original block is left unchanged.

Example

This program first allocates 17 characters, copies the string "this is 16 chars" into them and then uses **realloc( )** to increase the size to 18 in order to place a period at the end.

```
#include "stdlib.h"
#include "stdio.h"
#include "string.h"

void main(void)
{
  char *p;

  p = malloc(17);
  if(!p) {
    printf("allocation error - aborting");
    exit(1);
  }

  strcpy(p, "this is 16 chars");

  p = realloc(p, 18);
  if(!p) {
    printf("allocation error - aborting");
    exit(1);
  }

  strcat(p, ".");

  printf(p);

  free(p);
}
```

Related Functions

calloc( ), **free( )**, **malloc( )**

#include "malloc.h"
size _ t stackavail(void)

Description

The **stackavail( )** function is not defined by the ANSI C standard. It may also have a slightly different name, so check your user's manual.

The **stackavail( )** function returns the approximate number of bytes available on the stack for allocation with **alloca( )**.

You can also use **stackavail( )** to predict possible heap-stack collisions that could be generated by recursive routines, as illustrated by the example that follows.

Example

The function **recurse( )** calls itself indefinitely, using up stack space with each call, until the stack size has reached a dangerously low level. Free memory is not allowed to drop to zero because system interrupts could occur, unknown to the program, that would cause the stack to overrun the heap.

```
#include "malloc.h"
#include "stdio.h"

void recurse(void);

void main(void)
{
  recurse();
}

/* This routine will call itself until a heap-stack
   collision becomes a "real threat".
*/
void recurse(void)
{
  printf("%u\n", stackavail());
  if(stackavail() < 500) return;
  recurse();
}
```

Related Functions

alloca( ), **_freect( )**, **_memavl( )**

Screen and Graphics Functions

Although the ANSI standard for C does not define screen or graphics functions, they are important to most contemporary programming tasks. The ANSI standard does not define these functions because of wide differences between the capabilities and interfaces of different types of hardware. Even compilers designed for the same environment usually implement screen and graphics functions very differently. This chapter describes the most generalizable screen and graphics functions as supplied with Microsoft C version 5.1. These functions require a DOS-based PC environment operation. The graphics functions supplied with your compiler may differ, but the principles will be similar.

The prototypes for Microsoft's screen and graphics functions are contained in GRAPH.H, along with several structure types, which are discussed as required.

This chapter first discusses various video modes available for the PC line of computers. You need this background information to understand certain graphics functions.

As you probably know, there are several different types of video adapters currently available for PCs. The most common are the monochrome, the CGA (Color Graphics Adapter), PC*jr*, the EGA (Enhanced Graphics Adapter), and the VGA (Video Graphics Array). Together, these adapters support several different modes of video operation. Table 17-1 summarizes these video modes. As you can see, some modes are for text and some are for graphics. In a text mode, only text may be displayed. In a graphics mode, both text and graphics can be displayed.

The smallest user-addressable part of the screen in a text mode is one character. The smallest user-addressable part of the screen in a graphics mode is one pixel. Actually, the term *pixel* originally referred

Mode	Type	Graphics Dimensions	Text Dimensions
0	Text, b/w	n/a	40×25
1	Text, 16 colors	n/a	40×25
2	Text, b/w	n/a	80×25
3	Text, 16 colors	n/a	80×25
4	Graphics, 4 colors	320×200	40×25
5	Graphics, 4 gray tones	320×200	40×25
6	Graphics, 2 colors	640×200	80×25
7	Text, b/w	n/a	80×25
8	PC*jr* graphics 16 colors	160×200	20×25
9	PC*jr* graphics 16 colors	320×200	40×25
10	Graphics, 4 colors	640×200	80×25
11	Reserved		
12	Reserved		
13	Graphics, 16 colors	320×200	40×25
14	Graphics, 16 colors	640×200	80×25
15	Graphics, 2 colors	640×350	80×25
16	Graphics, 16 colors	640×350	80×25
17	Graphics, 2 colors	640×480	80×30
18	Graphics, 16 colors	640×480	80×30
19	Graphics, 256 colors	320×200	40×25

Table 17-1.   Screen Modes for Various Video Adapters

to the smallest individual phosphor element on the video monitor that could be individually energized by the scan beam. However, the term has been generalized to refer to the smallest addressable point on a graphics display.

In a text mode, individual character locations on the screen are referenced by their row and column numbers. In a graphics mode, individual pixels are referenced by their X,Y coordinates, with X being the horizontal axis. In any of the graphics modes, the upper-left corner of the screen is location 0,0.

The text screen examples in this chapter use video mode 3, the 80-column color mode. The graphics routines use EGA mode 16. If your hardware does not support one or both of these modes, you will have to make the appropriate changes to the examples.

When in a color text mode, you may specify what color the text is displayed in. The colors and their integer equivalents are shown here:

Text Color	Value
Blank	0
Blue	1
Green	2
Cyan	3
Red	4
Magenta	5
Brown	6
Lightgray	7
Darkgray	8
Lightblue	9
Lightgreen	10
Lightcyan	11
Lightred	12
Lightmagenta	13
Yellow	14
White	15

Setting the high-order bit by adding 128 to the color makes the text blink.

The text background colors are shown here:

Background Color	Value
Blank	0
Blue	1
Green	2
Cyan	3
Red	4

Magenta	5
Brown	6

For the color graphics modes, the background colors are shown here:

Background Color	Value
Blank	0
Blue	1
Green	2
Cyan	3
Red	4
Magenta	5
Brown	6
Lightgray	7
Darkgray	8
Lightblue	9
Lightgreen	10
Lightcyan	11
Lightred	12
Lightmagenta	13
Yellow	14
White	15

In a color graphics mode, the foreground color is determined by both the value of the color and the currently selected palette. In CGA four-color graphics video mode 4, you have four colors per palette and four palettes from which to choose. The colors are numbered 0 through 3, with 0 always being the background color. The palettes are also numbered 0 through 3. The palettes and their associated colors are shown in Table 17-2. The _selectpalette( ) function allows you to change palettes.

In EGA/VGA 16-color mode, a palette consists of 16 colors, selected out of a possible 64 colors. The default values are shown here:

Color	Value
Blank	0
Blue	1
Green	2
Cyan	3
Red	4
Magenta	5
Brown	6
Lightgray	7
Darkgray	8
Lightblue	9
Lightgreen	10
Lightcyan	11
Lightred	12
Lightmagenta	13
Yellow	14
White	15

To change an EGA/VGA palette, use **_remapallpalette**( ), which maps the colors that you select onto the palette.

Palette	Color Number		
	1	2	3
0	Green	Red	Yellow
1	Cyan	Magenta	White
2	Lightgreen	Lightred	Yellow
3	Lightcyan	Lightmagenta	White

Table 17-2.   The Palettes and Colors in Video Mode 4

#include "graph.h"
short far _arc(short x1, short y1, short x2, short y2, short x3, short y3, short x4, short y4);

Description

The _arc( ) function draws an arc whose center is the center of the bounding rectangle defined by $x1,y1$ and $x2,y2$. (The rectangle is not displayed.) The arc begins at the point defined by $x3,y3$ and ends at $x4,y4$. The arc is displayed in the current drawing color.

The _arc( ) function returns true if successful; it returns zero if an error occurs.

Example

This program displays an arc:

```
#include "graph.h"
#include "conio.h"

void main(void)
{
  _setvideomode(_VRES16COLOR);

  _arc(100, 100, 200, 200, 100, 100, 200, 200);
  getche();

  _setvideomode(_DEFAULTMODE);
}
```

Related Functions

_ellipse( ), _lineto( ), _rectangle( )

#include "graph.h"
void far _clearscreen(short region);

Description

The _clearscreen( ) function clears the specified region of the screen using the current background color. This function works for both text and graphics video modes. The values of *region* are _GCLEAR-

SCREEN, which clears the entire screen, **_GVIEWPORT**, which clears a graphics viewport, and **_GWINDOW**, which clears a text window. These macros are defined by Microsoft in GRAPH.H.

Example

This program clears the screen:

```
#include "graph.h"

void main(void)
{
    _clearscreen(_GCLEARSCREEN);
}
```

Related Functions

_settextwindow( ), _setviewport( )

#include "graph.h"
short far _ellipse(short fill, short x1, short y1,
short x2, short y2);

Description

The **_ellipse( )** function draws an ellipse using the current drawing color bounded by the rectangle defined by $x1,y1$ and $x2,y2$. (The rectangle is not displayed.) If *fill* has the value **_GFILLINTERIOR**, the ellipse is filled using the current fill color and style. If *fill* has the value **_GBORDER**, the ellipse is not filled. These macros are defined by Microsoft in GRAPH.H.

If the ellipse can be drawn, **_ellipse( )** returns true. Otherwise, it returns zero.

Example

The following program draws an ellipse.

```
#include "graph.h"
#include "conio.h"

void main(void)
{
  _setvideomode(_VRES16COLOR);
  _setcolor(3);
  _ellipse(_GBORDER, 100, 100, 300, 200);
  getche();

  _setvideomode(_DEFAULTMODE);
}
```

Related Functions

_arc( ), _lineto( ), _rectangle( )

#include "graph.h"
short far _floodfill(short x, short y, short color);

Description

The _floodfill( ) function fills an enclosed region with the current fill color and style. The region filled must be completely enclosed by the color specifed by *color*. The point specified by *x,y* must be inside the region to be filled.

The _floodfill( ) function returns true if successful, and zero if an error occurs.

Example

This program draws an ellipse and then uses _floodfill( ) to fill it:

```
#include "graph.h"
#include "conio.h"

void main(void)
{
  short color;

  _setvideomode(_VRES16COLOR);
```

```
    color = _getcolor();
    _ellipse(_GBORDER, 100, 100, 300, 200);
    _setcolor(2);
    _floodfill(150, 150, color);
    getche();

    _setvideomode(_DEFAULTMODE);
}
```

Related Function

_ setfillmask( )

#include "graph.h"
long far _getbkcolor(void);

Description

The _ **getbkcolor**( ) function returns the value of the current background color.

Example

This program displays the default background color:

```
#include "graph.h"
#include "conio.h"
#include "stdio.h"

void main(void)
{
    _setvideomode(_VRES16COLOR);

    printf("background color is %ld", _getbkcolor());
    getche();

    _setvideomode(_DEFAULTMODE);
}
```

Related Function

_ setbkcolor( )

#include "graph.h"
short far _getcolor(void);

Description

The _getcolor( ) function returns the value of the current drawing color. By default, the current drawing color has the highest value allowed by the video mode currently in use. You can use this fact to determine the valid range of colors (starting at zero) for a given mode.

Example

This program displays the value of the maximum drawing color:

```
#include "graph.h"
#include "conio.h"
#include "stdio.h"

void main(void)
{
  short color;

  _setvideomode(_VRES16COLOR);

  color = _getcolor();
  printf("color is %hd", color);
  getche();

  _setvideomode(_DEFAULTMODE);
}
```

Related Function

_setcolor( )

#include "graph.h"
struct xycoord far _getcurrentposition(void);

Description

The _getcurrentposition( ) function returns the x,y location of the current graphics position. The current position is the point at which the next graphics output event will begin. The current graphics position is not related to the current text position in any way.

Microsoft defines the **xycoord( )** structure like this:

```
struct xycoord {
  short xcoord;
  short ycoord;
};
```

Example

This fragment displays the current graphics location:

```
struct xycoord xy;
  .
  .
  .
xy = _getcurrentposition();
printf("current X,Y is %d %d", xy.xcoord, xy.ycoord);
```

Related Functions

_ **gettextposition( )**, _ **moveto( )**

#include "graph.h"
unsigned char far *far _getfillmask(unsigned char far *buf);

Description

The _ **getfillmask( )** function copies the current fill pattern into the buffer pointed to by *buf.* The buffer must be 8 bytes long.

The fill pattern defines the way an object is filled by _ **floodfill( )** or one of the other functions that can fill an object. The mask is treated as an 8-byte by 8-bit array. This array is then repeatedly mapped onto the region being filled. When a bit is set, the corresponding pixel is set to the current fill color. If the bit is off, the pixel is left unchanged.

The _ **getfillmask( )** function returns **NULL** if no mask is available.

Example

The following program saves the original fill mask, generates a new one randomly, fills an ellipse using the new mask, and, finally, resets the fill mask to its previous value.

```
#include "graph.h"
#include "conio.h"
#include "stdlib.h"

void main(void)
{
  short color, i;
  unsigned char oldmask[8];
  unsigned char newmask[8];

  /* obtain some random values for newmask */
  for(i=0; i<8; i++) newmask[i] = rand()%255;

  _setvideomode(_VRES16COLOR);

  color = _getcolor();
  _ellipse(_GBORDER, 100, 100, 300, 200);
  _setcolor(2);
  _getfillmask(oldmask);
  _setfillmask(newmask);
  _floodfill(150, 150, color);
  _setfillmask(oldmask);
  getche();

  _setvideomode(_DEFAULTMODE);
}
```

Related Function

_setfillmask( )

#include "graph.h"
void far _getimage(short x1, short y1,
short x2, short y2,
char far *buf);

Description

The _getimage( ) function copies the contents of the rectangle defined by *x1,y1* and *x2,y2* into the buffer pointed to by *buf*. To determine how big in bytes, the buffer must be, use the _imagesize( ) function.

Example

This program copies the image of an ellipse from one part of the screen to another:

```
#include "stdio.h"
#include "graph.h"
#include "conio.h"
#include "stdlib.h"

void main(void)
{
  long size;
  char far *buf;

  _setvideomode(_VRES16COLOR);

  size = _imagesize(100, 100, 300, 200);
  buf = malloc(size);
  if(!buf) {
    printf("allocation error\n");
    exit(1);
  }

  _ellipse(_GBORDER, 100, 100, 300, 200);
  _getimage(100, 100, 300, 200, buf);
  _putimage(0, 0, buf, _GPSET);
  getche();

  _setvideomode(_DEFAULTMODE);
}
```

Related Functions

_ imagesize( ), _ putimage( )

#include "graph.h"
unsigned short far _ getlinestyle(void);

Description

The _ getlinestyle( ) function returns the current line style. This mask determines how lines will appear. The line style mask is 16 bits long. If a bit is set, the pixel corresponding to that bit is set to the current drawing color. If the bit is off, the pixel is left unchanged.

Example

The following program saves the current line style, uses a new style to draw a rectangle, restores the old line style, and draws another rectangle.

```
#include "graph.h"
#include "conio.h"

void main(void)
{
  short oldstyle;

  _setvideomode(_VRES16COLOR);

  oldstyle = _getlinestyle();
  _moveto(0, 0);

  /* default line style */
  _lineto(100, 100);

  /* new line style */
  _setlinestyle(12345);
  _rectangle(_GBORDER, 100, 100, 200, 200);

  /* old style restored */
  _setlinestyle(oldstyle);
  _rectangle(_GBORDER, 200, 200, 300, 300);
  getche();

  _setvideomode(_DEFAULTMODE);
}
```

Related Function

_setlinestyle( )

#include "graph.h"
short far _getpixel(short x, short y);

Description

The _getpixel( ) function returns the color of the pixel specified by x,y.
If the value of either x or y is invalid, _getpixel( ) returns -1.

Example

This code fragment prints the current color of the pixel at 0,0:

```
printf("%d", _getpixel(0, 0));
```

Related Function

_setpixel( )

#Include "graph.h"
short far _gettextcolor(void);

Description

The _gettextcolor( ) function returns the current text color. This is the color that textual output will be written in.

Example

The following code fragment displays text in the default color and a new color. It then resets the text color to the default.

```
#include "graph.h"
#include "conio.h"
#include "stdio.h"

void main(void)
{
  int color;

  _setvideomode(_VRES16COLOR);

  color = _gettextcolor();
  printf("default text color is %d", color);
  _settextcolor(3);
  _settextposition(10, 1);
  _outtext("this is in a different color\n");
  getche();

  _setvideomode(_DEFAULTMODE);
}
```

Related Function

_settextcolor( )

#include "graph.h"
struct rccoord far _gettextposition(void);

Description

The _gettextposition( ) function returns the current text position. The current text position is the location at which the next textual output will begin. The current text position does not relate to the current graphics position.

The _gettextposition( ) function returns the row and column coordinates in a structure of type **rccoord**, defined by Microsoft like this:

```
struct rccoord {
  short row;
  short col;
};
```

Example

This fragment displays the current text position.

```
struct rccoord loc;

loc = _gettextposition();

printf("%d,%d", loc.row, loc.col);
```

Related Function

_settextposition( )

#include "graph.h"
struct videoconfig far *far _getvideoconfig(
struct videoconfig far *buf);

Description

The _getvideoconfig( ) function copies the system's current video configuration into the structure pointed to by *buf*. The configuration information includes the dimension of the screen in pixels, the number of text columns and rows, the number of different colors, the bits per pixel, and the number of video pages.

Microsoft defines the **videoconfig** structure as follows:

```
struct videoconfig {
  short numxpixels; /* number of pixels horizontally */
  short numypixels; /* number of pixels vertically */
  short numtextcols; /* number of text columns */
  short numtextrows; /* number of text rows */
  short numcolors;  /* number of colors */
  short bitsperpixel; /* number bits in a pixel */
  short numvideopages; /* number of video pages */
};
```

Example

This fragment displays the number of text columns available in the current video mode:

```
struct videoconfig c;

_getvideoconfig(&c);

printf("text columns: %d", c.numtextcols);
```

Related Function

_ setvideomode( )

#include "graph.h"
long far _imagesize(short x1, short y1,
short x2, short y2);

Description

The _**imagesize**( ) function returns the size, in bytes, of memory needed to hold the rectangular region of the screen defined by *x1,y1* and *x2,y2* relative to the current video mode. It is principally used in conjunction with _**getimage**( ).

Example

The following code fragment returns the number of bytes of memory needed to store an image.

```
size = _imagesize(0, 0, 10, 10);
```

Related Functions

_getimage( ), _setimage( )

#include "graph.h"
short far _lineto(short x, short y);

Description

The _lineto( ) function draws a line in the current drawing color from the current graphics position to that specified by x,y. The current graphics position is then set to x,y.

The _lineto( ) function returns true if successful. If the coordinates specified by x,y are invalid for the current video mode, _lineto( ) returns zero.

Example

This program draws a diagonal line starting in the upper-left corner of the screen:

```
#include "graph.h"
#include "conio.h"

void main(void)
{
  _setvideomode(_VRES16COLOR);

  _moveto(0, 0);
  _setcolor(3);
  _lineto(600, 400);
  getche();

  _setvideomode(_DEFAULTMODE);
}
```

Related Functions

_ellipse( ), _moveto( ), _rectangle( )

#include "graph.h"
struct xycoord far _moveto(short x, short y);

Description

The **_moveto( )** function changes the current graphics position to that specified by *x,y*. It does not affect the current text position. The **_moveto( )** function returns a structure of type **xycoord** that holds the coordinates of the previous graphics position.

The **xycoord** structure is defined by Microsoft as

```
struct xycoord {
  short xcoord;
  short ycoord;
};
```

Example

This fragment makes the upper-left corner of the screen the current graphics location:

```
_moveto(0, 0);
```

Related Functions

_lineto( ), **_settextposition( )**

#include "graph.h"
void far _outtext(char far *str);

Description

The **_outtext( )** function outputs the string pointed to by *str* to the screen at the current text position in the current text foreground and background colors. It also recognizes viewport and window boundaries.

Example

The following fragment outputs **Hello** to the screen.

```
_outtext("Hello");
```

Related Functions

_gettextposition( ), _settextposition( )

#include "graph.h"
short far _pie(short fill, short x1, short y1,
short x2, short y2, short x3, short y3,
short x4, short y4);

Description

The _pie( ) function draws a slice of a pie graph. The center of the pie
is at the center of the bounding rectangle defined by $x1,y1$ and $x2,y2$.
The rectangle is not displayed. The pie slice begins at point $x3,y3$ and
ends at $x4,y4$. The pie slice is displayed in the current drawing color. If
fill has the value **_GBORDER**, the pie slice is not filled. If *fill* has the
value **_GFILLINTERIOR**, the slice is filled using the current fill color
and style. (These macros are defined by Microsoft in GRAPH.H.)

Example

This program draws a pie slice:

```
#include "graph.h"
#include "conio.h"

void main(void)
{
  _setvideomode(_VRES16COLOR);

  _pie(_GBORDER, 100, 100, 300, 300, 300, 10, 100, 300);
  getche();

  _setvideomode(_DEFAULTMODE);
}
```


Related Functions

_ellipse( ), _rectangle( )

#include "graph.h"
void far _putimage(short x, short y, char far *buf,
short how);

Description

The _putimage( ) function copies an image previously saved by _getimage( ) to the screen. The memory that holds the image is pointed to by *buf*. The image is copied to the screen with its upper-left corner positioned at location *x,y*.

How the image will be copied to the screen is determined by *how*. Microsoft defines in GRAPH.H the five values it may have. If it is _GPSET, the image is copied to the screen, overwriting any previous contents. If *how* is _GPRESET, the image is copied to the screen in reverse video. If *how* is _GXOR, each pixel in the the image is XORed with the current contents of the screen. If *how* is _GOR, each pixel is ORed with the current contents of the screen. Finally, if *how* is _GAND, each pixel in the image is ANDed with the current contents of the screen.

Example

This program copies the image of an ellipse from one part of the screen to another:

```
#include "stdio.h"
#include "graph.h"
#include "conio.h"
#include "stdlib.h"

void main(void)
{
  long size;
  char far *buf;

  _setvideomode(_VRES16COLOR);

  size = _imagesize(100, 100, 300, 200);
  buf = malloc(size);
  if(!buf) {
    printf("allocation error\n");
    exit(1);
  }
```

```
_ellipse(_GBORDER, 100, 100, 300, 200);
_getimage(100, 100, 300, 200, buf);
_putimage(0, 0, buf, _GPSET);
getche();

_setvideomode(_DEFAULTMODE);
}
```

Related Function

_getimage( )

#include "graph.h"
short far _rectangle(short fill, short x1, short y1,
short x2, short y2);

Description

The _rectangle( ) function draws a rectangle in the current drawing color. The upper-left corner of the rectangle is specified by *x1,y1* and the lower-right corner by *x2,y2*.

If *fill* has the value _GFILLINTERIOR, the rectangle is filled using the current fill color. If *fill* has the value _GBORDER, the rectangle is not filled. (These macros are defined by Microsoft in GRAPH.H.)

The _rectangle( ) function returns true if the coordinates are within range, and zero otherwise.

Example

This code fragment draws a rectangle on the screen:

```
#include "graph.h"
#include "conio.h"

void main(void)
{
  _setvideomode(_VRES16COLOR);
  _rectangle(_GBORDER, 0, 0, 100, 100);
  getche();
```

```
    _setvideomode(_DEFAULTMODE);
}
```

Related Functions

 _ ellipse( ), _ lineto( )

#include "graph.h"
short far _ remapallpalette(long far *colors);
long far _ remappalette(short oldcolor, short newcolor);

Description

The _ **remapallpalette**( ) function changes the values of the colors supported by the current video mode to the values specified in the array pointed to by *colors*, which must contain as many colors as there are in the current palette. The _ **remappalette**( ) function changes the value of one color, specified by *oldcolor*, to that specified by *newcolor*.

Both of these functions require either an EGA or VGA video adapter.

When successful, _ **remappalette**( ) returns the color previously associated with *oldcolor*. When successful, _ **remapallpalette**( ) returns zero. Upon failure, both functions return −1.

Example

The following fragment maps color 4 onto color 3:

```
_remappalette(4, 3);
```

Related Function

 _ **selectpalette**( )

#include "graph.h"
short far _selectpalette(short palette);

Description

The _selectpalette( ) function selects one of four palettes when the video system is in mode 4 (four-color, medium resolution). The current palette determines exactly what colors are available for display.

This function works only when the video system is in mode 4.

Example

This fragment selects palette 0:

```
_selectpalette(0);
```

Related Functions

_remapallpalette( ), _remappalette( )

#include "graph.h"
long far _setbkcolor(long color);

Description

The _setbkcolor( ) function sets the background color to that specified by *color*. It returns the previous background color.

Example

This program displays **this is on cyan** on a cyan background:

```
#include "graph.h"
#include "conio.h"

void main(void)
```

```
{
  _setbkcolor(3L);
  _outtext("This is on cyan");
  getche();
}
```

Related Function

_getbkcolor( )

#include ''graph.h''
short far _setcolor(short color);

Description

The _setcolor( ) function changes the current drawing color to that specified by *color*. It returns the previous drawing color.

Example

This program prints a line in each available foreground color:

```
#include "graph.h"
#include "conio.h"

void main(void)
{
  int i;

  _setvideomode(_VRES16COLOR);

  i = _getcolor();
  for( ; i; i--) {
    _setcolor(i);
    _moveto(i*10, 0);
    _lineto(i*10, 100);
  }
  getche();

  _setvideomode(_DEFAULTMODE);
}
```

Related Functions

_getbkcolor( ), _getcolor( ), _setbkcolor( )

#include "graph.h"
void far _ setfillmask(unsigned char far *buf);

Description

The _setfillmask( ) function sets the fill mask used by those routines
that fill areas to that pointed to by *buf*, which must be an 8-byte by 8-bit
array. This array is then repeatedly mapped onto the region being filled.
When a bit is set, the corresponding pixel is set to the current fill color.
If the bit is off, the pixel is left unchanged.

Example

This program creates a new randomly generated fill mask and uses it to
fill an ellipse:

```
#include "graph.h"
#include "conio.h"
#include "stdlib.h"

void main(void)
{
  short  i;
  unsigned char newmask[8];

  /* obtain some random values for newmask */
  for(i=0; i<8; i++) newmask[i] = rand()%255;

  _setvideomode(_VRES16COLOR);

  _setfillmask(newmask);
  _ellipse(_GFILLINTERIOR, 100, 100, 300, 200);
  getche();

  _setvideomode(_DEFAULTMODE);
}
```

Related Function

_ getfillmask( )

#include "graph.h"
void far __setlinestyle(unsigned short mask);

Description

The __setlinestyle( ) function sets the current line style to that specified by *mask*. A line style mask is 16 bits long. If a bit is set, the pixel corresponding to that bit is set to the current drawing color. If the bit is off, the pixel is left unchanged.

Example

This program saves the current line style, uses a new one to draw a rectangle, restores the old line style, and draws another rectangle:

```
#include "graph.h"
#include "conio.h"

void main(void)
{
  short oldstyle;

  _setvideomode(_VRES16COLOR);

  oldstyle = _getlinestyle();
  _moveto(0, 0);

  /* default line style */
  _lineto(100, 100);

  /* new line style */
  _setlinestyle(12345);
  _rectangle(_GBORDER, 100, 100, 200, 200);

  /* old style restored */
  _setlinestyle(oldstyle);
  _rectangle(_GBORDER, 200, 200, 300, 300);
  getche();

  _setvideomode(_DEFAULTMODE);
}
```

Related Functions

__getlinestyle( ), __setfillmask( )

#include "graph.h"
short far _setpixel(short x, short y);

Description

The _setpixel( ) function changes the pixel specified by x,y to the current drawing color. It returns the pixel's previous color. If a coordinate specified is out of bounds, _setpixel( ) returns −1.

Example

This fragment sets the pixel at location 10,20 to the current drawing color:

```
_setpixel(10, 20);
```

Related Function

_getpixel( )

#include "graph.h"
short far _settextcolor(short color);

Description

The _settextcolor( ) function changes the current text color to that specified by *color*. It returns the previous text color.

Example

This program displays **this is in red** in red:

```
#include "graph.h"
#include "conio.h"
#include "stdio.h"
```

```
void main(void)
{
  _setvideomode(_VRES16COLOR);

  _settextcolor(4);
  _outtext("this is in red\n");
  getche();

  _setvideomode(_DEFAULTMODE);
}
```

Related Functions

_gettextcolor( ), _setcolor( )

#include "graph.h"
struct rccoord far _settextposition(short row,
short col);

Description

The _settextposition( ) function sets the current text position to that specified by *row* and *col.* The current text position is the location at which the next textual output will begin. The current text position is not related to the current graphics position.

The _settextposition( ) function returns the previous text position in the row and column coordinates in a structure of type **rccoord**, defined by Microsoft like this in GRAPH.H:

```
struct rccoord {
  short row;
  short col;
};
```

Example

This fragment sets the current text position to row 10, column 40:

```
_settextposition(10, 40);
```

Related Function

_gettextposition( )

#include "graph.h"
void far _settextwindow(short row1, short col1,
short row2, short col2);

Description

The _settextwindow( ) function defines a text window specified by
row1, col1 and *row2, col2* — the upper-left and lower-right corners of the
window. Text written to the window with _outtext( ) will appear relative to the window and not the screen. This means that text will scroll
when the bottom of the window is written to. Also, text will be wrapped
around to the next line when it attempts to go past the right edge of the
window. The rest of the screen outside the window is untouched.

The standard console output functions ignore text windows.

Example

This function creates a small text window and writes output to it. Text
will wrap and scroll within the window, but the rest of the screen will
remain untouched.

```
#include "graph.h"
#include "conio.h"

void main(void)
{
  int i;

  _settextwindow(1, 1, 5, 40);

  for(i=0; i<100; i++)
    _outtext("this is a test ");
}
```

Related Functions

_outtext( ), _setviewport( )

#include "graph.h"
short far _setvideomode(short mode);

Description

The _setvideomode( ) function activates the video mode specified by
mode. The valid modes are shown here. (The macros are defined by

Microsoft in GRAPH.H.) You can restore the default video mode by calling _ **setvideomode**( ) with _ **DEFAULTMODE**.

Macro Name

_ TEXTBW40

_ TEXTC40

_ TEXTBW80

_ TEXTC80

_ MRES4COLOR

_ MRESNOCOLOR

_ HRESNOCOLOR

_ HRESBW

_ TEXTMONO

_ MRES16COLOR

_ HRES16COLOR

_ ERESNOCOLOR

_ ERESCOLOR

_ VRES2COLOR

_ VRES16COLOR

_ MRES256COLOR

_ DEFAULTMODE

The _ **setvideomode**( ) function returns true if the mode change was succesful. If the specified mode is not supported by the system's hardware, _ **setvideomode**( ) returns zero.

Example

The following fragment sets the video mode to 80-column color text:

```
_setvideomode(_TEXTC80);
```

Related Function

_ **getvideoconfig**( )

#include "graph.h"
void far _setviewport(short x1, short y1, short x2, short y2);

Description

The _setviewport( ) function creates a graphics window called a *viewport* whose upper-left corner is specified by *x1,y1* and whose lower-right corner is specified by *x2,y2*. Once a viewport has been defined, the graphics functions operate relative to it rather than the screen. Output is automatically clipped at the edges of the viewport.

Example

```
#include "graph.h"
#include "conio.h"

void main(void)
{
  _setvideomode(_VRES16COLOR);

  _setviewport(200, 200, 300, 300);
  _moveto(0, 0);  _setcolor(3);
  _lineto(600, 400); /* this line will be clipped */
  getche();

  _setvideomode(_DEFAULTMODE);
}
```

Related Function

_settextwindow( )

Miscellaneous Functions

This chapter discusses all of the ANSI standard functions that don't fit easily in any other category. They include various conversion, variable-length argument processing, sorting, and other functions.

Many of these functions require the use of the header STDLIB.H. This header defines two types, **div_t** and **ldiv_t** which are the types of the values returned by **div( )** and **ldiv( )**, respectively. STDLIB.H also defines the type **size_t** which is the unsigned value returned by **sizeof**. The header also defines these macros:

NULL	A null pointer
RAND_MAX	The maximum value that can be returned by the **rand( )** function
EXIT_FAILURE	The value returned to calling process if program termination is unsuccessful
EXIT_SUCCESS	The value returned to calling process if program termination is successful

If a function requires a different header file, that function description will discuss it.

#include "stdlib.h"
void abort(void);

Description

The **abort( )** function causes immediate abnormal termination of a program. Generally, no files are flushed. In environments that support it,

abort( ) returns an implementation-defined value to the calling process (usually the operating system) indicating failure.

Example

In this program, the program terminates if the user enters an **A**:

```
#include "stdlib.h"
#include "stdio.h"

void main(void)
{
  for(;;)
    if(getchar()=='A') abort();
}
```

Related Functions

atexit( ), exit( )

#include "stdlib.h"
int abs(int num);

Description

The **abs( )** function returns the absolute value of the integer *num*.

Example

This function converts the user-entered numbers into their absolute values:

```
#include "stdlib.h"
#include "stdio.h"

get_abs(void)
{
  char num[80];

  gets(num);
```

```
   return abs(atoi(num));
}
```

Related Function

labs( )

#include "assert.h"
void assert(int exp);

Description

The **assert( )** macro, defined in its header ASSERT.H, writes error information to **stderr** and then aborts program execution if the expression *exp* evaluates to zero. Otherwise, **assert( )** does nothing. Although the exact output is implementation defined, many compilers use a message similar to this:

Assertion failed: < *expression* >, file < *file* >, line < *linenum* >

The **assert( )** macro is generally used to help verify that a program is operating correctly. The expression is devised so that it evaluates to true only when no errors have taken place.

You need not remove the **assert( )** statements from the source code once a program is debugged because, if the macro **NDEBUG** is defined (as anything), the **assert( )** macros are ignored.

Example

This code fragment tests if the data read from a serial port is ASCII (that is, that it does not use the seventh bit):

```
   .
   .
   .
ch = read_port();
assert(!(ch & 128)); /* check bit 7 */
   .
   .
   .
```

Related Function

abort( )

#include "stdlib.h"
int atexit(void (*func)(void));

Description

The **atexit( )** function registers the function pointed to by *func* as a function to be called upon normal program termination. That is, at the end of a program run, the specified function is called.

The **atexit( )** function returns zero if the function is successfully registered as a termination function; otherwise, it returns nonzero.

The ANSI standard specifies that at least 32 termination functions may be established and that they be called in the reverse order of their establishment. In other words, the registration process is stack-like.

Example

This program prints **hello there** on the screen when it terminates.

```
#include "stdlib.h"
#include "stdio.h"

void done(void);

void main(void)
{
   if(atexit(done)) printf("error in atexit()");
}

void done(void)
{
   printf("hello there");
}
```

Related Functions

abort( ), **exit( )**

#include "stdlib.h"
double atof(const char *str);

Description

The **atof( )** function converts the string pointed to by *str* into a **double** value. The string must contain a valid floating-point number. If not, the returned value is undefined.

The number may be terminated by any character that cannot be part of a valid floating-point number. This includes white space, punctuation other than periods, and characters other than "E" or "e." This means that if **atof( )** is called with ″100.00HELLO″, the value **100.00** is returned.

Example

This program reads two floating-point numbers and displays their sum:

```
#include "stdlib.h"
#include "stdio.h"

void main(void)
{
  char num1[80], num2[80];

  printf("enter first: ");
  gets(num1);
  printf("enter second: ");
  gets(num2);
  printf("the sum is: %lf", atof(num1) + atof(num2));
}
```

Related Functions

atoi( ), atol( )

#include ″stdlib.h″
int atoi(const char *str);

Description

The **atoi( )** function converts the string pointed to by *str* into an integer value. The string must contain a valid integer. If not, the returned value is undefined; however, most implementations return zero.

The number may be terminated by any character that cannot be part of an integer. This includes white space, punctuation, and characters other than "E" or "e." If **atoi( )** is called with ″123.23″, the integer value **123** is returned and 0.23 is ignored.

Example

The following program reads two integers and displays their sum.

```
#include "stdlib.h"
#include "stdio.h"

void main(void)
{
  char num1[80], num2[80];

  printf("enter first: ");
  gets(num1);
  printf("enter second: ");
  gets(num2);
  printf("the sum is: %d", atoi(num1)+atoi(num2));
}
```

Related Functions

atof( ), atol( )

#include "stdlib.h"
int atol(char *str);

Description

The atol( ) function converts the string pointed to by *str* into a **long int** value. The string must contain a valid **long** integer. If not, the returned value is undefined; however, most implementations return zero.

The number may be terminated by any character that cannot be part of an integer. This includes white space, punctuation, and characters other than "E" or "e." If **atol( )** is called with "123.23", for example, the integer value **123** is returned and 0.23 is ignored.

Example

This program reads two **long** integers and displays their sum:

```
#include "stdlib.h"
#include "stdio.h"

void main(void)
{
  char num1[80], num2[80];
```

```
    printf("enter first: ");
    gets(num1);
    printf("enter second: ");
    gets(num2);
    printf("the sum is: %ld", atol(num1)+atol(num2));
}
```

Related Functions

atof( ), atoi( )

#include "stdlib.h"
void *bsearch(const void *key, const void *buf,
size_t num, size_t size,
int (*compare)(const void *, const void *));

Description

The **bsearch( )** function performs a binary search on the sorted array pointed to by *buf,* returning a pointer to the first member that matches the key pointed to by *key.* The number of elements in the array is specified by *num* and the size (in bytes) of each element is described by *size.*

The function pointed to by *compare* compares an element of the array with the key. The form of the *compare* function must be

int *func_name*(const void *arg1, const *arg2);

It must return the following values:

If *arg1* is less than *arg2,* return less than zero.
If *arg1* is equal to *arg2,* return zero.
If *arg1* is greater than *arg2,* return greater than zero.

The array must be sorted in ascending order with the lowest address containing the lowest element. If the array does not contain the key, a null pointer is returned.

Example

The following program reads characters entered at the keyboard (assuming buffered keyboard I/O) and determines whether they belong to the alphabet.

```
#include "stdlib.h"
#include "ctype.h"
#include "stdio.h"
#include "conio.h"

char *alpha="abcdefghijklmnopqrstuvwxyz";

int comp(const char *ch, const char *s);

void main(void)
{
  char ch;
  char *p;

  do {
    printf("enter a character: ");
    ch = getche();
    ch = tolower(ch);
    p = (char *) bsearch(&ch, alpha, 26, 1, comp);
    if(p) printf("is in alphabet\n");
    else printf("is not in alphabet\n");
  } while(p);
}

/* compare two characters */
comp(const char *ch, const char *s)
{
  return *ch-*s;
}
```

Related Function

qsort( )

#include "stdlib.h"
div_t div(int numerator, int denominator);

Description

The **div( )** function returns the quotient and the remainder of the opera-tion *numerator/denominator* in a structure of type **div_t**.

The structure type **div_t** is defined in STDLIB.H and has at least these two fields:

```
int quot;   /* the quotient */
int rem;    /* the remainder */
```

Example

This program displays the quotient and remainder of 10/3:

```
#include "stdlib.h"
#include "stdio.h"

void main(void)
{
  div_t n;

  n = div(10, 3);

  printf("quotient and remainder: %d %d\n", n.quot, n.rem);

}
```

Related Function

ldiv( )

#include "stdlib.h"
void exit(int exit _ code);

Description

The **exit( )** function causes immediate, normal termination of a program.

The value of *exit _ code* is passed to the calling process, usually the operating system, if the environment supports it. By convention, if the value of *status* is zero, normal program termination is assumed. A nonzero value may indicate an implementation-defined error.

Example

This function performs menu selection for a mailing list program. If **Q** is selected, the program is terminated.

```
menu(void)
{
  char choice;

  do {
    printf("Enter names (E)\n");
    printf("Delete name (D)\n");
    printf("Print (P)\n");
    printf("Quit (Q)\n");
    choice = getche();
  } while(!strchr("EDPQ", toupper(choice)));
  if(choice=='Q') exit(0);
  return ch;
}
```

Related Functions

abort( ), atexit( )

#include "stdlib.h"
char *getenv(const char *name);

Description

The **getenv( )** function returns a pointer to environmental information associated with the string pointed to by *name* in the implementation-defined environmental information table. The string returned must never be changed by the program.

The environment of a program may include such things as path names and on-line devices. The exact nature of this data is implementation defined. Refer to your compiler's user manual for details.

If a call is made to **getenv( )** with an argument that does not match any of the environment data, a null pointer is returned.

Example

Assuming that a specific compiler maintains environmental information about the devices connected to the system, the following fragment returns a pointer to the list of devices:

```
      .
      .
      .
p = getevn("DEVICES");
      .
      .
      .
```

Related Function

system( )

#include "stdlib.h"
char *itoa(int num, const char *str, int radix);

Description

The **itoa**( ) function is not currently defined by the ANSI standard, but is found with many compilers.

The **itoa**( ) function converts the integer *num* into its string equivalent and places the result in the string pointed to by *str*. The base of the output string is determined by *radix*, which is generally in the range 2 through 16.

The **itoa**( ) function returns a pointer to *str*. Usually, there is no error return value. Be sure to call **itoa**( ) with a string of sufficient length to hold the converted result.

Example

This program displays the value of 1423 in hexadecimal (58F):

```
#include "stdlib.h"
#include "stdio.h"

void main(void)
{
  char p[20];

  itoa(1423, p, 16);

  printf(p);
}
```

Related Functions

atoi( ), sscanf( )

#include "stdlib.h"
long labs(long num);

Description

The **labs( )** function returns the absolute value of *num.*

Example

This function converts the number entered at the keyboard into its absolute value:

```
#include "stdlib.h"

long int get_labs()
{
  char num[80];

  gets(num)

  return labs(atol(num));
}
```

Related Function

abs( )

#include "stdlib.h"
ldiv_t ldiv(long numerator, long denominator);

Description

The **ldiv( )** function returns the quotient and remainder of the operation *numerator/denominator.*

The structure type **ldiv_t** is defined in STDLIB.H and has at least these two fields:

```
long quot;    /* the quotient */
long rem;     /* the remainder */
```

Example

This program displays the quotient and remainder of 100000L/3L:

```
#include "stdlib.h"
#include "stdio.h"

void main(void)
{
  ldiv_t n;

  n = ldiv(100000L, 3L);

  printf("quotient & remainder: %ld %ld\n", n.quot, n.rem);

}
```

Related Function

div( )

#include "setjmp.h"
void longjmp(jmp_buf envbuf, int status);

Description

The **longjmp( )** function causes program execution to resume at the point of the last call to **setjmp( )**. These two functions are C's way of providing for a jump between functions. Notice that the header SET-JUMP.H is required.

The **longjmp( )** function resets the stack as described in *envbuf*, which must have been set by a prior call to **setjmp( )**. This causes program execution to resume at the statement following the **setjmp( )** invocation. That is, the computer is "tricked" into thinking that it never left the function that called **setjmp( )**. In effect, **longjmp( )** "warps" across time and (memory) space to a previous point in your program without having to perform the normal function return process.

The buffer *evnbuf* is of type **jmp_buf**, which is defined in the header SETJMP.H. The buffer must have been set through a call to setjmp( ) prior to calling **longjmp( )**.

The value of *status* becomes the return value of **setjump( )** and may be interrogated to determine where the long jump came from. The only value not allowed is zero.

The **longjmp( )** function must be called before the function that called **setjmp( )** returns. If not, the result is technically undefined. (Actually, a crash will almost certainly occur.)

By far the most common use of **longjmp( )** is to return from a deeply nested set of routines when an error occurs.

Example

This program prints **1 2 3**:

```
#include "setjmp.h"
#include "stdio.h"

jmp_buf ebuf;
void f2(void);

void main(void)
{
  char first=1;
  int i;

  printf("1 ");
  i = setjmp(ebuf);
  if(first) {
    first =! first;
    f2();
    printf("this will not be printed");
  }
  printf("%d", i);
}

void f2(void)
{
  printf("2 ");
  longjmp(ebuf, 3);
}
```

Related Function

setjmp( )

#include "stdlib.h"
char *ltoa(int long num, const char *str, int radix);

Description

The **ltoa( )** function is not currently defined by the ANSI standard but is found in many C compilers.

The **ltoa( )** function converts the **long** integer *num* into its string equivalent, placing the result in the string pointed to by *str*. The base of the output string is determined by *radix*, which is usually in the range 2 through 16.

The **ltoa( )** function returns a pointer to *str*. Generally, there is no error return value. Be sure to call **ltoa( )** with a string long enough to hold the converted result.

Example

This program displays the value of 1423 in hexadecimal (58F):

```
#include "stdlib.h"
#include "stdio.h"

void main(void)
{
  char p[20];

  ltoa(1423L, p, 16);

  printf(p);
}
```

Related Function

itoa( )

#include "stdlib.h"
void qsort(void *buf, size_t num, size_t size,
int (*compare)(const void *, const void *));

Description

The **qsort( )** function sorts the array pointed to by *buf* using a quicksort. The quicksort is generally considered the best general-purpose sorting algorithm. (See Chapter 19 for full coverage of sorting and searching in

C.) Upon termination, the array is sorted. The number of elements in the array is specified by *num* and the size (in bytes) of each element is described by *size*.

The function pointed to by *compare* is used to compare an element of the array with the key. The form of *compare* must be

func_name(const void *arg1, const void *arg2);

It must return the following values:

If *arg1* is less than *arg2*, return less than zero.
If *arg1* is equal to *arg2*, return zero.
If *arg1* is greater than *arg2*, return greater than zero.

The array is sorted into ascending order with the lowest address containing the lowest element.

Example

This program sorts a list of integers and displays the result:

```
#include "stdlib.h"
#include "stdio.h"

int num[10]= {
  1, 3, 6, 5, 8, 7, 9, 6, 2, 0
};

int comp(const int *, const int *);

void main(void)
{
  int i;

  printf("original array: ");
  for(i=0; i<10; i++) printf("%d ", num[i]);

  qsort(num, 10, sizeof(int), comp);

  printf("sorted array: ");
  for(i=0; i<10; i++) printf("%d ", num[i]);
}

/* compare the integers */
comp(const int *i, const int *j)
{
```

```
    return *i-*j;
}
```

Related Function

bsearch( )

#include "signal.h"
int raise(int signal);

Description

The **raise( )** function sends the signal specified by *signal* to the executing program. It returns zero if successful; otherwise, it returns nonzero. Its uses the header file SIGNAL.H.

Example

The **raise( )** function is somewhat implementation-specific. Refer to your compiler's user's manual for details and examples.

Related Function

signal( )

#include "stdlib.h"
int rand(void);

Description

The **rand( )** function generates a sequence of pseudorandom numbers. Each time it is called, an integer between zero and **RAND_MAX** is returned.

Example

The following program displays ten pseudorandom numbers.

```
#include "stdlib.h"
#include "stdio.h"

void main(void)
{
  int i;

  for(i=0; i<10; i++)
    printf("%d ", rand());
}
```

Related Function

srand( )

#include "setjmp.h"
int setjmp(jmp_buf envbuf);

Description

The **setjmp( )** function saves the contents of the system stack in the buffer *envbuf* for later use by **longjmp( )**. It uses the header file SETJMP.H.

The **setjmp( )** function returns zero upon invocation. However, a **longjmp( )** passes an argument to **setjmp( )** when it executes; this value (always nonzero) appears to be **setjmp( )**'s value after a call to **longjmp( )**. See **longjmp( )** for addition information.

Example

This program prints **1 2 3**:

```
#include "setjmp.h"
#include "stdio.h"

jmp_buf ebuf;
void f2(void);

void main(void)
{
  char first=1;
  int i;
```

```
  printf("1 ");
  i = setjmp(ebuf);
  if(first) {
    first = !first;
    f2();
    printf("this will not be printed");
  }
  printf("%d",i);
}

void f2(void)
{
 printf("2 ");
 longjmp(ebuf,3);
}
```

Related Function

longjmp( )

#include "signal.h"
void (*signal(int signal, void (*func)(int))) (int);

Description

The **signal( )** function defines the function, *func,* to be executed if the specified signal *signal* is received. This function is somewhat implementation-specific. However, the value for *func* must be one of the following macros, defined in SIGNAL.H, or the address of a function:

Macro	**Meaning**
SIG_DFL	Use default signal handling
SIG_IGN	Ignore the signal

If a function address is used, the specified function is executed. On MS-DOS machines, **signal( )** is used in setting up critical error handlers, and control-C handlers.

Example

See your compiler's user's manual for details and examples relative to your system.

Related Function

raise( )

#include "stdlib.h"
void srand(unsigned seed);

Description

The **srand( )** function sets a starting point for the sequence generated by **rand( )**, which returns pseudorandom numbers.

srand( ) is generally used to allow multiple program runs to use different sequences of pseudorandom numbers by specifying different starting points. However, you can generate the same pseudorandom sequence over and over by calling **srand( )** with the same seed before starting the sequence each time.

Example

This program uses the system time to randomly initialize the **rand( )** function by using **srand( )**:

```
#include "stdio.h"
#include "stdlib.h"
#include "time.h"

/* Seed rand with the system time
   and display the first 10 numbers.
*/
void main(void)
{
  int i, stime;
  long ltime;

  /* get the current calendar time */
```

```
    ltime = time(NULL);
    stime = (unsigned) ltime/2;
    srand(stime);
    for(i=0; i<10; i++) printf("%d ", rand());
}
```

Related Function

rand( )

#include "stdlib.h"
double strtod(const char *start, char **end);

Description

The **strtod( )** function converts the string representation of a number stored in the string pointed to by *start* into a **double** and returns the result.

The **strtod( )** function works as follows. First, any white space in the string pointed to by *start* is stripped. Next, each character that constitutes the number is read. Any character that cannot be part of a floating-point number causes this process to stop. This includes white space, punctuation (other than periods), and characters other than "E" or "e." Finally, *end* is set to point to the remainder, if any, of the original string. This means that if **strtod( )** is called with " 100.00 Pliers", the value **100.00** is returned and *end* points to the space that precedes the word "Pliers."

If a conversion error occurs, **strtod( )** returns either **HUGE_VAL** for overflow or **−HUGE_VAL** for underflow. If no conversion could take place, zero is returned. In either case, the global variable **errno** is set to **ERANGE**, indicating a range error.

Example

This program reads floating-point numbers from a character array:

```
#include "stdlib.h"
#include "ctype.h"
#include "stdio.h"
```

```
void main(void)
{
  char *end, *start="100.00 pliers 200.00 hammers";

  end = start;
  while(*start) {
    printf("%f, ", strtod(start, &end));
    printf("remainder: %s\n" ,end);
    start = end;
    /* move past the non-digits */
    while(!isdigit(*start) && *start) start++;
  }
}
```

The output is

> 100.00000, remainder: pliers 200.00 hammers
> 200.00000, remainder: hammers

Related Function

atof( )

#include ''stdlib.h''
long strtol(const char *start, char **end, int radix);

Description

The **strtol( )** function converts the string representation of a number stored in the string pointed to by *start* into a **long** and returns the result. The base of the number is determined by *radix*. If *radix* is zero, the base is determined by rules that govern constant specification. If the radix is other than zero, it must be in the range 2 through 36.

The **strtol( )** function works as follows. First, any white space in the string pointed to by *start* is stripped. Next, each character that constitutes the number is read. Any character that cannot be part of a **long** integer number causes this process to stop. This includes white space, punctuation, and characters. Finally, *end* is set to point to the remainder, if any, of the original string. This means that if **strtol( )** is called with " 100 Pliers", the value **100L** will be returned and *end* will point to the space that precedes the word "Pliers."

If a conversion error occurs, **strtol( )** returns either **LONG_MAX** for overflow or **LONG_MIN** for underflow. The global **errno** is also set to **ERANGE**, indicating a range error. If no conversion could take place, zero is returned.

Example

This function reads base 10 numbers from standard input and returns their **long** equivalent.

```
#include "stdlib.h"
#include "stdio.h"

long read_long(void)
{
  char start[80], *end;

  printf("enter a number: ");
  gets(start);
  return strtol(start, &end,10);
}
```

Related Function

atol( )

#include "stdlib.h"
unsigned long strtoul(char *start, char **end, int radix);

Description

The **strtoul( )** function converts the string representation of a number stored in the string pointed to by *start* into an **unsigned long** and returns the result. The base of the number is determined by *radix*. If *radix* is zero, the base is determined by rules that govern constant specification. If *radix* is specified, it must be in the range 2 through 36.

The **strtoul( )** function works as follows. First, any white space in the string pointed to by *start* is stripped. Next, each character that comprises the number is read. Any character that cannot be part of an **unsigned long** integer causes this process to stop. This includes white space, punctuation, and characters. Finally, *end* is set to point to the remainder, if any, of the original string. This means that if **strtoul( )** is called with " 100 Pliers", the value **100L** will be returned and *end* will point to the space that precedes the word "Pliers."

If a conversion error occurs, then **strtoul( )** will return either **ULONG_MAX** for overflow or **ULONG_MIN** for underflow. The global variable **errno** is also set to **ERANGE**, indicating a range error. If no conversion could take place, zero is returned.

Example

This function reads unsigned base 16 (hexadecimal) numbers from standard input and returns their **unsigned long** equivalent:

```
#include "stdlib.h"

unsigned long read_unsigned_long(void)
{
  char start[80], *end;

  printf("enter a hex number: ");
  gets(start);
  return strtoul(start, &end, 16);
}
```

Related Function

strtol( )

#include "stdlib.h"
int system(const char *str);

Description

The **system( )** function passes the string pointed to by *str* as a command to the command processor of the operating system.

If **system( )** is called with a null pointer, it returns nonzero if a command processor is present, zero otherwise. (Remember, some C code will be executed in dedicated systems that do not have operating systems and command processors.) The return value of **system( )** is implementation defined when called with a pointer to a command string. However, generally it returns zero if the command was successfully executed, nonzero otherwise.

Example

Using the DOS operating system, this program displays the contents of the current working directory:

```
#include "stdlib.h"

void main(void)
{
  system("dir");
}
```

Related Function

exit( )

#include ''stdarg.h''
void va＿arg(va＿list argptr, type);
type va＿start(va＿list argptr, last＿parm);
void va＿end(va＿list argptr);

Description

The **va＿arg( )**, **va＿start( )**, and **va＿end( )** macros work together to allow a variable number of arguments to be passed to a function. The most common example of a function that takes a variable number of arguments is **printf( )**. The type **va＿list** is defined by STDARG.H.

The general procedure for creating a function that can take a variable number of arguments is as follows. The function must have at least one known parameter prior to the variable parameter list, but may have more. The rightmost known parameter is *last_parm*. Before any of the variable length parameters may be accessed, the argument pointer *argptr* must be initialized through a call to **va_start( )**. After that, parameters are returned via calls to **va_arg( )**, with *type* being the type of the next parameter. Finally, after all of the parameters have been read and before returning from the function, a call to **va_end( )** must be made to ensure that the stack is properly restored. If **va_end( )** is not called, a program crash is very likely.

Example

This program uses **sum_series( )** to return the sum of a series of numbers. The first argument contains a count of the number of arguments to follow. In this example, the program sums the first five elements of the series:

$$\frac{1}{2} + \frac{1}{4} + \frac{1}{8} + \frac{1}{16} + \dots \frac{1}{2^N}$$

The output displayed is **0.968750**.

```
#include "stdio.h"
#include "stdarg.h"

double sum_series(int num, ...);

/* variable length argument example - sum a series */
void main(void)
{
  double d, sum_series();

  d = sum_series(5, 0.5, 0.25, 0.125, 0.0625, 0.03125);

  printf("sum of series is %f\n", d);
}

double sum_series(int num, ...)
{
  double sum=0.0, t;
  va_list argptr;
```

```
   /* initialize argptr */
   va_start(argptr, num);

   /* sum the series */
   for( ; num; num--) {
     t = va_arg(argptr, double);
     sum += t;
   }

   /* do orderly shutdown */
   va_end(argptr);
   return sum;
}
```

Related Function

vprintf( )

Algorithms and Applications

Sorting and Searching
Queues, Stacks, Linked Lists, and Trees
Sparse Arrays
Expression Parsing and Evaluation
AI-Based Problem Solving
Using System Resources
Graphics

Part Three presents many common and useful algorithms and applications that illustrate many aspects of the C language. The code conforms closely with the ANSI standard. However, if your compiler does not support the entire standard, you will have to make only minor alterations. For the most part these alterations will consist of the substitution of **int** for **void** and **char *** for **void ***.

Sorting and Searching

In the world of computers, sorting and searching are perhaps the most fundamental and extensively analyzed tasks. These routines are used in almost all database programs as well as in compilers, interpreters, and operating systems. This chapter introduces the basics of sorting and searching. Since the point of sorting data is generally to make searching that data easier and faster, sorting is discussed first.

Sorting

Sorting is the process of arranging a set of similar information into an increasing or decreasing order. Specifically, given a sorted list i of n elements, then

$$i_1 <= i_2 <= \ldots <= i_n$$

Even though most C compilers supply the function **qsort( )** as part of the standard library, you should understand sorting for three reasons. First, you cannot apply a generalized function like **qsort( )** to all situations. Second, because **qsort( )** is parameterized to operate on a wide variety of data, it runs more slowly than a similar sort that operates on only one type of data. (Generalization inherently increases run time because of the extra processing time needed to handle various data types.) Finally, as you will see, although the quicksort algorithm (used by **qsort( )**) is very effective in the general case, it may not be the best sort for specialized situations.

There are two general categories of sorting algorithms: algorithms that sort arrays (both in memory and in random-access disk files), and algorithms that sort sequential disk or tape files. This chapter is concerned only with the first category because it is most relevant to the average programmer.

Generally, when information is sorted, only a portion of that information is used as the sort *key*. This key is used in comparisons, but when an exchange is made, the entire data structure is swapped. For example, in a mailing list the ZIP code field might be used as the key, but the entire address is sorted. For the sake of simplicity, the examples will sort character arrays as you learn about the various sorting methods. Later, you will learn how to adapt these methods to any type of data structure.

Classes of Sorting Algorithms

There are three general methods for sorting arrays:

- Exchange
- Selection
- Insertion

To understand these three methods, imagine a deck of cards. To sort the cards by using *exchange*, spread them on a table, face up, and then exchange out-of-order cards until the deck is ordered. Using *selection*, spread the cards on the table, select the card of lowest value, take it out of the deck, and hold it in your hand. Then, from the remaining cards on the table, select the lowest card and place it behind the one already in your hand. This process continues until all the cards are in your hand. The cards in your hand will be sorted when you finish the process. To sort the cards by using *insertion*, hold all the cards in your hand. Place one card at a time on the table, always inserting it in the correct position. The deck will be sorted when you have no cards in your hand.

Judging Sorting Algorithms

There are many different algorithms for each sorting method. They all have some merits, but the general criteria for judging a sorting algorithm are

- How fast can it sort information in an average case?

- How fast are its best and worst cases?

- Does it exhibit natural or unnatural behavior?

- Does it rearrange elements with equal keys?

Look closely at these criteria now. Clearly, how fast a particular algorithm sorts is of great concern. The speed with which an array can be sorted is directly related to the number of comparisons and the number of exchanges that take place, with exchanges taking more time. A *comparison* occurs when one array element is compared to another; an *exchange* happens when two elements in the array are swapped. As you will soon see, some sorts require an exponential amount of time per element to sort and some require logarithmic time.

The best- and worst-case run times are important if you expect to encounter one of these situations, frequently. Often a sort has a good average case but a terrible worst case.

A sort is said to exhibit *natural* behavior if it works least when the list is already in order, works harder as the list becomes less ordered, and works hardest when a list is in inverse order. How hard a sort works is based on the number of comparisons and exchanges that it executes.

To understand why rearranging elements with equal keys may be important, imagine a database such as a mailing list, which is sorted on a main key and a subkey. The main key is the ZIP code, and within ZIP codes the last name is the subkey. When a new address is added to the list and the list is re-sorted, you do not want the subkeys (that is, the last names within ZIP codes) to be rearranged. To guarantee that this doesn't happen, a sort must not exchange main keys of equal value.

The discussion that follows first examines the representative sorts from each category and then analyzes the efficiency of each. Later, you'll learn improved sorting methods.

The Bubble Sort—The Demon of Exchange

The most well-known (and infamous) sort is the *bubble sort*. Its popularity is derived from its catchy name and its simplicity. However, it is one of the worst sorts ever conceived.

The bubble sort is an exchange sort. It involves the repeated comparison and, if necessary, the exchange of adjacent elements. The elements are like bubbles in a tank of water—each seeks its own level. The simplest form of the bubble sort is shown here:

```
/* The Bubble Sort. */
void bubble(char *item, int count)
{
  register int a, b;
  register char t;

  for(a=1; a<count; ++a)
    for(b=count-1; b>=a; --b) {
      if(item[b-1] > item[b]) {
        /* exchange elements */
        t = item[b-1];
        item[b-1] = item[b];
        item[b] = t;
      }
    }
}
```

In the preceding code **item** is a pointer to the character array to be sorted and **count** is the number of elements in the array. The bubble sort is driven by two loops. Given that there are **count** elements in the array, the outer loop causes the array to be scanned **count**−1 times. This ensures that, in the worst case, every element is in its proper position when the function terminates. The inner loop actually performs the comparisons and exchanges. (A slightly improved version of the bubble sort terminates if no exchanges occur, but this adds another comparison in each pass through the inner loop.)

You can use this version of the bubble sort to sort a character array into ascending order. For example, the following short program sorts a string typed in from the keyboard:

```
/* Sort Driver */

#include "string.h"
#include "stdio.h"
#include "stdlib.h"
```

```
void bubble(char *item, int count);

void main(void)
{
  char s[80];

  printf("enter a string:");
  gets(s);
  bubble(s, strlen(s));
  printf("the sorted string is: %s\n", s);
}
```

To see how the bubble sort works, assume that the array to be sorted is **dcab**. Each pass is shown here:

initial	d	c	a	b
pass 1	a	d	c	b
pass 2	a	b	d	c
pass 3	a	b	c	d

In analyzing any sort, you should determine how many comparisons and exchanges will be performed for the best, average, and worst case. With the bubble sort, the number of comparisons is always the same because the two **for** loops repeat the specified number of times whether the list is initially ordered or not. This means that the bubble sort always performs

$$1/2(n^2 - n)$$

comparisons, where n is the number of elements to be sorted. This formula is derived from the fact that the outer loop executes $n - 1$ times and the inner loop $n/2$ times. Multiplied together, these numbers result in the preceding formula.

The number of exchanges is zero for the best case, an already sorted list. The number of exchanges for the average- and worst-case exchanges are

average $3/4(n^2 - n)$

worst $3/2(n^2 - n)$

It is beyond the scope of this book to explain the derivation of the preceding formulas, but you can guess that as the list becomes less ordered, the number of elements out of order approaches the number of comparisons. (Remember that in a bubble sort, there are three exchanges for every element out of order.) The bubble sort is said to be an *n-squared algorithm* because its execution time is a multiple of the square of the number of elements. Frankly, this type of algorithm is very ineffective when applied to a large number of elements because execution time is directly related to the number of comparisons and exchanges. For example, ignoring the time that it takes to exchange any out-of-position element, assume that each comparison takes 0.001 seconds. Sorting ten elements takes about 0.05 seconds, sorting 100 elements takes about 5 seconds, and sorting 1000 elements takes about 500 seconds. A sort of 100,000 elements, the number in a small phone book, takes about 5,000,000 seconds or about 1,400 hours—that is two months of continuous sorting! Figure 19-1 shows how execution time increases relative to the size of the array.

You can make slight improvements to the bubble sort in an attempt to speed it up. For example, the bubble sort has one peculiarity: An

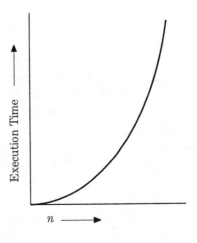

Figure 19-1.   Execution time of an n^2 sort in relation to array size

out-of-order element at the large end (such as "a" in the **dcab** example) goes to its proper position in one pass, but a misplaced element in the small end (such as "d") rises very slowly to its proper place. This suggests an improvement to the bubble sort.

Instead of always reading the array in the same direction, subsequent passes could reverse direction. In this way greatly out-of-place elements travel quickly to their correct position. This version of the bubble sort is called the *shaker sort* because it imparts the effect of a shaking motion to the array. The code that follows shows how a shaker sort works.

```
/* The Shaker Sort. */
void shaker(char *item, int count)
{
  register int a;
  int exchange;
  char t;

  do {
    exchange = 0;
    for(a=count-1; a>0; --a) {
      if(item[a-1]>item[a]) {
        t = item[a-1];
        item[a-1] = item[a];
        item[a] = t;
        exchange = 1;
      }
    }

    for(a=1; a<count; ++a) {
      if(item[a-1]>item[a]) {
        t = item[a-1];
        item[a-1] = item[a];
        item[a] = t;
        exchange = 1;
      }
    }
  } while(exchange); /* sort until no exchages
                        take place */
}
```

Although the shaker sort improves the bubble sort, it still executes on the order of an *n*-squared algorithm. This is because the number of comparisons has not been changed and the number of exchanges has only been reduced by a relatively small constant. The shaker sort is better than the bubble sort, but better sorts exist.

Sorting by Selection

A selection sort selects the element with the lowest value and exchanges it with the first element. Then from the remaining $n-1$ elements, the element with the smallest key is found and exchanged with the second element, and so forth. The exchanges continue to the last two elements. For example, if the selection method were used on the array **bdac**, each pass would look like this:

initial	b d a c
pass 1	a d b c
pass 2	a b d c
pass 3	a b c d

The code that follows shows the basic selection sort.

```
/* The Selection Sort. */
void select(char *item, int count)
{
  register int a, b, c;
  int exchange;
  char t;

  for(a=0; a<count-1; ++a) {
    exchange = 0;
    c = a;
    t = item[a];
    for(b=a+1; b<count; ++b) {
      if(item[b]<t) {
        c = b;
        t = item[b];
        exchange = 1;
      }
    }
    if(exchange) {
      item[c] = item[a];
      item[a] = t;
    }
  }
}
```

Unfortunately, as with the bubble sort, the outer loop executes $n-1$ times and the inner loop $1/2(n)$ times. As a result, the selection sort requires

$$1/2(n^2-n)$$

comparisons, making it too slow for a large number of items. The number of exchanges for the best and worst cases are

best $3(n-1)$
worst $n^2/4+3\ (n-1)$

For the best case, only $n-1$ elements need to be moved if the list is ordered, and each move requires three exchanges. The worst case approximates the number of comparisons. The average case is difficult to determine and its derivation is beyond the scope of this book. However, it is

$$n(\ln n + y)$$

where y is Euler's constant, about 0.577216.

Although the number of comparisons for both the bubble sort and the selection sort are the same, the number of exchanges in the average case is far less for the selection sort. However, better sorts exist.

Sorting by Insertion

The insertion sort is the third and last of the simple sorting algorithms. It initially sorts the first two members of the array. Next, the algorithm inserts the third member into its sorted position in relation to the first two members. Then it inserts the fourth element into the list of three elements. The process continues until all elements have been sorted. For example, given the array **dcab**, each pass of the insertion sort is shown here:

initial   d c a b
pass 1   c d a b
pass 3   a c d b
pass 4   a b c d

The code for a version of the insertion sort is

```
/* The Insertion Sort. */
void insert(char *item, int count)
{

  register int a, b;
  char t;

  for(a=1; a<count; ++a) {
    t = item[a];
    for(b=a-1; b>=0 && t<item[b]; b--)
      item[b+1] = item[b];
    item[b+1] = t;
  }
}
```

Unlike the bubble and selection sorts, the number of comparisons that occurs during insertion sorts depends upon how the list is initially ordered. If the list is in order, the number of comparisons is $n-1$. If it is out of order, it is

$$1/2(n^2+n)-1$$

The average case is

$$1/4(n^2+n-2)$$

The number of exchanges are

best	$2(n-1)$
average	$1/4(n^2+9n-10)$
worst	$1/2(n^2+3n-4)$

Therefore, for worst cases the insertion sort is as bad as the bubble sort and selection sort, and for average cases it is only slightly better. However, the insertion sort does have two advantages. First, it behaves naturally. That is, it works the least when the array is already sorted and the hardest when the array is sorted in inverse order. This makes the insertion sort excellent for lists that are almost in order. The second advantage is that it leaves the order of equal keys the same. This means that if a list is sorted by two keys, it remains sorted for both keys after an insertion sort.

Even though the number of comparisons may be fairly low for certain sets of data, the array must always be shifted over each time an element is placed in its proper location. As a result, the number of moves can be significant. However, still better sorts exist.

Improved Sorts

All of the algorithms in the preceding section had the fatal flaw of executing in n-squared time. For large amounts of data, this makes the sorts very slow. In fact, at some point, the sorts would be too slow to use. Unfortunately, horror stories of "the sort that took three days" are often real. When a sort takes too long, it is usually the fault of the underlying algorithm. However, the first response is often "let's write it in assembly code." Assembly language does sometimes speed up a routine by a constant factor. If the underlying algorithm is inefficient, however, the sort will be slow no matter how optimal the coding. Remember: When a routine is running relative to n^2, increasing the speed of the code or the computer only causes a small improvement because the rate at which the run time is increasing is exponential. (In essence, the n^2 curve in Figure 19-1 is shifted to the right slightly, but is otherwise unchanged.) The rule of thumb is that if the routine is not fast enough when written in C, it will not be fast enough in assembly language. The solution is to use a better sorting algorithm.

This section describes two excellent sorts. The first is the Shell sort. The second, the quicksort, is usually considered the best sorting routine. These sorts run so fast that if you blink, you miss them!

The Shell Sort

The Shell sort is named after its inventor, D. L. Shell. However, the name probably stuck because its method of operation is often described in terms of seashells piled upon one another.

The general sorting method is derived from the insertion sort and is based on diminishing increments. Consider the diagram in Figure 19-2. First, all elements that are three positions apart are sorted. Then, all elements that are two positions apart are sorted. Finally, all elements adjacent to each other are sorted.

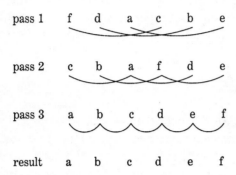

Figure 19-2.   The Shell sort

It is not easy to see that this method yields good results, or in fact that it even sorts the array. But it does. Each sorting pass involves relatively few elements, or elements that are already in reasonable order, so the Shell sort is efficient and each pass increases order.

The exact sequence for the increments can be changed. The only rule is that the last increment must be 1. For example, the sequence

9, 5, 3, 2, 1

works well and is used in the Shell sort shown here. Avoid sequences that are powers of 2—for mathematically complex reasons, they reduce the efficiency of the sorting algorithm (but the sort still works).

```
/* The Shell Sort. */
void shell(char *item, int count)
{
  register int i, j, gap, k;
  char x, a[5];

  a[0]=9; a[1]=5; a[2]=3; a[3]=2; a[4]=1;

  for(k=0; k<5; k++) {
    gap = a[k];
    for(i=gap; i<count; ++i) {
      x = item[i];
```

```
    for(j=i-gap; x<item[j] && j>=0; j=j-gap)
      item[j+gap] = item[j];
    item[j+gap] = x;
  }
 }
}
```

You may have noticed that the inner **for** loop has two test conditions. The comparison **x < item[j]** is obviously necessary for the sorting process. The test **j > = 0** keeps the sort from overrunning the boundary of the array **item**. These extra checks will degrade the performance of the Shell sort to some extent.

Slightly different versions of the sort employ special array elements called sentinels, which are not actually part of the array to be sorted. *Sentinels* hold special termination values that indicate the least and greatest possible element. In this way, the bounds checks are unnecessary. However, using sentinels requires a specific knowledge of the data, which limits the generality of the sort function.

The Shell sort presents some very difficult mathematical problems that are far beyond the scope of this discussion. Take it on faith that execution time is proportional to

$$n^{1.2}$$

for sorting n elements. This is a significant improvement over the n-squared sorts. To understand how great the improvement is, see Figure 19-3, which graphs both an n^2 and an $n^{1.2}$ sort. However, before getting too excited about the Shell sort, you should know that the quicksort is even better.

The Quicksort

The quicksort, invented and named by C.A.R. Hoare, is superior to all others in this book, and it is generally considered the best general-purpose sorting algorithm currently available. It is based on the exchange sort—surprising in light of the terrible performance of the bubble sort!

The quicksort is built on the idea of partitions. The general procedure is to select a value, called the *comparand,* and then to partition the array into two sections. All elements greater than or equal to the partition value are on one side and those less than the value are on the other. This process is then repeated for each remaining section until the

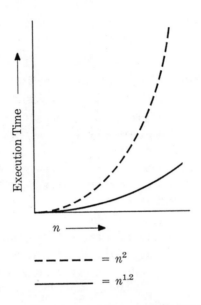

Figure 19-3.   The n^2 and $n^{1.2}$ curves

array is sorted. For example, given the array **fedacb** and using the value **d**, the first pass of the quicksort would rearrange the array as follows:

initial   f e d a c b

pass1   b c a d e f

This process is then repeated for each section—that is, **bca** and **def**. As you can see, the process is essentially recursive in nature and, indeed, the cleanest implementations of quicksort are recursive algorithms.

You can select the middle comparand value in two ways. You can either choose it at random or you can select it by averaging a small set of values taken from the array. For optimal sorting, you should select a value that is precisely in the middle of the range of values. However, this is not easy to do for most sets of data. In the worst case, the value chosen is at one extremity. Even in this case, however, quicksort still performs well. The following version of quicksort selects the middle element of the array. Although this may not always result in a good choice, the sort still performs correctly.

```
/* Quicksort setup function. */
void quick(char *item, int count)
{
  qs(item, 0, count-1);
}

/* The Quicksort. */
void qs(char *item, int left, int right)
{

  register int i, j;
  char x, y;

  i = left; j = right;
  x = item[(left+right)/2];

  do {
    while(item[i]<x && i<right) i++;
    while(x<item[j] && j>left) j--;

    if(i<=j) {
      y = item[i];
      item[i] = item[j];
      item[j] = y;
      i++; j--;
    }
  } while(i<=j);

  if(left<j)  qs(item, left, j);
  if(i<right) qs(item, i, right);
}
```

In this version, the function **quick( )** sets up a call to the main sorting function **qs( )**. This enables the same common interface of **item** and **count** to be maintained, but it is not essential because **qs( )** could have been called directly by using three arguments.

Deriving the number of comparisons and exchanges that quicksort performs requires mathematics beyond the scope of this book. However, the average number of comparisons is

$$n \log n$$

and the average number of exchanges is approximately

$n/6 \log n$

These numbers are significantly lower than those provided by any of the previous sorts.

Recall that

$$N = a^x$$

can be rewritten as

$$x = \log_x N$$

This means that if 100 elements were sorted, quicksort would require

$$100 * 2$$

or 200 comparisons because log 100 is 2. Compared with the bubble sort's 990 comparisons, this is quite good indeed.

You should be aware of one particularly problematic aspect to quicksort. If the comparand value for each partition is the largest value, quicksort degenerates into "slowsort" with an n-squared run time. Generally, however, this does not happen.

You must choose a method of defining the value of the comparand carefully. The method is frequently determined by the data that you are sorting. In very large mailing lists, where the sorting is often by ZIP code, the selection is simple because the ZIP codes are fairly evenly distributed — and a simple algebraic function can determine a suitable comparand. However, in certain databases, the keys may be the same or so close in value that a random selection is often the best one. A common and fairly effective method is to sample three elements from a partition and take the middle value.

Choosing a Sort

Generally, quicksort is the optimum sort because it is so fast. However, when only very small lists of data are to be sorted (less than 100), the overhead created by quicksort's recursive calls may offset the benefits of a superior algorithm. In rare cases like this, one of the simpler sorts — perhaps even the bubble sort — may be quicker.

Sorting Other Data Structures

Until now, you have been sorting only arrays of characters. Obviously, arrays of any of the built-in data types may be sorted by simply changing the data types of the parameters and variables to the sort function. Generally, however, complex data types like strings or groupings of information like structures need to be sorted. Most sorting involves a key and information linked to that key. To change the algorithms to accommodate a key, you need to alter the comparison section, the exchange section, or both. The algorithm itself remains unchanged.

Because quicksort is one of the best general-purpose routines available at this time, it is used in the following examples. However, the same techniques apply to any of the sorts described earlier.

Sorting Strings

The easiest way to sort strings is to create an array of character pointers to those strings. This allows you to maintain easy indexing and keeps the basic quicksort algorithm unchanged. The string version of quicksort that follows accepts an array of strings, each up to ten characters long. (You can change this length if you want.) This version sorts the strings in dictionary order.

```
/* A Quicksort for strings. */
void quick_string(char item[][10], int count)
{
  qs_string(item, 0, count-1);
}

void qs_string(char item[][10], int left, int right)
{
  register int i, j;
  char *x;
  char temp[10];
```

```
  i = left; j = right;
  x = item[(left+right)/2];

  do {
    while(strcmp(item[i],x)<0 && i<right) i++;
    while(strcmp(item[j],x)>0 && j>left) j--;
    if(i<=j) {
      strcpy(temp, item[i]);
      strcpy(item[i], item[j]);
      strcpy(item[j], temp);
      i++; j--;
    }
  } while(i<=j);

  if(left<j)  qs_string(item, left, j);
  if(i<right) qs_string(item, i, right);
}
```

Notice that the comparison step has been changed to use the function **strcmp( )**. The function returns a negative number if the first string is lexicographically less than the second, zero if the strings are equal, and a positive number if the first string is lexicographically greater than the second.

Be aware that **strcmp( )** slows down the sort for two reasons. First it involves a function call, which always takes time. Second, **strcmp( )** itself performs several comparisons to determine the relationship of the two strings. In the first case, if speed is absolutely critical, place the code for **strcmp( )** in line inside the routine by duplicating the **strcmp( )** code. In the second case, there is no way to avoid comparing the strings since, by definition, this is what the task involves.

Sorting Structures

Most application programs that require a sort probably need to have a grouping of data sorted. A mailing list is an excellent example because a name, street, city, state, and ZIP code are all linked together. When this conglomerate unit of data is sorted, a sort key is used but the entire structure is exchanged. To see how this is done, first create a structure. A convenient structure is

```
struct address {
        char name[40];
        char street[40];
        char city[20];
```

```
      char state[3];
      char zip[10];
};
```

state is three characters long and **ZIP** is ten characters long because, to store a null terminator, a string array always needs one more character than the maximum length of any string.

Since it is reasonable to arrange a mailing list as an array of structures, assume for this example that the sort routine will sort an array of structures of type **address**. Such a routine is shown here:

```
/* A Quicksort for structures of type address. */
void quick_struct(struct address item[], int count)
{
  qs_struct(item,0,count-1);
}

void qs_struct(struct address item[], int left, int right)
{

  register int i, j;
  char *x;
  struct address temp;

  i = left; j = right;
  x = item[(left+right)/2].zip;

  do {
    while(strcmp(item[i].zip,x)<0 && i<right) i++;
    while(strcmp(item[j].zip,x)>0 && j>left) j--;
    if(i<=j) {
      temp = item[i];
      item[i] = item[j];
      item[j] = temp;
      i++; j--;
    }
  } while(i<=j);

  if(left<j)  qs_struct(item, left, j);
  if(i<right) qs_struct(item, i, right);
}
```

Sorting Random-Access Disk Files

There are two types of disk files: *sequential* and *random access*. If either type of disk file is small enough, it may be read into memory and the array sorting routines presented earlier will be able to sort it. However, many disk files are too large to be sorted easily in memory and require special techniques. Most database applications use random-access disk files. This section shows one way random-access disk files may be sorted.

Random-access disk files have two major advantages over sequential disk files. First, they are easy to maintain. You can update information without having to copy the entire list. Second, they can be treated as a very large array on disk, which greatly simplifies sorting.

Treating a random-access file as an array means that you can use the basic quicksort with just a few modifications. Instead of indexing an array, the disk version of the quicksort must use **fseek( )** to seek the appropriate records on the disk.

In reality, each sorting situation differs in relation to the exact data structure that is sorted and the key that is used. However, you can learn the general idea of sorting random-access disk files by developing a sort program to sort structures of type **address**, the mailing-list structure defined earlier. The sample program that follows assumes that the number of elements is fixed at 100. In reality, a record count would have to be maintained dynamically.

```c
/* Disk sort for structures of type address */
#include "stdio.h"
#include "stdlib.h"
#include "string.h"

#define NUM_ELEMENTS 100   /* this is an arbitrary number
                              that should be determined
                              dynamically for each list */

struct address {
  char name[30];
  char street[40];
  char city[20];
  char state[3];
  char zip[10];
}ainfo;

void quick_disk(FILE *fp, int count);
void qs_disk(FILE *fp, int left, int right);
void swap_all_fields(FILE *fp, long i, long j);
char *get_zip(FILE *fp, long rec);

void main(void)
{
  FILE *fp;

  if((fp=fopen("mlist","rb+"))==NULL) {
```

```
      printf("cannot open file for read/write\n");
      exit(1);
   }

   quick_disk(fp, NUM_ELEMENTS);
   fclose(fp);
   printf("List sorted.\n");
}

/* A Quicksort for files. */
void quick_disk(FILE *fp, int count)
{
   qs_disk(fp, 0, count-1);
}

void qs_disk(FILE *fp, int left, int right)
{

   long int i, j;
   char x[100];

   i = left; j = right;

   strcpy(x, get_zip(fp,(long)(i+j)/2)); /* get the middle zip */

   do {
      while(strcmp(get_zip(fp,i),x)<0 && i<right) i++;
      while(strcmp(get_zip(fp,j),x)>0 && j>left) j--;

      if(i<=j) {
         swap_all_fields(fp, i, j);
         i++; j--;
      }
   } while(i<=j);

   if(left<j)  qs_disk(fp, left, (int) j);
   if(i<right) qs_disk(fp, (int) i, right);
}

void swap_all_fields(FILE *fp, long i, long j)
{

   char a[sizeof(ainfo)], b[sizeof(ainfo)];

   /* first read in record i and j */
   fseek(fp, sizeof(ainfo)*i, 0);
   fread(a, sizeof(ainfo), 1, fp);

   fseek(fp, sizeof(ainfo)*j, 0);
   fread(b, sizeof(ainfo), 1, fp);

   /* then write them back in opposite slots */
   fseek(fp, sizeof(ainfo)*j, 0);
   fwrite(a, sizeof(ainfo), 1, fp);

   fseek(fp, sizeof(ainfo)*i, 0);
   fwrite(b, sizeof(ainfo), 1, fp);
```

```
}

/* Return a pointer to the zip code */
char *get_zip(FILE *fp, long rec)
{
  struct address *p;

  p = &ainfo;

  fseek(fp, rec*sizeof(ainfo), 0);
  fread(p, sizeof(ainfo), 1, fp);

  return ainfo.zip;
}
```

As you can see, several support functions had to be written to sort the address records. In the comparison section of the sort, the function **get_zip( )** was used to return a pointer to the ZIP code of the comparand and the record being checked. The function **swap_all_fields( )** performs the actual data exchange. Note that under most operating systems, the order of the reads and writes has a great impact on the speed of this sort. When an exchange occurs, the code, as it is written, forces a seek to record **i**, then to **j**. While the head of the disk drive is still positioned at **j**, **i**'s data is written. This means that the head does not need to move a great distance. Had the code been written with **i**'s data first, an extra seek would have been necessary.

Searching

Databases of information exist so that, from time to time, a user can locate a record by entering its key. There is only one method of finding information in an unsorted file (array) and another for a sorted file (array). Many compilers supply search functions as part of the standard library. However, as with sorting, general-purpose routines sometimes are simply too inefficient for use in demanding situations because of the extra overhead created by their generalization.

Searching Methods

Finding information in an unsorted array requires a sequential search starting at the first element and stopping either when a match is found or at the end of the array. This method must be used on unsorted data but can be applied to sorted data as well. If the data has been sorted, you can use a binary search, which helps you locate the data more quickly.

The Sequential Search

The sequential search is simple to code. The following function searches a character array of known length until a match of the specified key is found:

```
sequential_search(char *item, int count, char key)
{
  register int t;
  for(t=0; t<count; ++t)
    if(key==item[t]) return t;
  return -1;  /* no match */
}
```

This function returns the index number of the matching entry if there is one; otherwise, it returns -1.

It is easy to see that a straight sequential search will, on the average, test $1/2n$ elements. In the best case, it tests only one element and in the worst case it tests n elements. If the information is stored on disk, the search time can be lengthy. But if the data is unsorted, you can only search sequentially.

The Binary Search

If the data to be searched is sorted, you can use a vastly superior method to find a match. It is the *binary search*, which uses the divide-and-conquer approach. To employ this method, test the middle element. If it is larger than the key, then test the middle element of the first half; otherwise, test the middle element of the second half. Repeat this procedure until a match is found or there are no more elements to test.

For example, to find the number 4 given the array

1 2 3 4 5 6 7 8 9

a binary search first tests the middle, which is 5. Since this is greater than 4, the search continues with the first half, or

1 2 3 4 5

The middle element is now 3. This is less than 4, so the first half is discarded. The search continues with

4 5

This time the match is found.

In a binary search, the number of comparisons in the worst case is

$$\log_2 n$$

In the average case, the number is somewhat lower and in the best case the number of comparisons is one.

A binary search function for character arrays follows. You can make this search for any arbitrary data structure by changing the comparison portion of the routine.

```
/* The Binary search. */
binary(char *item, int count, char key)
{
  int low,high, mid;

  low = 0; high = count-1;
  while(low<=high) {
    mid = (low+high)/2;
    if(key<item[mid]) high = mid-1;
    else if(key>item[mid]) low = mid+1;
    else return mid;  /* found */
  }
  return -1;
}
```

Queues, Stacks, Linked Lists, and Trees

Programs consist of two things: algorithms and data structures. A good program is a blend of both. The choice and implementation of a data structure is as important as the routines that manipulate it. How information is organized and accessed is usually determined by the nature of the programming problem. For this reason, it is important for you to have the right storage and retrieval method for a variety of situations in your bag of tricks.

How closely the logical concept of an item of data is bound to its machine representation is in inverse correlation to its abstraction. That is, as data types become more complex, the way the programmer thinks of them bears an ever decreasing resemblance to the way they are actually represented in memory. For example, simple types such as **char** and **int** are tightly bound to their machine representation, and the value an integer has in its machine representation closely approximates that which the programmer thinks it has. Simple arrays, which are organized collections of simple data types, are not quite as tightly bound as simple types because an array may not appear in memory the way the programmer thinks of it.

Even less tightly bound are **float**s. The actual representation inside the machine is little like the average programmer's conception of a floating-point number. The structure, which is a conglomerate data type accessed under one name, is even more abstracted from the machine

545

representation. The final level of abstraction transcends the mere physical aspects of the data and concentrates instead upon the sequence in which the data will be accessed—that is, stored and retrieved. In essence, the physical data is linked with a *data engine,* which controls the way information can be accessed by your program. There are basically four of these engines:

- A queue

- A stack

- A linked list

- A binary tree

Each of these methods provides a solution to a class of problems. These methods are essentially devices that perform a specific storage-and-retrieval operation on the information that they are given and the requests that they receive. They all store an item and retrieve an item, where an item is one informational unit. The rest of this chapter shows you how to build these data engines for use in your own programs.

Queues

A *queue* is simply a linear list of information that is accessed in *first-in, first-out* order, which is sometimes called FIFO. That is, the first item placed on the queue is the first item retrieved, the second item put in is the second item retrieved, and so on. This is the only means of storage and retrieval in a queue; random access of any specific item is not allowed.

Queues are very common in real life. For example, lines at a bank or a fast-food restaurant are queues (except when rude patrons push their way to the front!). To visualize how a queue works, consider two functions: **qstore( )** and **qretrieve( )**. The **qstore( )** function places an item onto the end of the queue and **qretrieve( )** removes the first item from the queue and returns its value. Table 20-1 shows the effect of a series of these operations.

Action	Contents of Queue
qstore(A)	A
qstore(B)	A B
qstore(C)	A B C
qretrieve( ) returns **A**	B C
qstore(D)	B C D
qretrieve( ) returns **B**	C D
qretrieve( ) returns **C**	D

Table 20-1.   A Queue in Action

Keep in mind that a retrieval operation removes an item from the queue and destroys it if it is not stored elsewhere. Therefore, a queue may be empty because all items have been removed, even though the program using it is still active.

Queues are used in many programming situations. One of the most common is in simulations. Queues are also used for event scheduling, as in a PERT or Gantt chart, and for I/O buffering.

As an example, consider a simple appointment-scheduler program. This program allows you to enter a number of appointments; then, as each event is performed, it is taken off the list and the description of the next event is displayed. For the sake of simplicity, an array of pointers to the appointment strings will be used and each appointment description will be limited to 256 characters. The number of appointments is arbitrarily limited to 100.

First, the functions **qstore( )** and **qretrieve( )** shown here are needed for the simple scheduling program:

```
#define MAX 100

char *p[MAX];
int spos;
int rpos;

/* Store an appointment. */
void qstore(char *q)
{
  if(spos==MAX) {
    printf("list full\n");
    return;
  }
  p[spos] = q;
```

```
    spos++;
  }

  /* Retrieve an appointment. */
  char *qretrieve()
  {
    if(rpos==spos) {
      printf("No (more) appointments.\n");
      return NULL;
    }
    rpos++;
    return p[rpos-1];
  }
```

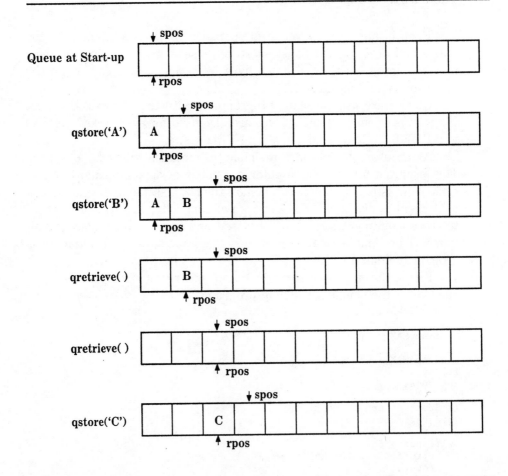

Figure 20-1.   The retrieve index chases the store index

Notice that these functions require two global variables: **spos** (which holds the index of the next free storage location) and **rpos** (which holds the index of the next item to retrieve). You can use these functions to maintain a queue of other data types by simply changing the base type of the array that they operate on.

The function **qstore( )** places pointers to new appointments on the end of the list and checks to see if the list is full. The function **qretrieve( )** takes appointments off the queue while there are events to perform. With each new appointment scheduled, **spos** is incremented and with each appointment completed, **rpos** is incremented. In essence, **rpos** chases **spos** through the queue. Figure 20-1 shows how this may appear in memory as the program executes. If **rpos** and **spos** are equal, there are no events left in the schedule. Even though the information stored in the queue is not actually destroyed by **qretrieve( )**, it is effectively destroyed because it can never be accessed again.

The entire program for this simple appointment scheduler is listed here. You may want to enhance this program for your own use.

```
/* Mini Appointment-Scheduler */

#include "string.h"
#include "stdlib.h"
#include "stdio.h"
#include "ctype.h"

#define MAX 100

char *p[MAX], *qretrieve(void);
int spos;
int rpos;
void enter(void), qstore(char *q), review(void), delete(void);

void main(void)
{
  char s[80];
  register int t;

  for(t=0; t<MAX; ++t) p[t] = NULL; /* init array to nulls */
  spos = 0; rpos = 0;

  for(;;) {
    printf("Enter, List, Remove, Quit: ");
    gets(s);
    *s = toupper(*s);

    switch(*s) {
```

```
        case 'E':
          enter();
          break;
        case 'L':
          review();
          break;
        case 'R':
          delete();
          break;
        case 'Q':
          exit(0);
    }
  }
}

/* Enter appointments in queue. */
void enter(void)
{
  char s[256], *p;

  do {
    printf("enter appointment %d: ", spos+1);
    gets(s);
    if(*s==0) break;   /* no entry */
    p = malloc(strlen(s));
    if(!p) {
      printf("out of memory.\n");
      return;
    }
    strcpy(p, s);
    if(*s) qstore(p);
  }while(*s);
}

/* See what's in the queue. */
void review(void)
{
  register int t;

  for(t=rpos; t<spos; ++t)
    printf("%d. %s\n", t+1, p[t]);
}

/* Delete an appointment from the queue. */
void delete(void)
{
  char *p;

  if((p=qretrieve())==NULL) return;
  printf("%s\n", p);
}

/* Store an appointment. */
void qstore(char *q)
{
  if(spos==MAX) {
```

```
        printf("list full\n");
        return;
      }
      p[spos] = q;
      spos++;
    }

    /* Retrieve an appointment. */
    char *qretrieve(void)
    {
      if(rpos==spos) {
        printf("No (more) appointments.\n");
        return NULL;
      }
      rpos++;
      return p[rpos-1];
    }
```

The Circular Queue

In studying the preceding appointment scheduler program, an improvement may have occurred to you. Instead of having the program stop
when the limit of the array used to store the queue is reached, you could
have both the store index (**spos**) and the retrieve index (**rpos**) loop back
to the start of the array. In this way, any number of items could be
placed on the queue, so long as items were also being taken off. This
implementation of a queue is called a *circular queue* because it uses its
storage array as if it were a circle instead of a linear list.

To create a circular queue for use in the scheduler program, you
need to change the functions **qstore( )** and **qretrieve( )** as shown here:

```
void qstore(char *q)
{
  /* The queue is full if either spos is one less than rpos
     or if spos is at the end of the queue array and rpos
     is at the beginning.
  */
  if(spos+1==rpos ¦¦ (spos+1==MAX && !rpos)) {
    printf("list full\n");
    return;
  }
  p[spos] = q;
  spos++;
  if(spos==MAX) spos = 0; /* loop back */
}
char *qretrieve(void)
```

```
{
  if(rpos==MAX) rpos = 0; /* loop back */
  if(rpos==spos) {
    printf("No events to perform.\n");
    return NULL;
  }
  rpos++;
  return p[rpos-1];
}
```

In essence, the queue is full only when both the store index and the retrieve index are equal; otherwise, there is room in the queue for another event. Conceptually, the array used for the circular version of the scheduler program looks like Figure 20-2.

Perhaps the most common use of a circular queue is in operating systems, where the circular queue holds the information read from and written to disk files or the console. Circular queues are also used in real-time application programs, which must continue to process information while buffering I/O requests. Many word processors do this when they reformat a paragraph or justify a line. What is being typed is not displayed until the other process is complete. To accomplish this, the application program needs to check for keyboard entry during the other process's execution. If a key has been typed, it is quickly placed in the

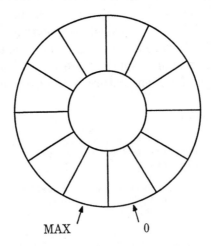

MAX   0

Figure 20-2.   The array in the circular version of the scheduler program queue and the process continues. Once the process is complete, the characters are retrieved from the queue.

For example, consider a simple program that contains two processes. The first process in the program prints the numbers 1 to 32,000 on the screen. The second process places characters into a circular queue as they are typed, without echoing them to the screen, until you press ENTER. The characters you type are not displayed because the first process is given priority over the screen. Once you have pressed ENTER, the characters in the queue are retrieved and printed.

For the program to function as described, it must use two functions not defined by the ANSI C standard: **kbhit( )** and **getch( )**. The **kbhit( )** function returns true if a key has been pressed; otherwise, it returns false. The **getch( )** function reads a keystroke but does not echo the character to the screen. The ANSI C standard does not define the library functions that check keyboard status or read keyboard characters without echoing them to the display because these functions are highly operating system dependent. Nonetheless, most compilers supply routines to do these things. The short program shown here works with most compilers; however, the two nonstandard functions might have different names.

```c
/* A circular queue example using a keyboard buffer. */
#include "stdio.h"
#include "conio.h"
#include "stdlib.h"

#define MAX 80

char buf[MAX+1];
int spos=0;
int rpos=0;

void qstore(char q);
char qretrieve(void);

void main(void)
{
  register char ch;
  int t;

  buf[80] = NULL;

  /* input characters until a carriage return is typed */
  for(ch=' ',t=0; t<32000 && ch!='\r'; ++t) {
    if(kbhit()) {
```

```
        ch = getch();
        qstore(ch);
      }
      printf("%d ", t);
      if(ch=='\r') {
        /* display and emtpy the key buffer */
        printf("\n");
        while((ch=qretrieve())!=NULL) printf("%c", ch);
        printf("\n");
      }
    }
  }
}

/* Store characters in the queue. */
void qstore(char q)
{
  if(spos+1==rpos || (spos+1==MAX && !rpos)) {
    printf("list full\n");
    return;
  }
  buf[spos] = q;
  spos++;
  if(spos==MAX) spos = 0; /* loop back */
}

/* Retrieve a character. */
char qretrieve(void)
{
  if(rpos==MAX) rpos = 0; /* loop back */
  if(rpos==spos) return NULL;

  rpos++;
  return buf[rpos-1];
}
```

Stacks

A stack is the opposite of a queue because it uses *last-in, first-out* accessing, which is sometimes called LIFO. To visualize a stack, just imagine a stack of plates. The first plate on the table is the last to be used and the last plate placed on the stack is the first to be used. Stacks are used a great deal in system software, including compilers and interpreters. In fact, most C compilers use a stack when passing arguments to functions.

The two basic operations—store and retrieve—are traditionally called *push* and *pop*, respectively. Therefore, to implement a stack you need two functions: **push( )** (which places a value on the stack) and

pop( ) (which retrieves a value from the stack). You also need a region of memory to use as the stack. You can use an array for this purpose or allocate a region of memory using C's dynamic allocation functions. As in the queue, the retrieval function takes a value off the list and destroys it if it is not stored elsewhere. The general forms of **push( )** and **pop( )** that use an integer array follow. You may maintain stacks of other data types by changing the base type of the array on which **push( )** and **pop( )** operate.

```c
int stack[MAX];
int tos=0;    /* top of stack */

/* Put an element on the stack. */
void push(int i)
{
  if(tos>=MAX) {
    printf("stack full\n");
    return;
  }
  stack[tos] = i;
  tos++;
}

/* Retrieve the top element from the stack. */
pop(void)
{
  tos--;
  if(tos<0) {
    printf("stack underflow\n");
    return HUGE_VAL;
  }
  return stack[tos];
}
```

The variable **tos** is the index of the next open stack location. When implementing these functions, you must remember to prevent overflow and underflow. In these routines, an empty stack is signaled by **tos** being zero and a full stack by **tos** being greater than the last storage location. To see how a stack works, see Table 20-2.

An excellent example of stack usage is a four-function calculator. Most calculators today accept a standard form of expression called *infix notation*, which takes the general form *operand-operator-operand*. For example, to add 200 to 100, enter **100**, then press the PLUS (+) key, then **200**, and press the EQUAL (=) key. In contrast, many early calculators used a form of expression evaluation called *postfix notation*, in which

Action	Contents of Stack
push(A)	A
push(B)	B A
push(C)	C B A
pop( ) retrieves C	B A
push(F)	F B A
pop( ) retrieves F	B A
pop( ) retrieves B	A
pop( ) retrieves A	*empty*

Table 20-2.   A Stack in Action

both operands are entered first and then the operator is entered. For example, to add 200 to 100 by using postfix notation, you enter **100**, then **200**, and then press the PLUS key. As operands are entered, they are placed on a stack. Each time an operator is entered, two operands are removed from the stack and the result is pushed back on the stack. The advantage of the postfix form is that very complex expressions can be easily evaluated by the calculator without much code.

Before you read about the full four-function calculator for postfix expressions, you need to modify the basic functions **push( )** and **pop( )**. The modification, which follows, uses C's dynamic memory-allocation routines to provide memory for the stack:

```
int *p;    /* will point to a region of free memory */
int *tos; /* points to top of stack */
int *bos; /* points to bottom of stack */

/* Store an element on the stack. */
void push(int i)
{
  if(p>bos) {
    printf("stack full\n");
    return;
  }
  *p = i;
  p++;
}

/* Retrieve the top element from the stack. */
pop(void)
{
  p--;
  if(p<tos) {
```

```
    printf("stack underflow\n");
    return 0;
  }
  return *p;
}
```

Before these functions can be used, a region of free memory must be allocated with **malloc( )**, the address of the beginning of that region assigned to **tos**, and the address of the end assigned to **bos**.

The entire postfix-based calculator program is shown here:

```
/* A simple four-function calculator. */

#include "stdio.h"
#include "stdlib.h"

#define MAX 100

int *p;    /* will point to a region of free memory */
int *tos; /* points to top of stack */
int *bos; /* points to bottom of stack */
void push(int i);
int pop(void);

void main(void)
{
  int a, b;
  char s[80];

  p = (int *) malloc(MAX*sizeof(int));   /* get stack memory */
  if(!p) {
    printf("allocation failure\n");
    exit(1);
  }
  tos = p;
  bos = p+MAX-1;

  printf("Four Function Calculator\n");
  printf("Enter 'q' to quit\n");

  do {
    printf(": ");
    gets(s);
    switch(*s) {
      case '+':
        a = pop();
        b = pop();
        printf("%d\n", a+b);
        push(a+b);
        break;
      case '-':
        a = pop();
        b = pop();
```

```
            printf("%d\n", b-a);
            push(b-a);
            break;
          case '*':
            a = pop();
            b = pop();
            printf("%d\n", b*a);
            push(b*a);
            break;
          case '/':
            a = pop();
            b = pop();
            if(a==0) {
              printf("divide by 0\n");
              break;
            }
            printf("%d\n", b/a);
            push(b/a);
            break;
          case '.': /* show  contents of top of stack */
            a = pop();
            push(a);
            printf("Current value on top of stack: %d\n", a);
            break;
          default:
            push(atoi(s));
      }
  } while(*s!='q');
}

/* Put an element on the stack. */
void push(int i)
{
  if(p>bos) {
    printf("stack full\n");
    return;
  }
  *p = i;
  p++;
}

/* Retrieve the top element from the stack. */
pop(void)
{
  p--;
  if(p<tos) {
    printf("stack underflow\n");
    return 0;
  }
  return *p;
}
```

Linked Lists

Queues and stacks share two common traits: They both have very strict rules for referencing the data stored in them, and the retrieval operations are, by nature, consumptive. In other words, accessing an item in a stack or queue requires its removal, and unless the item is stored elsewhere it is destroyed. Also, stacks and queues both use a contiguous region of memory. Unlike a stack or a queue, a linked list may access its storage in a random fashion because each piece of information carries with it a link to the next data item in the chain. That is, a linked list requires a complex data structure—as opposed to a stack or queue, which can operate on both simple and complex data items. In addition, a linked-list retrieval operation does not remove and destroy an item from the list. In fact, you need to add a specific deletion operation to do this.

Linked lists are used for two main purposes. The first is to create arrays of unknown size in memory. Linked lists are also used in disk-file storage of databases. The linked list allows items to be inserted and deleted quickly and easily, without rearranging the entire disk file. For these reasons, linked lists are used extensively in database managers.

Linked lists can be either singly linked or doubly linked. A singly linked list contains a link to the next data item. A doubly linked list contains links to both the next and the previous element in the list. You will use one or the other of these linked list types, depending upon your application.

Singly Linked Lists

A singly linked list requires that each item of information contain a link to the next element in the list. Each data item usually consists of a structure that includes information fields and a link pointer. Conceptually, a singly linked list looks like what is shown in Figure 20-3.

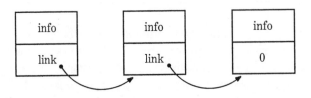

Figure 20-3.   A singly linked list in memory

Basically, there are two ways to build a singly linked list. The first is to simply put each new item on the end of the list. The other is to add items into specific places in the list—in ascending sorted order, for example. How you build the list determines the way the storage function is coded. Look at the simpler case of creating a linked list by adding items on the end.

Before beginning, you need to define a data structure to hold the information and the links. Mailing lists are common, so consider one in this case. The data structure for each element in the mailing list is defined here:

```
struct address {
  char name[40];
  char street[40];
  char city[20];
  char state[3];
  char zip[10];
  struct address *next;
} info;
```

The **slstore( )** function builds a singly linked list by placing each new element on the end. It must be passed a pointer to a structure of type **address** as well as a pointer to the last element, as shown here:

```
void slstore(struct address *i,
             struct address **last)
{
  if(!*last) *last = i; /* first item in list */
  else (*last)->next = i;
  i->next = NULL;
  *last = i;
}
```

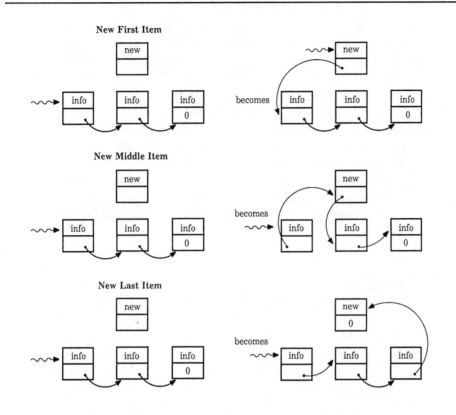

Figure 20-4.   Inserting an item into a singly linked list

Although you can sort the list created with the function **slstore( )** as a separate operation, it is easier to sort the list while building it by inserting each new item in the proper sequence of the chain. Also, if the list is already sorted, it would be advantageous to keep it sorted by inserting new items in their proper location. You do this by sequentially scanning the list until the proper location is found, inserting the new address at that point, and rearranging the links as necessary.

Three possible situations can occur when you insert an item in a singly linked list. First, it may become the new first item; second, it can go between two other items; or third, it can become the last element. Figure 20-4 diagrams how the links are changed for each case.

Keep in mind that if you change the first item in the list, you must update the entry point to the list elsewhere in your program. To avoid this overhead, you can use a sentinel as a first item. In this case, choose a special value that will always be first in the list to keep the entry point to the list from changing. This method has the disadvantage of using one extra storage location to hold the sentinel.

The function shown next, **sls_store( )**, will insert addresses into the mailing list in ascending order based on the **name** field. It must be passed a pointer to the pointer to the first element and the last element in the list along with a pointer to the information to be stored. Since the first or last element in the list could change, **sls_store( )** automatically updates the pointers to the beginning and end of the list if they change. The first time your program calls **sls_store( )**, **first** and **last** must point to **NULL**.

```c
/* Store in sorted order. */
void sls_store(struct address *i, /* new element to store */
               struct address **start, /* start of list */
               struct address **last) /* end of list */
{
  struct address *old, *p;

  p = *start;

  if(!*last) {  /* first element in list */
    i->next = NULL;
    *last = i;
    *start = i;
    return;
  }

  old = NULL;
  while(p) {
    if(strcmp(p->name, i->name)<0) {
      old = p;
      p = p->next;
    }
    else {
      if(old) {  /* goes in middle */
        old->next = i;
        i->next = p;
        return;
      }
      i->next = p; /* new first element */
      *start = i;
      return;
    }
  }
  (*last)->next = i; /* put on end */
```

```
  i->next = NULL;
  *last = i;
}
```

A linked list will rarely have a specific function dedicated to the retrieval process—that is, to returning item after item in list order. Usually this code is so short that it is simply placed inside another routine such as a search, delete, or display function. For example, the routine shown here displays all of the names in a mailing list:

```
void display(struct address *start)
{
  while(start) {
    printf(start->name);
    start = start->next;
  }.
}
```

When **display( )** is called, **start** must be a pointer to the first structure in the list.

Retrieving items from the list is as simple as following a chain. A search routine based on the **name** field could be written like this:

```
struct address *search(struct address *start, char *n)
{
  while(start) {
    if(!strcmp(n, start->name)) return start;
    start = start->next;
  }
  return NULL;  /* no match */
}
```

Because **search( )** is returning a pointer to the list item that matches the search name, it must be declared as returning a structure pointer of type **address**. If there is no match, a null is returned.

Deleting an item from a singly linked list is straightforward. As with insertion, there are three cases: deleting the first item, deleting an item in the middle, and deleting the last item. Figure 20-5 shows each of these operations.

The function that follows deletes a given item from a list of structures of type **address**:

```
void sldelete(
    struct address *p, /* previous item */
    struct address *i, /* item to delete */
```

```
       struct address **start,  /* start of list */
       struct address **last)   /* end of list */
{
  if(p) p->next = i->next;
  else  *start = i->next;

  if(i==*last && p) *last = p;

}
```

sldelete( ) must be sent pointers to the deleted item, the item before it in the chain, and the first and last items in the list. If the first item is to be removed, the previous pointer must be null. The function automatically updates **start** and **last** in the case where the item one of them points to is deleted.

Singly linked lists have one major drawback that prevents their extensive use: The list cannot be read in reverse order. For this reason, doubly linked lists are usually used.

Doubly Linked Lists

Doubly linked lists consist of data plus links to the next item as well as the preceding item. Figure 20-6 shows how these links are arranged.

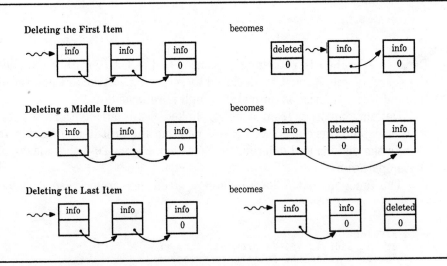

Figure 20-5.   Deleting an item from a singly linked list

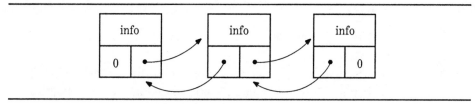

Figure 20-6. A doubly linked list

Having two links instead of just one has two major advantages. First, the list can be read in either direction. This not only simplifies managing the list but, in the case of a database, allows a user to scan the list in either direction. The second advantage is meaningful only in the case of equipment failure. Either forward links or backward links can read the entire list; therefore, should one of the links become invalid, the list can be reconstructed by using the other.

There are three ways a new element can be inserted into a doubly linked list: insert a new first element, insert in the middle, and insert a new last element. These operations are illustrated in Figure 20-7.

Building a doubly linked list is similar to building a singly linked list except that two links are maintained. Therefore, the structure must have room for both links. Using the mailing-list example again, you can modify structure **address** as shown here to accommodate both links:

```
struct address {
  char name[40];
  char street[40];
  char city[20];
  char state[3];
  char zip[10];
  struct address *next;
  struct address *prior;
} info;
```

Using **address** as the basic data item, the following function, **dlstore( )**, builds a doubly linked list:

```
void dlstore(struct address *i, struct address **last)
{

  if(!*last) *last = i; /* is first item in list */
  else (*last)->next = i;
  i->next = NULL;
```

```
   i->prior = *last;
   *last = i;
}
```

The function **dlstore( )** places each new entry on the end of the list. You must call it with a pointer to the data to be stored as well as a pointer to the end of the list, which must be null on the first call.

Like singly linked lists, a doubly linked list can contain a function that stores each element in a specific location in the list instead of always placing each new item on the end. The function shown here, **dls_store( )**, creates a list that is sorted in ascending order:

Figure 20-7.   Operations on a doubly linked list

```
/* Create a doubly linked list in sorted order.
*/
void dls_store(
  struct address *i,    /* new element */
  struct address **start, /* first element in list */
  struct address **last /* last element in list */
)
{
  struct address *old, *p;

  if(*last==NULL) {  /* first element in list */
    i->next = NULL;
    i->prior = NULL;
    *last = i;
    *start = i;
    return;
  }

  p = *start; /* start at top of list */

  old = NULL;
  while(p) {
    if(strcmp(p->name, i->name)<0){
      old = p;
      p = p->next;
    }
    else {
      if(p->prior) {
        p->prior->next = i;
        i->next = p;
        i->prior = p->prior;
        p->prior = i;
        return;
      }
      i->next = p; /* new first element */
      i->prior = NULL;
      p->prior = i;
      *start = i;
      return;
    }
  }
  old->next = i; /* put on end */
  i->next = NULL;
  i->prior = old;
  *last = i;
}
```

Because the first or last element in the list can change, the **dls_store( )** function automatically updates pointers to the beginning and ending elements of the list through the **start** and **last** parameters. You must call the function with a pointer to the data to be stored, and a pointer to the pointers to the first and last items in the list. When called the first time, the objects pointed to by **first** and **last** must be **NULL**.

As in singly linked lists, retrieving a specific data item in a doubly linked list is simply the process of following the links until the proper element is found.

There are three cases to consider when deleting an element from a doubly linked list: deleting the first item, deleting an item from the middle, and deleting the last item. Figure 20-8 shows how the links are rearranged.

```
void dldelete(
  struct address *i, /* item to delete */
  struct address **start,  /* first item */
  struct address **last)  /* last item */
{
  if(i->prior) i->prior->next = i->next;
  else { /* new first item */
    *start = i->next;
    if(start) start->prior = '\0';
  }

  if(i->next) i->next->prior = i->prior;
  else    /* deleting last element */
    *last = i->prior;
}
```

Because the first or last element in the list could be deleted, the **dldelete( )** function automatically updates pointers to the beginning and ending elements of the list through the **start** and **last** parameters. You must call the function with a pointer to the data to be deleted, and a pointer to the pointers to the first and last items in the list.

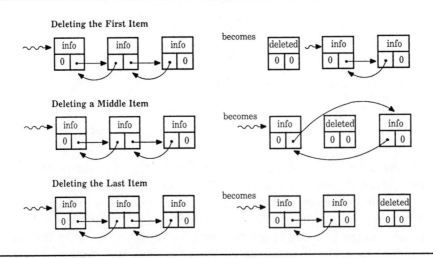

Figure 20-8.   Deletion in a doubly linked list

A Mailing-List Example

To finish the discussion of doubly linked lists, this section presents a simple but complete mailing-list program. The entire list is kept in memory while in use. However, it can be stored in a disk file and loaded for later use.

```c
/* A simple mailing list program that illustrates the
   use and maintenance of doubly linked lists.
*/
#include "stdio.h"
#include "stdlib.h"
#include "string.h"

struct address {
  char name[30];
  char street[40];
  char city[20];
  char state[3];
  char zip[10]; /* hold US and Canadian zips */
  struct address *next;  /* pointer to next entry */
  struct address *prior;  /* pointer to previous record */
} list_entry;

struct address *start; /* pointer to first entry in list */
struct address *last;  /* pointer to last entry */
struct address *find(char *);

void enter(void), search(void), save(void);
void load(void), list(void);
void delete(struct address **, struct address **);
void dls_store(struct address *i, struct address **start,
                          struct address **last);
void inputs(char *, char *, int), display(struct address *);

int menu_select(void);

void main(void)
{

  start = last = NULL;  /* initialize top and bottom pointers */
  for(;;) {
    switch(menu_select()) {
      case 1: enter();
        break;
      case 2: delete(&start, &last);
        break;
      case 3: list();
        break;
      case 4: search(); /* find a street */
        break;
      case 5: save();  /* save list to disk */
        break;
```

```
      case 6: load();   /* read from disk */
        break;
      case 7: exit(0);
    }
  }
}

/* Select an operation. */
menu_select(void)
{
  char s[80];
  int c;

  printf("1. Enter a name\n");
  printf("2. Delete a name\n");
  printf("3. List the file\n");
  printf("4. Search\n");
  printf("5. Save the file\n");
  printf("6. Load the file\n");
  printf("7. Quit\n");
  do {
    printf("\nEnter your choice: ");
    gets(s);
    c = atoi(s);
  } while(c<0 || c>7);
  return c;
}

/* Enter names and addresses. */
void enter(void)
{
  struct address *info;

  for(;;) {
    info = (struct address *)malloc(sizeof(list_entry));
    if(!info) {
      printf("\nout of memory");
      return;
    }

    inputs("enter name: ", info->name,30);
    if(!info->name[0]) break;  /* stop entering */
    inputs("enter street: ", info->street,40);
    inputs("enter city: ", info->city,20);
    inputs("enter state: ", info->state,3);
    inputs("enter zip: ", info->zip,10);

    dls_store(info, &start, &last);
  } /* entry loop */
}

/* This function will input a string up to
   the length in count and will prevent
   the string from being overrun.  It will also
   display a prompting message. */
void inputs(char *prompt, char *s, int count)
{
```

```
  char p[255];

  do {
    printf(prompt);
    gets(p);
    if(strlen(p)>count) printf("\ntoo long\n");
  } while(strlen(p)>count);
  strcpy(s, p);
}

/* Create a doubly linked list in sorted order.
*/
void dls_store(
  struct address *i,    /* new element */
  struct address **start, /* first element in list */
  struct address **last /* last element in list */
)
{
  struct address *old, *p;

  if(*last==NULL) {  /* first element in list */
    i->next = NULL;
    i->prior = NULL;
    *last = i;
    *start = i;
    return;
  }

  p = *start; /* start at top of list */

  old = NULL;
  while(p) {
    if(strcmp(p->name, i->name)<0){
      old = p;
      p = p->next;
    }
    else {
      if(p->prior) {
        p->prior->next = i;
        i->next = p;
        i->prior = p->prior;
        p->prior = i;
        return;
      }
      i->next = p; /* new first element */
      i->prior = NULL;
      p->prior = i;
      *start = i;
      return;
    }
  }
  old->next = i; /* put on end */
  i->next = NULL;
  i->prior = old;
  *last = i;
}
```

```
/* Remove an element from the list. */
void delete(struct address **start, struct address **last)
{
  struct address *info, *find();
  char s[80];

  printf("enter name: ");
  gets(s);
  info = find(s);
  if(info) {
    if(*start==info) {
      *start=info->next;
      if(*start) (*start)->prior = NULL;
      else *last = NULL;
    }
    else {
      info->prior->next = info->next;
      if(info!=*last)
          info->next->prior = info->prior;
      else
        *last = info->prior;
    }
    free(info);  /* return memory to system */
  }
}

/* Find an address. */
struct address *find( char *name)
{
  struct address *info;

  info = start;
  while(info) {
    if(!strcmp(name, info->name)) return info;
    info = info->next;  /* get next address */
  }
  printf("name not found\n");
  return NULL;  /* not found */
}

/* Display the entire list. */
void list(void)
{
  struct address *info;

  info = start;
  while(info) {
    display(info);
    info = info->next;  /* get next address */
  }
  printf("\n\n");
}

/* This function actually prints the fields in each address. */
void display(struct address *info)
{
    printf("%s\n", info->name);
```

```
    printf("%s\n", info->street);
    printf("%s\n", info->city);
    printf("%s\n", info->state);
    printf("%s\n", info->zip);
    printf("\n\n");
}

/* Look for a name in the list. */
void search(void)
{
  char name[40];
  struct address *info, *find();

  printf("enter name to find: ");
  gets(name);
  info = find(name);
  if(!info) printf("not found\n");
  else display(info);
}

/* Save the file to disk. */
void save(void)
{
  struct address *info;

  FILE *fp;

  fp = fopen("mlist", "wb");
  if(!fp) {
    printf("cannot open file\n");
    exit(1);
  }
  printf("\nsaving file\n");

  info = start;
  while(info) {
    fwrite(info, sizeof(struct address), 1, fp);
    info = info->next;  /* get next address */
  }
  fclose(fp);
}

/* Load the address file. */
void load()
{
  struct address *info;
  FILE *fp;

  fp = fopen("mlist", "rb");
  if(!fp) {
    printf("cannot open file\n");
    exit(1);
  }

  /* free any previously allocated memory */
  while(start) {
    info = start->next;
```

```
    free(info);
    start = info;
  }

  /* reset top and bottom pointers */
  start = last = NULL;

  printf("\nloading file\n");
  while(!feof(fp)) {
    info = (struct address *) malloc(sizeof(struct address));
    if(!info) {
      printf("out of memory");
      return;
    }
    if(1!=fread(info, sizeof(struct address), 1, fp)) break;
    dls_store(info, &start, &last);
  }
  fclose(fp);
}
```

Binary Trees

The final data structure to be examined is the *binary tree*. Although there can be many different types of trees, binary trees are special because, when sorted, they lend themselves to rapid searches, insertions, and deletions. Each item in a tree consists of information along with a link to the left member and a link to the right member. Figure 20-9 shows a small tree.

Special terminology is needed when discussing trees. Computer scientists are not known for their grammar, and terminology for trees is a classic case of a confused metaphor. The *root* is the first item in the tree. Each data item is called a *node* (or sometimes a *leaf*) of the tree, and any piece of the tree is called a *subtree*. A node that has no subtrees attached to it is called a *terminal node*. The *height* of the tree is equal to the number of layers that its roots grow. Think of binary trees in memory as looking the way they do on paper. Remember, however, that a tree is only a way to structure data in memory and memory is linear in form.

In a sense, the binary tree is a special form of linked list. Items can be inserted, deleted, and accessed in any order. Also, the retrieval operation is nondestructive. Although trees are easy to visualize, they present some very difficult programming problems. This discussion only scratches the surface.

Most functions that use trees are recursive because the tree itself is a recursive data structure. That is, each subtree is itself a tree. Therefore, the routines that this discussion develops will be recursive. Remember, nonrecursive versions of these functions exist, but their code is much harder to understand.

How a tree is ordered depends on how it is going to be referenced. The process of accessing each node in a tree is called a *tree traversal.* Consider the following tree:

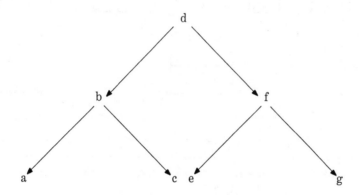

There are three ways to traverse a tree: *inorder, preorder,* and *postorder.* Using inorder, you visit the left subtree, the root, and then the right subtree. In preorder, you visit the root, the left subtree, and then the right subtree. With postorder, you visit the left subtree, the right subtree, and then the root. The order of access for the tree shown using each method is

inorder	a b c d e f g
preorder	d b a c f e g
postorder	a c b e g f d

Although a tree need not be sorted, most uses require this. Of course, what constitutes a sorted tree depends on how you will be traversing the tree. The rest of this chapter assumes inorder. Therefore, a sorted binary tree is one where the subtree on the left contains nodes

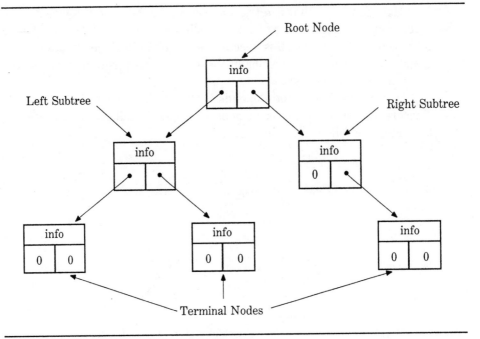

Figure 20-9.   A sample binary tree with height of three

that are less than or equal to the root, and those on the right are greater than the root.

The following function, **stree( )**, builds a sorted binary tree:

```
struct tree {
  char info;
  struct tree *left;
  struct tree *right;
}

struct tree *stree(
  struct tree *root,
  struct tree *r,
  char info)
{
  if(!r) {
    r = (struct tree *) malloc(sizeof(struct tree));
    if(!r) {
      printf("out of memory\n");
      exit(0);
    }
    r->left = NULL;
    r->right = NULL;
    r->info = info;
    if(!root) return r; /* first entry */
```

```
    if(info<root->info) root->left = r;
    else root->right = r;
    return r;
  }

  if(info<r->info) stree(r,r->left,info);
  else
    stree(r,r->right,info);
}
```

The preceding algorithm simply follows the links through the tree going left or right based on the **info** field. To use this function, you need a global variable that holds the root of the tree. This global must initially be set to **NULL** and a pointer to the root assigned on the first call to **stree( )**. Subsequent calls do not need to reassign the root. Assuming the name of this global is **rt**, to call the function **stree( )** you use

```
/* call stree() */
if(!rt) rt = stree(rt, rt, info);
else stree(rt, rt, info);
```

In this way, both the first and subsequent elements can be inserted correctly.

The function **stree( )** is a recursive algorithm, as are most tree routines. The same routine would be several times longer if you employ straight iterative methods. The function must be called with a pointer to the root, the left or right node, and the information. For the sake of clarity, only a character is used as the information. However, you could substitute any simple or complex data type.

To traverse in order the tree built by using **stree( )**, and to print the **info** field of each node, you could use the **inorder( )** function shown here:

```
void inorder(struct tree *root)
{
  if(!root) return;

  inorder(root->left);
  printf("%c ", root->info);
  inorder(root->right);
}
```

This recursive function returns when a terminal node (a null pointer) is encountered.

The functions for transversing the tree in preorder and postorder are shown in the following listing.

```
void preorder(struct tree *root)
{
  if(!root) return;

  printf("%c ", root->info);
  preorder(root->left);
  preorder(root->right);
}

void postorder(struct tree *root)
{
  if(!root) return;

  postorder(root->left);
  postorder(root->right);
  printf("%c ", root->info);
}
```

Now consider a short but interesting program to build a sorted binary tree and print that tree sideways on your screen. The program requires only a small modification to the function **inorder( )**. This new function is called **print_tree( )** and prints a tree inorder, as shown here:

```
void print_tree(struct tree *r, int l)
{
  int i;

  if(r==NULL) return;

  print_tree(r->left, l+1);
  for(i=0; i<l; ++i) printf("    ");
  printf("%c\n", r->info);
  print_tree(r->right, l+1);
}
```

The entire tree-printing program follows. Try entering various trees to see how each one is built.

```
/* This program displays a binary tree. */

#include "stdlib.h"
#include "stdio.h"

struct tree {
  char info;
  struct tree *left;
  struct tree *right;
};

struct tree *root;  /* first node in tree */
```

```
struct tree *stree(struct tree *root,
                   struct tree *r, char info);
void print_tree(struct tree *root, int l);

void main(void)
{
  char s[80];

  root = NULL;  /* initialize the root */

  do {
    printf("enter a letter: ");
    gets(s);
    if(!root) root = stree(root, root, *s);
    else stree(root, root, *s);
  } while(*s);

  print_tree(root, NULL);
}

struct tree *stree(
  struct tree *root,
  struct tree *r,
  char info)
{

  if(!r) {
    r = (struct tree *) malloc(sizeof(struct tree));
    if(!r) {
      printf("out of memory\n");
      exit(0);
    }
    r->left = NULL;
    r->right = NULL;
    r->info = info;
    if(!root) return r; /* first entry */
    if(info<root->info) root->left = r;
    else root->right = r;
    return r;
  }

  if(info<r->info) stree(r, r->left, info);
  else
    stree(r, r->right, info);
}

void print_tree(struct tree *r, int l)
{
  int i;

  if(!r) return;

  print_tree(r->left, l+1);
  for(i=0; i<l; ++i) printf("   ");
  printf("%c\n", r->info);
  print_tree(r->right, l+1);
}
```

This program is actually sorting the information that you give it. It is essentially a variation of the insertion sort that you saw in the previous chapter. In the average case, its performance can be quite good, but the quicksort is still a better general-purpose sorting method because it uses less memory and has lower processing overhead. However, if you have to build a tree from scratch or maintain an already sorted tree, you should always insert new entries in sorted order by using the **stree( )** function.

If you have run the tree-printing program, you have probably noticed that some trees are *balanced*—that is, that each subtree is the same or nearly the same height as any other—and that others are very far out of balance. In fact, if you entered the tree **abcd**, it would have looked like this:

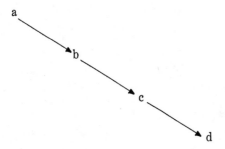

There would have been no right subtrees. This is called a *degenerate tree* because it has degenerated into a linear list. In general, if the data you are using as input to build a binary tree is fairly random, the tree produced approximates a balanced tree. However, if the information is already sorted, a degenerate tree results. (It is possible to readjust the tree with each insertion to keep the tree in balance but the necessary algorithms are fairly complex. Interested readers should refer to books about advanced programming algorithms.)

Search functions are easy to implement for binary trees. The following function returns a pointer to the node in the tree that matches the key; otherwise, it returns a null.

```
struct tree *search_tree(struct tree *root, char key)
{
  if(!root) return root;  /* empty tree */
  while(root->info!=key) {
    if(key<root->info) root = root->left;
```

```
      else root = root->right;
      if(root==NULL) break;
    }
  return root;
}
```

Unfortunately, deleting a node from a tree is not as simple as searching a tree. The deleted node may be either the root, a left node, or a right node. Also, the node may have from zero to two subtrees attached to it. The process of rearranging the pointers lends itself to a recursive algorithm, which is shown here:

```
struct tree *dtree(struct tree *root, char key)
{
  struct tree *p,*p2;

  if(root->info==key) { /* delete root */
    /* this means an empty tree */
    if(root->left==root->right){
      free(root);
      return NULL;
    }
    /* or if one subtree is null */
    else if(root->left==NULL) {
      p = root->right;
      free(root);
      return p;
    }
    else if(root->right==NULL) {
      p = root->left;
      free(root);
      return p;
    }
    /* or both subtrees present */
    else {
      p2 = root->right;
      p = root->right;
      while(p->left) p = p->left;
      p->left = root->left;
      free(root);
      return p2;
    }
  }
  if(root->info<key) root->right = dtree(root->right, key);
  else root->left = dtree(root->left, key);
  return root;
}
```

Remember to update the pointer to the root in the rest of your program code because the node deleted could be the root of the tree.

Binary trees offer tremendous power, flexibility, and efficiency when used with database management programs. This is because the information for these databases must reside on disk, and access times are important. Because a balanced binary tree has, as a worst case, $\log_2 n$ comparisons in searching, it is far better than a linked list, which must rely on a sequential search.

Sparse Arrays

The Linked-List Sparse Array
The Binary-Tree Approach to Sparse Arrays
The Pointer-Array Approach to Sparse Arrays
Hashing
Choosing an Approach

There are two major uses for C's dynamic allocation system. You can use it to create variable-length lists of information, as in a database application. You can also use it to support sparse arrays. A *sparse array* is one in which not all the elements of the array are actually present or necessary. You will need to create a sparse array when the array dimensions required by the application exceed the memory of the machine, but not all array locations will be used. Recall that arrays—especially multidimensional arrays—can consume vast quantities of memory because their storage needs are exponentially related to their size. For example, a character array of 10 by 10 needs only 100 bytes of memory, a 100-by-100 array needs 10,000, but a 1000-by-1000 array needs 1,000,000 bytes of memory—clearly too much for most computers.

There are numerous examples of applications that require sparse-array processing. Many apply to scientific and engineering problems that are easily understood only by experts. However, there is one very familiar application that uses sparse arrays: a spreadsheet program. Even though the matrix of the average spreadsheet is very large, say 999 by 999, only a portion of the matrix may actually be in use at any one time. Spreadsheets use the matrix to hold formulas, values, and strings associated with each location. In a sparse array, storage for each element is allocated from the pool of free memory as it is needed. Although only a small portion of the elements are actually in use, the array may appear very large—larger than would usually fit in the memory of the computer.

The rest of this discussion uses the terms logical array and physical array. The *logical array* is the array that you think of as existing in the

```
         ————A————    ————B————    ————C————
    1
    2                      X
    3
    4
    5
    6
    7

    .
    .
    .
```

Figure 21-1.   The organization of a sample spreadsheet

system. For example, the spreadsheet matrix is a logical array. The *physical array* is the array that actually exists inside the computer. The sparse-array support routines link these two arrays.

This chapter examines four distinct techniques for creating a sparse array: the linked list, the binary tree, a pointer array, and hashing. Although no spreadsheet program is developed, all examples relate to a spreadsheet matrix that is organized as shown in Figure 21-1. In the figure, the X is located in cell B2.

The Linked-List Sparse Array

When a you implement sparse array by using a linked list, a structure holds the information, its logical position in the array, and links to the previous and next element. Each structure is placed in the list with the elements inserted in sorted order based on the array index. The array is accessed by following the links.

For example, you can use the following structure as the basis of a sparse array in a spreadsheet program:

```
struct cell {
    char cell_name[9];   /* cell name e.g., A1, B34 */
    char  formula[128];  /* info e.g., 10/B2 */
```

```
   struct cell *next;  /* pointer to next entry */
   struct cell *prior; /* pointer to previous record */
} list_entry;
```

The field **cell_name** holds a string that contains a cell name such as A1, B34, Z19, or the like. The string **formula** holds the formula that is assigned to each spreadsheet location.

An entire spreadsheet program would be far too large to use as an example. Instead this chapter examines the key functions that support the linked-list sparse array. Remember, there are many ways to implement a spreadsheet program. The data structure and routines here are just examples of sparse-array techniques.

The following global variables point to the beginning and end of the linked-list array.

```
struct cell *start;  /* first element in list */
struct cell *last;   /* last element in list */
```

When you enter a formula into a cell in most spreadsheets, you are, in effect, creating a new element in the sparse array. If the spreadsheet uses a linked list, that new cell is inserted into it via a function similar to **dls_store( )**, which was developed in Chapter 20. Remember that the list is sorted according to the cell name; that is, A12 precedes A13, and so on.

```
/* Store cells in sorted order. */
void dls_store(struct cell *i,
               struct cell **start,
               struct cell **last)
{
  struct cell *old, *p;

  if(!*last) {  /* first element in list */
    i->next = NULL;
    i->prior = NULL;
    *last = i;
    *start = i;
    return;
  }

  p = *start; /* start at top of list */

  old = NULL;
  while(p) {
    if(strcmp(p->cell_name, i->cell_name)<0){
      old = p;
```

```
      p = p->next;
  }
  else { /* is a middle element */
    if(p->prior) {
      p->prior->next = i;
      i->next = p;
      i->prior = p->prior;
      p->prior = i;
      return;
    }
    i->next = p; /* new first element */
    i->prior = NULL;
    p->prior = i;
    *start = i;
    return;
  }
}
old->next = i; /* put on end */
i->next = NULL;
i->prior = old;
*last = i;
return;
}
```

The **delete( )** function, which follows, removes from the list the cell whose name is an argument to the function:

```
void delete(char *cell_name,
            struct cell **start,
            struct cell **last)
{
  struct cell *info;

  info = find(cell_name, *start);
  if(info) {
    if(*start==info) {
      *start = info->next;
      if(*start) (*start)->prior = NULL;
      else *last = NULL;
    }
    else {
      if(info->prior) info->prior->next = info->next;
      if(info!=*last)
          info->next->prior = info->prior;
      else
        *last = info->prior;
    }
    free(info);  /* return memory to system */
  }
}
```

The final function that you need to support a linked-list sparse array is **find( )**, which locates any specific cell. The function requires a linear search to locate each item and, as you saw in Chapter 19, the average number of comparisons in a linear search is $n/2$, where n is the number of elements in the list. In addition, a significant loss of performance occurs because each cell may contain references to other cells in the formula, and each of these cells must be found. Here is **find( )**:

```
struct cell *find(char *cell_name, struct cell *start)
{
  struct cell *info;

  info = start;
  while(info) {
    if(!strcmp(cell_name, info->cell_name)) return info;
    info = info->next;  /* get next cell */
  }
  printf("cell not found\n");
  return NULL;  /* not found */
}
```

Analysis of the Linked-List Approach

The principal advantage of the linked-list method is that it makes efficient use of memory. However, it has one major drawback: It must use a linear search to access cells in the list. Without the use of additional information, which requires additional memory, there is no way to perform a binary search to locate a cell. Also, the store routine uses a linear search to find the proper place to insert a new cell into the list. You can solve these problems by using a binary tree to support the sparse array.

The Binary-Tree Approach to Sparse Arrays

In essence, the binary tree is simply a modified doubly linked list. Its major advantage over a list is that it can be searched quickly, which means that insertions and lookups can be very fast. In applications where you want a linked-list structure but need fast search times, the binary tree is perfect.

To use a binary tree to support the spreadsheet example, you must change the structure **cell** as shown in the code that follows:

```
struct cell {
  char cell_name[9];   /* cell name e.g., A1, B34 */
  char  formula[128];  /* info e.g., 10/B2 */
  struct cell *left;   /* pointer to left subtree */
  struct cell *right;  /* pointer to right subtree */
} list_entry;
```

You can modify the **stree( )** function from Chapter 19 so that it builds a tree based on the cell name. Notice that the following assumes that the parameter **new** is a pointer to a new entry in the tree.

```
struct cell *stree(
        struct cell *root,
        struct cell *r,
        struct cell *new)
{
  if(!r) {      /* first node in subtree */
    new->left = NULL;
    new->right = NULL;
    if(!root) return new;  /* first entry in tree */
    if(strcmp(new->cell_name, root->cell_name)<0)
      root->left = new;
    else
      root->right = new;
    return new;
  }

  if(strcmp(r->cell_name, new->cell_name)<=0)
    stree(r, r->right, new);
  else
    stree(r, r->left, new);

  return root;
}
```

The **stree( )** function must be called with a pointer to the root node for the first two parameters and a pointer to the new cell for the third. It returns a pointer to the root.

To delete a cell from the spreadsheet, modify the **dtree( )** function as shown here to accept the name of the cell as a key:

```
struct cell *dtree(
        struct cell *root,
        char *key)
```

```
{
  struct cell *p, *p2;

  if(!strcmp(root->cell_name, key)) { /* delete root */
    /* this means an empty tree */
    if(root->left==root->right){
      free(root);
      return NULL;
    }
    /* or if one subtree is null */
    else if(root->left==NULL) {
      p = root->right;
      free(root);
      return p;
    }
    else if(root->right==NULL) {
      p = root->left;
      free(root);
      return p;
    }
    /* or both subtrees present */
    else {
      p2 = root->right;
      p = root->right;
      while(p->left) p = p->left;
      p->left = root->left;
      free(root);
      return p2;
    }
  }
  if(strcmp(root->cell_name, key)<=0)
    root->right = dtree(root->right, key);
  else root->left = dtree(root->left, key);
  return root;
}
```

Finally, you can use a modified version of the **search( )** function to locate quickly any cell in the spreadsheet if you specify the cell name.

```
struct cell *search_tree(
        struct cell *root,
        char *key)
{
  if(!root) return root;  /* empty tree */
  while(strcmp(root->cell_name, key)) {
    if(strcmp(root->cell_name, key)<=0)
      root = root->right;
    else root = root->left;
    if(root==NULL) break;
  }
  return root;
}
```

Analysis of the Binary-Tree Approach

A binary tree results in much faster insert and search times than a linked list. Remember, a sequential search requires, on average, $n/2$ comparisons, where n is the number of elements in the list. A binary search, in contrast, requires only $\log_2 n$ comparisons. Also, the binary tree is as memory efficient as a doubly linked list. However, in some situations, there is a better alternative than the binary tree.

The Pointer-Array Approach to Sparse Arrays

Suppose that your spreadsheet had the dimensions 26 by 100 (A1 through Z100), or a total of 2600 elements. In theory, you could use the following array of structures to hold the spreadsheet entries:

```
struct cell {
  char cell_name[9];
  char  formula[128];
} list_entry[2600];    /* 2,600 cells */
```

However, 2600 multiplied by 137 (the raw size of the structure — some machines require data to be aligned on even boundaries, thus increasing the number of bytes actually needed) amounts to 356,200 bytes of memory. This is too big for many systems. Also, on processors that use segment architecture, such as the 8088, memory access to such a large array is very slow because 32-bit pointers are required. So, this approach is often impractical. However, you could create an array of pointers to structures. This array of pointers would require significantly less permanent storage than an entire array, and would offer superior performance over the linked-list and binary-tree methods. The declaration that creates such an array of pointers is

```
struct cell {
  char cell_name[9];
  char  formula[128];
} list_entry;

struct cell *sheet[2600]; /* array of 2,600 pointers */
```

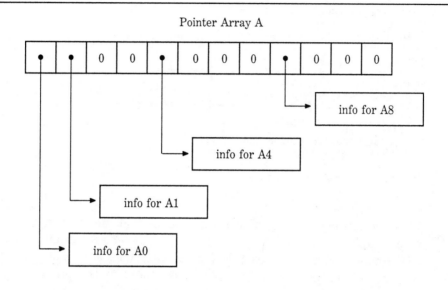

Figure 21-2.   A pointer array as support for a sparse array

You can use this smaller array to hold pointers to the information that is actually entered by the spreadsheet user. As each entry is made, a pointer to the information about the cell is stored in the proper location in the array. Figure 21-2 shows how this might appear in memory, with the pointer array providing support for the sparse array.

Before the pointer array can be used, each element must must be initialized to null, which indicates that there is no entry in that location. The function that does this is

```
void init_sheet(void)
{
  register int t;

  for(t=0; t<2600; ++t) sheet[t] = NULL;
}
```

When the user enters a formula for a cell, the cell location (which is defined by its name) is used to produce an index for the pointer array **sheet**. The index is derived from the cell name by converting the name into a number, as shown in the following listing.

```
void store(struct cell *i)
{
  int loc;
  char *p;

  /* compute location given point name */
  loc = (*(i->cell_name)-'A');
  p = &(i->cell_name[1]);
  loc += (atoi(p)-1) * 26;    /* WIDTH * rows */

  if(loc>=2600) {
    printf("cell out of bounds\n");
    return;
  }
  sheet[loc] = i; /* place pointer in the array */
}
```

When computing the index, **store()** assumes that all cell names start with a capital letter and are followed by an integer—for example, B34, C19, and so on. Because each cell name is unique, each index is also unique and the pointer to each entry is stored in the proper array element. If you compare this procedure to the linked-list or binary-tree version, you will see how much shorter and simpler it is.

The **delete()** function also becomes very short. Called with the name of the cell to remove, it simply zeros the pointer to the element and returns the memory to the system.

```
void delete(struct cell *i)
{
  int loc;
  char *p;

  /* compute location given point name */
  loc = (*(i->cell_name)-'A');
  p = &(i->cell_name[1]);
  loc += (atoi(p)-1) * 26;    /* WIDTH * rows */

  if(loc>=2600) {
    printf("cell out of bounds\n");
    return;
  }
  if(!sheet[loc]) return; /* don't free a null pointer */

  free(sheet[loc]);  /* return memory to system */
  sheet[loc] = NULL;
}
```

Once again, this code is much faster and simpler than the linked-list version.

The process of locating a cell given its name is simple because the name itself directly produces the array index. Therefore, the function **find( )** becomes

```
struct cell *find(char *cell_name)
{
  int loc;
  char *p;

  /* compute location given name */
  loc = (*(cell_name)-'A');
  p = &(cell_name[1]);
  loc += (atoi(p)-1) * 26;   /* WIDTH * rows */

  if(loc>=2600 || !sheet[loc]) {  /* no entry in that cell */
    printf("cell not found\n");
    return NULL;  /* not found */
  }
  else return sheet[loc];
}
```

Analysis of the Pointer-Array Approach

The pointer-array method of sparse-array handling provides much faster accessing to array elements than either the linked-list or binary-tree method. Unless the array is very large, the memory used by the pointer array is not usually a significant drain on the free memory of the system. However, the pointer array itself uses some memory for every location—whether the pointers are pointing to actual information or not. This may be a serious limitation for certain applications, although in general it is not a problem.

Hashing

Hashing is the process of extracting the index of an array element directly from the information that is stored there. The index generated is called the *hash*. Traditionally, hashing has been applied to disk files as a means of decreasing access time. However, you can use the same general methods to implement sparse arrays. The preceding pointer-array example used a special form of hashing called *direct indexing*, where each key maps onto one and only one array location. That is, each hashed index is unique. (The pointer-array approach does not require a direct indexing hash—this was just an obvious approach given the spreadsheet problem.) In actual practice, such direct hashing schemes are few, and a more flexible method is required. This section shows how hashing can be generalized to allow greater power and flexibility.

The spreadsheet example makes clear that even in the most rigorous environments, not every cell in the sheet will be used. Suppose that for virtually all cases, no more than 10% of the potential locations are occupied by actual entries. That is, if the spreadsheet has dimensions 26×100 (2600 locations), only about 260 are actually used at any one time and the largest array necessary to hold all the entries will normally consist of only 260 elements. But how do the logical array locations get mapped onto and accessed from this smaller physical array? And what happens when this array is full?

When a formula for a cell is entered by the user of the spreadsheet, which is the logical array, the cell location, defined by its name, is used to produce an index (a hash) into the smaller physical array, sometimes called the *primary array*. The index is derived from the cell name, which is converted into a number, as in the pointer-array example. However, this number is then divided by 10 to produce an initial entry point into the array. (Remember, in this example the size of the physical array is only 10% of the logical array.) If the location referenced by this index is free, the logical index and the value are stored there. However, since ten logical locations actually map onto one physical location, hash collisions can occur. When this happens, a linked list, sometimes called the *collision list*, is used to hold the entry. A separate collision list is associated with each entry in the primary array. Of course, these lists are zero length until a collision occurs, as depicted in Figure 21-3.

Suppose you want to find an element in the physical array, given its logical array index. First, transform the logical index into its hash value and check the physical array at the index generated by the hash to see if the logical index stored there matches the one that you are searching for. If it does, return the information. Otherwise, follow the collision list until either the proper index is found or the end of the chain is reached.

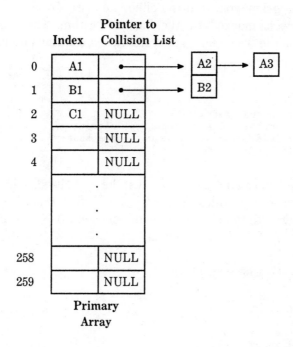

given entries in this order: A1
                           A2
                           B1
                           B2
                           A3
                           C1

Figure 21-3.   A hashing example

Before you can understand how this procedure applies to the spreadsheet program, you need to define two arrays of structures. One, called **primary**, is indexed by the hash algorithm. The other, called **collision**, holds the hash chain generated when collisions occur.

```
#define MAX 260

struct htype {
  int index; /* actual index */
  int val;   /* actual value of the array element */
  int next; /* index of next value with same hash */
} primary[MAX];
```

Before this array can be used, it must be initialized. The following function initializes the **index** field to −1 (a value that, by definition, cannot be generated) to indicate an empty element. A **NULL** in the **next** field indicates the end of a hash chain.

```
/* Initialize the hash array. */
void init()
{
  register int i;

  for (i=0; i<MAX; i++) {
    primary[i].index = -1;
    primary[i].next = NULL;   /* null chain */
    primary[i].val = 0;
  }
}
```

The **store( )** procedure converts a cell name into a hashed index into the **primary** array. If the location directly pointed to by the hashed value is occupied, the procedure automatically adds the entry to the collision list using a modified version of **slstore( )** developed in the preceding chapter. The logical index must be stored because it will be needed when that element is accessed again. These functions are shown here:

```
/* Compute hash and store value. */
void store(char *cell_name, int v)
{
  int h, loc;
  struct htype *p;

  /* produce the hash value */
  loc = *cell_name-'A';
```

```
  loc += (atoi(&cell_name[1])-1) * 26;    /* WIDTH * rows */
  h = loc/10;

  /* store in the location unless full or
     store there if logical indexes agree - i.e., update.
  */
  if(primary[h].index==-1 || primary[h].index==loc) {
    primary[h].index = loc;
    primary[h].val = v;
    return;
  }

  /* otherwise, create or add to collision list */
  p = malloc(sizeof(struct htype));
  if(!p) {
    printf("out of memory\n");
    return;
  }
  p->index = loc;
  p->val = v;
  slstore(p, &primary[h]);
}

/* Add elements to the collision list. */
void slstore(struct htype *i,
             struct htype *start)
{
  struct htype *old, *p;

  old = start;
  /* find end of list */
  while(start) {
    old = start;
    start = start->next;
  }
  /* link in new entry */
  old->next = i;
  i->next = NULL;
}
```

Before finding the value of an element, your program must first compute the hash and then check to see if the logical index stored in the physical array matches the index of the logical array that is requested. If it does, that value is returned; otherwise, the collision chain is searched. The **find( )** function, which performs these tasks, is shown here:

```
/* Compute hash and return value. */
int find(char *cell_name)
{
  int h, loc;
  struct htype *p;
```

```
/* produce the hash value */
loc = *cell_name-'A';
loc += (atoi(&cell_name[1])-1) * 26;    /* WIDTH * rows */
h = loc/10;

/* return the value if found */
if(primary[h].index==loc)  return(primary[h].val);
else { /* look in collision list */
  p = primary[h].next;
  while(p) {
    if(p->index == loc) return p->val;
    p = p->next;
  }
  printf("not in array\n");
  return -1;
}
}
```

Creating a deletion function is left to you as an exercise. (Hint: Just reverse the insertion process.)

Keep in mind that the preceding hashing algorithm is very simple. Generally, you would use a more complex method to provide a more even distribution of indexes in the primary array, thus avoiding very long hash chains. However, the basic principle is the same.

Analysis of Hashing

In its best case (quite rare), each physical index created by the hash is unique and access times approximate that of direct indexing. This means that no collision lists are created and all lookups are essentially direct accesses. However, this will seldom be the case because it requires that the logical indexes be evenly distributed throughout the logical index space. In a worst case (also rare), a hashed scheme degenerates into a linked list. This can happen when the hashed values of the logical indexes are all the same. In the average (and the most likely) case, the hash method can access any specific element in the amount of time it takes to use a direct index divided by some constant that is proportional to the average length of the hash chains. The most critical factor in using hashing to support a sparse array, is to make sure that the hashing algorithm spreads the physical index evenly so that long collision lists are avoided.

Choosing an Approach

You must consider speed and memory efficiency when deciding whether to use a linked list, a binary tree, a pointer array, or a hashing approach to implement a sparse array.

When the array is very sparse, the most memory-efficient approaches are the linked lists and binary trees, because only array elements that are actually in use have memory allocated to them. The links themselves require very little additional memory and generally have a negligible effect. The pointer-array design requires that the entire pointer array exists, even if some of its elements are not used. Not only must the entire pointer array fit in memory, but enough memory must be left over for the application to use. This could be a serious problem for certain applications, whereas it may not be a problem at all for others. Usually you can calculate the approximate amount of free memory and determine whether it is sufficient for your program. The hashing method lies somewhere between the pointer-array and the linked-list/binary-tree approaches. Although it requires that all of the physical array exist even if it is not all used, it may still be smaller than a pointer array, which needs at least one pointer for each logical array location.

However, when the array is fairly full, the pointer array makes better use of memory. This is because the binary-tree and linked-list implementations need two pointers for each element, whereas the pointer array only has one pointer. For example, suppose that a 1000-element array were full and pointers were two bytes long. Both the binary tree and linked list would use 4000 bytes for pointers, but the pointer array would only need 2000 — a savings of 2000 bytes. In the hashing method, even more memory is wasted to support the array.

By far the fastest approach, in terms of execution speed, is the pointer array. As in the spreadsheet example, there is often an easy method for indexing the pointer array and linking it with the sparse array elements. This makes accessing the elements of the sparse array nearly as fast as accessing a normal array. The linked-list version is very slow by comparison because it must use a linear search to locate each element. Even if extra information were added to the linked list to allow faster accessing of elements, it would still be slower than the pointer array's direct accessing capability. The binary tree certainly speeds up the search time, but is sluggish compared with the pointer array's direct indexing capability. If you choose the hashing algorithm properly, the hashing method can often beat the binary tree in access times, but it will never be faster than the pointer-array approach.

The rule of thumb is to use a pointer-array implementation when possible because this method has the fastest access times. However, if memory usage is critical, you must use the linked-list or binary-tree approach.

Expression Parsing and Evaluation

Expressions
Disssecting an Expression
Expression Parsing
A Simple Expression Parser
Adding Variables to the Parser
Syntax Checking in a Recursive-Descent Parser

How do you write a program that will take as input a string containing a numeric expression, such as (10 − 5) * 3, and compute the proper answer? If there is still a "high priesthood" among programmers, it must be those few who know how to do this. Many who use computers are mystified by the way a high-level language converts complex expressions, such as 10 * 3 − (4 + count)/12, into instructions that a computer can execute. This procedure is called *expression parsing*, and it is the backbone of all language compilers and interpreters, spreadsheet programs, and anything else that needs to convert numeric expressions into a form that the computer can use. Expression parsing is generally thought of as off limits except to the enlightened few, but this need not be the case.

Expression parsing is actually very straightforward, and in a way it is easier than other programming tasks in that it works according to the strict rules of algebra. This chapter will develop what is commonly referred to as a recursive-descent parser and all the necessary support routines that enable you to evaluate complex numeric expressions. Once you have mastered the operation of the parser, you can easily enhance and modify it to suit your needs. What's more, other programmers will think that you have entered the high priesthood!

Expressions

Although expressions can be made up of all types of information, this chapter deals only with numeric expressions. For our purposes *numeric expressions* can be made up of the following items:

- Numbers
- The operators +, −, /, *, ^, %, =
- Parentheses
- Variables

The operator ^ indicates exponentiation, as in BASIC, and = is the assignment operator. These items can be combined in expressions according to the rules of algebra. Here are some examples:

```
10 − 8
(100 − 5) * 14/6
a + b − c
10^5
a = 10 − b
```

Assume this precedence for each operator:

```
highest      ^
             *, /, %
             +, −
lowest       =
```

Operators of equal precedence evaluate from left to right.

In the examples in this chapter, all variables are single letters (in other words, 26 variables, **A** through **Z**, are available). The variables are not case sensitive (**a** and **A** are treated as the same variable). Each number is a **double**, although you could easily write the routines to handle other types of numbers. Finally, to keep the logic clear and easy to understand, only a minimal amount of error checking is included in the routines.

In case you have not thought about expression parsing, try to evaluate this sample expression:

```
10 − 2 * 3
```

You know that this expression is equal to the value 4. Although you could easily create a program that would compute that *specific* expression, the question is how to create a program that gives the correct answer for any arbitrary expression. At first you might think of a routine something like this:

```
a = get first operand
while(operands present) {
        op = get operator
        b = get second operand
        a = a op b
}
```

This routine gets the first operand, the operator, and the second operand to perform the first operation and then gets the next operator and operand—if any—to perform the next operation, and so on. However, if you use this basic approach, the expression 10 − 2 * 3 evaluates to 24 (that is, 8 * 3) instead of 4 because this procedure neglects the precedence of the operators. You cannot just take the operands and operators in order from left to right because multiplication must be done before subtraction. Some beginners think that this can be easily overcome, and sometimes—in very restricted cases—it can. But the problem only gets worse when you add parentheses, exponentiation, variables, function calls, and the like.

Although there are a few ways to write a routine that evaluates expressions of this sort, the one developed here is most easily written by a person. It is also the most common. (Some of the other methods used to write parsers employ complex tables that must be generated by another computer program. These are sometimes called *table-driven parsers.*) The method used here is called a *recursive-descent parser*, and in the course of this chapter you will see how it got its name.

Dissecting an Expression

Before you can develop a parser to evaluate expressions, you need to be able to break an expression into its components. For example, the expression

$$A * B - (W + 10)$$

contains the components A, *, B, −, (, W, +, 10, and). Each component represents an indivisible unit of the expression. In general, you need a routine that returns each item in the expression individually. The routine must also be able to skip over spaces and tabs and detect the end of the expression.

Each component of an expression is called a *token*. Therefore, the function that returns the next token in the expression is often called **get_token( )**. You need a global character pointer to hold the expression string. In the version of **get_token( )** shown here, the global character pointer is **prog**. **prog** is global because it must maintain its value between calls to **get_token( )** and allow other functions to use it. Besides returning a token, you need to know what type of token is being returned. For the parser developed in this chapter, you need only three types: **VARIABLE**, **NUMBER**, and **DELIMITER**. (**DELIMITER** is used for both operators and parentheses.) Here is **get_token( )** along with its necessary globals, **#define**s, and support function:

```c
#define DELIMITER  1
#define VARIABLE   2
#define NUMBER     3

extern char *prog;   /* holds expression to be analyzed */
char token[80];
char tok_type;

/* Return the next token. */
void get_token(void)
{

  register char *temp;

  tok_type = 0;
  temp = token;
  *temp = '\0';

  if(!*prog) return; /* at end of expression */
  while(isspace(*prog)) ++prog;   /* skip over white space */

  if(strchr("+-*/%^=()", *prog)){
    tok_type = DELIMITER;
    /* advance to next char */
    *temp++ = *prog++;
  }
  else if(isalpha(*prog)) {
    while(!isdelim(*prog)) *temp++ = *prog++;
```

```
      tok_type = VARIABLE;
  }
  else if(isdigit(*prog)) {
    while(!isdelim(*prog)) *temp++ = *prog++;
    tok_type = NUMBER;
  }

  *temp = '\0';
}

/* Return true if c is a delimiter. */
isdelim(char c)
{
  if(strchr(" +-/*%^=()", c) || c==9 || c=='\r' || c==0)
    return 1;
  return 0;
}
```

Look closely at the preceding functions. After the first few initializations, **get_token( )** checks to see if the **NULL** terminating the expression has been found. Next, leading spaces are skipped. Once the spaces have been skipped, **prog** is pointing to either a number, a variable, an operator, or — if trailing spaces end the expression — a null. If the next character is an operator, it is returned as a string in the global variable **token**, and **DELIMITER** is placed in **tok_type**. If the next character is a letter instead, it is assumed to be one of the variables. It is returned as a string in **token** and **tok_type** is assigned the value **VARIABLE**. If the next character is a digit, the entire number is read and placed in the string **token** as the type **NUMBER**. Finally, if the next character is none of the preceding, it is assumed that the end of the expression has been reached. In this case, **token** is null, which signals the end of the expression.

As stated earlier, to keep the code in this function clean, a certain amount of error checking has been omitted and some assumptions have been made. For example, any unrecognized character may end an expression. Also, in this version, variables may be of any length, but only the first letter is significant. You can add more error checking and other details as your specific application dictates. You can easily modify or enhance **get_token( )** to enable character strings, other types of numbers, or whatever to be returned one token at a time from an input string.

To understand better how **get_token( )** works, study what it returns for each token and type in the following expression:

A + 100 − (B * C) /2

Token	Token type
A	VARIABLE
+	DELIMITER
100	NUMBER
–	DELIMITER
(	DELIMITER
B	VARIABLE
*	DELIMITER
C	VARIABLE
)	DELIMITER
/	DELIMITER
2	NUMBER
null	Null

Remember that **token** always holds a null-terminated string, even if it contains just a single character.

Expression Parsing

There are a number of ways to parse and evaluate an expression. For use with a recursive-descent parser, think of expressions as *recursive data structures*—that is, expressions that are defined in terms of themselves. If, for the moment, expressions can only use **+**, **–**, *****, **/**, and parentheses, all expressions can be defined with the following rules:

    expression → term [+ term] [– term]
    term → factor [* factor] [/ factor]
    factor → variable, number, or (expression)

The square brackets designate an optional element, and → means produces. In fact, the rules are usually called the *production rules* of the expression. Therefore, you could say: "Term produces factor times factor or factor divided by factor" for the definition of *term*. Notice that the precedence of the operators is implicit in the way an expression is defined.

The expression

$$10 + 5 * B$$

has two terms: 10, and 5 * B. It has three factors: 10, 5, and B. These factors consist of two numbers and one variable.

On the other hand, the expression

$$14 * (7 - C)$$

has two terms: 14 and (7 − C). The terms consist of one number and one parenthesized expression. The parenthesized expression evaluates to one number and one variable.

This process forms the basis for a *recursive-descent parser*, which is basically a set of mutually recursive functions that work in a chainlike fashion. At each appropriate step, the parser performs the specified operations in the algebraically correct sequence. To see how this process works, parse the input expression that follows and perform the arithmetic operations at the right time:

$$9/3 - (100 + 56)$$

If you parsed the expression correctly, you followed these steps:

1. Get the first term, 9/3.

2. Get each factor and divide the integers. The resulting value is 3.

3. Get the second term, (100 + 56). At this point, start recursively analyzing the second subexpression.

4. Get each factor and add. The resulting value is 156.

5. Return from the recursive call and subtract 156 from 3. The answer is −153.

If you are a little confused at this point, don't feel bad. This is a fairly complex concept that takes some getting used to. There are two basic things to remember about this recursive view of expressions. First, the precedence of the operators is implicit in the way the production rules are defined. Second, this method of parsing and evaluating expressions is very similar to the way humans evaluate mathematical expressions.

A Simple Expression Parser

The remainder of this chapter develops two parsers. The first will parse and evaluate only constant expressions—that is, expressions with no variables. This example shows the parser in its simplest form. The second parser will include the 26 variables **A** through **Z**.

Here is the entire version of the simple recursive-descent parser for floating-point expressions:

```c
/* This module contains a simple expression parser
   that does not recognize variables.
*/

#include "stdlib.h"
#include "ctype.h"
#include "stdio.h"
#include "string.h"

#define DELIMITER  1
#define VARIABLE   2
#define NUMBER     3

extern char *prog;   /* holds expression to be analyzed */
char token[80];
char tok_type;

void eval_exp(double *answer), eval_exp2(double *answer);
void eval_exp3(double *answer), eval_exp4(double *answer);
void eval_exp5(double *answer);
void eval_exp6(double *answer), atom(double *answer);
void get_token(void), putback(void);
void unary(char o, double *r);
void serror(int error);
int isdelim(char c);

/* Parser entry point. */
void eval_exp(double *answer)
{
```

```
    get_token();
    if(!*token) {
      serror(2);
      return;
    }
    eval_exp2(answer);
}

/* Add or subtract two terms. */
void eval_exp2(double *answer)
{
  register char  op;
  double temp;

  eval_exp3(answer);
  while((op = *token) == '+' || op == '-') {
    get_token();
    eval_exp3(&temp);
    switch(op) {
      case '-':
        *answer = *answer - temp;
        break;
      case '+':
        *answer = *answer + temp;
        break;
    }
  }
}

/* Multiply or divide two factors. */
void eval_exp3(double *answer)
{
  register char  op;
  double temp;

  eval_exp4(answer);
  while((op = *token) == '*' || op == '/' || op == '%') {
    get_token();
    eval_exp4(&temp);
    switch(op) {
      case '*':
        *answer = *answer * temp;
        break;
      case '/':
        *answer = *answer / temp;
        break;
      case '%':
        *answer = (int) *answer % (int) temp;
        break;
    }
  }
}

/* Process an exponent */
void eval_exp4(double *answer)
{
  double temp, ex;
```

```
    register int t;

  eval_exp5(answer);
  if(*token== '^') {
    get_token();
    eval_exp4(&temp);
    ex = *answer;
    if(temp==0.0) {
      *answer = 1.0;
      return;
    }
    for(t=temp-1; t>0; --t) *answer = (*answer) * (double)ex;
  }
}

/* Evaluate a unary + or -. */
void eval_exp5(double *answer)
{
  register char  op;

  op = 0;
  if((tok_type == DELIMITER) && *token=='+' || *token == '-') {
    op = *token;
    get_token();
  }
  eval_exp6(answer);
  if(op=='-') *answer = -(*answer);
}

/* Process a parenthesized expression. */
void eval_exp6(double *answer)
{
  if((*token == '(')) {
    get_token();
    eval_exp2(answer);
    if(*token != ')')
      serror(1);
    get_token();
  }
  else
    atom(answer);
}

/* Get the actual value of a number. */
void atom(double *answer)
{

  if(tok_type==NUMBER) {
    *answer = atof(token);
    get_token();
    return;
  }
  serror(0);  /* otherwise syntax error in expression */
}

/* Return a token to its resting place. */
void putback(void)
```

```
{
  char *t;

  t = token;
  for(; *t; t++) prog--;
}

/* Display a syntax error. */
void serror(int error)
{
  static char *e[]= {
      "syntax error",
      "unbalanced parentheses",
      "no expression present"
  };
  printf("%s\n", e[error]);
}

/* Return the next token. */
void get_token(void)
{

  register char *temp;

  tok_type = 0;
  temp = token;
  *temp = '\0';

  if(!*prog) return; /* at end of expression */
  while(isspace(*prog)) ++prog;   /* skip over white space */

  if(strchr("+-*/%^=()", *prog)){
    tok_type = DELIMITER;
    /* advance to next char */
    *temp++ = *prog++;
  }
  else if(isalpha(*prog)) {
    while(!isdelim(*prog)) *temp++ = *prog++;
    tok_type = VARIABLE;
  }
  else if(isdigit(*prog)) {
    while(!isdelim(*prog)) *temp++ = *prog++;
    tok_type = NUMBER;
  }

  *temp = '\0';
}

/* Return true if c is a delimiter. */
isdelim(char c)
{
  if(strchr(" +-/*%^=()", c) || c==9 || c=='\r' || c==0)
    return 1;
  return 0;
}
```

The parser as it is shown can handle the following operators: **+**, **−**, *****, **/**, **%**. In addition, it can handle integer exponentiation (**^**) and the unary minus. The parser can also deal with parentheses correctly. Notice that it has six levels as well as the **atom( )** function, which returns the value of a number. As discussed, the two globals **token** and **tok_type** return, respectively, the next token and its type from the expression string. The pointer **extern prog** points to the string that holds the expression.

The simple **main( )** function that follows demonstrates the use of the parser:

```
/* Parser demo program. */
#include "stdlib.h"
#include "ctype.h"
#include "stdio.h"
#include "string.h"

char *prog;
void eval_exp(double *answer);

void main(void)
{
  double answer;
  char *p;

  p = malloc(100);
  if(!p) {
    printf("allocation failure\n");
    exit(1);
  }

  /* Process expressions until a blank line
     is entered.
  */
  do {
    prog = p;
    printf("enter expression: ");
    gets(prog);
    if(!*prog) break;
    eval_exp(&answer);
    printf("answer is: %.2f\n", answer);
  } while(*p);
}
```

To understand exactly how the parser evaluates an expression, work through the following expression, which **prog** points to:

10 − 3 * 2

When **eval_exp( )**, the entry routine into the parser, is called, it gets the first token. If the token is null, the routine prints the message **no expression present** and returns. If the token is not null, **eval_exp2( )** is called (**eval_exp1( )** is used when the assignment operator is added; it is not needed here). At this point, the token contains the number 10. As a result, **eval_exp2( )** calls **eval_exp3( )** and **eval_exp3( )** calls **eval_exp4( )**, which in turn calls **eval_exp5( )**. Then **eval_exp5( )** checks whether the token is a unary plus or minus, which in this case, it is not, so **eval_exp6( )** is called. At this point **eval_exp6( )** either recursively calls **eval_exp2( )** (in the case of a parenthesized expression) or **atom( )** to find the value of the integer. Finally, **atom( )** is executed and **answer** contains the number 10. Another token is retrieved, and the functions begin to return up the chain. The token is now the operator −, and the functions return up to **eval_exp2( )**.

What happens at this point is very important. Because the token is −, it is saved. The parser gets the new token 3, and the descent down the chain begins again. Again, **atom( )** is entered. The integer 3 is returned in **answer** and the token * is read. This causes a return back up the chain to **eval_exp3( )**, where the final token 2 is read. At this point, the first arithmetic operation occurs—the multiplication of 2 and 3. The result is returned to **eval_exp2( )** and the subtraction is performed. The subtraction yields the answer 4. Although the process may at first seem complicated, work through some other examples to verify that this method functions correctly every time.

This parser would be suitable for use by a desktop calculator, as is illustrated by the previous program. It also could be used in a limited database. Before it could be used in a computer language or in a sophisticated calculator, however, it would need the ability to handle variables. This is the subject of the next section.

Adding Variables to the Parser

All programming languages, many calculators, and spreadsheets use variables to store values for later use. The simple parser in the preceding section needs to be expanded to include variables before it can store values. To include variables, you need to add several things to the parser. First, of course, are the variables themselves. As stated earlier, the parser only recognizes the variables **A** through **Z** (although you could expand that capability if you wanted to). Each variable uses one array location in a 26-element array of **double**s. Therefore, add the following to the parser:

```
double vars[26]= {     /* 26 user variables,  A-Z */
  0.0, 0.0, 0.0, 0.0, 0.0, 0.0, 0.0, 0.0, 0.0, 0.0,
  0.0, 0.0, 0.0, 0.0, 0.0, 0.0, 0.0, 0.0, 0.0, 0.0,
  0.0, 0.0, 0.0, 0.0, 0.0, 0.0
};
```

As you can see, the variables are initialized to 0 as a courtesy to the user.

You also need a routine to look up the value of a given variable. Because the variables are named **A** through **Z**, they can easily be used to index the array **vars** by subtracting the ASCII value for **A** from the variable name. The function **find_var( )** is shown here:

```
double find_var(char *s)
{
  if(!isalpha(*s)){
    serror(1);
    return 0;
  }
  return vars[toupper(*token)-'A'];
}
```

As this function is written, it will actually accept long variable names, but only the first letter is significant. You may modify this to fit your needs.

You must also modify the **atom( )** function to handle both numbers and variables. The new version is shown here:

```
void atom(double *answer)
{

  switch(tok_type) {
    case VARIABLE:
      *answer = find_var(token);
      get_token();
      return;
    case NUMBER:
      *answer = atof(token);
```

```
       get_token();
       return;
     default:
       serror(0);
   }
}
```

Technically, these additions are all that is needed for the parser to use variables correctly; however, there is no way for these variables to be assigned a value. Often this is done outside the parser, but you can treat the equal sign as an assignment operator and make it part of the parser. There are various ways to do this. One method is to add **eval _ exp1( )** to the parser, as shown here:

```
/* Process an assignment. */
void eval_exp1(double *result)
{
  int slot, ttok_type;
  char temp_token[80];

  if(tok_type==VARIABLE) {
    /* save old token */
    strcpy(temp_token, token);
    ttok_type = tok_type;

    /* compute the index of the variable */
    slot = toupper(*token)-'A';

    get_token();
    if(*token != '=') {
      putback(); /* return current token */
      /* restore old token - not assignment */
      strcpy(token, temp_token);
      tok_type = ttok_type;
    }
    else {
      get_token(); /* get next part of exp */
      eval_exp2(result);
      vars[slot] = *result;
      return;
    }
  }

  eval_exp2(result);
}
```

As you can see, the function needs to look ahead to determine whether an assignment is actually being made. This is because a variable name always precedes an assignment, but a variable name alone does not guarantee that an assignment expression follows. That is, the parser will accept A = 100 as an assignment, but is also smart enough to know that A/10 is an expression. To accomplish this, **eval_exp1( )** reads the next token from the input stream. If it is not an equal sign, the token is returned to the input stream for later use by calling **putback( )**, shown here:

```
/* Return a token to the input stream. */
void putback(void)
{
  char *t;

  t = token;
  for(; *t; t++) prog--;
}
```

Here is the entire enhanced parser:

```
/* This module contains the recursive descent
   parser that recognizes variables.
*/

#include "stdlib.h"
#include "ctype.h"
#include "stdio.h"
#include "string.h"

#define DELIMITER  1
#define VARIABLE   2
#define NUMBER     3

extern char *prog;  /* holds expression to be analyzed */
char token[80];
char tok_type;

double vars[26]= {     /* 26 user variables,  A-Z */
  0.0, 0.0, 0.0, 0.0, 0.0, 0.0, 0.0, 0.0, 0.0, 0.0,
  0.0, 0.0, 0.0, 0.0, 0.0, 0.0, 0.0, 0.0, 0.0, 0.0,
  0.0, 0.0, 0.0, 0.0, 0.0, 0.0
};

void eval_exp(double *answer), eval_exp2(double *answer);
void eval_exp1(double *result);
void eval_exp3(double *answer), eval_exp4(double *answer);
void eval_exp5(double *answer);
void eval_exp6(double *answer), atom(double *answer);
void get_token(void), putback(void);
void unary(char o, double *r);
void serror(int error);
double find_var(char *s);
int isdelim(char c);

/* Parser entry point. */
void eval_exp(double *answer)
```

```
{
  get_token();
  if(!*token) {
    serror(2);
    return;
  }
  eval_exp1(answer);
}

/* Process an assignment. */
void eval_exp1(double *answer)
{
  int slot;
  char ttok_type;
  char temp_token[80];

  if(tok_type==VARIABLE) {
    /* save old token */
    strcpy(temp_token, token);
    ttok_type = tok_type;

    /* compute the index of the variable */
    slot = toupper(*token)-'A';

    get_token();
    if(*token != '=') {
      putback(); /* return current token */
      /* restore old token - not assignment */
      strcpy(token, temp_token);
      tok_type = ttok_type;
    }
    else {
      get_token(); /* get next part of exp */
      eval_exp2(answer);
      vars[slot] = *answer;
      return;
    }
  }

  eval_exp2(answer);
}

/* Add or subtract two terms. */
void eval_exp2(double *answer)
{
  register char  op;
  double temp;

  eval_exp3(answer);
  while((op = *token) == '+' || op == '-') {
    get_token();
    eval_exp3(&temp);
    switch(op) {
      case '-':
        *answer = *answer - temp;
        break;
      case '+':
```

```
      *answer = *answer + temp;
      break;
  }
 }
}

/* Multiply or divide two factors. */
void eval_exp3(double *answer)
{
  register char  op;
  double temp;

  eval_exp4(answer);
  while((op = *token) == '*' || op == '/' || op == '%') {
    get_token();
    eval_exp4(&temp);
    switch(op) {
      case '*':
        *answer = *answer * temp;
        break;
      case '/':
        *answer = *answer / temp;
        break;
      case '%':
        *answer = (int) *answer % (int) temp;
        break;
    }
  }
}

/* Process an exponent */
void eval_exp4(double *answer)
{
  double temp, ex;
  register int t;

  eval_exp5(answer);
  if(*token== '^') {
    get_token();
    eval_exp4(&temp);
    ex = *answer;
    if(temp==0.0) {
      *answer = 1.0;
      return;
    }
    for(t=temp-1; t>0; --t) *answer = (*answer) * (double)ex;
  }
}

/* Evaluate a unary + or -. */
void eval_exp5(double *answer)
{
  register char  op;

  op = 0;
  if((tok_type == DELIMITER) && *token=='+' || *token == '-') {
    op = *token;
```

```
      get_token();
    }
    eval_exp6(answer);
    if(op=='-') *answer = -(*answer);
}

/* Process a parenthesized expression. */
void eval_exp6(double *answer)
{
    if((*token == '(')) {
      get_token();
      eval_exp2(answer);
      if(*token != ')')
        serror(1);
      get_token();
    }
    else
      atom(answer);
}

void atom(double *answer)
{

    switch(tok_type) {
      case VARIABLE:
        *answer = find_var(token);
        get_token();
        return;
      case NUMBER:
        *answer = atof(token);
        get_token();
        return;
      default:
        serror(0);
    }
}

/* Return a token to the input stream. */
void putback(void)
{
    char *t;

    t = token;
    for(; *t; t++) prog--;
}

/* Display a syntax error. */
void serror(int error)
{
    static char *e[]= {
        "syntax error",
        "unbalanced parentheses",
        "no expression present"
    };
    printf("%s\n", e[error]);
}
```

```
/* Return the next token. */
void get_token(void)
{

  register char *temp;

  tok_type = 0;
  temp = token;
  *temp = '\0';

  if(!*prog) return; /* at end of expression */

  while(isspace(*prog)) ++prog;   /* skip over white space */

  if(strchr("+-*/%^=()", *prog)){
    tok_type = DELIMITER;
    /* advance to next char */
    *temp++ = *prog++;
  }
  else if(isalpha(*prog)) {
    while(!isdelim(*prog)) *temp++ = *prog++;
    tok_type = VARIABLE;
  }
  else if(isdigit(*prog)) {
    while(!isdelim(*prog)) *temp++ = *prog++;
    tok_type = NUMBER;
  }

  *temp = '\0';
}

/* Return true if c is a delimiter. */
isdelim(char c)
{
  if(strchr(" +-/*%^=()", c) || c==9 || c=='\r' || c==0)
    return 1;
  return 0;
}

double find_var(char *s)
{
  if(!isalpha(*s)){
    serror(1);
    return 0.0;
  }
  return vars[toupper(*token)-'A'];
}
```

You may still use the same **main( )** function that you used for the simple parser. With the enhanced parser, you can now enter expressions like

    A = 10/4
    A - B
    C = A * (F - 21)

Syntax Checking in a Recursive-Descent Parser

In expression parsing, a syntax error is simply a situation in which the input expression does not conform to the strict rules required by the parser. Most of the time, this is caused by human error—usually typing mistakes. For example, the following expressions are not valid for the parsers in this chapter:

    10 ** 8
    (10 − 5) * 9)
    /8

The first contains two operators in a row, the second has unbalanced parentheses, and the last has a division sign at the start of an expression. None of these conditions is allowed by the parsers in this chapter. Because syntax errors can cause the parser to give erroneous results, you need to guard against them.

As you studied the code of the parsers, you probably noticed the **serror( )** function, which is called under certain situations. Unlike many other parsers, the recursive-descent method makes syntax checking easy because, for the most part, it occurs in **atom( )**, **find_var( )**, or **eval_exp6( )**, where parentheses are checked. The only problem with the syntax checking as it now stands is that the entire parser is not aborted on syntax error. This can lead to multiple error messages.

The best way to implement the **serror( )** routine is to have it execute a reset routine. ANSI standard compilers come with a pair of companion functions called **setjmp( )** and **longjmp( )**. These two functions allow a program to branch to a *different* function. Therefore, in **serror( )**, execute a **longjmp( )** to some safe point in your program outside the parser.

If your compiler does not have **setjmp( )** and **longjump( )**, the only other option is to add a global variable that is checked at each level. Initially, the variable would be **false** and any call to **serror( )** would set it to **true**, causing the parser to abort one function at a time.

If you leave the code the way it is, multiple syntax-error messages may be issued. This can be an annoyance in some situations, but it can be a blessing in others because multiple errors may be caught. Generally, however, you will want to enhance the syntax checking before using it in commercial programs.

AI-Based Problem Solving

The field of artificial intelligence (AI) is composed of several different exciting aspects.[*] However, fundamental to most AI applications is problem solving.

Basically, there are two types of problems. The first type can be solved through the use of some sort of deterministic procedure that is guaranteed success—in other words, a computation. The methods used to solve these types of problems are often easily translated into an algorithm that a computer can execute. However, few real-world problems lend themselves to computational solutions. In fact, most problems are noncomputational. These problems are solved by searching for a solution—the method of problem solving with which AI is concerned.

One of the dreams of AI research is a general problem solver. A *general problem solver* is a program that can produce solutions to all sorts of different problems about which it has no specific designed-in knowledge. This chapter shows why the dream is as tantalizing as it is

[*]See the book *Artificial Intelligence Using C* (Berkeley, Calif.: Osborne/McGraw-Hill, 1987) by Herbert Schildt. The book discusses such things as expert systems, robotics, natural language processing, vision, and machine logic.

difficult to realize.

In early AI research, developing good search methods was a primary goal. There are two reasons for this: necessity and desire. One of the most difficult obstacles when applying AI techniques to real-world problems is the sheer magnitude and complexity of most situations. Solving these problems requires good search techniques. In addition, researchers believed then as they do now that searching is central to problem solving, which is a crucial ingredient of intelligence.

Representation and Terminology

Imagine that you have lost your car keys. You know that they are somewhere in your house, which looks like this:

You are standing at the front door (where the *X* is). As you begin your search, you check the living room. Then you go down the hall to the first bedroom, to the hall to the second bedroom, back to the hall, and to the master bedroom. Not having found your keys, you backtrack further by going back through the living room. You find your keys in the kitchen. This situation is easily represented by a graph, as shown in Figure 23-1.

The fact that problems can be represented by a graph is important because a graph provides a means to visualize the way the different search techniques work. (Also, being able to represent problems by graphs allows AI researchers to apply various theorems from graph theory. However, these theorems are beyond the scope of this book.) With this in mind, study the following definitions:

Node	A discrete point and possible goal
Terminal node	A node that ends a path
Search space	The set of all nodes
Goal	The node that is the object of the search
Heuristics	Information about whether any specific node is a better next choice than another
Solution path	A directed graph of the nodes visited en route to a solution

In the example of the lost keys, each room in the house is a node; the entire house is the search space; the goal, as it turns out, is the kitchen; and the solution path is shown in Figure 23-1. The bedrooms and the bath are terminal nodes because they lead nowhere. This example doesn't use heuristics, but you will see some later on in this chapter.

Combinatorial Explosions

At this point, you may think that searching for a solution is easy—you start at the beginning and work your way to the conclusion. In the

Figure 23-1.   The solution path to find the missing keys

extremely simple case of the lost keys, this is not a bad method. But in most problems that you would use a computer to solve, the situation is much different. In general, you use a computer to solve problems where the number of nodes in the search space is very large, and as the search space grows, so does the number of different possible paths to the goal. The trouble is that each node added to the search space adds more than one path. That is, the number of pathways to the goal increases faster as each node is added.

For instance, consider the number of ways three objects — A, B, and C — can be arranged on a table. The six possible arrangements are

A	B	C
A	C	B
B	C	A
B	A	C
C	B	A
C	A	B

You can quickly prove to yourself that these six are the only ways that A, B, and C can be arranged. However, you can derive the same number by using a theorem from the branch of mathematics called *combinatorics* — the study of the way that things can be combined. According to the theorem, the number of ways that N objects can be combined (or arranged) is equal to N! (N factorial). The factorial of a number is the product of all whole numbers equal to or less than itself down to 1. Therefore, 3! is $3 \times 2 \times 1$, or 6. If you had four objects to arrange, there would be 4!, or 24, combinations. With five objects, the number is 120, and with six it is 720. With 1000 objects the number of possible combinations is huge! The graph in Figure 23-2 gives you a visual feel for what AI researchers commonly refer to as a *combinatoric explosion.* Once there are more than a handful of possibilities, it very quickly becomes impossible to examine (indeed, even to enumerate) all the combinations.

In other words, each additional node in the search space increases the number of possible solutions by a number far greater than one. Hence, at some point there are too many possibilities to work with. Because the number of possibilities grows so quickly, only the simplest of problems lend themselves to exhaustive searches. An *exhaustive*

Figure 23-2.   A combinatoric explosion with factorials

search is one that examines all nodes—think of it as a "brute-force" technique. Brute force always works, but is not often practical because it consumes far too much time, too many computing resources, or both. For this reason, researchers developed other search techniques.

Search Techniques

There are several ways to search for a possible solution. The most important and common are

- Depth-first searches
- Breadth-first searches
- Hill-climbing searches
- Least-cost searches

This chapter examines each of these searches.

Evaluating a Search

Evaluating the performance of a search technique can be very complicated. In fact, the evaluation of searches forms a large part of AI. However, for our purposes there are two important measurements:

- How quickly the search finds a solution
- How good the solution is

There are several types of problems for which all that matters is that a solution, any solution, be found with the minimum effort. For these problems, the first measurement is important. However, in other situations, the solution must be good, perhaps even optimal.

The speed of a search is determined both by the length of the solution path and by the actual number of nodes traversed. Remember that backtracking from dead ends is essentially wasted effort, so you want a search that seldom backtracks.

You should understand that there is a difference between finding an optimal solution and finding a good solution. Finding an optimal solution usually entails an exhaustive search because this is the only way to know that the best solution has been found. Finding a good solution, in contrast, means finding a solution that is within a set of constraints — it does not matter if a better solution exists.

As you will see, the search techniques described in this chapter all work better in certain situations than others. So, it is difficult to say whether one search method is *always* superior to another. But some search techniques have a greater probability of being better for the average case. In addition, the way a problem is defined can sometimes help you choose an appropriate search method.

First, consider a problem that we will use various searches to solve. Imagine that you are a travel agent and a rather quarrelsome customer wants you to book a flight from New York to Los Angeles with XYZ Airlines. You try to tell the customer that XYZ does not have a direct flight from New York to Los Angeles, but the customer insists that XYZ is the only airline that he will fly. XYZ's scheduled flights are as follows:

New York to Chicago	1000 miles
Chicago to Denver	1000 miles
New York to Toronto	800 miles
New York to Denver	1900 miles
Toronto to Calgary	1500 miles
Toronto to Los Angeles	1800 miles
Toronto to Chicago	500 miles
Denver to Urbana	1000 miles
Denver to Houston	1500 miles
Houston to Los Angeles	1500 miles
Denver to Los Angeles	1000 miles

You quickly see that there is a way to fly from New York to Los Angeles by using XYZ if you book connecting flights. You book the fellow his flights.

Your task is to write C programs that do the same thing even better.

A Graphic Representation

The flight information in XYZ's schedule book can be translated into the directed graph shown in Figure 23-3. A *directed graph* is simply a graph in which the lines connecting each node include an arrow to indicate the direction of motion. In a directed graph, you cannot travel in the direction against the arrow.

To make things easier to understand, this graph is redrawn as the tree in Figure 23-4. Refer to this version for the rest of this chapter. The goal, Los Angeles, is circled. Also notice that various cities appear more than once to simplify the construction of the graph.

Now you are ready to develop the various search programs that will find paths from New York to Los Angeles.

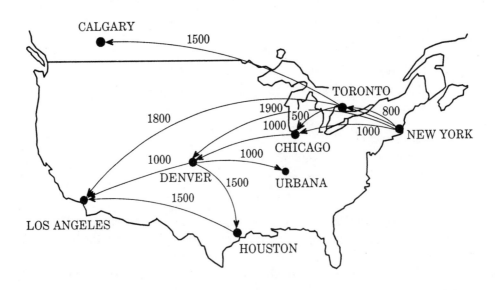

Figure 23-3.   A directed graph of XYZ's flight schedule

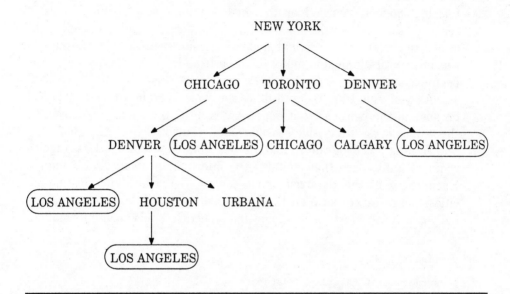

Figure 23-4.   A tree version of XYZ's flight schedule

The Depth-First Search

The *depth-first search* explores each possible path to the conclusion (or goal) before another path is tried. To understand exactly how this works, consider the tree that follows. F is the goal.

A depth-first search traverses the graph in the following order: ABDBEBACF. If you are familiar with trees, you recognize this type of

search as an inorder tree traversal. That is, the path goes left until a terminal node is reached or the goal is found. If a terminal node is reached, the path backs up one level, goes right, and then left until either the goal or a terminal node is encountered. This procedure is repeated until the goal is found or the last node in the search space has been examined.

As you can see, a depth-first search is certain to find the goal because in the worst case it degenerates into an exhaustive search. In this example, an exhaustive search would result if G were the goal.

Writing a C program to find a route from New York to Los Angeles requires a database that contains the information about XYZ's flights. Each entry in the database must contain departure and destination cities, the distance between them, and a flag that aids in backtracking (as you will see shortly). The following structure holds such information:

```
#define MAX 100

/* structure of the flight database */
struct FL {
  char from[20];
  char to[20];
  int distance;
  char skip;  /* used in backtracking */
};

struct FL flight[MAX];  /* array of db structures */

int f_pos=0; /* number of entries in flight db */
int find_pos=0; /* index for searching flight db */
```

Entries are placed into the database function **assert_flight( )**, and **setup( )** initializes the information. The global **f_pos** holds the index of the last item in the database. These routines are shown here:

```
void setup(void)
{
  assert_flight("New York", "Chicago", 1000);
  assert_flight("Chicago", "Denver", 1000);
  assert_flight("New York", "Toronto", 800);
  assert_flight("New York", "Denver", 1900);
  assert_flight("Toronto", "Calgary", 1500);
  assert_flight("Toronto", "Los Angeles", 1800);
  assert_flight("Toronto", "Chicago", 500);
  assert_flight("Denver", "Urbana", 1000);
  assert_flight("Denver", "Houston", 1500);
  assert_flight("Houston", "Los Angeles", 1500);
```

```
    assert_flight("Denver", "Los Angeles", 1000);
}

/* Put facts into the database. */
void assert_flight(char *from, char *to, int dist)
{

  if(f_pos<MAX) {
    strcpy(flight[f_pos].from, from);
    strcpy(flight[f_pos].to, to);
    flight[f_pos].distance = dist;
    flight[f_pos].skip = 0;
    f_pos++;
  }
  else printf("Flight database full.\n");
}
```

In keeping with the spirit of AI, think of the database as containing facts. The program to be developed will use these facts to arrive at a solution. For this reason, many AI researchers refer to the database as a *knowledge base*. This book uses the two terms interchangeably.

Before you can write the actual code to find a route between New York and Los Angeles, you need several support functions. First, you need a routine that determines if there is a flight between the two cities. This function is called **match( )**, and it returns zero if no such flight exists or returns the distance between the two cities if there is a flight. This routine is shown here:

```
/* If flight between from and to, then return
   the distance of flight; otherwise, return 0. */
match(char *from, char *to)
{
  register int t;

  for(t=f_pos-1; t>-1; t--)
    if(!strcmp(flight[t].from, from) &&
       !strcmp(flight[t].to, to)) return flight[t].distance;

  return 0;   /* not found */
}
```

Another necessary routine is **find( )**. Given a city, **find( )** searches the database for any connection. If a connection is found, the name of the destination city and its distance are returned; otherwise, zero is returned. The **find( )** routine follows:

```
/* Given from, find anywhere. */
find(char *from, char *anywhere)
{
```

```
  find_pos = 0;
  while(find_pos<f_pos) {
    if(!strcmp(flight[find_pos].from, from) &&
      !flight[find_pos].skip) {
        strcpy(anywhere, flight[find_pos].to);
        flight[find_pos].skip = 1; /* make active */
        return flight[find_pos].distance;
    }
    find_pos++;
  }
  return 0;
}
```

As you can see, cities that have the **skip** field set to 1 are not valid connections. Also, if a connection is found, its **skip** field is marked as active—this controls backtracking from dead ends.

Backtracking is a crucial ingredient in many AI techniques. Backtracking is accomplished through the use of recursive routines and a backtrack stack. Almost all backtracking situations are stacklike in operation—that is, they are first-in, last-out. As a path is explored, nodes are pushed onto the stack as they are encountered. At each dead end, the last node is popped off the stack and a new path, from that point, is tried. This process continues until either the goal is reached or all paths have been exhausted. The functions **push( )** and **pop( )**, which manage the backtrack stack, follow. They use the globals **tos** and **bt _ stack** to hold the top-of-stack pointer and the stack array, respectively.

```
/* stack routines */
void push(char *from, char *to, int dist)
{
  if(tos<MAX) {
    strcpy(bt_stack[tos].from, from);
    strcpy(bt_stack[tos].to, to);
    bt_stack[tos].dist = dist;
    tos++;
  }
  else printf("Stack full.\n");
}

void pop(char *from, char *to, int *dist)
{
  if(tos>0) {
    tos--;
    strcpy(from, bt_stack[tos].from);
    strcpy(to, bt_stack[tos].to);
    *dist = bt_stack[tos].dist;
  }
  else printf("Stack underflow.\n");
}
```

Now that the required support routines have been developed, consider the code that follows. It is **isflight( )**, the key routine in finding a route between New York and Los Angeles.

```
/* Determine if there is a route between from and to. */
void isflight(char *from, char *to)
{
  int d, dist;
  char anywhere[20];

  /* see if at destination */
  if(d=match(from, to)) {
    push(from, to, d);
    return;
  }

  /* try another connection */
  if(dist=find(from, anywhere)) {
    push(from, to, dist);
    isflight(anywhere, to);
  }
  else if(tos>0) {
    /* backtrack */
    pop(from, to, &dist);
    isflight(from, to);
  }
}
```

The routine works as follows: First, the database is checked by **match( )** to see if there is a flight between **from** and **to**. If there is, the goal has been reached—the connection is pushed onto the stack and the function returns. Otherwise, **find( )** checks if there is a connection between **from** and any place else. If there is, this connection is pushed onto the stack and **isflight( )** is called recursively. Otherwise, backtracking takes place. The previous node is removed from the stack and **isflight( )** is called recursively. This process continues until the goal is found. The **skip** field is necessary to backtracking to prevent the same connections from being tried over and over again.

Hence, if called with Denver and Houston, the first part of the routine would succeed and **isflight( )** would terminate. Say, however, that **isflight( )** were called Chicago and Houston. In this case, the first part would fail because there is no direct flight connecting these two cities. The second part is tried by attempting to find a connection between the origin city and any other city. In this case, Chicago connects with Denver; therefore, **isflight( )** is called recursively with Denver and Houston. Once again, the first condition is tested. A connection is found this time. Finally, the recursive calls unravel and **isflight( )** terminates. Verify in your mind that, as **isflight( )** is presented here, it performs a depth-first search of the knowledge base.

It is important to understand that **isflight( )** does not actually return the solution—it generates it. Upon exit from **isflight( )**, the backtrack stack contains the route between Chicago and Houston—that is, the solution. In fact, the success or failure of **isflight( )** is determined by the state of the stack. An empty stack indicates failure; otherwise, the stack holds a solution. Hence, you need one more function to complete the entire program. The function is called **route( )**, and it prints both the path to follow as well as the total distance. The **route( )** function is shown here:

```
/* Show the route and total distance. */
void route(char *to)
{
  int dist, t;

  dist = 0;
  t = 0;
  while(t<tos) {
    printf("%s to ", bt_stack[t].from);
    dist += bt_stack[t].dist;
    t++;
  }
  printf("%s\n", to);
  printf("distance is %d\n", dist);
}
```

The entire depth-first search program follows. Enter this program into your computer at this time.

```
/* Depth-first search. */
#include "stdio.h"
#include "string.h"

#define MAX 100

/* structure of the flight database */
struct FL {
  char from[20];
  char to[20];
  int distance;
  char skip; /* used in backtracking */
};

struct FL flight[MAX]; /* array of db structures */

int f_pos=0; /* number of entries in flight db */
int find_pos=0; /* index for searching flight db */
```

```c
int tos=0;        /* top of stack */
struct stack {
  char from[20];
  char to[20];
  int dist;
} ;
struct stack bt_stack[MAX]; /* backtrack stack */

void setup(void), route(char *to);
void assert_flight(char *from, char *to, int dist);
void push(char *from, char *to, int dist);
void pop(char *from, char *to, int *dist);
void isflight(char *from, char *to);
int find(char *from, char *anywhere);
int match(char *from, char *to);

void main(void)
{
  char from[20], to[20];

  setup();

  printf("from?");
  gets(from);
  printf("to? ");
  gets(to);

  isflight(from,to);
  route(to);
}

void setup(void)
{
  assert_flight("New York","Chicago",1000);
  assert_flight("Chicago","Denver",1000);
  assert_flight("New York","Toronto", 800);
  assert_flight("New York","Denver", 1900);
  assert_flight("Toronto","Calgary",1500);
  assert_flight("Toronto","Los Angeles",1800);
  assert_flight("Toronto","Chicago",500);
  assert_flight("Denver","Urbana",1000);
  assert_flight("Denver","Houston",1500);
  assert_flight("Houston","Los Angeles",1500);
  assert_flight("Denver","Los Angeles",1000);
}

/* Put facts into the database. */
void assert_flight(char *from, char *to, int dist)
{

  if(f_pos<MAX) {
    strcpy(flight[f_pos].from, from);
    strcpy(flight[f_pos].to, to);
    flight[f_pos].distance = dist;
    flight[f_pos].skip = 0;
    f_pos++;
  }
  else printf("Flight database full.\n");
```

```
}

/* Show the route and total distance. */
void route(char *to)
{
  int dist, t;

  dist = 0;
  t = 0;
  while(t<tos) {
    printf("%s to ", bt_stack[t].from);
    dist += bt_stack[t].dist;
    t++;
  }
  printf("%s\n", to);
  printf("distance is %d\n", dist);
}

/* If flight between from and to, then return
   the distance of flight; otherwise, return 0. */
match(char *from, char *to)
{
  register int t;

  for(t=f_pos-1; t>-1; t--)
    if(!strcmp(flight[t].from, from) &&
      !strcmp(flight[t].to, to)) return flight[t].distance;

  return 0; /* not found */
}

/* Given from, find anywhere. */
find(char *from, char *anywhere)
{
  find_pos=0;
  while(find_pos<f_pos) {
    if(!strcmp(flight[find_pos].from,from) &&
      !flight[find_pos].skip) {
        strcpy(anywhere,flight[find_pos].to);
        flight[find_pos].skip=1; /* make active */
        return flight[find_pos].distance;
      }
    find_pos++;
  }
  return 0;
}

/* Determine if there is a route between from and to. */
void isflight(char *from, char *to)
{
  int d, dist;
  char anywhere[20];

  /* see if at destination */
  if(d=match(from, to)) {
    push(from, to, d);
    return;
  }
```

```
/* try another connection */
if(dist=find(from, anywhere)) {
  push(from, to, dist);
  isflight(anywhere, to);
}
else if(tos>0) {
  /* backtrack */
  pop(from, to, &dist);
  isflight(from, to);
}
}

/* stack routines */
void push(char *from, char *to, int dist)
{
  if(tos<MAX) {
    strcpy(bt_stack[tos].from,from);
    strcpy(bt_stack[tos].to,to);
    bt_stack[tos].dist=dist;
    tos++;
  }
  else printf("Stack full.\n");
}

void pop(char *from, char *to, int *dist)
{
  if(tos>0) {
    tos--;
    strcpy(from,bt_stack[tos].from);
    strcpy(to,bt_stack[tos].to);
    * dist=bt_stack[tos].dist;
  }
  else printf("Stack underflow.\n");
}
```

Notice that **main( )** prompts you for both the city of origin and the destination. This means that you can use the program to find routes between any two cities. However, the rest of this chapter assumes that New York is the origin and Los Angeles is the destination.

Compile the program now. For certain compilers, including Microsoft C, you will need to increase the amount of memory allocated for the stack because, for certain solutions, the routines are highly recursive.

When run with New York as the origin and Los Angeles as the destination, the solution is

New York to Chicago to Denver to Los Angeles
distance is 3000

Figure 23-5 shows the path of the search.

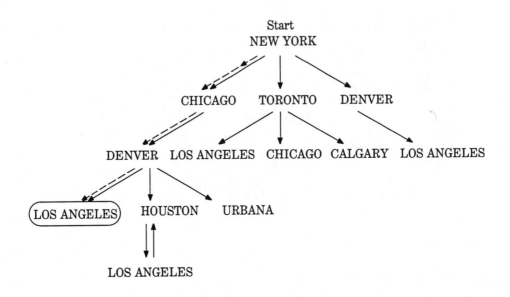

Figure 23-5.   The depth-first path to a solution

If you refer to Figure 23-5 you see that this is indeed the first solution that would be found by a depth-first search. It is not the optimal solution—which is New York to Toronto to Los Angeles with a distance of 2600 miles—but it is not bad.

An Analysis of the Depth-First Search

As you can see, the depth-first approach found a fairly good solution. Also, relative to this specific problem, depth-first searching found a solution on its first try with no backtracking—this is very good. But, it would have had to traverse nearly all the nodes to arrive at the optimal solution—this is not so good.

Note that the performance of depth-first searches can be quite poor when a particularly long branch with no solution at the end is explored. In this case, a depth-first search wastes considerable time not only exploring this chain, but also backtracking to the goal.

The Breadth-First Search

The opposite of the depth-first search is the *breadth-first search*. In this method, each node on the same level is checked before the search proceeds to the next deeper level. This traversal method is shown here with C as the goal:

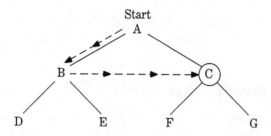

As you can see, the nodes A, B, and C are visited. Like a depth-first search, a breadth-first search guarantees a solution, if one exists, because it eventually degenerates into an exhaustive search.

To make the route-seeking program perform a breadth-first search, you only need to alter the procedure **isflight( )** as shown here:

```
void isflight(char *from, char *to)
{
  int d, dist;
  char anywhere[20];

  while(dist=find(from, anywhere)) {
    /* breadth-first modification */
    if(d=match(anywhere, to)) {
      push(from, to, dist);
      push(anywhere, to, d);
      return;
    }
  }
  /* try any connection */
  if(dist=find(from, anywhere)) {
    push(from, to, dist);
    isflight(anywhere, to);
  }
  else if(tos>0) {
    pop(from, to, &dist);
    isflight(from, to);
  }
}
```

As you can see, only the first condition has been altered. Now all connecting cities to the departure city are checked to see if they connect with the destination city.

Substitute this version of **isflight( )** in the program and run it. The solution is

New York to Toronto to Los Angeles
distance is 2600

The solution is optimal. Figure 23-6 shows the breadth-first path to the solution.

An Analysis of the Breadth-First Search

In this example, the breadth-first search performed very well by finding the first solution without backtracking. As it turned out, this was also the optimal solution. In fact, the first three solutions that would be found are the best three routes there are. However, remember that this result does not generalize to other situations because the path depends

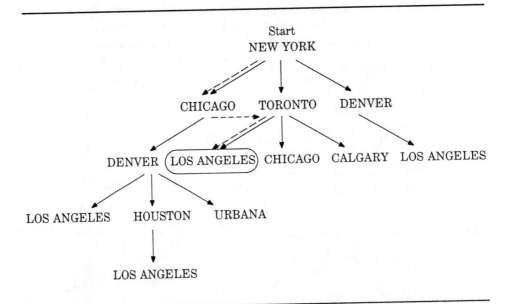

Figure 23-6. The breadth-first path to a solution

upon the physical organization of the information as it is stored in the computer. The example does illustrate, however, how radically different depth-first and breadth-first searches are.

A disadvantage to breadth-first searching becomes apparent when the goal is several layers deep. In this case a breadth-first search expends substantial effort to find the goal. In general, you choose between depth-first and breadth-first searching by making an educated guess about the most likely position of the goal.

Adding Heuristics

You have probably guessed by now that both the depth-first and breadth-first search routines are blind. They are methods of looking for a solution that rely solely upon moving from one goal to the other without any educated guesswork on the part of the computer. This may be fine for certain controlled situations where you know that one method is better than the other. However, a generalized AI program needs a search procedure that is on the average superior to either of these two techniques. The only way to achieve such a search is to add heuristic capabilities.

Recall that heuristics are simply rules that qualify the possibility that a search is proceeding in the correct direction. For example, imagine that you are lost in the woods and need a drink of water. The woods are so thick that you cannot see far ahead, and the trees are too big to climb and get a look around. However, you know that rivers, streams, and ponds are most likely in valleys; that animals frequently make paths to their watering places; that when you are near water it is possible to "smell" it; and that you can hear running water. So, you begin by moving downhill because water is unlikely to be uphill. Next you come across a deer trail that also runs downhill. Knowing that this may lead to water, you follow it. You begin to hear a slight rushing off to your left. Knowing that this may be water, you cautiously move in that direction. As you move, you begin to detect the increased humidity in the air; you can smell the water. Finally, you find a stream and have your drink. As you can see, heuristic information, although neither precise nor guaranteed, increases the chances that a search method will find a goal quickly, optimally, or both. In short, it ups the odds in favor of a quick success.

You may think that heuristic information could easily be included in programs designed for specific applications, but that it would be impossible to create generalized heuristic searches. This is not the case, as you will see.

Most often, heuristic search methods are based on maximizing or minimizing some aspect of the problem. In fact, the two heuristic approaches that we will look at use opposite heuristics and yield different results. Both of these searches will be built upon the depth-first search routines.

The Hill-Climbing Search

In the problem of scheduling a flight from New York to Los Angeles, there are two possible constraints that a passenger may want to minimize. The first is the number of connections that have to be made. The second is the length of the route. Remember, the shortest route does not necessarily imply the fewest connections. A search algorithm that attempts to find as a first solution a route that minimizes the number of connections uses the heuristics that the longer the distance of the flight, the greater the likelihood that it takes the traveler closer to the destination; therefore, the number of connections is minimized.

In the language of AI, this is called *hill climbing*. The hill-climbing algorithm chooses as its next step the node that appears to place it closest to the goal (that is, farthest away from the current position). It derives its name from the analogy of a hiker being lost in the dark halfway up a mountain. Assuming that the hiker's camp is at the top of the mountain, even in the dark the hiker knows that each step that goes up is a step in the right direction.

Working only with the information contained in the flight-scheduling knowledge base, here is how to incorporate the hill-climbing heuristics into the routing program: Choose the connecting flight that is as far away as possible from the current position in the hope that it will be closer to the destination. To do this, modify the **find( )** routine as shown here:

```
/* Given from, find the farthest away "anywhere". */
find(char *from, char *anywhere)
{
  int pos, dist;

  pos=dist = 0;
  find_pos = 0;

  while(find_pos<f_pos) {
    if(!strcmp(flight[find_pos].from, from) &&
       !flight[find_pos].skip) {
         if(flight[find_pos].distance>dist) {
         pos = find_pos;
         dist = flight[find_pos].distance;
       }
    }
    find_pos++;
  }
  if(pos) {
    strcpy(anywhere, flight[pos].to);
    flight[pos].skip = 1;
    return flight[pos].distance;
  }
  return 0;
}
```

The **find( )** routine now searches the entire database, looking for the connection that is farthest away from the departure city.

The entire hill-climbing program follows. Enter this program into your computer at this time:

```
/* Hill-climbing */
#include "stdio.h"
#include "string.h"

#define MAX 100

/* structure of the flight database */
struct FL {
  char from[20];
  char to[20];
  int distance;
  char skip; /* used for backtracking */
};

struct FL flight[MAX];   /* array of db structures */

int f_pos=0; /* number of entries in flight db */
int find_pos=0; /* index for searching flight db */

int tos=0;       /* top of stack */
struct stack {
  char from[20];
```

```
  char to[20];
  int dist;
} ;
struct stack bt_stack[MAX]; /* backtrack stack */

void setup(void), route(char *to);
void assert_flight(char *from, char *to, int dist);
void push(char *from, char *to, int dist);
void pop(char *from, char *to, int *dist);
void isflight(char *from, char *to);
int find(char *from, char *anywhere);
int match(char *from, char *to);

void main(void)
{
  char from[20], to[20];

  setup();

  printf("from? ");
  gets(from);
  printf("to? ");
  gets(to);

  isflight(from,to);
  route(to);
}

void setup(void)
{
  assert_flight("New York", "Chicago", 1000);
  assert_flight("Chicago", "Denver", 1000);
  assert_flight("New York", "Toronto", 800);
  assert_flight("New York", "Denver", 1900);
  assert_flight("Toronto", "Calgary", 1500);
  assert_flight("Toronto", "Los Angeles", 1800);
  assert_flight("Toronto", "Chicago", 500);
  assert_flight("Denver", "Urbana", 1000);
  assert_flight("Denver", "Houston", 1500);
  assert_flight("Houston", "Los Angeles", 1500);
  assert_flight("Denver", "Los Angeles", 1000);
}

/* Put facts into the database. */
void assert_flight(char *from, char *to, int dist)
{

  if(f_pos<MAX) {
    strcpy(flight[f_pos].from, from);
    strcpy(flight[f_pos].to, to);
    flight[f_pos].distance = dist;
    flight[f_pos].skip = 0;
    f_pos++;
  }
  else printf("Flight database full.\n");
}
```

```
/* Show the route and the total distance. */
void route(char *to)
{
  int dist, t;

  dist = 0;
  t = 0;
  while(t<tos) {
    printf("%s to ", bt_stack[t].from);
    dist += bt_stack[t].dist;
    t++;
  }
  printf("%s\n", to);
  printf("distance is %d\n", dist);
}

/* If flight between from and to, then return
   the distance of flight; otherwise, return 0. */
match(char *from, char *to)
{
  register int t;

  for(t=f_pos-1; t>-1; t--)
    if(!strcmp(flight[t].from, from) &&
      !strcmp(flight[t].to, to)) return flight[t].distance;

  return 0;   /* not found */
}

/* Given from, find the farthest away "anywhere". */
find(char *from, char *anywhere)
{
  int pos, dist;

  pos=dist = 0;
  find_pos = 0;

  while(find_pos<f_pos) {
    if(!strcmp(flight[find_pos].from, from) &&
      !flight[find_pos].skip) {
        if(flight[find_pos].distance>dist) {
          pos = find_pos;
          dist = flight[find_pos].distance;
        }
    }
    find_pos++;
  }
  if(pos) {
    strcpy(anywhere, flight[pos].to);
    flight[pos].skip = 1;
    return flight[pos].distance;
  }
  return 0;
}

/* Determine if there is a route between from and to. */
void isflight(char *from, char *to)
```

```
{
  int d, dist;
  char anywhere[20];

  if(d=match(from, to)) {
    /* is goal */
    push(from, to, d);
    return;
  }

  /* find any connection */
  if(dist=find(from, anywhere)) {
    push(from, to, dist);
    isflight(anywhere, to);
  }
  else if(tos>0) {
    pop(from, to, &dist);
    isflight(from, to);
  }
}

/* stack routines */
void push(char *from, char *to, int dist)
{
  if(tos<MAX) {
    strcpy(bt_stack[tos].from, from);
    strcpy(bt_stack[tos].to, to);
    bt_stack[tos].dist = dist;
    tos++;
  }
  else printf("Stack full.\n");
}

void pop(char *from, char *to, int *dist)
{
  if(tos>0) {
    tos--;
    strcpy(from, bt_stack[tos].from);
    strcpy(to, bt_stack[tos].to);
    *dist = bt_stack[tos].dist;
  }
  else printf("Stack underflow.\n");
}
```

When the program is run, the solution is

New York to Denver to Los Angeles
distance is 2900

This is quite good! The route contains the minimal number of stops on the way (only one) and it is really quite close to the shortest route. Furthermore, the program arrives at the solution with no time or effort wasted through extensive backtracking.

However, if the Denver to Los Angeles connection did not exist, the solution would not be quite so good. It would be New York to Denver to Houston to Los Angeles — a distance of 4900 miles! This solution climbs a "false peak." As you can easily see, the route to Houston does not take us closer to the goal of Los Angeles. Figure 23-7 shows the first solution as well as the path to the false peak.

An Analysis of Hill Climbing

Actually, hill cimbing provides fairly good solutions in many circumstances because it tends to reduce the number of nodes that need to be visited before a solution is reached. However, it can suffer from three maladies. First, there is the problem of false peaks, as you saw in the second solution in the example. In this case, extensive backtracking must be used to find the solution. The second problem relates to plateaus, a situation in which all next steps look equally good (or bad). In this case hill climbing is no better than depth-first searching. The final

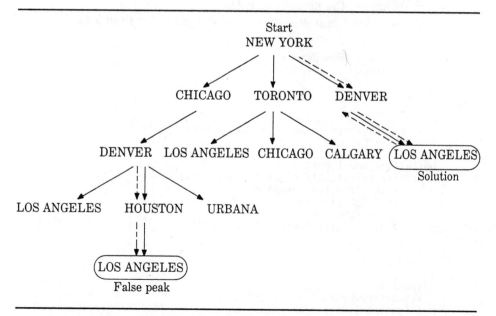

Figure 23-7.   The hill-climbing path to a solution and to a false peak

problem is that of a ridge. In this case, hill climbing really performs poorly because the algorithm causes the ridge to be crossed several times as backtracking occurs.

In spite of these potential troubles, hill climbing generally leads to a closer-to-optimal solution more quickly than any of the nonheuristic methods.

The Least-Cost Search

The opposite of a hill-climbing search is a *least-cost search*. This strategy is similar to standing in the middle of a street on a big hill while wearing roller skates. You have the definite feeling that it's a lot easier to go down rather than up! In other words, a least-cost search takes the path of least resistance.

Applying a least-cost search to the flight-scheduling problem implies that the shortest connecting flight is taken in all cases so that the route found has a good chance of covering the shortest distance. Unlike hill climbing, which minimized the number of connections, a least-cost search minimizes the number of miles.

To use a least-cost search, you must again alter **find( )** as shown:

```
/* Find closest "anywhere". */
find(char *from, char *anywhere)
{
  int pos, dist;

  pos = 0;
  dist = 32000;   /* larger than the longest route */
  find_pos = 0;

  while(find_pos<f_pos) {
    if(!strcmp(flight[find_pos].from, from) &&
      !flight[find_pos].skip) {
        if(flight[find_pos].distance<dist) {
        pos = find_pos;
        dist = flight[find_pos].distance;
      }
    }
    find_pos++;
  }
  if(pos) {
    strcpy(anywhere, flight[pos].to);
    flight[pos].skip = 1;
```

```
      return flight[pos].distance;
   }
   return 0;
}
```

Using this version of **find( )**, the solution is

> New York to Toronto to Los Angeles
> distance is 2600

As you can see, the search actually found the shortest route. Figure 23-8 shows the least-cost path to the goal.

An Analysis of the Least-Cost Search

The least-cost search and hill climbing have the same advantages and disadvantages, but in reverse. There can be false valleys, lowlands, and gorges, but a least-cost search usually works fairly well. However, don't assume that just because the least-cost search performed better than

Figure 23-8.   The least-cost path to a solution

hill climbing in this problem that it is better. All that can be said is that on average it will outperform a blind search.

Choosing a Search Technique

As you have seen, the heuristic techniques tend, on the average, to work better than blind searching. However, it is not always possible to use a heuristic search because there may not be enough information to qualify the likelihood of the next node being on a path to the goal. Therefore, the rules for choosing a search method are separated into two categories: one for problems that can utilize a heuristic search and one for those that cannot.

If you cannot apply heuristics to a problem, depth-first searching is usually the best approach. The only exception to this is when you know something that indicates that a breadth-first search will be better.

The choice between hill climbing and a least-cost search is really one of deciding what constraint you are trying to minimize or maximize. In general, hill climbing produces a solution with the least nodes visited, but a least-cost search finds a path that requires the least effort.

If you are seeking a near-optimal solution but cannot apply an exhaustive search for the reasons already stated, an effective method is to apply each of the four searches and then use the best solution. Since the searches all work in substantially different ways, one should produce better results than the others.

Finding Multiple Solutions

Sometimes it is valuable to find several solutions to the same problem. This is not the same as finding all solutions (an exhaustive search), however. For instance, think about designing your dream house. You want to sketch several different floor plans to help you decide upon the best design, but you don't need sketches of all possible houses. In essence, multiple solutions can help you see many different ways to approach a solution before implementing it.

There are several ways to generate multiple solutions, but only two are examined here. The first is path removal and the second is node removal. As their names imply, generating multiple solutions without redundancy requires that already found solutions be removed from the system. Remember that neither of these methods attempts (or can even be used) to find all solutions. Finding all solutions is a different problem that is usually not attempted because it implies an exhaustive search.

Path Removal

The *path-removal method* of generating multiple solutions removes all nodes that form a current solution from the database and then attempts to find another. In essence, path removal prunes limbs from the tree.

To find multiple solutions by using path removal, you just need to alter **main( )** in the depth-first search, as shown here:

```
void main(void)
{
  char from[20], to[20];

  setup();

  printf("from? ");
  gets(from);
  printf("to? ");
  gets(to);
  do {
    isflight(from, to);
    route(to);
    tos = 0;   /* reset the backtrack stack */
  } while(getche()!='q');
}
```

Any connection that is part of a solution will have its **skip** field marked. Consequently, such a connection can no longer be found by **find( )** and all connections in a solution are effectively removed. You just need to reset **tos**, which effectively clears the backtrack stack.

The path-removal method finds the following solutions:

New York to Chicago to Denver to Los Angeles
distance is 3000

New York to Toronto to Los Angeles
distance is 2600

New York to Denver to Los Angeles
distance is 2900

The search found the three best solutions. However, this result cannot be generalized because it is based upon how the data is placed in the database and the actual situation under study.

Node Removal

The second way to force the generation of additional solutions, *node removal*, simply removes the last node in the current solution path and tries again. To do this, the function **main( )** must pop the last node off the backtrack stack and remove it from the database by using a new function called **retract( )**. Also, all the **skip** fields must be reset by using **clearmarkers( )** and the backtrack stack must be cleared. The functions **main( )**, **clearmarkers( )**, and **retract( )** are shown here:

```
void main(void)
{
  char from[20], to[20], cl[20], c2[20];
  int d;

  setup();

  printf("from? ");
  gets(from);
  printf("to? ");
  gets(to);
  do {
    isflight(from, to);
    route(to);
    clearmarkers();   /* reset the database */
    if(tos>0) pop(cl, c2, &d);
    retract(cl, c2);  /* remove last node from database */
    tos = 0;  /* reset the backtrack stack */
  } while(getche()!='q');
}

/* Reset the "skip" field - i.e., re-activate all nodes, */
void clearmarkers()
{
```

```
    int t;

    for(t=0; t<f_pos; ++t) flight[t].skip = 0;
}

/* Remove an entry from the database. */
void retract(char *from, char *to)
{
    int t;

    for(t=0; t<f_pos; t++)
      if(!strcmp(flight[t].from, from) &&
        !strcmp(flight[t].to, to)) {
          strcpy(flight[t].from, "");
          return;
      }
}
```

As you can see, retracting an entry is accomplished by simply using zero-length strings for the names of the cities. For your convenience, the entire node-removal program is shown here:

```
/* Depth-first with multiple solutions
    using node removal */
#include "stdio.h"
#include "string.h"
#include "conio.h"

#define MAX 100

/* structure of the flight database */
struct FL {
  char from[20];
  char to[20];
  int distance;
  char skip;    /* used in backtracking */
};

struct FL flight[MAX];

int f_pos=0; /* number of entries in flight db */
int find_pos=0; /* index for searching flight db */

int tos=0;     /* top of stack */
struct stack {
        char from[20];
        char to[20];
        int dist;
} ;
struct stack bt_stack[MAX]; /* backtrack stack */

void retract(char *from, char *to);
void clearmarkers(void);
```

```
void setup(void), route(char *to);
void assert_flight(char *from, char *to, int dist);
void push(char *from, char *to, int dist);
void pop(char *from, char *to, int *dist);
void isflight(char *from, char *to);
int find(char *from, char *anywhere);
int match(char *from, char *to);

void main(void)
{
  char from[20],to[20], c1[20], c2[20];
  int d;

  setup();

  printf("from? ");
  gets(from);
  printf("to? ");
  gets(to);
  do {
    isflight(from,to);
    route(to);
    clearmarkers();  /* reset the database */
    if(tos>0) pop(c1,c2,&d);
    retract(c1,c2);  /* remove last node from database */
    tos=0;  /* reset the backtrack stack */
  } while(getche()!='q');
}


void setup(void)
{
  assert_flight("New York","Chicago",1000);
  assert_flight("Chicago","Denver",1000);
  assert_flight("New York","Toronto", 800);
  assert_flight("New York","Denver", 1900);
  assert_flight("Toronto","Calgary",1500);
  assert_flight("Toronto","Los Angeles",1800);
  assert_flight("Toronto","Chicago",500);
  assert_flight("Denver","Urbana",1000);
  assert_flight("Denver","Houston",1500);
  assert_flight("Houston","Los Angeles",1500);
  assert_flight("Denver","Los Angeles",1000);
}

/* Put facts into the database. */
void assert_flight(char *from, char *to, int dist)
{
  if(f_pos<MAX) {
    strcpy(flight[f_pos].from, from);
    strcpy(flight[f_pos].to, to);
    flight[f_pos].distance = dist;
    flight[f_pos].skip = 0;
    f_pos++;
  }
  else printf("Flight database full.\n");
}
```

```
/* Reset the "skip" field - i.e., re-activate all nodes. */
void clearmarkers()
{
  int t;

  for(t=0; t<f_pos; ++t) flight[t].skip = 0;
}

/* Remove an entry from the database. */
void retract(char *from, char *to)
{
  int t;

  for(t=0; t<f_pos; t++)
    if(!strcmp(flight[t].from, from) &&
       !strcmp(flight[t].to, to)) {
         strcpy(flight[t].from,"");
         return;
    }
}

/* Show the route and the total distance. */
void route(char *to)
{
  int dist, t;

  dist=0;
  t=0;
  while(t<tos) {
    printf("%s to ", bt_stack[t].from);
    dist += bt_stack[t].dist;
    t++;
  }
  printf("%s\n",to);
  printf("distance is %d\n", dist);
}

/* Given from, find anywhere. */
find(char *from, char *anywhere)
{
  find_pos = 0;
  while(find_pos<f_pos) {
    if(!strcmp(flight[find_pos].from, from) &&
       !flight[find_pos].skip) {
         strcpy(anywhere, flight[find_pos].to);
         flight[find_pos].skip = 1;
         return flight[find_pos].distance;
    }
    find_pos++;
  }
  return 0;
}

/* If flight between from and to, then return
   the distance of flight; otherwise, return 0. */
match(char *from, char *to)
{
```

```
  register int t;

  for(t=f_pos-1; t>-1; t--)
    if(!strcmp(flight[t].from, from) &&
       !strcmp(flight[t].to, to)) return flight[t].distance;

  return 0;  /* not found */
}

/* Determine if there is a route between from and to. */
void isflight(char *from, char *to)
{
  int d, dist;
  char anywhere[20];

  if(d=match(from, to)) {
    push(from, to, d); /* distance */
    return;
  }

  if(dist=find(from, anywhere)) {
    push(from, to, dist);
    isflight(anywhere, to);
  }
  else if(tos>0) {
    pop(from, to, &dist);
    isflight(from, to);
  }
}

/* stack routines */
void push(char *from, char *to, int dist)
{
  if(tos<MAX) {
    strcpy(bt_stack[tos].from, from);
    strcpy(bt_stack[tos].to, to);
    bt_stack[tos].dist = dist;
    tos++;
  }
  else printf("Stack full.\n");
}

void pop(char *from, char *to, int *dist)
{
  if(tos>0) {
    tos--;
    strcpy(from, bt_stack[tos].from);
    strcpy(to, bt_stack[tos].to);
    *dist = bt_stack[tos].dist;
  }
  else printf("Stack underflow.\n");
}
```

Using this method produces the following solutions:

New York to Chicago to Denver to Los Angeles
distance is 3000

New York to Chicago to Denver to Houston to Los Angeles
distance is 5000

New York to Toronto to Los Angeles
distance is 2600

In this case, the second solution is the worst possible route, but the optimal solution is still found. However, remember that you cannot generalize these results because they are based upon both the physical organization of data in the database and the specific situation under study.

Finding the "Optimal" Solution

All of the previous search techniques were concerned with finding a solution. As you saw with the heuristic searches, there were efforts to improve the likelihood of finding a good (and, hopefully, the optimal) solution. However, at times you may only want the optimal solution. Keep in mind, however, that *optimal*, as it is used here, simply means the best route that can be found by using one of the various multiple-solution generation techniques — it may not actually be the best solution. (Finding the true optimal solution would, of course, require the prohibitively time-consuming exhaustive search.)

Before leaving the well-worked scheduling example, consider a program that finds the optimal schedule with the condition that distance is to be minimized. Employ the path-removal method of generating multiple solutions, and use a least-cost search to minimize distance.

The key to finding the shortest schedule is to keep a solution that has a distance less than the previous one. Hence, when there are no more solutions to generate, the optimal solution remains.

To accomplish this, you must make a major change to the function **route( )** and create an additional stack. The new stack holds the current solution and, upon completion, the optimal solution. The new stack is called **solution**, and the modified **route( )** is shown here:

```
/* Find the shortest distance. */
route(void)
{
```

```
  int dist, t;
  static int old_dist=32000;

  if(!tos) return 0;   /* all done */
  t = 0;
  dist = 0;
  while(t<tos) {
    dist += bt_stack[t].dist;
    t++;
  }

  /* if shorter, then make new solution */
  if(dist<old_dist && dist) {
    t = 0;
    old_dist = dist;
    stos = 0; /* clear old route from location stack */
    while(t<tos)  {
      spush(bt_stack[t].from, bt_stack[t].to, bt_stack[t].dist);
      t++;
    }
  }
  return dist;
}
```

The entire program follows. Notice the changes in **main( )** and the
addition of **spush( )**, which places the new solution nodes onto the
solution stack.

```
/* Optimal solution using least-cost with
    route removal.
*/
#include "stdio.h"
#include "string.h"

#define MAX 100

/* structure of the flight database */
struct FL {
  char from[20];
  char to[20];
  int distance;
  char skip;   /* used for backtracking */
};

struct FL flight[MAX];   /* array of db structures */

int f_pos=0; /* number of entries in flight db */
int find_pos=0; /* index for searching flight db */

int tos=0;      /* top of stack */
int stos=0;     /* top of solution stack */

struct stack {
    char from[20];
    char to[20];
```

```
     int dist;
} ;

struct stack bt_stack[MAX]; /* backtrack stack */
struct stack solution[MAX]; /* hold temporary solutions */

void setup(void);
int route(void);
void assert_flight(char *from, char *to, int dist);
void push(char *from, char *to, int dist);
void pop(char *from, char *to, int *dist);
void isflight(char *from, char *to);
void spush(char *from, char *to, int dist);
int find(char *from, char *anywhere);
int match(char *from, char *to);

void main(void)
{
  char from[20], to[20];
  int t, d;

  setup();

  printf("from? ");
  gets(from);
  printf("to? ");
  gets(to);
  do {
    isflight(from, to);
    d = route();
    tos = 0;  /* reset the backtrack stack */
  } while(d!=0);  /* while still finding solutions */

  t = 0;
  printf("Optimal solution is:\n");
  while(t<stos) {
    printf("%s to ", solution[t].from);
    d += solution[t].dist;
    t++;
  }
  printf("%s\n", to);
  printf("distance is %d\n", d);
}

void setup(void)
{
  assert_flight("New York", "Chicago", 1000);
  assert_flight("Chicago", "Denver", 1000);
  assert_flight("New York", "Toronto", 800);
  assert_flight("New York", "Denver", 1900);
  assert_flight("Toronto", "Calgary", 1500);
  assert_flight("Toronto", "Los Angeles", 1800);
  assert_flight("Toronto", "Chicago", 500);
  assert_flight("Denver", "Urbana", 1000);
  assert_flight("Denver", "Houston", 1500);
  assert_flight("Houston", "Los Angeles", 1500);
  assert_flight("Denver", "Los Angeles", 1000);
```

```
}

/* Put facts into the database. */
void assert_flight(char *from, char *to, int dist)
{
  if(f_pos<MAX) {
    strcpy(flight[f_pos].from, from);
    strcpy(flight[f_pos].to, to);
    flight[f_pos].distance = dist;
    flight[f_pos].skip = 0;
    f_pos++;
  }
  else printf("Flight database full.\n");
}

/* Find the shortest distance. */
route(void)
{
  int dist, t;
  static int old_dist=32000;

  if(!tos) return 0;  /* all done */
  t = 0;
  dist = 0;
  while(t<tos) {
    dist += bt_stack[t].dist;
    t++;
  }

  /* if shorter then make new solution */
  if(dist<old_dist && dist) {
    t = 0;
    old_dist = dist;
    stos = 0; /* clear old route from location stack */
    while(t<tos)  {
      spush(bt_stack[t].from, bt_stack[t].to, bt_stack[t].dist);
      t++;
    }
  }
  return dist;
}

/* If flight between from and to, then return
   the distance of flight; otherwise, return 0. */
match(char *from, char *to)
{
  register int t;

  for(t=f_pos-1; t>-1; t--)
    if(!strcmp(flight[t].from, from) &&
       !strcmp(flight[t].to, to)) return flight[t].distance;

  return 0;  /* not found */
}

/* Given from, find anywhere. */
find(char *from, char *anywhere)
```

```
{
  find_pos=0;
  while(find_pos<f_pos) {
    if(!strcmp(flight[find_pos].from, from) &&
       !flight[find_pos].skip) {
        strcpy(anywhere, flight[find_pos].to);
        flight[find_pos].skip = 1;
        return flight[find_pos].distance;
    }
    find_pos++;
  }
  return 0;
}

/* Determine if there is a route between from and to. */
void isflight(char *from, char *to)
{
  int d, dist;
  char anywhere[20];

  if(d=match(from, to)) {
    push(from, to, d); /* distance */
    return;
  }

  if(dist=find(from, anywhere)) {
    push(from, to, dist);
    isflight(anywhere, to);
  }
  else if(tos>0) {
    pop(from, to, &dist);
    isflight(from, to);
  }
}

/* stack routines */
void push(char *from, char *to, int dist)
{
  if(tos<MAX) {
    strcpy(bt_stack[tos].from, from);
    strcpy(bt_stack[tos].to, to);
    bt_stack[tos].dist = dist;
    tos++;
  }
  else printf("Stack full.\n");
}

void pop(char *from, char *to, int *dist)
{
  if(tos>0) {
    tos--;
    strcpy(from, bt_stack[tos].from);
    strcpy(to, bt_stack[tos].to);
    *dist = bt_stack[tos].dist;
  }
  else printf("Stack underflow.\n");
}
```

```
/* solution stack */
void spush(char *from, char *to, int dist)
{
  if(stos<MAX) {
    strcpy(solution[stos].from, from);
    strcpy(solution[stos].to, to);
    solution[stos].dist = dist;
    stos++;
  }
  else printf("Shortest distance stack full.\n");
}
```

The one inefficiency in the preceding method is that all paths are followed to their conclusion. An improved method would stop following a path as soon as the length equaled or exceeded the current minimum. You might want to modify this program to accommodate such an enhancement.

Back to the Lost Keys

To conclude this chapter on problem solving it seems only fitting to provide a C program that finds the lost car keys described in the first example. The accompanying code employs the same techniques used in the problem of finding a route between two cities. By now, you should have a fairly good understanding of how to use C to solve problems, so the program is presented without further explanation.

```
/* Find the keys using a depth-first search. */
#include "stdio.h"
#include "string.h"

#define MAX 100

/* structure of the keys database */
struct FL {
  char from[20];
  char to[20];
  char skip;
};

struct FL keys[MAX];  /* array of db structures */

int f_pos=0; /* number of rooms in house */
int find_pos=0; /* index for searching keys db */
```

```
  int tos=0;          /* top of stack */
  struct stack {
    char from[20];
    char to[20];
  } ;
  struct stack bt_stack[MAX]; /* backtrack stack */

  void setup(void), route(void);
  void assert_keys(char *from, char *to);
  void push(char *from, char *to);
  void pop(char *from, char *to);
  void iskeys(char *from, char *to);
  int find(char *from, char *anywhere);
  int match(char *from, char *to);

  void main(void)
  {
    setup();
    iskeys("front_door", "keys");
    route();
  }

  void setup(void)
  {
    assert_keys("front_door", "lr");
    assert_keys("lr", "bath");
    assert_keys("lr", "hall");
    assert_keys("hall", "bd1");
    assert_keys("hall", "bd2");
    assert_keys("hall", "mb");
    assert_keys("lr", "kitchen");
    assert_keys("kitchen", "keys");
  }

  /* Put facts into the database. */
  void assert_keys(char *from, char *to)
  {
    if(f_pos<MAX) {
      strcpy(keys[f_pos].from, from);
      strcpy(keys[f_pos].to, to);
      keys[f_pos].skip = 0;
      f_pos++;
    }
    else printf("Keys database full.\n");
  }

  /* Show the route to the keys. */
  void route(void)
  {
    int t;

    t = 0;
    while(t<tos) {
      printf("%s", bt_stack[t].from);
      t++;
      if(t<tos) printf(" to ");
    }
```

```
  printf("\n");
}

match(char *from, char *to)
{
  register int t;

  for(t=f_pos-1; t>-1; t--)
    if(!strcmp(keys[t].from, from) &&
      !strcmp(keys[t].to, to)) return 1;

  return 0;   /* not found */
}

/* Given from, find anywhere. */
find(char *from, char *anywhere)
{
  find_pos = 0;
  while(find_pos<f_pos) {
    if(!strcmp(keys[find_pos].from, from) &&
      !keys[find_pos].skip) {
        strcpy(anywhere, keys[find_pos].to);
        keys[find_pos].skip = 1;
        return 1;
    }
    find_pos++;
  }
  return 0;
}

/* Determine if there is a route between from and to. */
void iskeys(char *from, char *to)
{
  char anywhere[20];

  if(match(from, to)) {
    push(from, to); /* distance */
    return;
  }

  if(find(from, anywhere)) {
    push(from, to);
    iskeys(anywhere, to);
  }
  else if(tos>0) {
    pop(from, to);
    iskeys(from, to);
  }
}

/* stack routines */
void push(char *from, char *to)
{
  if(tos<MAX) {
    strcpy(bt_stack[tos].from, from);
    strcpy(bt_stack[tos].to, to);
```

```
    tos++;
  }
  else printf("Stack full.\n");
}

void pop(char *from, char *to)
{
  if(tos>0) {
    tos--;
    strcpy(from, bt_stack[tos].from);
    strcpy(to, bt_stack[tos].to);
  }
  else printf("Stack underflow.\n");
}
```

Using System Resources

The 8086 Family of Processors
The 8086 Interrupts and DOS
Accessing System Resources in the BIOS
Using DOS to Access System Functions
Final Thoughts on Using System Resources

As powerful as C is, at times you may want or need to access directly the resources of both the operating system and the host environment. Often a specific device or operating-system function must be utilized, yet there is no way to do so with any existing library routine. Also, to achieve increased performance, you may need to bypass a standard library routine, directly manipulating a device or operating-system function yourself.

Each processor, operating system, and environment has its own methods of accessing system resources. The remainder of this chapter assumes that you have the DOS operating system and the Microsoft functions **bdos( )** and **int86( )** to access system functions. The detailed workings of the 8086 family of processors are beyond the scope of this book. However, the following discussion gives you a brief overview.

The 8086 Family of Processors

The 8086 family of processors includes the 8086, 8088, 80186, 80286, 80386, and 80486. Although the 80286, 80386, and 80486 have modes of operating that exceed the 8086, they all can emulate the 8086. Since DOS is an 8086-based operating system, all processors behave the same when running DOS. For the rest of this discussion, the term *8086* stands for the entire family of processors.

The 8086 contains 14 registers into which information is placed for processing or program control. The registers fall into the following categories.

- General-purpose registers
- Base-pointer and index registers
- Segment registers
- Special-purpose registers

All of the registers in the 8086 CPU are 16 bits (2 bytes) wide.

The *general-purpose registers* are the workhorse registers of the CPU. It is in these registers that values are placed for processing. This processing includes arithmetic operations, such as adding or multiplying; comparisons, including equality, less than, greater than, and the like; and branch (jump) instructions. Each of the general-purpose registers may be accessed either as one 16-bit register or as two 8-bit registers.

The *base-pointer* and *index registers* provide support for such things as relative addressing, the stack pointer, and block move instructions.

The *segment registers* support the 8086's segmented memory scheme. The **CS** register holds the current code segment, **DS** holds the current data segment, **ES** holds the extra segment, and **SS** holds the stack segment.

Finally, the *special-purpose registers* are the flag register (which holds the state of the CPU) and the instruction pointer (which points to the next instruction for the CPU to execute).

Figure 24-1 shows the layout of the 8086 registers.

The 8086 Interrupts and DOS

An *interrupt* is a special instruction that halts the execution of the current program, saves the current state of the system on the stack, and then jumps to an interrupt-handling routine that is determined by the number of the interrupt. After the interrupt routine has finished, it performs an *interrupt return*, which causes the previously executing program to resume. There are two basic type of interrupts: those generated by hardware and those caused by software. It is the latter that is of interest at this time.

General-purpose registers

	AH	AL			CH	CL
AX				CX		

	BH	BL			DH	DL
BX				DX		

Base-pointer and index registers

SP [ ]   SI [ ]
Stack pointer   Source index

BP [ ]   DI [ ]
Base pointer   Destination index

Segment registers

CS [ ]   SS [ ]
Code segment   Stack segment

DS [ ]   ES [ ]
Data segment   Extra segment

Special-purpose registers

[ ]   IP [ ]
Flag register   Instruction pointer

Figure 24-1.   The 8086 CPU registers

The 8086 CPU allows a program to execute a *software interrupt* via the INT instruction. The number that follows the instruction determines the number of the interrupt. For example, INT 21H causes interrupt 21H to be executed. The number of the interrupt is used to find the proper interrupt handler. The 8086 reserves the first 1K in memory for an *interrupt vector table*. This table contains the addresses (in segment/offset form) of the interrupt handlers. This means that each address requires 4 bytes. Thus, the 8086 supports 256 interrupt vectors. For example, the INT 5 instruction tells the CPU to use the address found at the 5 × 4 byte in memory as the location of the interrupt routine. (By the way, INT 5 calls the print-screen utility). Figure 24-2 depicts this situation.

DOS has reserved a number of these vectors for its own use. In DOS, operating system functions are accessed through software interrupts. Each interrupt accesses its own category of functions, which are determined by the value of the **AH** register. If additional information is needed, it is passed in the **AL**, **BX**, **CX**, and **DX** registers.

The PC operating environment separates itself into the BIOS (Basic I/O System) and DOS (Disk Operating System). BIOS provides the lowest-level routines, which DOS uses to provide the higher-level functions. There is overlap, however, between the two systems. Fortunately, for our purposes they are accessed in basically the same way—through software interrupts.

The chapter begins with the BIOS routines and ends with a discussion of the DOS services.

Accessing System Resources in the BIOS

There are twelve BIOS interrupts, as shown in Table 24-1.

Each interrupt is associated with a number of options that can be accessed depending upon the value of the **AH** register when called. Table 24-2 shows a partial list of the options available for several of the interrupts. (For a complete list and explanation, refer to the appropriate IBM *Technical Reference Manual*.)

001Eh
001Ch
001Ah
0018h
0016h
0014h
0012h
0010h
000Eh
000Ch
000Dh
0008h
0006h
0004h
0002h
0000h

INT 5
(5 × 4 = 20)

Memory

Figure 24-2.   The interrupt vector table for the 8086

Interrupt	Function
5H	Print screen utility
10H	Video I/O
11H	Equipment list
12H	Memory size
13H	Disk I/O
14H	Serial port I/O
15H	Cassette control
16H	Keyboard I/O
17H	Printer I/O
18H	Execute ROM BASIC
19H	Execute bootstrap loader
1AH	Time and date

Table 24-1.   BIOS Interrupts

Video I/O functions—Interrupt 10H

AH register	Function
0	Sets video mode if AL = video mode
1	Sets cursor lines CH: bits 0-4 contain start of line bits 5-7 are 0 CL: bits 0-4 contain end of line bits 5-7 are 0
2	Sets cursor position DH: row DL: column BH: video page number

Table 24-2.   Partial List of BIOS Interrupt Options

Video I/O functions — Interrupt 10H (*continued*)

AH register	Function
3	Reads cursor position
	BH: video page number
	Returns:
	DH: row
	DL: column
	CX: mode
4	Reads light-pen position
	Returns:
	if AH = 0 pen not triggered
	if AH = 1 pen triggered
	DH: row
	DL: column
	CH: raster line (0-199)
	BX: pixel column (0-319 or 0-639)
5	Sets active video page
	AL: may be 0-7
6	Scrolls page up
	AL: number of lines to scroll, 0 for all
	CH: row of upper-left corner of scroll
	CL: column of upper-left corner of scroll
	DH: row of lower-right corner of scroll
	DL: column of lower-right corner of scroll
	BH: attribute to be used on blank line
7	Scrolls page down
	same as 6
8	Reads character at cursor position
	BH: video page
	Returns
	AL: character read
	AH: attribute

Table 24-2. Partial List of BIOS Interrupt Options (*continued*)

Video I/O functions—Interrupt 10H (*continued*)

AH register	Function
9	Writes character and attribute at cursor position
	BH: video page
	BL: attribute
	CX: number of characters to write
	AL: character
AH	Writes character at current cursor position
	BH: video page
	CX: number of characters to write
	AL: character
BH	Sets color palette
	BH: palette number
	BL: color
CH	Writes a pixel
	DX: row number
	CX: column number
	AL: color
DH	Reads a pixel
	DX: row number
	CX: column number
	Returns
	AL: dot read
EH	Writes character to screen and advances cursor
	AL: character
	BL: foreground color
	BH: video page
FH	Reads video state
	Returns
	AL: current mode
	AH: number of columns on screen
	BH: current active video page

Table 24-2.   Partial List of BIOS Interrupt Options (*continued*)

Equipment list — Interrupt 11H

AH register   **Function**

Reads equipment list
Returns
    AX: list of equipment installed
        bit 0: 1 of diskettes present
        bit 1: not used
        bits 2,3: system board RAM, 11 = 64K
        bits 4,5: initial video mode,
            10 = 80 column color, 11 = monochrome,
            01 = 40 column
        bits 6,7: number of disk drives, 0 = 1
        bits 8: DMA chip installed, 0 = installed
        bits 9,10,11: number of RS-232 ports
        bit 12: 1 = game adapter installed
        bit 13: 1 = serial printer (PCjr only)
        bits 14,15: number of printers

Memory Size — Interrupt 12H

AH register   **Function**

Returns the number of kilobytes of RAM that are resident in
the system
Returns:
    AX: number of kilobytes of RAM

Disk I/O functions — Interrupt 13H

AH register   **Function**

0   Resets disk system

1   Reads disk status
                        Returns
                            AL: status (see IBM *Technical Reference*)

2   Reads sectors into memory
                            DL: drive number
                            DH: head number

Table 24-2.   Partial List of BIOS Interrupt Options (*continued*)

Disk I/O functions — Interrupt 13H (*continued*)

AH register   **Function**

CH: track number
CL: sector number
AL: number of sectors to read
ES:BX: address of buffer
Returns
AL: number of sectors read
AH: 0 on success, otherwise status

3   Writes sectors to disk
(same as 2)

4   Verifies
(same as 2)

5   Formats a track
DL: drive number
DH: head number
CH: track number
ES:BX: sector information

Keyboard I/O functions — Interrupt 16H

AH register   **Function**

0   Reads scan code
Returns
AH: scan code
AL: character code

1   Gets status of buffer
Returns
ZF: 1 then buffer empty
0 then characters waiting
with next char in AX as
described above

2   Gets status of keyboard
(see IBM *Technical Reference Manual*)

Table 24-2.   Partial List of BIOS Interrupt Options (*continued*)

BIOS Printer I/O functions – Interrupt 17H

AH register	Function

0	Prints a character
	    AL: character
	    DX: printer number
	Returns
	    AH: status

1	Initializes Printer
	    DX: printer number
	Returns
	    AH: status

2	Reads status
	    DX: printer number
	Returns
	    AH: status

Table 24-2.   Partial List of BIOS Interrupt Options (*continued*)

The Microsoft C compiler supplies the library routine called **int86( )**, which is used to execute software interrupts. This function was discussed in Chapter 15. Its prototype is

```
#include "dos.h"
int int86(int intnum, union REGS *in, union REGS *out);
```

Here, *intnum* is the number of the interrupt, *in* is a **union** containing the registers used to pass information to the interrupt handlers, and *out* is the **union** that will hold the values, if any, returned by the interrupt routine. However, the value of the **AX** register is also returned by **int86( )**. The type **REGS** is supplied in the header DOS.H. This section uses the **int86( )** function to access the various BIOS functions, examining a few of the more interesting BIOS functions.

Mode	Type	Graphics Dimensions	Text Dimensions
0	Text, B/W	n/a	40×25
1	Text, 16 colors	n/a	40×25
2	Text, B/W	n/a	80×25
3	Text, 16 colors	n/a	80×25
4	Graphics, 4 colors	320×200	40×25
5	Graphics, 4 grey tones	320×200	40×25
6	Graphics, 2 colors	640×200	80×25
7	Text, B/W	n/a	80×25
8	PC*jr* Graphics 16 colors	160×200	20×25
9	PC*jr* Graphics 16 colors	320×200	40×25
10	Graphics, 4 colors	640×200	80×25
11	Reserved		
12	Reserved		
13	Graphics, 16 colors	320×200	40×25
14	Graphics, 16 colors	640×200	80×25
15	Graphics, 2 colors	640×350	80×25
16	Graphics, 16 colors	640×350	80×25
17	Graphics, 2 colors	640×480	80×30
18	Graphics, 16 colors	640×480	80×30
19	Graphics, 256 colors	640×200	40×25

Table 24-3. Screen Modes for the Various Video Adapters

Changing the Screen Mode

Suppose that you wish to change the screen mode during program execution. The 19 modes that the screen can display are shown in Table 24-3.

Using the **int86( )** function, you can create the following function, **setmode( )**, which changes the mode of the screen to the specified type:

```
#include "dos.h"

/* Set the video mode. */
void setmode(int mode)
{
  union REGS r;
```

```
  r.h.al = mode;
  r.h.ah = 0;
  int86(0x10, &r, &r);
}
```

Clearing the Screen

To clear the screen, execute BIOS interrupt 10H, function 6, as shown here:

```
#include "dos.h"

/* Clear the screen. */
void cls(void)
{
  union REGS r;

  r.h.ah = 6;   /* screen scroll code */
  r.h.al = 0;   /* clear screen code */
  r.h.ch = 0;   /* start row */
  r.h.cl = 0;   /* start column */
  r.h.dh = 24;  /* end row */
  r.h.dl = 79;  /* end column */
  r.h.bh = 7;   /* blank line is black */
  int86(0x10, &r, &r);
}
```

The value placed in **AL** determines the number of lines to scroll the screen, given the starting and ending coordinates. However, if **AL** is 0, the entire screen is erased. The **BH** register determines the attribute of a blank line. Since 7 is used in this case, blank lines will be black.

Cursor Positioning

goto_xy( ) is another useful function left out of some C compilers' libraries. This function locates the cursor at the specified X and Y coordinates. Fortunately, you can easily create this function by using the BIOS interrupt 0x10, function 2, which places the cursor at the location specified by the **DL** and **DH** registers. The **goto_xy( )** function is shown here:

```
#include "dos.h"

/* Position the cursor to x,y. */
```

```
void goto_xy(int x, int y)
{
  union REGS r;

  r.h.ah = 2; /* cursor addressing function */
  r.h.dl = y; /* column coordinate */
  r.h.dh = x; /* row coordinate */
  r.h.bh = 0; /* video page */
  int86(0x10, &r, &r);
}
```

For the PC, 0,0 is the upper-left corner of the screen.

To see how this function works, try the following short program, which first clears the screen and then prints Xs diagonally across it:

```
#include "dos.h"
#include "stdio.h"

void cls(void), goto_xy(int x, int y);

/* Clear the screen and print Xs. */
void main(void)
{
  register int x, y;

  cls();
  for(x=0, y=0; x<25; x++, y+=3) {
    goto_xy(x, y);
    printf("X");
  }
}

/* Clear the screen. */
void cls(void)
{
  union REGS r;

  r.h.ah=6; /* screen scroll code */
  r.h.al=0; /* clear screen code */
  r.h.ch=0; /* start row */
  r.h.cl=0; /* start column */
  r.h.dh=24; /* end row */
  r.h.dl=79; /* end column */
  r.h.bh=7;  /* blank line is black */
  int86(0x10, &r, &r);
}

/* Send the cursor to x,y. */
void goto_xy(int x, int y)
{
  union REGS r;

  r.h.ah = 2; /* cursor addressing function */
  r.h.dl = y; /* column coordinate */
```

```
   r.h.dh = x; /* row coordinate */
   r.h.bh = 0; /* video page */
   int86(0x10, &r, &r);
}
```

Using the Scan Codes from the PC Keyboard

With the PC, one of the most frustrating experiences is trying to use the arrow keys (as well as INS, DEL, PGUP, PGDN, END, and HOME) and the function keys. The problem is that these special keys do not return the normal 8-bit (1-byte) character, as does the rest of the keyboard. When you press a key on the PC, you are actually generating a 2-byte (16-bit) value called a *scan code*. The scan code consists of two pieces: the low-order byte (which, if a normal key, contains the ASCII code for the key) and a high-order byte (which contains the key's position code on the keyboard). For most keys on the keyboard, these scan codes are converted into 8-bit ASCII values by the operating system. However, this is not done for the special keys because the character code for a special key is 0. This means that you must use the position code to determine which key was pressed. (The standard character-input routine to read a character from the keyboard supported by DOS function call number 1 does not allow you to read the special keys.)

The easiest way to access the special keys is to write a small function that calls interrupt 16H, which returns the scan code of any key that is pressed. After a call to interrupt 16H function 0, the position code is in **AH** and the character code is in **AL**. The function **get_key( )** shown here returns these codes as an integer:

```
#include "dos.h"

/* Read the 16-bit scan code. */
get_key(void)
{
  union REGS r;

  r.h.ah = 0;
  return int86(0x16, &r, &r);
}
```

The trick to using **get_key( )** is to remember that when a special key is struck, the character code is 0. In this case, you then decode the position code to determine which key was actually typed. If you want to use **get_key( )** to do all keyboard input, the calling routine must make decisions based on the contents of **AH** and **AL**. What follows is a short program that illustrates one way to do this:

```
/* Scan code example. */
#include "dos.h"
#include "stdio.h"

void main(void)
{
  union scan {
    int c;
    char ch[2];
  } sc;

  do { /* read the keyboard */
    sc.c = get_key();
    if(sc.ch[0]==0)   /* is special key */
      printf("special key number %d", sc.ch[1]);
    else /* regular key */
      putchar(sc.ch[0]);
  } while(sc.ch[0]!='q');
}
```

Notice the use of the **union** to allow the two halves of the scan code returned by **get_key( )** to be decoded.

There are basically two ways to decode a scan code. You can look in the IBM *Technical Reference Manual*, or you can use the preceding program to determine the values experimentally. The program is more fun! To help you get started, here are the scan codes for the arrow keys:

LEFT ARROW	75
RIGHT ARROW	77
UP ARROW	72
DOWN ARROW	80

Unfortunately, fully integrating the special keys with the normal keys requires writing special input functions and bypassing the normal **gets( )** type functions found in the standard library. The reward is that your programs will look professional and be much easier to use.

Using DOS to Access System Functions

The part of the DOS operating system that is loaded and executed by the BIOS bootstrap loader is called DOS. It contains various functions that are, for the most part, of a higher level than those in the BIOS routines (although there is some overlap). All the DOS functions are accessed through interrupt 21H, which uses the **AH** register to pass the requested DOS function number. Table 24-4 shows a partial list of the DOS functions.

AH register	Function
1	Reads character from the keyboard Returns AL: character
2	Displays a character on the screen DL: character
3	Reads a character from async port Returns AL: character
4	Writes a character to async port DL: character
5	Prints a character to list device DL: character
7	Reads a character from keyboard but doesn't display it Returns AL: character
B	Checks keyboard status Returns AL: 0FFH if key struck; 0 otherwise
D	Resets disk
E	Sets default drive DL: Drive Number (0 = A, 1 = B,...)

Table 24-4.   High Level DOS Functions Calls—Interrupt 21H (partial list)

AH register	Function
1A	Sets disk transfer address DX: disk transfer address

2A	Gets system date
	Returns
	    CX: year (1980-2099)
	    DH: month (1-12)
	    DL: day (1-31)

2B	Sets system date
	    CX: year (1980-2099)
	    DH: month (1-12)
	    DL: day (1-31)

2C	Gets system time
	Returns
	    CH: hours (0-23)
	    CL: minutes (0-59)
	    DH: seconds (0-59)
	    DL: hundredths of seconds (0-99)

2D	Sets system time
	    CH: hours (0-23)
	    CL: minutes (0-59)
	    DH: seconds (0-59)
	    DL: hundredths of seconds (0-99)

4E	Searches for file name
	    DX: address of FCB
	    CX: file attribute
	Returns
	    AL: 2 if file not found
	        18 if no more files found

4F	Finds next occurrence of file name and continues search begun using 4E Returns AL: 18 if no more files found

Table 24-4.   High Level DOS Functions Calls—Interrupt 21H (partial list)
           (*continued*)

Most compilers for the DOS operating system provide in the standard library a function often called **bdos( )**. This function performs an interrupt 21H to access one of the higher-level functions in the operating system. (This function may have a different name, so check your user's manual.) This discussion uses the function **bdos( )** in Microsoft C. **bdos( )** is discussed in detail in Chapter 15. Its prototype is

```
#include "dos.h"
int bdos(int fnum, unsigned Reg_DX, unsigned Reg_AL)
```

where *fnum* is the number of the DOS function. The values of Reg_DX and Reg_AL are assigned to the **DX** and **AL** registers, respectively. Upon return, **bdos( )** returns the value of the **AX** register.

Checking Keyboard Status

kbhit( ) is a useful function that employs DOS and the **bdos( )** function. This function returns true if a key has been struck and false otherwise. **kbhit( )** uses interrupt 21H, function number BH, as shown here:

```
#include "dos.h"

/* Return 0 if no key struck; non-zero otherwise. */
kbhit(void)
{
  return((char) bdos(0xB, 0, 0));
}
```

Notice that zeroes were used for all but the first argument because no other information was needed. This is the usual procedure. When a specific register is not used in the call, it may have any value assigned to it as a placeholder. The cast to **char** is necessary because the status is returned in **AL** and **AH** is not defined.

Using the Printer

Often you will need to interface to the operating system to use a function not in the standard library. One function that is omitted from the library for many C compilers for the PC is one that sends characters to the printer. However, you can develop a function to do this by using the DOS function number 5, which prints one character to the printer. The short function shown here prints a null-terminated string:

```
#include "dos.h"

/* Send a string to the printer. */
void prints(char *s)
{
  while(*s) bdos(0x5, *s++, 0);
}
```

Reading and Writing the Serial Port

You can use DOS to read or write characters from or to the asynchronous serial port using DOS functions 3 to read a character and 4 to write a character. You would use this port if you wanted to write a modem program, for example. The functions that read and write the serial port are shown here:

```
#include "dos.h"

/* Send a character out the port. */
void put_async(char ch)
{
  bdos(0x4, ch, 0);
}

/* return a character read from the port */
get_async(void)
{
  return((char) bdos(0x3, 0, 0));
}
```

Notice once again the use of the **char** cast to ensure that any value in **AH** does not confuse any calling routine.

Listing the Directory

A more complex example using interrupt 21H is the function **dir_list( )**, shown here. It lists all files in the current working directory, and works for DOS 2.0 and greater.

```
/* list entire directory for DOS 2 and greater. */

void dir_list(void)
{
  char pp[44];  /* disk transfer array */

  bdos(0x1a, pp, 0);  /* set disk transfer address */

  bdos(0x4e, "*.*", 0);  /* find first */
  printf("%s\n", &pp[30]);
  for(;;) {
    if(18==bdos(0x4f, 0, 0)) break;
    printf("%s\n", &pp[30]);
  }
}
```

This function works as follows. First, a disk transfer buffer must be initialized. You do this by passing the address of array **pp** to DOS in the **DX** register. Because the **AL** register is not used, zeroes are substituted. Next, the function executes function 4EH to find the first file that matches the wild card ***.***. Subsequent files are found using function 4FH to find the next occurrence. When the function returns 18, the last file has been found. The file names are placed in the disk-transfer buffer that was defined with the first DOS call. These are printed by using a normal **printf( )** statement, except that the file name starts at byte 30 in the disk-transfer buffer, so a little pointer arithmetic must be done.

You can use the **bdos( )** function to execute any 21H interrupt, but interrupts returning information in registers other than **AX** will not work because the information will be lost. For those DOS calls, either an additional special function is supplied by the compiler manufacturer, or you can use the **int86( )** function.

Final Thoughts on Using System Resources

This chapter has only scratched the surface of what you can do through the creative use of system resources. To fully integrate your program with the operating system, you need information that describes all the functions in detail.

You should remember two things before using operating-system functions. First, they can make your program look very professional. Bypassing some of C's built-in functions in favor of the operating-system functions can create programs that run faster and use less memory. Also, you have access to functions that are not available through C's standard library. Second, when you use the operating-system functions instead of C's standard functions your code is no longer portable. You may also become dependent on specific versions of a given operating system and a C compiler, creating compatibility problems when you distribute your program. However, only you can decide when and if you should introduce machine and operating-system dependencies into your programs.

Graphics

Modes and Palettes
Writing Pixels
Drawing Lines
Drawing and Filling Boxes
Putting It All Together

Graphics rank high on the list of exciting things that you can do with a computer. One reason for this is the vast number of different ways that you can use graphics. A CAD/CAM system can present detailed three-dimensional models that you can rotate to provide various views. A statistical package can display business graphics illustrating a company's sales growth. A graphic artist might create a new company logo on the screen of a personal computer. Given the wide range of applications, you might think that an entire book would be necessary to even approach the subject of graphics. However, what all graphics applications have in common is the ability to draw points, lines, and boxes. It is this ability that is the concern of this chapter.

Although most PC-based C compilers provide complete graphics libraries, you might want your own set of graphics functions for several reasons. First, some commercial graphics systems are so sophisticated that using even a few simple graphical functions links a large amount of code to your program. Second, you might need to create graphics routines for a graphics adapter that is not supported by your compiler's graphics library. Finally, controlling your own graphics functions allows you to optimize them for your own purposes.

This chapter's main emphasis is not on how graphics hardware works, but on the creation of a few core graphics routines that you can use, enhance, and evolve.

For the routines developed in this chapter to run correctly, you need an IBM PC/XT/AT or compatible and either a CGA, EGA, or VGA graphics board. However, beyond the writing of a pixel, the routines in the chapter are hardware independent and you should have little trouble

TWENTY FIVE

making them work on other systems. The examples in this chapter use graphics mode 4, which works with all graphics adapters. You can easily use a higher resolution mode if you like.

Modes and Palettes

Before you can use any graphics functions, you must place the computer into the appropriate video mode. For the IBM PC, this means selecting the proper mode and palette.

There are several different video modes available on the IBM PC. (There is a summary of all the modes in Chapter 17.) The functions developed in this chapter require screen mode 4, which is 320 × 200 four-color graphics. This mode works with PC graphics adapters. The last chapter developed the **mode( )** function, which sets the current video mode through a call to the ROM-BIOS. The **mode( )** function is repeated here for your convenience. (Several of the functions developed in this chapter interface to the ROM-BIOS, so you may want to read Chapter 24 if you haven't already done so.)

```
/* Set the video mode. */
void mode(int mode_code)
{
  union REGS r;

  r.h.al = mode_code;
  r.h.ah = 0;
  int86(0x10, &r, &r);
}
```

Keep in mind that in all modes, the upper-left corner is location 0,0.

There are two palettes available in mode 4 graphics. The palette determines which four colors are displayed. On the IBM PC, palette 0 provides the colors red, green, and yellow; palette 1 provides white, magenta, and cyan. For each, the fourth color is the same and is the color of the background—usually black. The function **palette( )**, shown here, selects the palette specified in its argument:

```
/* Set the palette. */
void palette(int pnum)
{
```

```
      union REGS r;

      r.h.bh = 1;    /* code for mode 4 graphics */
      r.h.bl = pnum;
      r.h.ah = 11;   /* set palette function */
      int86(0x10, &r, &r);
    }
```

Writing Pixels

The most fundamental graphics routine is the one that actually writes a pixel. Because it is used by higher-level routines, its efficiency is very important to the overall speed of the graphics functions. On the IBM PC and compatibles, you can write information to a pixel in two ways. The first is through a ROM-BIOS routine. This is the easiest but also the slowest method. The second and faster method is to place information directly into the video-display RAM.

Writing a Pixel Using ROM-BIOS

The ROM-BIOS interrupt 10H, function 12, writes the color specified in **AL** into the pixel at the row value in **DX** and the column number in **CX**. The function **writepoint( )**, shown here, writes the specified color to the specified location. Notice that it also prevents you from using out-of-range locations.

```
#define XMAX 199
#define YMAX 319

/* Write a pixel at x,y in the specified color. */
void writepoint(int x, int y, int color_code)
{
  union REGS r;

  /* don't display if out-of-range */
  if(x<0 || x>XMAX || y<0 || y>YMAX) return;

  r.h.ah = 12; /* set for write */
  r.h.al = color_code; /* color */
  r.x.dx = x; /* set row */
  r.x.cx = y; /* set column */
```

```
    int86(0x10, &r, &r); /* call BIOS */
}
```

To use **writepoint( )**, simply call it with the coordinates of the pixel and the color you want written there. For example, this program prints three diagonal lines, each of a different color and each 100 pixels long. (For the shorter examples in this chapter, only the **main( )** function is shown, but be sure to include the necessary functions—in this case **mode( )**, **palette( )**, and **writepoint( )**.)

```
#include "dos.h"
#include "stdio.h"

void main(void)
{
  int i, color;

  mode(4);
  palette(0);

  for(i=0;i<100;i++)
    for(color=1; color<4; color++)
      writepoint(i, i+(color*4), color);

  getchar();
  mode(2); /* return to standard text mode */
}
```

Figure 25-1 shows this program's output.

There is one very interesting feature of the ROM-BIOS function that writes to a pixel. If the seventh bit (the leftmost one) of the color code is 1, the color specified is XORed with the existing color at the specified location; it does not simply overwrite the previous color. This guarantees that the pixel will be visible. You will see the value of this feature a little later in this chapter.

Writing Pixels Directly

You can bypass the ROM-BIOS and write information directly into the video RAM used by the CGA, EGA, or VGA while operating in mode 4. You may want to do this because the graphics routines that access the graphics adapter directly run much faster than those that use the ROM-BIOS routines. (However, to write directly to the video RAM, your compiler must support **far** pointers.)

Figure 25-1.   Drawing points in graphics mode

In mode 4, the CGA, EGA, and VGA video controllers map the contents of the video-display RAM onto the screen. The CGA video RAM always starts at location B8000H. The EGA and VGA use the same location for those modes that are compatible with the CGA modes. (For higher resolution EGA and VGA modes, a quite different approach is used.) Each byte holds the color information for 4 pixels. Because 2 bits can hold only four different values, there can be only four colors in mode 4. A quirk in the CGA stores the even-numbered pixels in memory beginning at B8000H, but the odd-numbered pixels 2000H bytes higher, at BA000H. Therefore, each row of pixels requires 80 bytes—40 for the even pixels and 40 for the odd. Within each byte, the pixels are stored left to right as they appear on the screen. This means that pixel number 0 occupies bits 6 and 7, while pixel number 3 uses bits 0 and 1.

Because there are 4 pixels encoded into each byte, you need to preserve the value of the other three when changing the value of one. The best way to do this is to create a bit mask that contains all 1's except in the location of the pixel to be changed. This value is ANDed with the original byte, and then the new value is ORed with the new information. However, the situation is slightly different if you want to XOR the new value with the old. In this case, you simply OR the original byte with 0 and then XOR that result with the new color.

You locate the address of the proper byte by first dividing the x coordinate by 40 and then adding the value of the y coordinate divided by 4. By finding the remainder of an integer division by 2, you can determine which video bank is required. If the remainder is zero, the number is even so the first bank is used; otherwise, the number is odd and the second bank must be used. The proper bits within the byte are computed by performing a modulus division by 4. The remainder is the number of the 2-bit packet that contains the desired pixel. Bit-shift operations are used to arrange the **color_code** byte and the bit mask into their proper positions. The bit manipulations in the function **mempoint( )**, shown here, are fairly intimidating. But you should have no trouble understanding the code if you study it carefully.

```c
/* Write a point directly to the CGA. */
void mempoint(int x, int y, int color_code)
{
  union {
   unsigned char bits;
   unsigned i;
  } bit_mask;

  int index, loc;
  unsigned char t;
  char xor; /* xor color in or overwrite */
  char far *ptr = (char far *) 0xB8000000; /* pointer
                                         to CGA memory */

  bit_mask.i = 0xFF3F;  /* 11111111 00111111 in binary */

  /* check range for mode 4 */
  if(x<0 || x>199 || y<0 || y>319) return;

  xor = color_code & 128; /* see if xor mode is set */
  color_code = color_code & 127; /* mask off high bit */

  /* set bit_mask and color_code bits to the right location */
  loc = y%4;
  color_code <<= 2*(3-loc);
  bit_mask.i >>= 2*loc;

 /* find the correct byte in screen memory */
  index = x*40 +(y >> 2);
  if(x % 2) index += 8152; /* if odd use 2nd bank */

  /* write the color */
  if(!xor) { /* overwrite mode */
    t = *(ptr+index) & bit_mask.bits;
    *(ptr+index) = t | color_code;
  }
  else { /* xor mode */
    t = *(ptr+index) | (char)0;
    *(ptr+index) = t ^ color_code;
  }
}
```

Notice that the special XOR write mode available in the ROM-BIOS function has been preserved in **mempoint( )**.

The **mempoint( )** function is used in subsequent examples because it is much faster. If your compiler does not support **far** pointers, however, you should use the slower **writepoint( )** function. (You will also need to use **writepoint( )** if you use a higher resolution EGA or VGA mode.)

Drawing Lines

Another fundamental graphics routine is the line-drawing function. It draws a line in the specified color given the beginning and ending coordinates of the line. Although you can easily draw lines that are either vertical or horizontal, it is a little harder to create a function that draws lines along any diagonal. For example, to draw a line from 0,0 to 80,120, what are the points in between? There are various methods of drawing lines, but this chapter examines only two.

One approach to creating a line-drawing function uses the ratio between the change in the x and y dimensions. To see how this works, consider a line from 0,0 to 5,10. The change in x is 5 and the change in y is 10—a ratio of 1/2. This ratio is used to determine the rate at which the x and y coordinates change as the line is drawn. In this case, the x coordinate is incremented only half as frequently as the y coordinate. This is the strategy that novice programmers often choose when creating a line-drawing function. This method is mathematically simple and easy to understand. However, if it is to work properly in all situations, floating-point variables and arithmetic must be used to avoid serious round-off errors. This means that the line-drawing function runs quite slowly unless there is a math coprocessor, such as the 8087, installed in the system. The function **slowline( )**, shown here, uses ratios to draw lines on the screen. It illustrates how *not* to implement a line-drawing function.

```
/* Draw a line in specified color using floating point
   ratios.  This function is too slow for most
   applications.
```

```c
*/
void slowline(int startx, int starty,
              int endx, int endy, int color)
{
  register int t;
  int delta_x, delta_y;
  int incx, incy, run, cx, cy;
  float ratio_x, ratio_y;

  /* compute the increments */
  delta_x = endx-startx;
  delta_y = endy-starty;

  /* Compute the direction of the increment,
     an increment of 0 means either a vertical or horizontal
     line.
  */
  if(delta_x>0) incx = 1;
  else if(delta_x==0) incx = 0;
  else incx = -1;

  if(delta_y>0) incy = 1;
  else if(delta_y==0) incy = 0;
  else incy = -1;

  delta_x = abs(delta_x);
  delta_y = abs(delta_y);

  /* determine which coordinate governs the line
  */
  if(delta_x > delta_y)
    run = delta_x;
  else
    run = delta_y;

  /* Draw the line.  This routine uses the ratios
     between the changes in X and Y to compute
     the next move.
  */
  ratio_x = ratio_y = 1.0;
  for (t=0, cx=0, cy=0; t<=run; t++) {
    mempoint(startx, starty, color);
    if(delta_x) ratio_x = (float)cx / (float)delta_x;
    else ratio_x = 0.0;
    if(delta_y) ratio_y = (float)cy / (float)delta_y;
    else ratio_y = 0.0;
    if(run==delta_x) {
      startx += incx;
      cx++;
    }
    else if(ratio_x<ratio_y) {
      startx += incx;
      cx++;
    }
    if(run==delta_y) {
      starty += incy;
```

```
      cy++;
    }
    else if(ratio_-y < ratio_x) {
      starty += incy;
      cy++;
    }
  }
}
```

Notice that **mempoint( )** actually writes points to the screen. Much of the routine's code is used to determine such things as the direction of the line, the magnitude of the change to both the X and Y coordinate components, and the appropriate increment. However, it is the floating-point calculations in the loop that actually draws the line that cause this algorithm to perform so poorly. For this reason, this approach is seldom used.

By far the most common method for drawing a line employs Bresenham's algorithm. Although still based upon the ratios between the x and y distances, no divisions or floating-point calculations are required. Instead, the ratio between the change in the X and Y directions is handled implicitly through a series of additions and subtractions. The basic idea behind Bresenham's approach is to keep track of how wide the error is between where each point should go and where it must be displayed. The error is introduced because no display has infinite precision. Therefore, the actual location of each dot on the line is the best approximation. In each iteration through the line-drawing loop, two variables—**xerr** and **yerr**—are incremented by the changes in magnitude of X and Y, respectively. When an error value reaches a predetermined limit, it is reset and the appropriate coordinate counter is incremented. This process continues until the entire line is drawn. The **line( )** function, shown here, implements this method. Study it until you understand how it works. Notice that it uses the **mempoint( )** function to write dots to the screen.

```
/* Draw a line in specified color
   using Bresenham's integer based algorithm.
*/
void line(int startx, int starty,
          int endx, int endy, int color)
{
  register int t, distance;
  int xerr=0, yerr=0, delta_x, delta_y;
```

```
int incx, incy;

/* compute the distances in both directions */
delta_x = endx-startx;
delta_y = endy-starty;

/* Compute the direction of the increment,
   an increment of 0 means either a vertical or horizontal
   line.
*/
if(delta_x>0) incx = 1;
else if(delta_x==0) incx = 0;
else incx = -1;

if(delta_y>0) incy = 1;
else if(delta_y==0) incy = 0;
else incy = -1;

/* determine which distance is greater */
delta_x = abs(delta_x);
delta_y = abs(delta_y);
if(delta_x > delta_y) distance = delta_x;
else distance = delta_y;

/* draw the line */
for(t=0; t<=distance+1; t++) {
  mempoint(startx, starty, color);
  xerr += delta_x;
  yerr += delta_y;
  if(xerr > distance) {
    xerr -= distance;
    startx += incx;
  }
  if(yerr > distance) {
    yerr -= distance;
    starty += incy;
  }
 }
}
```

The following program shows how you can use the **line( )** function to display lines on the screen. Figure 25-2 shows this program's output.

```
#include "dos.h"
#include "stdio.h"

void main(void)
{
  mode(4);
  palette(0);

  line(0, 0, 100, 100, 1);
  line(50, 90, 180, 300, 2);
  line(10, 10, 20, 200, 3);
```

```
   getchar();
   mode(2); /* return to standard text mode */
}
```

Drawing and Filling Boxes

Once you have a line-drawing function, it is easy to create a box-drawing function. The one shown here draws the outline of a box in the specified color when given the coordinates of two opposing corners:

```
/* draw a box */
void box(int startx, int starty,
         int endx, int endy, int color_code)
{
   line(startx,starty, endx,starty, color_code);
   line(startx,starty, startx,endy, color_code);
   line(startx,endy, endx,endy, color_code);
   line(endx,starty, endx,endy, color_code);
}
```

Using **box( )**, this program draws the boxes shown in Figure 25-3.

```
#include "dos.h"
#include "stdio.h"

void main(void)
{
   mode(4);    /* go to graphics mode */
   palette(0);

   box(0, 0, 40, 50, 1);
   box(100, 120, 140, 250, 2);
   box(150, 150, 90, 0, 3);

   getchar();
   mode(2); /* return to standard text mode */
}
```

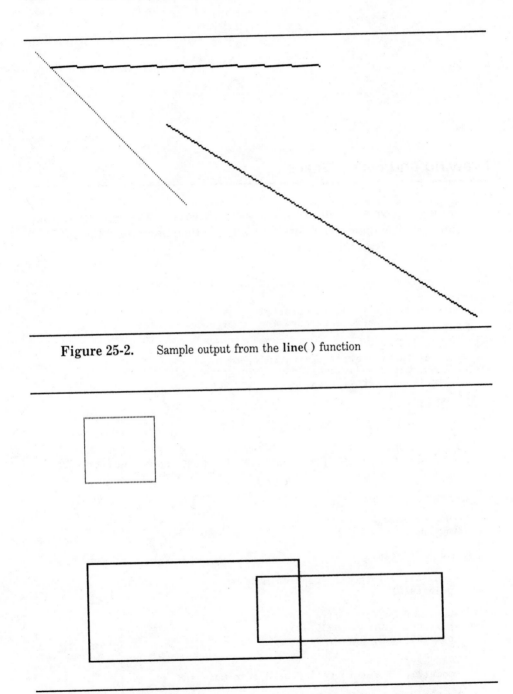

Figure 25-2. Sample output from the **line( )** function

Figure 25-3. Sample output using the **box( )** function

To fill a box, you must write to each pixel in the box. The **fill＿box( )** routine shown here fills a box with the specified color when given the coordinates of two opposing corners. It uses the **line( )** function to color in the box.

```
/* fill box with specified color */
void fill_box(int startx, int starty,
              int endx, int endy, int color_code)
{
  register int i,begin, end;

  /* Find starting points so that box is filled
     in the direction of increasing coordinates. */
  begin = startx<endx ? startx : endx;
  end = startx>endx ? startx : endx;

  for(i=begin; i<=end;i++)
    line(i, starty, i, endy, color_code);
}
```

The next program produced the sample output shown in Figure 25-4.

```
#include "dos.h"
#include "stdio.h"

void main(void)
{
  mode(4);  /* go to graphics mode */
  palette(0);

  fill_box(0, 0, 40, 50, 1);
  fill_box(100, 120, 140, 250, 2);
  fill_box(150, 150, 90, 0, 3);

  getchar();
  mode(2); /* return to standard text mode */
}
```

Putting It All Together

The chapter concludes with a simple "paint" program that uses the graphics routines already developed. You may be familiar with paint

Figure 25-4.   Sample output using **fill＿box( )**

programs because they are quite popular. These programs generally use a mouse to allow you to "brush" lines onto the computer screen. However, since not everyone has a mouse, the paint program developed here relies on the cursor keys.

The program requires two routines that have not yet been developed. The first, **get＿key( )**, reads the 16-bit scan code from the keyboard. (Scan codes were discussed in Chapter 24.) The cursor keys and the function keys return 0 for their character code (the low-order 8 bits), meaning that you must examine the position code (the high-order 8 bits) to determine what key was pressed. The **get＿key( )** function is shown here. It uses **int86( )** to access the ROM-BIOS routine that returns the scan code. (Some compilers call **int86( )** by a different name, so check your user's manual.)

```
/* Read the scan code. */
get_key(void)
{
  union REGS r;

  r.h.ah = 0;
  return int86(0x16, &r, &r);
}
```

In a paint program, you need to be able to see the current X,Y position. (Remember, in graphics mode there is no cursor.) This requires a locator, which resembles the cross hairs of a rifle scope. The function **xhairs( )**, shown here, places small cross hairs on the screen at the current X,Y position. Notice that the color code is ORed with 128, setting bit 7 to 1. This tells **mempoint( )** to XOR the color onto the screen instead of overwriting the current color, achieving two very important things: First, the locator is always visible because it always has a color other than what is around it. Second, it is easy to return the pixels occupied by the locator to their former color by simply writing them a second time. (Recall that two XOR operations with the same operands always produce the original value.)

```
/* Display cross hair locator. */
void xhairs(int x, int y)
{
  line(x-4, y, x+3, y, 1 | 128);
  line(x, y+4, x, y-3, 1 | 128);
}
```

The paint program lets you

- Draw lines

- Draw boxes

- Fill boxes

- Select color

- Select palette

- Turn the brush on and off

- Set a speed-of-motion parameter

The main loop of the program is shown here:

```
void main(void)
{
  union k{
    char c[2];
    int i;
  } key;

  int x=10, y=10, cc=2, on_flag=1, pal_num=1;
```

```
int startx=0, starty=0, endx=0, endy=0, first_point=1;
int inc=1;

mode(4);
palette(0);

xhairs(x, y);
do {
  key.i = get_key();
  xhairs(x, y);
  if(!key.c[0]) switch(key.c[1]) {
    case 75: /* left */
      if(on_flag) line(x, y, x, y-inc, cc);
      y -= inc;
      break;
    case 77: /* right */
      if(on_flag) line(x, y, x, y+inc, cc);
      y += inc;
      break;
    case 72: /* up */
      if(on_flag) line(x, y, x-inc, y, cc);
      x -= inc;
      break;
    case 80: /* down */
      if(on_flag) line(x, y, x+inc, y, cc);
      x += inc;
      break;
    case 71: /* up left - Home */
      if(on_flag) line(x, y, x-inc, y-inc, cc);
      x -= inc; y -= inc;
      break;
    case 73: /* up right - PgUp */
      if(on_flag) line(x, y, x-inc, y+inc, cc);
      x -= inc; y += inc;
      break;
    case 79: /* down left - End */
      if(on_flag) line(x, y, x+inc, y-inc, cc);
      x += inc; y -= inc;
      break;
    case 81: /* down right - PgDn */
      if(on_flag) line(x, y, x+inc, y+inc, cc);
      x += inc; y += inc;
      break;
    case 59: inc = 1;   /* F1 */
      break;
    case 60: inc = 5;   /* F2 */
      break;
  }
  else switch(tolower(key.c[0])) {
    case 'o': on_flag = !on_flag; /* brush on/off */
      break;
    case '1': cc = 1;   /* color 1 */
      break;
    case '2': cc = 2;   /* color 2 */
      break;
    case '3': cc = 3;   /* color 3 */
```

```
      break;
    case '0': cc = 0;   /* color 4 */
      break;
    case 'b': box(startx, starty, endx, endy, cc);
      break;
    case 'f': fill_box(startx, starty, endx, endy, cc);
      break;
    case 'l': line(startx, starty, endx, endy, cc);
      break;
    case '\r': /* set end points */
      if(first_point) {
        startx = x, starty = y;
      }
      else {
        endx = x; endy = y;
      }
      first_point = !first_point;
      break;
    case 'p': /* change palettes */
      pal_num = pal_num==1 ? 2:1;
      palette(pal_num);
    }
    xhairs(x, y);
  } while (key.c[0]!='q');
  mode(2);
}
```

The paint program works like this: Upon execution, the screen is set to graphics mode 4. Palette 0 is selected and the locator is displayed in the upper-left corner. The brush is on with a default color of 2 (red in palette 0). Therefore, moving the cursor leaves a trail of pixels. This is how color is brushed onto the screen. Each time you strike a cursor key, the locator moves one pixel in the indicated direction. This can be rather slow at times, so the program allows you to move five pixels at a time by striking the function key F2. To return to single-pixel moves, strike the function key F1. You can select different colors by typing the numbers 0 through 3 on the keyboard. In palette 0, 0 is blank, 1 is green, 2 is red, and 3 is yellow. You can turn the brush off and on by typing the letter **o**. The HOME, PGUP, PGDN, and END keys move the locator at 45-degree angles in the expected direction.

The program supports three special commands that draw boxes, fill boxes, and draw lines. To use these commands, you must first define two coordinates. To draw and fill boxes, you must specify the location of two opposing corners. To draw lines, select the beginning and ending points. You perform the selection process by pressing ENTER. Once the locations have been recorded, typing **b** draws a box, **f** draws a filled box, and **l** draws a line. You terminate the program by typing **q**.

The entire paint program is shown here. It might be fun to add other high-level commands or to interface it to a mouse. Sample output is shown in Figure 25-5.

```
/* A simple paint program. */

#include "dos.h"
#include "stdio.h"
#include "ctype.h"
#include "stdlib.h"

void palette(int pnum), mode(int mode_code);
void box(int startx, int starty,
        int endx, int endy, int color_code);
void line(int startx, int starty,
        int endx, int endy, int color);
void fill_box(int startx, int starty,
        int endx, int endy, int color_code);
void xhairs(int x, int y);
void mempoint(int x, int y, int color_code);
int get_key(void);
```

Figure 25-5.   Sample output from the paint program

```
void main(void)
{
  union k{
    char c[2];
    int i;
  } key;

  int x=10, y=10, cc=2, on_flag=1, pal_num=1;
  int startx=0, starty=0, endx=0, endy=0, first_point=1;
  int inc=1;

  mode(4);
  palette(0);

  xhairs(x, y);
  do {
    key.i = get_key();
    xhairs(x, y);
    if(!key.c[0]) switch(key.c[1]) {
      case 75: /* left */
        if(on_flag) line(x, y, x, y-inc, cc);
        y -= inc;
        break;
      case 77: /* right */
        if(on_flag) line(x, y, x, y+inc, cc);
        y += inc;
        break;
      case 72: /* up */
        if(on_flag) line(x, y, x-inc, y, cc);
        x -= inc;
        break;
      case 80: /* down */
        if(on_flag) line(x, y, x+inc, y, cc);
        x += inc;
        break;
      case 71: /* up left - Home */
        if(on_flag) line(x, y, x-inc, y-inc, cc);
        x -= inc; y -= inc;
        break;
      case 73: /* up right - PgUp */
        if(on_flag) line(x, y, x-inc, y+inc, cc);
        x -= inc; y += inc;
        break;
      case 79: /* down left - End */
        if(on_flag) line(x, y, x+inc, y-inc, cc);
        x += inc; y -= inc;
        break;
      case 81: /* down right - PgDn */
        if(on_flag) line(x, y, x+inc, y+inc, cc);
        x += inc; y += inc;
        break;
      case 59: inc = 1;   /* F1 */
        break;
      case 60: inc = 5;   /* F2 */
        break;
    }
    else switch(tolower(key.c[0])) {
```

```
         case 'o': on_flag = !on_flag; /* brush on/off */
           break;
         case '1': cc = 1;   /* color 1 */
           break;
         case '2': cc = 2;   /* color 2 */
           break;
         case '3': cc = 3;   /* color 3 */
           break;
         case '0': cc = 0;   /* color 4 */
           break;
         case 'b': box(startx, starty, endx, endy, cc);
           break;
         case 'f': fill_box(startx, starty, endx, endy, cc);
           break;
         case 'l': line(startx, starty, endx, endy, cc);
           break;
         case '\r': /* set end points */
           if(first_point) {
             startx = x, starty = y;
           }
           else {
             endx = x; endy = y;
           }
           first_point = !first_point;
           break;
         case 'p': /* change palettes */
           pal_num = pal_num==1 ? 2:1;
           palette(pal_num);
       }
     xhairs(x, y);
   } while (key.c[0]!='q');
   mode(2);
}

/* Set the palette. */
void palette(int pnum)
{
  union REGS r;

  r.h.bh = 1;    /* code for mode 4 graphics */
  r.h.bl = pnum;
  r.h.ah = 11;   /* set palette function */
  int86(0x10, &r, &r);
}

/* Set the video mode. */
void mode(int mode_code)
{
  union REGS r;

  r.h.al = mode_code;
  r.h.ah = 0;
  int86(0x10, &r, &r);
}

/* Draw a box. */
void box(int startx, int starty,
```

```
            int endx, int endy, int color_code)
{
  line(startx,starty, endx,starty, color_code);
  line(startx,starty, startx,endy, color_code);
  line(startx,endy, endx,endy, color_code);
  line(endx,starty, endx,endy, color_code);
}

/* Draw a line in specified color
   using Bresenham's integer based algorithm.
*/
void line(int startx, int starty,
          int endx, int endy, int color)
{
  register int t, distance;
  int xerr=0, yerr=0, delta_x, delta_y;
  int incx, incy;

  /* compute the distances in both directions */
  delta_x = endx-startx;
  delta_y = endy-starty;

  /* Compute the direction of the increment,
     an increment of 0 means either a vertical or horizontal
     line.
  */
  if(delta_x>0) incx = 1;
  else if(delta_x==0) incx = 0;
  else incx = -1;

  if(delta_y>0) incy = 1;
  else if(delta_y==0) incy = 0;
  else incy = -1;

  /* determine which distance is greater */
  delta_x = abs(delta_x);
  delta_y = abs(delta_y);
  if(delta_x > delta_y) distance = delta_x;
  else distance = delta_y;

  /* draw the line */
  for(t=0; t<=distance+1; t++) {
    mempoint(startx, starty, color);
    xerr += delta_x;
    yerr += delta_y;
    if(xerr > distance) {
      xerr -= distance;
      startx += incx;
    }
    if(yerr > distance) {
      yerr -= distance;
      starty += incy;
    }
  }
}

/* Fill box with specified color. */
```

```
void fill_box(int startx, int starty,
              int endx, int endy, int color_code)
{
  register int i,begin, end;

  begin = startx<endx ? startx : endx;
  end = startx>endx ? startx : endx;

  for(i=begin; i<=end;i++)
    line(i,starty,i,endy,color_code);
}

/* Display crosshair locator. */
void xhairs(int x, int y)
{
  line(x-4, y, x+3, y, 1 | 128);
  line(x, y+4, x, y-3, 1 | 128);
}

/* Read the scan code. */
get_key(void)
{
  union REGS r;

  r.h.ah = 0;
  return int86(0x16, &r, &r);
}

/* Write a point directly to the CGA. */
void mempoint(int x, int y, int color_code)
{
  union {
   unsigned char bits;
   unsigned i;
  } bit_mask;

  int index, loc;
  unsigned char t;
  char xor; /* xor color in or overwrite */
  char far *ptr = (char far *) 0xB8000000; /* pointer
                                     to CGA memory */

  bit_mask.i = 0xFF3F;   /* 11111111 00111111 in binary */

  /* check range for mode 4 */
  if(x<0 || x>199 || y<0 || y>319) return;

  xor = color_code & 128; /* see if xor mode is set */
  color_code = color_code & 127; /* mask off high bit */

  /* set bit_mask and color_code bits to the right location */
  loc = y%4;
  color_code <<= 2*(3-loc);
  bit_mask.i >>= 2*loc;

  /* find the correct byte in screen memory */
```

```
   index = x*40 +(y >> 2);
   if(x % 2) index += 8152; /* if odd use 2nd bank */

  /* write the color */
  if(!xor) { /* overwrite mode */
    t = *(ptr+index) & bit_mask.bits;
    *(ptr+index) = t | color_code;
  }
  else { /* xor mode */
    t = *(ptr+index) | (char)0;
    *(ptr+index) = t ^ color_code;
  }
}
```

Software Development Using C

Interfacing to Assembly-Language Routines
Software Engineering Using C
Efficiency, Porting, and Debugging

This part examines various aspects of the software-development process as they relate to the C programming environment. Chapter 26 covers the use of assembly-language subroutines and optimizations. Chapter 27 is an overview of the design process using C. Last, Chapter 28 provides a look at porting, efficiency, and debugging.

Interfacing to Assembly-Language Routines

Assembly-Language Interfacing
The Calling Conventions of a C Compiler
The Calling Conventions of Microsoft C
Creating an Assembly-Code Function
Creating an Assembly-Code Skeleton
Using asm
When to Code in Assembler

As powerful as C is, at times you must write a routine using assembler. The way you accomplish this will vary from compiler to compiler, but the general process described in this chapter applies to most compilers.

Each processor has a different assembly language and each operating system has a different interface structure. Also, each C compiler has a different calling convention, which defines how information is passed to and from a function. This chapter uses the DOS operating system and the 8086 assembly language. Many of the assembly-language interfacing examples use Microsoft C version 5.1, but you can generally apply the information to other C compilers. Even if you have a different computer or compiler, the following discussion can serve as a guide.

Assembly-Language Interfacing

There are three reasons you might want to use a routine written in assembler:

- To gain speed and efficiency

- To perform some machine-specific function unavailable in C

- To use a third-party assembly-language routine

Let's take a closer look at these now.

SIX

Although C compilers tend to produce extremely fast, compact object code, no compiler consistently creates code as fast or compact as that written by an excellent programmer using assembler. Most of the time, the small difference does not matter, nor does it warrant the extra time needed to write in assembler. However, in special cases a specific function must be coded in assembler so that it runs very quickly. For example, you might code a floating-point math package in assembly language because it is used frequently and greatly affects a program's execution speed. Also, special hardware devices may need exact timing, which means that you must code in assembler to meet the strict timing requirement.

Many computers, including 8086-based machines, have certain instructions that most C compilers cannot execute. For example, you cannot change data segments with any ANSI standard C instruction. Also, you cannot issue a software interrupt or control the contents of specific registers using a standard C statement.

It is very common in professional programming environments to purchase subroutine libraries for things like graphics, floating-point math, and the like. Sometimes it is necessary to take these in object format because the developer will not sell the source code. Occasionally, you can simply link these routines with code compiled by your compiler. At other times, you must write an interface module to correct any differences in the interface used by your compiler and the routines you purchased.

There are basically two ways to integrate assembly-code modules into your C programs. You can code the routine separately and link it with the rest of your program. Alternately, you can use the in-line assembly-code capabilities of many C compilers. This chapter explores both methods.

A word of warning: This chapter does *not* teach you how to code in assembler—it assumes that you already know how. If you do not, don't try the examples. It is extremely easy to do something slightly wrong and create a disaster. You could erase your hard disk, for example.

The Calling Conventions of a C Compiler

A *calling convention* is the method that a particular C compiler uses to pass information into functions and return values. Usually, either the internal registers of the CPU or the system stack are used to pass information between independent functions. Generally, C compilers use the stack to pass arguments to functions. If the argument is one of the seven built-in data types or a structure, union, or enumeration, the actual value is placed on the stack. If the argument is an array, its address is placed on the stack. When a C function begins execution, it retrieves its parameter's values from the stack. When a C function terminates, it passes a return value back to the calling routine. Typically, this return value is placed in a register, although it could theoretically be passed on the stack.

The calling convention also determines exactly what registers must be preserved and which ones you can use freely. Often a compiler produces object code that needs only a portion of the available registers. You must preserve the contents of the register used by your compiler, generally by pushing their contents on the stack before using them. Any other registers are usually free for your use.

When you write an assembly-language module that must interface to code compiled by your C compiler, you need to follow the conventions defined and used by your compiler. Only in this way can you hope to have assembly-language routines interface correctly to your C code. The next section examines in detail the calling conventions of Microsoft C.

The Calling Conventions of Microsoft C

Like most C compilers, Microsoft C passes arguments to functions on the stack. The arguments are pushed onto the stack from right to left. That is, given the call

func(a, b, c);

c is pushed first, followed by **b**, and **a**. Table 26-1 shows the number of bytes occupied on the stack by each type.

Upon entry into an assembly-code function, the contents of the **BP** register must be saved on the stack and the current value of the stack

Type	Number of Bytes
char	2
short	2
signed char	2
signed short	2
unsigned char	2
unsigned short	2
int	2
signed int	2
unsigned int	2
long	4
unsigned long	4
float	4
double	8
long double	8
(near) pointer	2 (offset only)
(far) pointer	4 (segment and offset)

Table 26-1.   The Number of Bytes on the Stack Required for Each Data Type When Passed to a Function for Microsoft C

pointer (**SP**) is placed into **BP**. The only other registers that you must preserve are **SI** and **DI** (if your routine uses them).

Before returning, your assembly-language function must restore the value of **BP**, **SI**, and **DI** and reset the stack pointer.

If your assembly-language function returns an 8- or 16-bit value, it is placed into the **AX** register. Otherwise, it is returned according to Table 26-2.

Creating an Assembly-Code Function

Without a doubt, seeing how your compiler generates code is the easiest way to learn to create assembly-language functions that are compatible with your compiler's calling convention. Virtually all C compilers have a compile-time option that causes the compiler to output an assembly-language listing of the code that it generates. By examining this file,

Type	Register(s) and Meaning
char	AX
unsigned char	AX
short	AX
unsigned short	AX
int	AX
unsigned int	AX
long	Low-order word in AX
	High-order word in DX
unsigned long	Low-order word in AX
	High-order word in DX
float & double	Address (offset only) to value
struct & union	Address (offset only) to value
(near) pointer	AX
(far) pointer	Offset in AX, segment in DX

Table 26-2.   Register Usage for Return Values Using Microsoft C

you can learn a great deal about not only how to interface to the compiler, but also how the compiler actually works.

The Microsoft C compiler option **−Fa** creates an assembly language file. **−Fc** creates a file that contains the assembly-language instructions, the actual hexadecimal codes for the instructions, and the lines of C code that generated those instructions. These two files have the extensions .ASM and .COD, respectively. This chapter uses these features to show how Microsoft C generates code for two short programs.

A Simple Assembly-Code Function

The first program, shown here, illustrates how code is generated for a function call with arguments:

```
int sum;

int add(int a, int b);
```

```
void main(void)
{
  sum = add(10,12);
}

add(int a, int b)
{
  int t;

  t = a+b;
  return t;
}
```

The variable **sum** is intentionally declared as global so that you can see examples of both local and global data. If this program is called **test**, the following command line creates **test.cod**:

>cl −Fc test.c

The contents of **test.cod** are shown here:

```
;       Static Name Aliases
;
        TITLE   test.c
        NAME    test

        .8087
_TEXT   SEGMENT  WORD PUBLIC 'CODE'
_TEXT   ENDS
_DATA   SEGMENT  WORD PUBLIC 'DATA'
_DATA   ENDS
CONST   SEGMENT  WORD PUBLIC 'CONST'
CONST   ENDS
_BSS    SEGMENT  WORD PUBLIC 'BSS'
_BSS    ENDS
DGROUP  GROUP   CONST, _BSS, _DATA
        ASSUME  CS: _TEXT, DS: DGROUP, SS: DGROUP
EXTRN   __acrtused:ABS
EXTRN   __chkstk:NEAR
_BSS        SEGMENT
COMM NEAR       _sum:  BYTE:    2
_BSS        ENDS
_TEXT       SEGMENT
        ASSUME  CS: _TEXT
;|***
;|*** int sum;
;|***
;|*** int add(int a, int b);
;|***
;|*** void main(void)
;|*** {
; Line 7
        PUBLIC  _main
```

```
_main    PROC NEAR
         *** 000000    33 c0          xor     ax,ax
         *** 000002    e8 00 00       call    __chkstk
;¦***    sum = add(10,12);
; Line 8
         *** 000005    b8 0c 00       mov     ax,12
         *** 000008    50             push    ax
         *** 000009    b8 0a 00       mov     ax,10
         *** 00000c    50             push    ax
         *** 00000d    e8 00 00       call    _ add
         *** 000010    83 c4 04       add     sp,4
         *** 000013    a3 00 00       mov     WORD PTR _sum,ax
;¦*** }
; Line 9
         *** 000016    c3             ret
         *** 000017    90             nop

_main    ENDP
;¦***
;¦*** add(int a, int b)
;¦*** {
; Line 12
         PUBLIC  _add
_add     PROC NEAR
         *** 000018    55             push    bp
         *** 000019    8b ec          mov     bp,sp
         *** 00001b    b8 02 00       mov     ax,2
         *** 00001e    e8 00 00       call    __chkstk
;          a = 4
;          b = 6
;          t = -2
;¦***      int t;
;¦***
;¦***      t = a+b;
; Line 15
         *** 000021    8b 46 04       mov     ax,WORD PTR [bp+4] ;a
         *** 000024    03 46 06       add     ax,WORD PTR [bp+6] ;b
         *** 000027    89 46 fe       mov     WORD PTR [bp-2],ax ;t
;¦***      return t;
; Line 16
         *** 00002a    8b e5          mov     sp,bp
         *** 00002c    5d             pop     bp
         *** 00002d    c3             ret

_add     ENDP
_TEXT    ENDS
END
;¦*** }
;¦***
;¦***
;¦***
```

The program first establishes the various segments required by a C program. These vary with different memory models. (This file was produced for the small memory model.) For the exact names, meaning, and usage of these segments, refer to your compiler's user's manual. Next, 2 bytes are allocated in the **_BSS** segment for the global variable **sum**. The compiler adds the underscore in front of **sum** to avoid confusion with any internal compiler names. In fact, the underscore is added to the front of all function and variable names. After this, the program code begins. In Microsoft C, the code segment is called **_TEXT**.

The first thing that **_main** does is call the compiler supplied routine named **_ _chkstk**, which checks to see if the stack has enough space in it to allocate the number of bytes contained in the **AX** register. Here, that value is 0 because there are no local variables for which to allocate space on the stack. Next, the two arguments to **_add** are pushed on the stack and **_add** is called. Finally, the value **_add** returns is moved into **_sum**, and **_main** returns.

The function **_add** begins by saving **BP**, placing the value of **SP** into **BP**, checking the stack, and allocating 2 bytes on the stack for the local variable **t**. The next three lines of code add the numbers and place their sum in **t**'s location on the stack. Notice, however, that the compiler detects that **AX** already has the value of **t** in it, so **AX** is not reloaded from memory before returning. This type of manipulation is called a *compiler optimization,* and is used to increase the efficiency of the code.

This same program in its straight assembly-language listing file is shown here:

```
;       Static Name Aliases
;
        TITLE   test.c
        NAME    test

        .8087
_TEXT   SEGMENT  WORD PUBLIC 'CODE'
_TEXT   ENDS
_DATA   SEGMENT  WORD PUBLIC 'DATA'
_DATA   ENDS
CONST   SEGMENT  WORD PUBLIC 'CONST'
CONST   ENDS
_BSS    SEGMENT  WORD PUBLIC 'BSS'
_BSS    ENDS
DGROUP  GROUP    CONST, _BSS, _DATA
        ASSUME  CS: _TEXT, DS: DGROUP, SS: DGROUP
EXTRN   __acrtused:ABS
EXTRN   __chkstk:NEAR
_BSS        SEGMENT
COMM NEAR       _sum:   BYTE:   2
_BSS        ENDS
_TEXT       SEGMENT
        ASSUME  CS: _TEXT
```

```
; Line 7
        PUBLIC  _main
_main   PROC NEAR
        xor     ax,ax
        call    __chkstk
; Line 8
        mov     ax,12
        push    ax
        mov     ax,10
        push    ax
        call    _add
        add     sp,4
        mov     WORD PTR _sum,ax
; Line 9
        ret
        nop

_main   ENDP
; Line 12
        PUBLIC  _add
_add    PROC NEAR
        push    bp
        mov     bp,sp
        mov     ax,2
        call    __chkstk
;       a = 4
;       b = 6
;       t = -2
; Line 15
        mov     ax,WORD PTR [bp+4]      ;a
        add     ax,WORD PTR [bp+6]      ;b
        mov     WORD PTR [bp-2],ax      ;t
; Line 16
        mov     sp,bp
        pop     bp
        ret

_add    ENDP
_TEXT   ENDS
END
```

You can literally assemble this file by using the Microsoft macro-assembler MASM (or a compatible assembler), link it by using the standard LINK utility, and run it. Moreover, you can modify the file to make it run faster but leave the C source code untouched. For example, you could remove the instructions that relate to the local variable **t**—they are not essential—and assemble the file. This is called *hand optimization*.

A Call-by-Reference Example

In the following program, the function **get_val( )** is called using the address of **a** to illustrate the code produced when pointers are used.

```
#include "stdio.h"

void get_val(int *x);

void main(void)
{
  int a;

  get_val(&a);
  printf("%d", a);
}

void get_val(int *x)
{
  *x = 100;
}
```

The assembly-language file is shown here:

```
;       Static Name Aliases
;
        TITLE   test.c
        NAME    test

        .8087
_TEXT   SEGMENT  WORD PUBLIC 'CODE'
_TEXT   ENDS
_DATA   SEGMENT  WORD PUBLIC 'DATA'
_DATA   ENDS
CONST   SEGMENT  WORD PUBLIC 'CONST'
CONST   ENDS
_BSS    SEGMENT  WORD PUBLIC 'BSS'
_BSS    ENDS
DGROUP  GROUP   CONST, _BSS, _DATA
        ASSUME  CS: _TEXT, DS: DGROUP, SS: DGROUP
EXTRN   __acrtused:ABS
EXTRN   _printf:NEAR
EXTRN   __chkstk:NEAR
_DATA       SEGMENT
$SG161  DB         '%d', 00H
_DATA       ENDS
_TEXT       SEGMENT
        ASSUME  CS: _TEXT
; Line 6
        PUBLIC  _main
_main   PROC NEAR
        push    bp
        mov     bp,sp
        mov     ax,2
        call    __chkstk
;       a = -2
; Line 9
        lea     ax,WORD PTR [bp-2]        ;a
        push    ax
```

```
        call    _get_val
        add     sp,2
; Line 10
        push    WORD PTR [bp-2] ;a
        mov     ax,OFFSET DGROUP:$SG161
        push    ax
        call    _printf
; Line 11
        mov     sp,bp
        pop     bp
        ret
        nop

_main   ENDP
; Line 15
        PUBLIC  _get_val
_get_val        PROC NEAR
        push    bp
        mov     bp,sp
        xor     ax,ax
        call    __chkstk
;       x = 4
; Line 16
        mov     bx,WORD PTR [bp+4]        ;x
        mov     WORD PTR [bx],100
; Line 17
        pop     bp
        ret
        nop

_get_val        ENDP
_TEXT   ENDS
END
```

As you can see, _ get _ val is called by using the address of **a**. The address of **a** is found by using the LEA (load effective address) assembly-language instruction. Inside _ get _ val, this address loads the value **100** into **a** by using the indirect addressing mode of the 8086.

Using the Large Code and Data Memory Model

As a final example of the way a C compiler generates code, let's compile the same test program used by the previous section using the huge memory model. This will cause references to library functions and global data to be **FAR**. To do this using the Microsoft compiler, specify the **-MH** compiler option. The following assembly-code module is produced:

```
;       Static Name Aliases
;
        TITLE   test.c
```

```
          NAME     test

          .8087
TEST_TEXT          SEGMENT  WORD PUBLIC 'CODE'
TEST_TEXT          ENDS
_DATA    SEGMENT  WORD PUBLIC 'DATA'
_DATA    ENDS
CONST    SEGMENT  WORD PUBLIC 'CONST'
CONST    ENDS
_BSS     SEGMENT  WORD PUBLIC 'BSS'
_BSS     ENDS
DGROUP   GROUP    CONST, _BSS, _DATA
          ASSUME  CS: TEST_TEXT, DS: DGROUP, SS: DGROUP
EXTRN    __acrtused:ABS
EXTRN    _printf:FAR
EXTRN    __chkstk:FAR
_DATA        SEGMENT
$SG161 DB        '%d',   00H
_DATA        ENDS
TEST_TEXT        SEGMENT
          ASSUME  CS: TEST_TEXT
; Line 6
          PUBLIC  _main
_main    PROC FAR
          push    bp
          mov     bp,sp
          mov     ax,2
          call    FAR PTR __chkstk
;        a = -2
; Line 9
          lea     ax,WORD PTR [bp-2]      ;a
          push    ss
          push    ax
          push    cs
          call    _get_val
          add     sp,4
; Line 10
          push    WORD PTR [bp-2  ;a
          mov     ax,OFFSET DGROUP:$SG161
          push    ds
          push    ax
          call    FAR PTR _printf
; Line 11
          mov     sp,bp
          pop     bp
          ret

_main    ENDP
; Line 15
          PUBLIC  _get_val
_get_val          PROC FAR
          push    bp
          mov     bp,sp
          xor     ax,ax
          call    FAR PTR __chkstk
;        x = 6
```

```
; Line 16
        les        bx,DWORD PTR [bp+6]      ;x
        mov        WORD PTR es:[bx],100
; Line 17
        pop        bp
        ret

_get_val           ENDP
TEST_TEXT          ENDS
END
```

Notice that now all calls to library functions are **FAR**. If you want to link your own assembly-language routines with C code compiled for a large code and data model, you must generate compatible return code when returning from a **FAR** call. When a procedure is called as **FAR**, both the segment and offset are placed on the stack. In the small code models, only the offset is placed on the stack. Confusing the two models will corrupt the stack and crash the program. Also, you must use **FAR** when referencing global data.

Creating An Assembly-Code Skeleton

Now that you have seen how C compilers call functions, it is just a short step to writing your own assembly-language functions. An easy method is to let the compiler generate an assembly-language skeleton for you. Once you have the skeleton, you just have to fill in the details. For example, suppose that you need to create an assembly-language routine that multiplies two integers. To have the compiler generate a skeleton for this function, first create a file that contains only this function.

```
mul(int a, int b)
{
}
```

Next, compile the file with the proper option to produce an assembly-language file. If you use the Microsoft compiler, this file is produced:

```
;       Static Name Aliases
;
        TITLE   mul.c
```

```
        NAME    mul

        .8087
_TEXT   SEGMENT  WORD PUBLIC 'CODE'
_TEXT   ENDS
_DATA   SEGMENT  WORD PUBLIC 'DATA'
_DATA   ENDS
CONST   SEGMENT  WORD PUBLIC 'CONST'
CONST   ENDS
_BSS    SEGMENT  WORD PUBLIC 'BSS'
_BSS    ENDS
DGROUP  GROUP    CONST, _BSS, _DATA
        ASSUME   CS: _TEXT, DS: DGROUP, SS: DGROUP
EXTRN   __acrtused:ABS
EXTRN   __chkstk:NEAR
_TEXT      SEGMENT
        ASSUME   CS: _TEXT
; Line 2
        PUBLIC  _mul
_mul    PROC NEAR
        push    bp
        mov     bp,sp
        xor     ax,ax
        call    __chkstk
;       a = 4
;       b = 6
; Line 3
        pop  bp
        ret

_mul    ENDP
_TEXT   ENDS
END
```

In this skeleton, the compiler has defined the proper segments and set up the stack and registers. All you have to do is fill in the details. The finished **mul( )** function is shown here:

```
;       Static Name Aliases
;
        TITLE   test.c
        NAME    test

        .8087
_TEXT   SEGMENT  WORD PUBLIC 'CODE'
_TEXT   ENDS
_DATA   SEGMENT  WORD PUBLIC 'DATA'
_DATA   ENDS
CONST   SEGMENT  WORD PUBLIC 'CONST'
CONST   ENDS
_BSS    SEGMENT  WORD PUBLIC 'BSS'
_BSS    ENDS
DGROUP  GROUP    CONST, _BSS, _DATA
```

```
        ASSUME  CS: _TEXT, DS: DGROUP, SS: DGROUP
EXTRN   __acrtused:ABS
EXTRN   __chkstk:NEAR
_TEXT       SEGMENT
        ASSUME  CS: _TEXT
; Line 2
        PUBLIC  _mul
_mul    PROC NEAR
        push    bp
        mov     bp,sp
        xor     ax,ax
        call    __chkstk
;       a = 4
;       b = 6
;
; here is where the actual multiplication takes place
        mov     ax,[bp+4]       ;a
        imul    ax,[bp+6]       ;b
;
;
; Line 3
        pop  bp
        ret

_mul    ENDP
_TEXT   ENDS
END
;
;
```

Once this file is assembled, you may link it to any C program that requires it. For example, this program prints the number 10 on the screen (remember to link in **mul( )**):

```
#include "stdio.h"

int mul(int a, int b);

void main(void)
{
  printf("%d ", mul(2,5));
}
```

However, don't forget that every compiler is different and every processor is different. Be sure to study your user's manuals.

The best way to learn more about interfacing assembly-language code with your C programs is to write short functions in C that do approximately what you want the assembly-language version to do. Then, by using the assembly-language compiler option, create an assembly-language file. Most of the time, you will just need to hand optimize this code instead of actually creating an assembly-language routine from the ground up.

Using asm

Although not supported by some compilers (including Microsoft's), many other C compilers, such as Turbo C, have added an extension to the C language that allows in-line assembly code to be part of a C program without using a completely separate module. The advantage to this is twofold. First, you don't need to write all of the interface code for each function. Second, all the code is in one place, which makes maintenance a little easier.

The extension added by Turbo C is called **asm**. To insert assembly code into a program, precede the assembly-code instruction with **asm**. That is, each line that contains assembly code must start with **asm**. The Turbo C compiler simply passes the assembly-code instruction through, untouched, to the assembler phase of the compiler.

For example, the following short function called **init_port1( )** sends a 255 and then a 0 to port 26 using 8086 assembly code:

```
void init_port1(void)
{
  printf("Initializing Port\n");
asm     out 26,255
asm     out 26,0
}
```

Here, Turbo C automatically provides the interface code to save registers and to return from the function. You just need to provide the code that runs inside the function.

You could use in-line assembly code to create a function that multiplies two numbers, called **mul( )**, without actually creating a separate assembly-language file. Using this approach, the code for **mul( )** is shown here:

```
mul(int a, int b)
{
asm     mov ax, word ptr 4[bp]
asm     imul ax, word ptr 6[bp]
}
```

Remember, the C compiler provides all customary support for setting up and returning from a function call. You must simply provide the body of the function and follow the calling conventions to access the arguments.

Keep in mind that, whatever method you use, you are creating machine dependencies that will make your program difficult to port to another machine. However, for the demanding situations that require assembly code, it is usually worth the effort.

When to Code in Assembler

Because it is difficult to code in assembler, most programmers only do this when absolutely necessary. The general rule is: Don't do it; it creates too many problems! Nevertheless, there are two situations in which coding in assembler makes sense. The first is when there is absolutely no other way to achieve the desired result. For example, you may have to interface directly to a hardware device that cannot be handled with C. The second situation is when you must reduce a C program's execution time.

When you need to speed up a program, you should choose carefully which functions you code in assembler. If you code the wrong ones, you will see very little speed increase. If you choose the right ones, your program will fly! You can easily determine which functions to recode by reviewing how your program runs. The functions that are used inside loops are generally the ones to program in assembler. This is because they are executed repeatedly. Coding in assembler a function used only once or twice does not speed up your program. But recoding a function used several times will. For example, consider the following **main( )** function:

```
#include "stdio.h"

void main(void)
{
  register int t;
```

```
init();

for(t=0; t<1000; ++t) {
  phase1();
  phase2();
  if(t==10) phase3();
}

byebye();
}
```

Clearly, recoding **init( )** and **byebye( )** will not measurably affect the speed of this program because these functions execute only once. However, **phase1( )** and **phase2( )** execute 1000 times and coding them in assembly language would definitely decrease this program's run time. **phase3( )** only executes once, even though it is inside the loop, so you should not recode this function into assembler.

With careful thought, you can make major improvements in the speed of your program by recoding only a few functions in assembler.

Software Engineering Using C

Top-Down Design
Bulletproof Functions
Function Prototypes
LINT and MAKE

The entire discipline of computer science has emerged with astonishing speed. Before 1970, little distinction was made between engineers who designed computers and those who programmed them. If you understood computers, it was assumed that you could engineer the hardware as well as the software. This situation changed radically during the 1970s. Now most colleges offer separate curricula for computer engineers and software engineers.

The art and science of software engineering encompass a wide range of topics. Creating a large computer program is a little like designing a large building. There are so many bits and pieces that it almost seems impossible to make everything work together. Of course, what makes the creation of a large program possible is the application of the proper engineering methods. In this chapter, several techniques and utilities that relate specifically to the C programming environment and that make the creation and maintenance of a program much easier will be examined.

Top-Down Design

Without a doubt the single most important thing that you can do to simplify the creation of a large program is to apply a solid approach. There are three general approaches to writing a program: top-down, bottom-up, and ad hoc. In the *top-down approach*, you start with the top-level routine and move down to the low-level routines. The *bottom-up approach* works in the opposite direction: you begin with specific routines and build them progressively into more complex structures, ending at the top-level routine. The *ad hoc approach* has no predetermined method.

As a structured language, C lends itself to a top-down approach. The top-down method can produce clean, readable code that you can easily maintain. This approach also helps you clarify the overall structure of the program before you code low-level functions, reducing time wasted by false starts.

Outlining Your Program

Like an outline, the top-down method starts with a general description and works toward specifics. In fact, a good way to design a program is to define exactly what the program will do at the top level. For example, assume that you have to write a mailing-list program. First you should make a list of what the program will do. Each entry in the list should contain only one functional unit. (You can think of a functional unit as a black box that performs a single task.) For example, your list might look like this:

- Enter a new name
- Delete a name
- Print the list
- Search for a name
- Save the list to a disk file
- Load the list
- Quit the program

These units can form the basis of functions in the program.

After you have defined the overall functionality of the program, you can sketch in the details of each functional unit, beginning with the main loop. The main loop of this program is

```
main loop
{
  do {
```

```
      display menu
      get user selection
      process the selection
    } while selection does not equal quit
}
```

This type of algorithmic notation (sometimes called *pseudocode*) can help you clarify the general structure of your program before you sit down at the computer. C syntax has been used because it is familiar, but you can use any type of syntax.

You should give a similar definition to each functional area. For example, you can define the function that writes the mailing list to a disk file like this:

```
save to disk  {
  open disk file
  while data left to write {
    write data to disk
  }
  close disk file
}
```

At this point, the save-to-disk function has created new, more specific functional units. You must define each of these. If, in the course of their definition, new functional units are created, they must also be defined, and so on. This process stops when no new functional units are created and all that is left to do is to actually code the routine.

Notice that the definition does not mention data structure or variables. This is intentional. So far, you only want to define what your program will do, not how it will actually do it. This definition process will help you decide on the actual structure of the data. However, you need to determine the data structure before you can code all functional units.

Choosing a Data Structure

After you have determined your program's general outline, you must decide how the data will be structured. The selections of data structure and its implementation are critical because they help determine the design limits of your program.

A mailing list deals with collections of information: names and addresses. Using a top-down approach, this immediately suggests the use of a structure to hold the information. However, how will these structures be stored and manipulated? For a mailing-list program, you could use a fixed-size array of structures. But a fixed-size array has two serious drawbacks. First, the size of the array arbitrarily limits the length of the mailing list. Second, a fixed-size array will not take advantage of additional memory you may add to your computer. On the other hand, if memory is subtracted (for example, if a memory card fails), the program may not work because the fixed-size array may not fit. Therefore, a mailing-list program should use dynamic memory allocation so that the list can be as large as free memory allows.

Although dynamic storage allocation has been chosen over a fixed-size array, the exact form of the data still has not been decided. There are several possibilities: You could use a singly linked list, a doubly linked list, a binary tree, or even a hashing method. Each method has its merits and its drawbacks. If you decide to use a binary tree for its fast search times, you can now define the structure that holds each name and address in the list, as shown here:

```
struct addr {
  char name[30];
  char street[40];
  char city[20];
  char state[3];
  char zip[10]; /* hold US and Canadian zips */
  struct addr *left;  /* pointer to left subtree */
  struct addr *right;  /* pointer to right subtree */
};
```

If you follow the top-down approach, your programs will not only be much easier to read, but will take less time to develop and less effort to maintain.

Bulletproof Functions

In large programs, especially those that control potentially life-threatening events, the potential for error has to be very slight. Although small programs can be verified as correct, this is not the case for large ones. (A verified program is proved to be free of errors and will never malfunction — in theory at least.) For example, consider a program that controls the wing flaps of a 767 jet. You cannot test all possible interactions of the numerous forces that will be exerted on the plane. This means that you cannot test the program exhaustively. At best, all that you can say is that it performed correctly in such and such situations. In a program of this type, the last thing that you (as a passenger or programmer) want is a crash (of the program or the plane).

After you have programmed for a few years, you learn that most program crashes outside the initial development stage occur because one function inadvertently interferes with another function's code or data. Therefore, to reduce the chance of a catastrophic failure, you will want your functions and their data to be as "bulletproof" as possible. The best way to achieve this is to keep the code and data related to each function hidden from the rest of the program. This is sometimes called *hiding code and data.*

Hiding code and data is similar to telling a secret only to those who need to know. Simply put, if a function does not need to know about another function or variable, don't let the function have access to it. You must follow three rules to accomplish this:

1. Each functional unit must have one entry point and one exit point.

2. Wherever possible, pass information to functions instead of using global variables.

3. Where global variables are required by a few related functions, you should place both the variables and the functions in a separate file. Also, the global variables must be declared as **static**.

Keep in mind that strict adherence to these rules will not be applicable in every situation. However, you must follow the rules when the highest degree of fault tolerance is required. The goal of this approach is to create a program that has the highest likelihood of recovering unharmed from an error condition. For example, if the program that controls the flaps on the 767 experiences an out-of-range condition, it must not crash. Rather, it should simply wait a few clock ticks and try again.

Rule 1 states that each functional area has one entry point and one exit point. This means that although a functional unit may contain several functions, the rest of the program only communicates through one of them. Think about the mailing-list program discussed earlier. There are seven functional areas. You could place all of the functions needed by each functional area in their own files and compile them separately. If done correctly, the only way in or out of each functional unit is through its top-level function. And, in the mailing-list program, these top-level functions are called only by **main( )**, thereby preventing one functional unit from accidentally damaging another. This situation is depicted in Figure 27-1.

Although it decreases performance, the best way to reduce the possibility of side effects is always to pass all information needed by a function to that function. Never use global data. This is rule 2, and if you have ever programmed a large program in standard BASIC—where every variable is global—you already understand its importance.

Rule 3 states that when global data must be used, the global data and the functions that need to access it should be placed in one file and compiled separately. The key is to declare the global data as **static**, thereby keeping knowledge of it from the other files.

Even if you follow these rules, you can still have a program crash, but it is less likely. Also, even though you still cannot *prove* that your

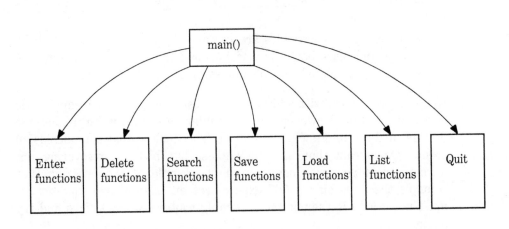

Figure 27-1.   Each functional unit has only one entry point

program is correct, you can more easily verify that it *should be* correct because of the controls that you have in place.

Function Prototypes

The ANSI standard added support for function prototypes. Although old-style compilers do not support this feature, most current compilers do. You should definitely use full function prototypes if your compiler supports them. Function prototypes help you trap bugs before they occur. Moreover, they help verify that your program is working correctly by not allowing functions to be called with mismatched arguments.

LINT and MAKE

LINT and MAKE are two important utility programs that are often supplied with the C compiler. They can greatly aid in the development of large programs. Although the exact implementation of these programs varies slightly, this section presents a general discussion of both utilities.

LINT

By nature, C is forgiving and tries to do something reasonable with what you have written. Although this is generally a virtue, it can also make certain bugs very hard to find. The LINT utility reads your C program, looking for suspicious or unnecessary code. For example, LINT checks for type mismatches between the arguments used to call a function and those expected. Although function prototyping also catches this type of error, it may not be supported by your compiler. The type checking provided by LINT may be the only way you can check type mismatches.

LINT also reports variables that are declared but never used. In large programs, it is easy to have unused variables because of changes made during development. Not only do unused variables take up space, but they confuse anyone that reads the code. For example, LINT reports that **count** is not used in the following function:

```
void f(void)
{
  int i, count;

  for(i=0; i<10; i++) printf("%d ", i);
}
```

LINT also spots unused functions.

A somewhat more complex thing that most LINTs find is the use of an uninitialized variable in the right-hand side of an assignment statement. For example,

```
void main(void)
{
  int num;
  char s[80];

  num = atoi(s);
}
```

causes LINT to display a warning message because **s** has never been assigned a value.

You can tell LINT to point out statements in your program that may cause portability problems—that is, things in your program that may work correctly in the current host environment but not in other environments. This feature is useful when you are writing for a variety of environments.

Depending upon the implementation, LINT may do several other checks on your program's source file. Be sure to check your compiler's user's manual.

Some compilers provide LINT-like checking during the compilation process. You generally turn on this extra checking by specifying that various warning messages be displayed. For example, most compilers allow you to request that unused variables or suspicious type conversions be reported.

MAKE

MAKE is a utility program that automates the recompilation process for large programs composed of several files. As you probably know, many small changes will be made to some files in the course of program development. Then the program is recompiled and tested. Unfortunately, it is easy to forget which of the files need to be recompiled. In this situation, you may either recompile all the files—a waste of time— or accidentally not recompile a file that should be, potentially adding several hours of frustrating debugging. The MAKE program solves this problem by automatically recompiling only those files that have been altered.

The examples presented here use the MAKE program supplied with Microsoft C. Although other implementations may vary, the general concepts are the same.

MAKE is driven by a *make file,* which contains a list of target files, dependent files, and commands. A *target file* requires its *dependent files* to produce it. For example, T.C would be the dependent file of T.OBJ because T.C is required to make T.OBJ. MAKE works by comparing the dates between a dependent file and its target file. (As used here, the term *date* includes both the calendar date and the time.) If the target file has a date that is older than its dependent file or if it does not exist, the specified command sequence is executed. The general form of the make file is

> *target_file1 : dependent_file list*
>   *command_sequence*
>
> *target_file2 : dependent_file list*
>   *command_sequence*
>
> *target_file3 : dependent_file list*
>   *command_sequence*
>
> .
> .
> .
>
> *target_fileN : dependent_file list*
>   *command_sequence*

TEST.H

```
extern int count;
```

TEST.C

```
#include "stdio.h"
void test2(void), test3(void);

int count=0;

void main(void)
{
  printf("count=%d\n", count);
  test2();
  printf("count=%d\n", count);
  test3();
  printf("count=%d\n", count);
}
```

TEST2.C

```
#include "stdio.h"
#include "test.h"

void test2(void)
{
  count = 30;
}
```

TEST3.C

```
#include "stdio.h"
#include "test.h"

void test3(void)
{
  count = -100;
}
```

Figure 27-2.   A simple four-file program

The target file name must start in the leftmost column and be followed by a colon and its list of dependent files. The command sequence associated with each target must be preceded by at least one space or a tab. Comments are preceded by a # and may follow the dependent file list and the command sequence. If they appear on a line of their own, they must start in the leftmost column. Each target-file specification must be separated from the next by at least one blank line.

To see how MAKE works, consider a very simple program. The program is divided into four files called TEST.H, TEST.C, TEST2.C, and TEST3.C. (To follow along, enter each part of the program into the indicated files.) This situation is illustrated in Figure 27-2.

A make file that you can use to recompile the program when you make changes looks like this:

```
test.exe:   test.h
        cl -c test.c
        cl -c test2.c
        cl -c test3.c

test.obj: test.c
        cl -c test.c

test2.obj: test2.c
        cl -c test2.c

test3.obj: test3.c
        cl -c test3.c

test.exe: test.obj test2.obj test3.obj
        cl test.obj test2.obj test3.obj
```

If the name of this file is TEST, you would type

```
make test
```

at the command prompt to compile the necessary modules and create an executable program.

Order is very important in the make file because many versions of MAKE only move through the list in the forward direction. For example, if the TEST make file were changed to look like this:

```
# this is an incorrect make file
test.obj: test.c
        cl -c test.c

test2.obj: test2.c
        cl -c test2.c

test3.obj: test3.c
        cl -c test3.c

test.exe: test.obj test2.obj test3.obj
        cl test.obj test2.obj test3.obj

test.exe:  test.h
        cl -c test.c
        cl -c test2.c
        cl -c test3.c
```

it would no longer work correctly when the file TEST.H and any other source file were changed. This is because changing a source file creates a new TEST.EXE. Therefore, its date will no longer be older than TEST.H.

MAKE allows macros to be defined in the make file. These macro names are simply placeholders for the information that will actually be determined either by a command-line specification or by the macro's definition in the make file. Macros are defined according to this general form:

$$macro\_name = definition$$

If there is to be any white space in the macro definition, you must enclose the definition within double quotes.

Once a macro has been defined, it is used in the make file like this:

$$\$(macro\_name)$$

Each time this statement is encountered, the definition linked to the macro is substituted.

For example, this make file uses the macro **LIBFIL** to determine which library is used by the linker:

```
LIBFIL = graphics

prog.exe: prog.obj prog2.obj prog3.obj
        link prog+prog2+prog3,,,$(LIBFIL);
```

If the name of the link file is GRCOMP, this command line links the program with the graphics library specified in the file:

```
>make grcomp
```

However, the following command line overrides the internal definition of **LIBFIL** and causes GRTEMP to be used as the library file:

```
>make LIBFIL=grtemp grcomp
```

Many MAKE programs have additional features, so it is very important to consult your user's manual.

Efficiency, Porting, and Debugging

Efficiency
Porting Programs
Debugging
The Art of Program Maintenance

The ability to write programs that make efficient use of system resources, are bug-free, and can be transported to a new computer is the mark of a professional programmer. It is also in these areas that computer science becomes the "art of computer science" because there are so few formal techniques that ensure success. This chapter presents some of the methods to achieve efficiency, enhance program debugging, and increase portability.

Efficiency

In programming, the term *efficiency* can refer to the speed of execution, the use of system resources, or both. System resources include such things as RAM, disk space, printer paper, and the like—basically anything that you can allocate and use up. Whether a program is efficient or not is sometimes a subjective judgment that can change from situation to situation. For example, consider a sorting program that uses 128K of RAM, requires 2MB of disk space, and whose average run time is seven hours. If this program is sorting only 100 addresses in a mailing-list database, it is not very efficient. However, if the program is sorting the New York telephone directory, it is probably quite efficient.

In addition, optimizing one aspect of a program often degrades another. For example, making a program execute faster also often means making it bigger when you use in-line code to eliminate the overhead of a function call. By the same token, making a program smaller by replacing in-line code with function calls makes the program run slower. In the same vein, making more efficient use of disk space means compacting the data, which can often make disk accesses slower. These and other types of efficiency trade-offs can be very frustrating—especially to nonprogrammers and end users who cannot see why one thing should affect the other.

Fortunately, there are some programming practices that are always efficient—or, at least, more efficient than others. Also, there are a few techniques that make programs both faster and smaller. This chapter examines these techniques.

The Increment and Decrement Operators

Discussions on the efficient use of C almost always start with the increment and decrement operators. In case you have forgotten, the increment operator, + +, increases its operand by one, and the decrement operator, − −, decreases it by one. For example, both of these statements are the same in final effect:

```
x = x + 1;

x++;
```

Both increase the value of **x** by one. However, the increment statement executes faster and requires less RAM than its assignment statement counterpart. This is because of the way object code is generated by the compiler. Often, as is the case for most microcomputers, you can increment or decrement a word of memory without using explicit load and store instructions. For example, by using an imaginary assembly language that loosely approximates that found on many microprocessors, the statement

```
x = x + 1;
```

generates object code that looks something like this:

```
move A, x   ; load value of x from memory into
            ;   accumulator
add A, 1    ; add 1 to the accumulator
store x     ; store new value back in x
```

If, however, you used the increment operator, the following code would be produced:

```
incr x    ; increase x by 1
```

As you can see, both the load and store instructions are eliminated, which means that the code executes faster and is smaller. Although many of the better compilers automatically optimize a statement like **x = x + 1** into **x + +**, you should not take this for granted.

Using Register Variables

Without a doubt, you should use **register** variables for loop control wherever possible. Any variable specified as **register** is stored in a manner that produces the shortest access time. For integer types, this usually means a register of the CPU. This is important because the speed with which the critical loops of a program execute sets the pace for the overall program speed.

To show how the code differs between a **register** variable and a regular memory variable, this program was compiled to an assembly-language file using Microsoft C version 5.1. (**j** is declared as a global variable because Microsoft C automatically makes the first two local integer variables into **register** types. Declaring it as a global variable prevents this.)

```
int j;

void main(void)
{
  register int i;

  for(i=0; i<100 ;i++) ;

  for(j=0; j<100; j++) ;
}
```

The assembly-code file produced is shown here. The comments beginning with asterisks were added by the author.

```
;          Static Name Aliases
;
           TITLE    test.c
           NAME     test

           .8087
_TEXT     SEGMENT  WORD PUBLIC 'CODE'
_TEXT     ENDS
_DATA     SEGMENT  WORD PUBLIC 'DATA'
_DATA     ENDS
CONST     SEGMENT  WORD PUBLIC 'CONST'
CONST     ENDS
_BSS      SEGMENT  WORD PUBLIC 'BSS'
_BSS      ENDS
DGROUP    GROUP    CONST, _BSS, _DATA
          ASSUME   CS: _TEXT, DS: DGROUP, SS: DGROUP
EXTRN     __acrtused:ABS
EXTRN     __chkstk:NEAR
_BSS         SEGMENT
COMM NEAR          _j:       BYTE:     2
_BSS         ENDS
_TEXT        SEGMENT
          ASSUME   CS: _TEXT
; Line 4
          PUBLIC   _main
_main     PROC NEAR
          push     bp
          mov      bp,sp
          mov      ax,2
          call     __chkstk
          push     si
;         register si = i
; Line 7
; ****** This is the initialization of the register
; ****** controlled loop.  Notice that SI is cleared
; ****** using a subtraction instruction.
          sub      si,si
          jmp      SHORT $F104
$FC105:
; ****** a register increment
          inc      si
$F104:
; ****** a register comparison
          cmp      si,100
          jl       $FC105
; Line 9
; ****** This is the initialization of the memory
; ****** controlled loop.  Notice that a memory access
; ****** is required to zero the variable.
          mov      WORD PTR _j,0
          jmp      SHORT $F107
$FC108:
; ****** Here, a memory access is required to increment
; ****** j.
          inc      WORD PTR _j
$F107:
```

```
; ****** Here, a memory access required to compare
; ****** j with the target value.
        cmp     WORD PTR _j,100
        jl      $FC108
; Line 10
        pop     si
        mov     sp,bp
        pop     bp
        ret

_main   ENDP
_TEXT   ENDS
END
```

To get an idea of the differences in execution time, assume that an 8086 processor executes this program. The register-controlled loop uses the instruction **cmp si, 100** to compare i's value against the target value of **100**. This requires only four system clock ticks. On the other hand, the memory-controlled loop must use **cmp WORD PTR _j,100**, which requires at least 20 clock ticks, and more if the program is compiled for a large data model!

Although you can declare as many variables as you like as **register**, in reality, most compilers can only optimize the access time of a few. For example, generally only two integer type variables can be held in registers of the CPU. In fact, the ANSI standard states, in effect, that the compiler can disregard the **register** specifier and simply handle the variable normally. The reason for this provision is that in many environments there are only a limited number of fast-access storage locations. Thus, it is best to choose carefully those variables that you want to be accessed the fastest.

Pointers Versus Array Indexing

You can also substitute pointer arithmetic for array indexing to produce both smaller and faster code. Pointers generally make your code run faster and take up less space. For example, the following two code fragments do the same thing:

```
array indexing          pointer arithmetic

                        p = array;
for(;;) {               for(;;) {
    a = array[t++];         a = *(p++);
```

```
    .                    .
    .                    .
    .                    .
}                    }
```

The advantage of the pointer method is that once **p** has been loaded with the address of **array** (perhaps in an index register such as **SI** on the 8086 processor), only an increment must be performed each time the loop repeats. However, the array index version must always compute the array index based on the value of **t** — a more complex task. The disparity in the execution speeds of array indexing and pointer arithmetic gets wider as you use multiple indexes. Each index requires its own sequence of instructions, whereas the pointer arithmetic equivalent can use simple addition.

Be careful. You should use array indexes when the index is derived through a very complex formula and pointer arithmetic would obscure the meaning of the program. It is usually better to degrade performance slightly than to sacrifice clarity.

Use of Functions

Remember at all times that the use of stand-alone functions with local variables helps form the basis of structured programming. Functions are the building blocks of C programs and are one of C's strongest assets. Do not let anything that is discussed in this chapter be construed otherwise. Having been warned, there are a few things that you should know about C functions and their ramifications on the size and speed of your code.

First and foremost, C is a stack-oriented language. This means that all local variables and parameters to functions use the stack for temporary storage. When a function is called, the return address of the calling routine is placed on the stack as well. This enables the subroutine to return to the location from which it was called. When a function returns, this address and all local variables and parameters have to be removed from the stack. The process of pushing this information is generally referred to as the *calling sequence,* and the popping process is called the *returning sequence.* These sequences take time — sometimes quite a bit of time.

To understand how a function call can slow down your program, look at these two code fragments:

```
version 1                         version 2

for(x=1; x<100; ++x) {            for(x=1; x<100; ++x) {
  t = compute(x);                   t = abs(sin(q)/100/3.1416);
}                                 }

float compute(int q)
{
  return abs(sin(q)/100/3.1416);
}
```

Although each loop performs the same function, version 2 is much faster because the overhead of the calling and returning sequence has been eliminated through the use of in-line code.

Look at another example, this time one that involves assembly code output by the Microsoft C version 5.1 compiler. This program

```
void main(void)
{
   int x;

   x = max(10, 20);
}

max(int a, int b)
{
  return a>b ? a : b;
}
```

produces the following assembly code. The calling and returning sequences are indicated by comments beginning with asterisks added by the author. As you can see, they amount to a sizable part of the program code.

```
;       Static Name Aliases
;
        TITLE   test.c
        NAME    test

        .8087
_TEXT   SEGMENT  WORD PUBLIC 'CODE'
_TEXT   ENDS
_DATA   SEGMENT  WORD PUBLIC 'DATA'
_DATA   ENDS
CONST   SEGMENT  WORD PUBLIC 'CONST'
CONST   ENDS
_BSS    SEGMENT  WORD PUBLIC 'BSS'
_BSS    ENDS
DGROUP  GROUP    CONST, _BSS, _DATA
```

```
        ASSUME  CS: _TEXT, DS: DGROUP, SS: DGROUP
EXTRN   __acrtused:ABS
EXTRN   __chkstk:NEAR
_TEXT       SEGMENT
        ASSUME  CS: _TEXT
; Line 3
        PUBLIC  _main
_main   PROC NEAR
        push    bp
        mov     bp,sp
        mov     ax,2
        call    __chkstk
;       x = -2
; Line 6
; ***** The calling sequence ****************
        mov     ax,20
        push    ax
        mov     ax,10
        push    ax
        call    _max
; ****************************************
        mov     WORD PTR [bp-2],ax      ;x
; Line 7
        mov     sp,bp
        pop     bp
        ret
        nop


_main   ENDP
; Line 10
        PUBLIC  _max
_max    PROC NEAR
; ***** More of the calling sequence ********
        push    bp
        mov     bp,sp
        xor     ax,ax
        call    __chkstk
; ****************************************
;       a = 4
;       b = 6
; Line 11
        mov     ax,WORD PTR [bp+4]      ;a
        cmp     ax,WORD PTR [bp+6]      ;b
        jge     $EX106
; ***** The returning sequence. *************
        mov     ax,WORD PTR [bp+6]      ;b
$EX106:
        pop     bp
        ret
; ****************************************
        nop


_max    ENDP
_TEXT   ENDS
END
```

The actual code produced depends on how the compiler is implemented and what processor is being used, but it will generally be similar to this.

Now you may think that you should write programs that have just a few very large functions so that they run quickly. This is probably not a good idea. First, in the vast majority of cases the slight time differential gained by using large functions is not meaningful and the loss of structure is acute. But there is another problem. Replacing functions that are used by several routines with in-line code causes your program to become very large because the same code is duplicated several times. Keep in mind that subroutines were invented largely as a way to make efficient use of memory. In fact, this is why, as a rule of thumb, making a program faster means making it bigger, while making it smaller means making it slower.

In the final analysis, it really makes sense to use in-line code instead of a function call only when speed is the overriding priority. Otherwise, the liberal use of functions is definitely recommended.

Porting Programs

It is common for a program written on one machine to be transported to another computer with a different processor, operating system, or both. This process is called *porting,* and can be very easy or extremely hard, depending upon how the program was originally written. A program that can be easily ported is called *portable.* When a program is not easily portable, this is usually because it contains numerous *machine dependencies*—that is, it has code fragments that work only with one specific operating system or processor. C allows you to create portable code, but achieving this goal still requires care and attention to detail. This section examines a few specific problem areas and offers some solutions.

Using #define

Perhaps the simplest way to make programs portable is to make every system- or processor-dependent "magic number" a **#define** macro substitution directive. These magic numbers include things like buffer sizes for disk accesses, special screen and keyboard commands, memory allocation information, and the like—that is, anything that has the slightest possibility of changing when the program is ported. These **#define**s not only make all magic numbers obvious to the person doing the porting, but also simplify the editing job because their values have to be changed only once instead of throughout the program.

For example, here is an **fread( )** statement that is inherently nonportable:

```
fread(buf, 128, 1, fp);
```

The problem is that the buffer size, 128, is hardcoded into **fread( )**. This might work for one operating system but be less than optimal for another. Here is a better way to code this function:

```
#define BUF_SIZE 128
fread(buf, BUF_SIZE, 1, fp);
```

In this case, when moving to a different system, only the **#define** has to change and all references to **BUF_SIZE** are automatically corrected. This not only makes it easier to change, but also avoids many editing errors. Remember that there will probably be many references to **BUF_SIZE** in a real program, so the gain in portability is often great.

Operating-System Dependencies

Virtually all commercial programs contain code specific to the operating system. For example, a spreadsheet program might use the PC's video memory to allow fast switching between screens, or a graphics package might use special graphics commands that are only applicable to that operating system. The point is that some operating-system dependencies are necessary for truly good, fast, and commercially viable programs. However, there is no reason to hard-code any more dependencies than necessary.

When you must use system calls to directly access the operating system, it is best to access them all through one master function. In this way, only the master function need be changed to accommodate a new operating system, and you can leave the rest of the code intact. For example, if system calls are needed to clear the screen, clear to the end of the line, and locate the cursor at an X,Y coordinate, you should create a master function, such as **op＿sys＿call**( ), shown here:

```
void op_sys_call(char op, int x, int y)
{
  switch(op) {
    case 1: clear_screen();
    break;
    case 2: clear_eol();
    break;
    case 3: goto_xy(x, y);
    break;
  }
}
```

In this way, only the code that forms the actual functions has to change, leaving a common interface intact.

Differences in Data Sizes

As you may know, the size of a word in a 16-bit processor is 16 bits; in a 32-bit processor it is 32 bits. Because the size of a word tends to be the size of an integer, you must never make assumptions about the size of a data type if you wish to write portable code. Therefore, use **sizeof**( ) whenever your program needs to know how many bytes long something is. For example, this function writes an integer to a disk file and works on any computer:

```
void write_int(int i)
{
  fwrite(&i, sizeof(int), 1, stream);
}
```

Sometimes, however, you cannot create portable code even with **sizeof**( ). For example, this function (which swaps the bytes in an integer) works on an 8086-based computer but fails on a 68000. This function cannot be made portable because in the 8086 integers are 2 bytes long.

```
void swap_bytes(int *x)
{
  union sb {
    int t;
    unsigned char c[2];
  } swap;

  unsigned char temp;

  swap.t = *x;
  temp = swap.c[1];
  swap.c[1] = swap.c[0];
  swap.c[0] = temp;
  *x = swap.t;
}
```

Debugging

To paraphrase Thomas Edison, programming is 10% inspiration and
90% debugging. All really good programmers are good debuggers. The
types of bugs that can occur easily while you are using C are the topic of
this section.

Order-of-Process Errors

The increment and decrement operators are used in most programs
written in C, and the order in which the operations take place is affected
by whether these operators precede or follow the variable. Consider the
following:

```
y = 10;          y = 10;

x = y++;         x = ++y;
```

These two statements are not the same. The first one assigns the value
of **10** to x and then increments y. The second increments y to **11** and
then assigns the value **11** to x. Therefore, in the first case x contains **10**;
in the second, x contains **11**. The rule is that increment and decrement
operations occur before other operations if they precede the operand;
otherwise, they happen afterwards.

The way an order-of-process error usually occurs is through changes to an existing statement. For example, you may enter the statement

```
x = *p++;
```

which assigns the value pointed to by **p** to **x** and then increments the pointer **p**. Say, however, that later you decide that **x** really needs the value pointed to by **p** times the value pointed to by **p**. To do this, you try

```
x = *p++ * (*p);
```

However, this can't work because **p** has already been incremented. The proper solution is to write

```
x = *p * (*p++);
```

Errors like this can be very hard to find. There may be clues such as loops that don't run right or routines that are off by one. If you have any doubt about a statement, recode it in a way that you are sure about.

Pointer Problems

A very common error in C programs is the misuse of pointers. Pointer problems fall into two general categories: misunderstanding indirection and the pointer operators, and accidentally using invalid pointers. The solution to the first problem is to understand the C language; the solution to the second is always to verify the validity of a pointer before it is used.

What follows is a typical C programming error:

```
/* This program has an error. */
#include "stdlib.h"
#include "stdio.h"

void main(void)
{
  char *p;

  *p = malloc(100); /* this line is wrong */
```

```
  gets(p);
  printf(p);
}
```

This program will most likely crash — probably taking the operating system with it. The reason is that the address returned by **malloc( )** was not assigned to **p** but rather to the memory location pointed to by **p**, which in this case is completely unknown. To correct this program, you must substitute

```
p = malloc(100); /* this is correct */
```

for the wrong line.

The program also contains a second and more insidious error. There is no run-time check on the address returned by **malloc( )**. Remember, if memory is exhausted, **malloc( )** returns **NULL**, which is never a valid pointer in C. The malfunction caused by this type of bug is difficult to find because it occurs rarely, when an allocation request fails. The best way to handle this problem is to prevent it. What follows is a corrected version of the program, which includes a check for pointer validity:

```
/* This program is now correct. */

#include "stdio.h"
#include "stdlib.h"

void main(void)
{
  char *p;

  p = malloc(100); /* this is correct */

  if(!p) {
    printf("out of memory\n");
    exit(1);
  }

  gets(p);
  printf(p);
}
```

The terrible thing about wild pointers is that they are so hard to track down. If you are making assignments to a pointer variable that does not contain a valid pointer address, your program may appear to function correctly some of the time and crash at other times. The smaller your program, the more likely that it will run correctly, even with a stray pointer. This is because very little memory is in use and the odds of that memory being used by something else is statistically small. As your program grows, failures will become more common, but you will be thinking about current additions or changes to your program, not about pointer errors. Hence, you will tend to look in the wrong spot for the bug.

The way to recognize a pointer problem is that errors tend to be erratic. Your program will work right one time, wrong another. Sometimes other variables will contain garbage for no apparent reason. If these problems begin to occur, check your pointers. As a matter of procedure, you should always check all pointers when bugs begin to occur.

As a consolation, remember that although pointers can be troublesome, they are also one of the most powerful aspects of the C language and are worth whatever trouble they may cause you. Make the effort early on to learn to use them correctly.

One final point to remember about pointers is that you must initialize them before they are used. Consider the following code fragment:

```
int *x;

*x = 100;
```

This will be a disaster because you don't know where **x** is pointing. Assigning a value to that unknown location is probably destroying something of value, such as other code or data for your program.

Bizarre Syntax Errors

Once in a while you will see a syntax error that you cannot understand or see why it is an error. Sometimes, the C compiler itself may have a bug that causes it to report false errors. The only way around this bug is to redesign your code. Finding other unusual errors simply requires some backtracking on your part.

One particularly unsettling error occurs when you try to compile the following code.

```
char *myfunc();

void main(void)
{
  char *p;

    .
    .
    .
}

myfunc()
{
    .
    .
    .
}
```

Most compilers issue an error message similar to **function redefined** and point to **myfunc( )**. How can this be? There are not two **myfunc( )**s. The answer is that you declared **myfunc( )** as returning a character pointer at the top of the program. This caused a symbol table entry to be made with that information. When the compiler encountered **myfunc( )** later in the program, there was no indication that it was to be returning anything other than an integer, the default type. Hence you were "redefining" the function.

Another syntax error that is difficult to understand is generated with the following code:

```
/* This program has a syntax error in it. */
#include "stdio.h"

void func1(void);

void main(void)
{
  func1();
}

void func1(void);
{
  printf("this is func1 \n");
}
```

The error here is the semicolon after the declaration of **func1( )**. The compiler will see this as a statement outside of any function, which is an error. However, the way that various compilers report this error differs.

Many compilers issue an error message like **bad declaration syntax** while pointing at the first open brace after **func1( )**. Because you are used to seeing semicolons after statements, it can be very hard to see the source of this error.

One-Off Errors

As you should know by now, in C all array indexes start at 0. A common error involves using a **for** loop to access the elements of an array. Consider the following program, which is supposed to initialize an array of 100 integers:

```
/* This program will not work. */

void main(void)
{
    int x, num[100];

    for(x=1; x<=100; ++x) num[x]=x;
}
```

The **for** loop in this program is wrong in two ways. First, it does not initialize **num[0]**, the first element of array **num**. Second, it goes one past the end of the array because **num[99]** is the last element in the array and the loop runs to 100. The correct way to write this program is

```
/* This is right. */

void main(void)
{
  int x, num[100];

    for(x=0; x<100; ++x) num[x]=x;
}
```

Remember, an array of 100 has elements 0 through 99.

Boundary Errors

Both the C run-time environment and many standard library functions have very little or no run-time bounds checking. For example, you can overwrite arrays. Consider the following program, which is supposed to read a string from the keyboard and display it on the screen:

```
#include "stdio.h"

void main(void)
{
  int var1;
  char s[10];
  int var2;

  var1 = 10;  var2 = 10;
  gets(s);
  printf("%s %d %s", s, var1, var2);
}
```

Here, there are no direct coding errors. Indirectly, however, calling **gets( )** with **s** may cause a bug. In the program, **s** is declared to be ten characters long, but what if the user enters more than ten characters? This causes **s** to be overwritten. The real problem is that **s** may display all characters, but either **var1** or **var2** will not contain the correct value. This is because virtually all C compilers use the stack to store local variables. The variables **var1**, **var2**, and **s** will be located in memory as shown in Figure 28-1.

Figure 28-1.   The variables **var1**, **var2**, and **s** in memory

Your C compiler may exchange the order of **var1** and **var2**, but they still bracket **s**. When **s** is overwritten, the additional information is placed into the area that is supposed to be **var2**, destroying any previous contents. Therefore, instead of printing the number **10** for both integer variables, the variable destroyed by the overrun of **s** displays something else. This makes you look for the problem in the wrong place. Also, in this specific instance the return address of the function call may also be overwritten, causing a crash.

Function-Prototype Omissions

Any time a function returns a value type other than integer, you must declare the function as such using its prototype. If you do not include a function's prototype, the compiler assumes that it returns an integer — whether or not it does. Consider the following program, which multiplies two floating-point numbers:

```
/* This program is wrong. */
#include "stdio.h"

void main(void)
{
  float x, y;

  scanf("%f%f", &x, &y);
  printf("%f", mul(x, y));
}

float mul(float a, float b)
{
  return a*b;
}
```

Here, **main( )** expects an integer value back from **mul( )**, but **mul( )** returns a floating-point number. You get meaningless answers because **main( )** only copies 2 bytes out of the 8 needed for a **float**. Although C catches this error if these functions are both in the same file, it cannot if they are in separately compiled modules and no prototype for **mul( )** was included. In fact, the preceding program is an excellent illustration of why you should prototype all functions in your program.

The way to correct this program is to prototype **mul( )**. The corrected version follows.

```
/* This program is correct. */
#include "stdio.h"
float mul(float a, float b);

void main(void)
{
 float x, y;

  scanf("%f%f", &x, &y);
  printf("%f", mul(x, y));
}

float mul(float a, float b)
{
  return a*b;
}
```

Here, the prototype tells **main( )** to expect **mul( )** to return a floating-point value.

Argument Errors

You must be sure to match whatever type of argument a function expects with the type you give it. An important example is **scanf( )**. Remember that **scanf( )** expects to receive the *addresses* of its arguments, not their values. For example,

```
int x;
char string[10];

scanf("%d%s", x, string);
```

is wrong, while

```
scanf("%d%s", &x, string);
```

is correct. Recall that strings already pass their addresses to functions, so you should not use the **&** operator on them.

Stack-Heap Collisions

Although some C compilers do not allow the stack to collide with the heap, many do. When this happens, the program either dies completely or continues executing at a bizarre point. This second symptom is due to data being used accidentally as a return address. The worst thing about stack-heap collisions is that they generally occur without any warning and kill the program so completely that debug code cannot execute. Another problem is that stack-heap collisions often appear to be wild pointers and thus mislead you. The only advice that can be offered is that most stack-heap collisions are caused by runaway recursive functions. If your program uses recursion and you experience unexplainable failures, check the terminating conditions in your recursive functions.

Debugging Theory in General

Everyone has a different approach to programming and debugging. However, certain techniques have, over time, proven to be better than others. In the case of debugging, incremental testing is considered to be the most cost- and time-effective method, even though it can appear to slow the development process at first. To understand what incremental testing is, you must first see what it is not.

In the early days of computers, programmers were taught to prepare their programs in advance, submit them for execution, and then interpret results. This is called *batch programming*, and was necessary when computers were scarce. Batch programming helped give computers a bad image in the early 1960s because it required programmers to expend an enormous amount of time and mental energy developing a program. Because all testing had to be done in batch mode as well, it was difficult to try all possible conditions in which a program could fail. This lack of thorough testing led to the pervasive "computer error" problems so common in many early computer installations.

Today, batch programming is almost extinct because it can not support an interactive incremental testing environment. *Incremental testing* is the process of always having a working program. That is, very early in the development process, an operational unit is established. An *operational unit* is simply a piece of working code. As new code is added to this unit, it is tested and debugged. In this way, the programmer can easily find errors because the errors probably occur in the newly added code or in the way that it interacts with the operational unit.

Debugging time is proportional to this formula:

$$\text{DebugTime} = T * (num\_lines)^2$$

where *num_lines* is the total number of lines of code that a bug could be in and T is some constant (programmer dependent) unit of time. As you can see, debugging time is a squared quantity. With incremental testing, you can restrict the number of lines of code to only those that are newly added—that is, not part of the operational unit. This situation is shown in Figure 28-2.

Incremental testing theory is generally based on probability and areas. As you know, area is a squared dimension. Therefore, as your program grows there is an n-squared area that you must search for bugs. As a programmer, you want to deal with the smallest possible area while debugging. Through incremental testing, you can subtract the area already tested from the total area, thereby reducing the region in which a bug may be found.

In large projects, there are often several modules that have little interaction. In these cases, you can establish several operational units to allow concurrent development.

There are two reasons that incremental testing is so important. First, it greatly reduces debugging time because errors are easier to find. Second, it speeds up the development process because design errors can be caught early on in the project—before all the code is written. (Of course, this should never take the place of a good design!)

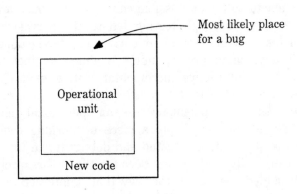

Figure 28-2. The most likely location of a bug when incremental testing is used

Incremental testing is simply the process of always having working code. As soon as it is possible to run a piece of your program, you should do so, testing that section completely. As you add to the program, continue to test the new sections as well as the way they connect to the known operational code. In this way, you concentrate any possible bugs in a small area of code.

The Art of Program Maintenance

Once a program has been written, tested, debugged, and—finally—judged ready for use, the program's development phase is over and its maintenance phase begins. Most programmers like the glamour and excitement of developing a new program but try to avoid being the one to maintain it. This is, in part, because the maintenance phase never ends. When a program is being developed, even a very large one, there is always light at the end of the tunnel. Someday the program will be done. However, the maintenance phase is a daily grind of quirks, anomalies, errors, and bugs. The maintenance programmer may never feel the thrill of accomplishment, and the only good part of the day may be quitting time. As bleak as it may seem, program maintenance can be a challenging and rewarding task if you approach it correctly.

The maintenance programmer has two responsibilities:

- Correcting bugs
- Providing source-code protection

Fixing Bugs

All nontrivial programs have bugs. This is one of the unprovable but irrefutable truths of computer science. The hard part about maintaining a program is that all of the easy bugs are found during the development stage. The bugs that the maintenance programmer must find and fix are often very obscure and only turn up under devilishly complex and difficult to re-create circumstances. If you like real challenges, perhaps program maintenance is for you.

There are basically three types of bugs: those that you must fix (category 1), those that you would like to fix (category 2), and those that you just plain aren't going to worry about (category 3). Category 1 bugs crash the system, scribble on the disk, or destroy data. For example, the bug that causes a database program to occasionally trash the database disk file simply must be fixed because it renders the program unusable. Category 2 bugs get fixed only when there are no category 1 bugs to fix. A category 2 bug is the bug that causes a word processor to, on rare occasions, incorrectly reformat a paragraph. Nothing is lost, the program doesn't die, and the user makes a manual adjustment. Category 2 bugs are, for the most part, annoyances to the user but they can be worked around. These bugs should be fixed, but they are not a number one priority. Finally, category 3 bugs are a nuisance, such as a word processor that always ejects an extra sheet of paper at the end of a print session. Sure, paper costs money, but not very much. Another type of category 3 bug is really not a bug at all, but a difference between the way the documentation says the program will work and the way it actually works. Category 3 bugs are rarely fixed; not because they shouldn't be, but because there are always too many category 1 and 2 bugs.

If you can organize the bugs you find into these three categories, you can budget your time accordingly.

Source-Code Protection

The maintenance programmer is often in charge of the source code to the program. Although most companies place a copy of the source code of the current version of the program in a bank box, it is usually out of date if it is ever needed. Generally, the code in the bank is viewed as the code of last resort. Actually, the maintenance programmer is in charge of protecting the company's source code. What this really means is not losing it!

The most common way that source code is lost is during the bug-fixing process. It works like this: Programmer A "fixes" a bug. In the process and unknown to A, an editing error deletes five lines of code elsewhere in the file. Programmer A compiles the program and checks to see if the bug is fixed. The bug appears to be fixed, so—and here is the important part—programmer A copies the "fixed" source code from the work directory back into the storage directory. Now five lines of code are missing and the program definitely has a new bug. But before this is discovered, programmer B, whose job it is to back up the hard disk, copies the new, mutilated copy of the program onto the off-site storage disk. Now the old source code is really gone.

There is only one way to prevent the preceding scenario: never destroy old versions of the program. The real error that occurred, aside from sloppy editing, was not that programmer A copied the altered source code back into the storage directory. The error was that programmer B overwrote the off-site storage media.

Here is how you must handle the source code to an evolving program to prevent its loss. First, create three directories. The first holds the currently released version of the program. This directory is only updated when a new release is made. The second directory contains the latest stable but unreleased version of the program. The third directory contains the evolving code. Next, perform off-site storage backups on a regular basis—for example, weekly—always using a new disk (or tape). Keep on file all previous backups. In this way, the off-site storage is never more than five days out of date if it is needed for a recovery.

New Directions

C++

Programming languages, like most things in life, are not static and unchanging but dynamic and evolving. No one language can be everything to every programmer for every situation. Although C is one of the best general-purpose programming languages, it is stretched to (and some would say beyond) its limits when used for very large programming efforts. The final part of this book contains an overview of the newest direction in C, one that addresses the programming of large projects: C++.

C++

Data Abstraction
Objects
Comments
Classes
Function Overloading
Operator Overloading
Other Features of C++

Originally called "C with classes," C++ was developed by Bjarne Stroustrup at Bell Laboratories in Murray Hill, New Jersey, in 1983. Since C++ is a superset of standard C, most of what you already know still applies. C++ was developed primarily to facilitate managing, programming, and maintaining large software systems.

One of the most criticized yet most loved aspects of C is that it gives you virtually unlimited freedom to do whatever you want without much complaint from the language. Unfortunately, in large projects in which many programmers use shared routines, this unlimited freedom can lead to major problems due to side effects. (*Large* as used here means software systems in excess of 50,000 to 100,000 lines of code.)

C++ attempts to keep the freedom and spirit of C by allowing you to create *black-box functional units* that have access strictly controlled. These black-box units are often called *objects*, and C++ is sometimes called an *object oriented language*. Unlike languages such as Ada or Modula-2, in C++ the use of these facilities is up to the programmer, in keeping with the original spirit of C. (If you know Modula-2, loosely speaking, C++ is to C what Modula-2 is to Pascal.)

All C keywords are also C++ keywords, including those added by the ANSI standard. However, C++ also adds the following keywords.

class	delete	friend
inline	overload	operator
new	public	this
virtual		

Although it is impossible to cover C++ in detail here, this chapter discusses a few of the more important and exciting parts. The three most important facilities that C++ adds to C are classes, function overloading, and operator overloading. Before discussing this in detail, a little background in data abstraction and object oriented languages is required.

Note: The examples in this chapter were tested using C++ version 1.07c for DOS by Zortech Incorporated. Zortech strayed only slightly from the original C++ in that it uses the extension .HPP for C++ header files instead of simply .H. If you are using a different C++ implementation, please make the appropriate change.

Data Abstraction

Imagine that your program requires two stack routines. One will be used to store integers and the other to store floating-point numbers. As you know, stack routines are composed of two basic functions: push and pop. However, because you need stacks for two separate data types, you must create four separate push and pop functions, all with different names. For example, you might call them **pushint( )**, **pushfloat( )**, **popint( )**, and **popfloat( )**. Although this works, you have created more complexity, on a conceptual level, than is inherent in the program. It would be much clearer simply to use the same function names—**push( )** and **pop( )**—with both **int**s and **float**s, and have the compiler automatically select the correct supporting routine. That is, it is conceptually clearer to disassociate the data type from the operation, a process called *data abstraction*. Figure 29-1 depicts this approach.

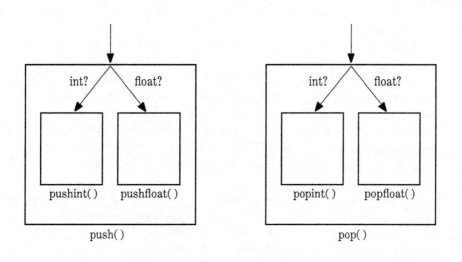

Figure 29-1.   **push( )** and **pop( )** for integers and floating-point numbers

Look at data abstraction from a different perspective. Imagine that you need to perform arithmetic operations on complex numbers. (Complex numbers have both a real and imaginary part. The imaginary part is in terms of the square root of −1.) You could create separate routines for the various operations. For example, **complex _ add( )** would add two complex numbers. However, it would be better if you could somehow use the plus sign, that is, if you could simply write

complex _ a = complex _ b + complex _ c;

In this situation, the compiler would automatically use an operation you previously defined for the addition of complex numbers.

All computer languages support limited amounts of data abstraction. For example, you use the same plus sign when adding **int**s or **float**s. The only thing you need to generalize this is some mechanism that allows you to define what a certain operation means relative to a programmer-defined type. As you will see shortly, C++ addresses this issue.

Objects

A key to managing a large program is to break it down into smaller pieces. The most fundamental level is the subroutine. Next comes separate files of related functions that form some functional unit. Although separate files definitely help manage a large program, they cannot control how the functions in the file are used. For example, say you need to create and maintain an integer stack. You must define two global variables: an integer array that is the stack space and an index into that array. You also need these three routines: **init_stack( )**, **push( )**, **pop( )**.

Using only C, the best protection you can give the elements that create and maintain the stack is to place them in a separate file and use the **static** modifier on the global data. However, this does not completely prevent the stack from being corrupted by a routine outside the file. For example, the function **init_stack( )** could be accidentally called while the stack still had items in it. The solution to this and other problems is to create an object that defines which functions and variables are known and accessible outside that object and those that are private. In this way, private routines cannot be called from outside the object. Likewise, variables that are not to be changed by routines outside the object are not visible.

A more important aspect of objects is that they provide a way of linking into a single unit variables and the functions that operate on them. For example, making the variables that hold the stack and the routines that manipulate a stack into a single object allows them to be thought of as a stack engine.

Keep in mind the concepts of objects and data abstraction as you look at a few of C++'s more important features in the sections that follow.

Comments

C++ allows the standard C comment mechanism **/*** and ***/** but also allows a second method. You may start a one-line comment with a **//** and terminate it with the end of the line. For example, these are valid C++ comments:

```
/* a C-like comment */

// this is a comment

a = b-c; // another comment
```

Classes

The single most important feature of C++ not found in regular C is the **class**. A **class** is similar to a **struct** in many ways and is used to allow the creation of objects. Essentially, a **class** permits the creation of a programmer-defined conglomerate type. In its definition, you may include information about variables, and you may also define precisely what functions have access to variables. For example, this **class** defines a data type called **over_drawn**, which holds the names of those unfortunates with overdrawn checking accounts.

```
class over_drawn {
   char name[30];
   char acc_num[10];
   float balance;
   int times_contacted;
   void delete_account(over_drawn bal);
public:
   void print_nasty_letter(over_drawn bal);
   void call_collection_agency(over_drawn bal);
   void cancel_account(over_drawn bal);
};
```

This example is somewhat similar to a structure. Any variable of type **over_drawn** has the fields **name**, **acc_num** and **times_contacted**. The two important differences, however, are the inclusion of function identifiers and the new keyword **public**.

The functions declared within the **class** are called *member functions*, which means that they may operate on any of the variables defined in the class. The keyword **public** controls access to the elements of a **class**. Identifiers that are declared before the word **public** can only be accessed by functions that are members of the **class**, and are called *private identifiers*. Identifiers that occur after **public** may be accessed by any other function in the program. Therefore, in this example, all variables of the **class** are private and can only be accessed through functions that are members of the **class**. Of the member functions, all are **public** except **delete_account( )**, which can only be called by one of the other member functions.

The fact that **delete_account( )** can only be called by another function that is a member of its **class** gives a clue about the benefit of classes. Imagine that you manage a team of programmers who are developing a bank accounting package (no small task). Because the deletion of an account is a serious event, you do not want every programmer to be able to call it. Making **delete_account( )** private helps to prevent its use.

Although all of the member functions are declared as taking **over_drawn** arguments, they could theoretically have taken any type of argument. If a function is a member of a **class** it has access to the private parts of that **class** — but this fact does not imply any restrictions.

Like a structure, the previous **class** definition does not create a variable. To create a variable, you would write something like this:

```
over_drawn x, y, z;
```

Look at another example. Chapter 20 developed various data engines for things like stacks and queues. You can further refine the implementation of these engines with the aid of classes. The basic **class** definition for an integer queue might look like this.

```
/* This class defines the queue and the functions
   that can access it.
*/
class queue {
  char q[MAX];
  int rpos, spos;
public:
  void q_init(void);
  void qstore(char ob);
  char qretrieve(void);
};
```

When you declare a variable of type **queue**, you instantiate storage for the queue and also create a link between that specific variable and the functions. For example, the declaration

```
queue a, b;
```

creates two variables with the members defined earlier. Because both the functions and variables of a class are inside the class, they must be de-referenced in the same way. For example,

```
a.rpos = 0;
b.rpos = 0;
```

initializes the **rpos** member for both **class** variables **a** and **b**. In a similar fashion, to store the value **X** on **a**'s queue and **Z** on **b**'s, you would write

```
a.qstore('X');
b.qstore('Z');
```

This may seem strange at first, but there must be some way to tell the compiler what queue **qstore( )** is supposed to use.

Declaring Member Functions

Before you can actually use a **class**, all of its members must be defined. In the **queue** example, the three functions must be written. When you define a member function, you must precede its name with the **class** name followed by two colons. For example, here are the three functions necessary to **queue**.

```
/* Store a character. */
void queue::qstore(char ob)
{
  if(spos==MAX) {
    printf("list full\n");
    return;
  }
  spos++;
  q[spos]=ob;
}

/* Retrieve a character. */
char queue::qretrieve(void)
{
  if(rpos==spos) {
    printf("No more characters in queue.\n");
    return (char) 0;
  }
  rpos++;
  return q[rpos];
```

```
}

/* Initialize the queue. */
void queue::q_init(void)
{
  spos = 0;
  rpos = 0;
  printf("queue initialized\n");
}
```

The **class** name is necessary because there could be other classes that define other types of queues that also use the same function names.

To illustrate how all this works, the following short program reads characters from the keyboard and places them in a queue. Typing **r** causes one character to be removed from the queue and typing **q** quits the program.

```
/* Black-box Queue routines. */
#include "stdio.h"

#define MAX 100

/* This class defines the queue and the functions
   that can access it.
*/
class queue {
  char q[MAX];
  int rpos, spos;
public:
  void q_init(void);
  void qstore(char ob);
  char qretrieve(void);
};

queue q_it;

/* read characters from console and store in queue */
void main(void)
{
  char str[80];

  q_it.q_init(); // init the queue
  for(;;) {
    gets(str);
    if(*str=='r') printf("-->%c\n", q_it.qretrieve());
    else if(*str=='q') break;
    else q_it.qstore(*str);
  }
}

/* Store a character. */
void queue::qstore(char ob)
```

```
{
  if(spos==MAX) {
    printf("list full\n");
    return;
  }
  spos++;
  q[spos]=ob;
}

/* Retrieve a character. */
char queue::qretrieve(void)
{
  if(rpos==spos) {
    printf("No more characters in queue.\n");
    return (char) 0;
  }
  rpos++;
  return q[rpos];
}

/* Initialize the queue. */
void queue::q_init(void)
{
  spos = 0;
  rpos = 0;
  printf("queue initialized\n");
}
```

Constructors and Destructors

In the preceding **queue** example, the **init( )** function initializes the head
and tail indexes into the queue. Many classes require an initialization
step at startup. C++ has a built-in mechanism that automatically provides the necessary initialization each time a variable of that class is
created, without an explicit call to the initialization function. C++ calls
the initialization function a *constructor function.*

All constructors have the same name as the **class** they initialize.
Therefore, the constructor function for **queue** is **queue( )**. The constructor function is made a member of the **class** like this:

```
class queue {
  char q[MAX];
  int rpos, spos;
public:
  queue(void);   // constructor
  void qstore(char ob);
  char qretrieve(void);
};
```

The **queue( )** function is defined like this.

```
// The constructor function.
queue::queue(void)
{
  spos = 0;
  rpos = 0;
  printf("queue initialized\n");
}
```

Notice that **queue( )** does not have a return type defined. This is necessary for constructor functions. Now, each time a variable of class **queue** is declared, the constructor function **queue( )** is automatically called to initialize it.

Although the **queue** class does not need one, a class often requires a de-initialization operation. In C++ this is called a *destructor function*. One of its most common uses is to deallocate any storage that was allocated by the constructor function. All destructor functions have the same name as the **class** they are associated with, but the name is preceded by a ~. The destructor function is called when a **class** variable goes out of existence. This happens either when its scope is terminated or when the program ends.

As written, the **queue** class does not require a destructor. For the sake of illustration, however, one is added that simply prints a message on the screen. The modified **queue** class that includes both the constructor and destructor functions and the ~**queue( )** function looks like this:

```
class queue {
  char q[MAX];
  int rpos, spos;
public:
  queue(void);  // constructor
  ~queue(void); // destructor
  void qstore(char ob);
  char qretrieve(void);
};

// illustration of a destructor function
queue::~queue(void)
{
  printf("queue destroyed\n");
}
```

Using the constructor and destructor functions, the earlier program that reads characters from the keyboard and places them in a queue looks like this:

```
/* Black-box Queue routines using constructor
   and desctructor functions
 */
#include "stdio.h"

#define MAX 100

class queue {
  char q[MAX];
  int rpos, spos;
public:
  queue(void); // initialize
  ~queue(void); // deinitialize
  void qstore(char ob);
  char qretrieve(void);
};

queue q_it;

void main(void)
{
  char str[80];

  for(;;) {
    gets(str);
    if(*str=='r') printf("-->%c\n", q_it.qretrieve());
    else if(*str=='q') break;
    else q_it.qstore(*str);
  }
}

// Store an event.
void queue::qstore(char ob)
{
  if(spos==MAX) {
    printf("list full\n");
    return;
  }
  spos++;
  q[spos]=ob;
}

// Retrieve an event.
char queue::qretrieve(void)
{
  if(rpos==spos) {
    printf("No more characters in queue.\n");
    return (char) 0;
  }
  rpos++;
```

```
    return q[rpos];
}

// The constructor function.
queue::queue(void)
{
  spos = 0;
  rpos = 0;
  printf("queue initialized\n");
}

// illustration of a destructor function
queue::~queue(void)
{
  printf("queue destroyed\n");
}
```

Notice that no explicit calls to **queue( )** or ~**queue( )** are made. However, at startup the message inside **queue( )** is printed, and at termination the ~**queue( )** message is displayed.

friends

You can give one or more functions access to the private part of a **class** without actually making them members of the **class** by preceding their declaration in the **class** by the keyword **friend**. A **friend** function is defined in the body of the program without being preceded by the class name. For example,

```
class x {
  int a, b;
public
  int func(void);
  friend float func2(void);
};
    .
    .
    .
float func2(void)
{
    .
    .
    .
}
```

friend functions have a special use in operator overloading, as you will see later in the chapter.

Function Overloading

As you know, standard C requires separate functions for similar operations that differ only in the types of data that they operate on. For example, the ANSI standard defines both **abs( )**, which returns the absolute value of an integer, and **labs( )**, which returns the absolute value of a **long** integer. Even though the operations are fundamentally the same, two separate function names are required and there is always the danger that you will accidentally use the wrong one. In relatively small projects, this type of a problem is not too likely. In very large projects, however, it is vital to remove the possibility for errors of this type.

C++'s answer is called *function overloading*, which allows one function name to be used to declare several functions that differ only in the type of data that they operate on. The compiler automatically uses the correct version of the function based upon the type of the arguments. In this way, you could use the name **abs( )** to call the absolute value function, regardless of the type of data you call it with.

The C++ compiler must be told in advance, using the keyword **overload**, that a function is going to be overloaded. Otherwise, it just assumes that you are making a multiple definition error. For example, to create two versions of **abs( )**, first write the following near the top of your program:

```
overload abs;
int abs(int);
long abs(long);
```

Next, define both versions of **abs( )** in the body of the program, as shown here.

```
int abs(int i)
{
   return i<0 ? -i : i;
}

long abs(long i)
{
   return i<0 ? -i : i;
}
```

For another example, the following program creates two versions of a function that returns the value of a number raised to an integer exponent. One version of the function accepts two integer arguments; the other accepts a floating-point base and an integer exponent.

```
/* A function overload example. */

#include "stdio.h"

overload power;
int power(int b, int e);
double power(double b, int e);

void main(void)
{
  printf("%d\n", power(10, 2));
  printf("%f", power(10.12, 2));
}

// integer power
int power(int b, int e)
{
  int t;

  t = b;
  for(e--; e; e--) b *= t;
  return b;
}

// double power
double power(double b, int e)
{
  double t;

  t = b;
  for(e--; e; e--) b *= t;
  return b;
}
```

Overloaded functions may not be the most memory-efficient way to accomplish some things because each version of the function is resident in the program. In the case of the **power( )** function, smaller code would result if only the **double** version were created and explicit type casts used when integer quantities were needed. Remember, however, that such memory considerations are becoming a thing of the past for most host environments, so the gain in control and structure often outweighs the use of extra memory.

Operator Overloading

One of C++'s most interesting aspects is called *operator overloading*. Simply put, an overloaded operator behaves differently for each type of data it is declared to work with. To begin, consider this simple C++ program.

```
#include "stream.hpp"

void main(void)
{
  char s[80];

  // write a string to the console
  cout << "this is an example of operator overloading\n";

  cout << "enter a word: ";

  cin >> s;   // read a string from console

  cout << s;  // write it back to console
}
```

As the comments indicate, this program first writes the message **this is an example of operator overloading** followed by **enter a word:**. Then, it waits for you to type a word, which it places into string **s**. Finally, it redisplays the word in **s**.

You are probably wondering about the statements that contain **>>** and **<<**. The **<<** and **>>** operators have been overloaded to allow console input and output. The code that overloads these operators is in the file STREAM.H (called STREAM.HPP by Zortech). The bit-shift meaning of the operators has not been lost; it is just that when the operators are applied to character strings, it specifies a different operation. (You are free to use the standard C console I/O functions, as in the previous examples, but most C++ programmers use the overloaded **<<** and **>>** operators.)

Operators are overloaded by creating an **operator( )** function that defines what action the specified operator should take with types of data defined by the arguments. All operator functions have this general form:

```
type operator#(arg_list)
{
  body
}
```

Here, # is a placeholder for the actual operator. For example, you might redefine the + operator to perform matrix addition on variables of type **matrix** as in the following.

```
matrix operator+(matrix x, matrix y)
{
    .
    .
    .
}
```

Unfortunately, creating overloaded operators is a little more tricky than creating overloaded functions. The process requires these steps:

1. First, create a **class** that defines the type of data the overloaded operator will be operating on.

2. In the **public** part of the **class**, include a **friend** or member **operator( )** function.

3. In the body of the program, define the **operator( )** function.

Consider an example of operator overloading and how it can sometimes be an alternative to function overloading. The ^ operator is overloaded so that it can be used to raise a number to a power. For example, 10^2 would be 100. (This is similar to the use of ^ in BASIC.)

First, you must create a **class** that defines the type of data that can be used with the overloaded ^ operator. The one shown here contains only two items: an integer variable and the declaration that **operator^( )** is a **friend**.

```
class pwr {
public:
  int num;
  friend int operator^(pwr b, pwr e);
};
```

The definition of the operator function is coded like this:

```
// x^y operation
int operator^(pwr b, pwr e)
{
  register int t,temp;

  temp = b.num;
  for(t=e.num-1; t; t--) b.num *= temp;
  return b.num;
}
```

Now, whenever you use variables of type **pwr** in an expression of the form **b^e**, the power is computed instead of an XOR bitwise operation taking place. Remember, the bitwise XOR operation still exists, but not for data of type **pwr**. This simple program illustrates the use of ^:

```
// Operator overloading example.

#include "stdio.h"

class pwr {
public:
  int num;
  friend int operator^(pwr b, pwr e);
};

pwr b, e;

void main(void)
{
  b.num = 2;
  e.num = 4;

  printf("%d", b^e);
}

// x^y operation
int operator^(pwr b, pwr e)
{
  register int t,temp;

  temp = b.num;
  for(t=e.num-1; t; t--) b.num *= temp;
  return b.num;
}
```

The operator function must be a **friend** of the **class** if you are overloading a binary operator; otherwise, the operator function may be a member.

You may only overload an existing operator—you cannot create new operators. Also, you may only overload binary operators with binary operations and unary operators with unary operations. For example, you cannot overload ! so that it takes two arguments. The ternary operator (?) may not be overloaded.

Data Abstraction and Operator Overloading

In the same way that function overloading abstracts data, so may overloaded operators. For example, by creating a new **class** and an additional definition for **operator^( )**, you can also raise **float**s to an integer power, as shown in this expanded version of the previous program:

```
// Operator overloading for multiple data types.

#include "stdio.h"

class intpwr {
public:
  int num;
  friend int operator^(intpwr b, intpwr e);
};

class floatpwr {
public:
  float num;
  friend float operator^(floatpwr b, intpwr e);
};

intpwr b, e;
floatpwr fb;

void main(void)
{
  b.num = 2;
  e.num = 4;

  printf("%d\n", b^e);

  fb.num = 9.3;
  printf("%f", fb^e);
}

// Integer b^e
int operator^(intpwr b, intpwr e)
{
  register int t, temp;

  temp = b.num;
  for(t=e.num-1; t; t--) b.num*=temp;
  return b.num;
}

// Float b^e
float operator^(floatpwr b, intpwr e)
{
  register int t;
  float temp;

  temp = b.num;
  for(t=e.num-1; t; t--) b.num *= temp;
  return b.num;
}
```

As you can see, the two classes **intpwr** and **floatpwr** define which **operator^( )** function is used for each type of data.

Other Features of C++

To finish, this chapter gives a brief description of some of C++'s other new features.

new and delete

Although the C++ environment still gives you access to **malloc( )** and **free( )** as library routines, the recommended way of allocating and deallocating dynamic storage in C++ is with the keywords **new** and **delete**. The **new** operator returns a pointer to an object of the specified type. For example, the following code fragment allocates space for a **double** and places its address in **p**:

```
double *p;

p = new double;
```

Like **malloc( )**, **new** returns 0 if the allocation request fails.

The **delete** operator frees memory previously allocated by **new**. For example, this code fragment frees the memory pointed to by **p**:

```
delete p;
```

inline

The **inline** statement causes the function that it modifies to be expanded in line rather than to be actually called each time it is encountered. This is similar to using a macro definition. For example, if this function

```
inline int abs(int x)
{
  return x<0 ? -x : x;
}
```

is used with this fragment

```
a = 10;
b = abs(10);
```

the compiler generates code as if the following code had been written:

```
a = 10;
b = a<0 ? -a : a;
```

Differences Between K&R C and ANSI-Standard C

Keyword Deletions
Keyword Extensions
Passing Structures
Function Prototypes
Modern Versus Classic Function Declarations
Standard Libraries
Additional Preprocessor Directives

As has been mentioned many times, the ANSI standard has defined a slightly different and expanded version of C than the de facto standard defined by Brian Kernighan and Dennis Ritchie in their book *The C Programming Language* (Englewood Cliffs, N.J.: Prentice-Hall, 1978). Each of these differences is thoroughly covered in the chapters of this book. This appendix provides a quick and convenient reference for the most important differences.

Keyword Deletions

The ANSI standard deletes the unused but previously reserved keyword **entry**.

Keyword Extensions

The ANSI standard adds the following five keywords:

const

enum

signed

void

volatile

Each is examined briefly.

const

The **const** type modifier informs the compiler that the value of the variable that follows it may not be changed by any program statement. (However, it may be initialized.) For example,

```
const int version=2;
```

informs the compiler that **version** may not occur on the left-hand side of an assignment statement and sets the initial value of **version** to 2.

Variables of type **const** have two main purposes. First, the compiler can place them in ROM (read-only memory). For example, the combination of a garage door opener may be in ROM to prevent tampering. Second, they ensure that when pointers are passed to a function, no code in the function can modify the objects pointed to. Consider this:

```
char *find_first_space(const char* p)
{
  .
  .
  .
}
```

Because **p** is declared as a **const**, no code in the function may modify the object that it points to.

enum

The **enum** type specifier creates *enumeration types*. An enumeration is a list of named constants that a variable of that type may have. For example, this declaration defines an enumeration type and two variables:

```
enum names = {Herb, Sherry, Jon, Rachel, Sasha, Josselyn};
enum names child, parent;
```

Now, the following statements are legal:

```
parent = Sherry;
child = Jon;
if(child == Jon && parent != Herb) ...;
```

The values associated with the named constants are integer values.

signed

The **signed** type modifier was added to the ANSI standard to allow you to specify the type **signed char**. Previously, some compilers defaulted to signed characters and others defaulted to unsigned. The **signed** modifier helps standardize the use of type **char**.

void

The **void** type is used in two ways. First, functions that do not return values may be declared to be of type **void**, which tells the compiler that no value will be returned. This prevents any accidental use in an expression. Second, generic pointers may be created as **void *** variables.

volatile

The **volatile** type modifier tells the compiler that the following variable may be modified in ways not under the direct control of the program. For example, a variable may be updated by the system clock every tenth second. Declaring a variable as **volatile** prevents certain compiler optimizations from being made that might prevent the value of the variable from being accessed precisely as the expression indicates. For example, given this fragment

```
volatile int clck;
int timel;

timel = clck;
if(timel==clck) ...;
```

if **clck** were not declared as **volatile**, some compilers might optimize the two expressions such that the value of **clck** was only examined once.

Passing Structures

Some early versions of C could not pass structures to functions. Rather, they would only pass the address of the structure, much as arrays are passed. However, in newer versions and in the ANSI standard, structures are passed to a function in their entirety on the stack. If you wish to pass the address instead, you must precede the structure name with the **&** operator.

Function Prototypes

The ANSI standard allows the types of the arguments as well as the return type of a function to be declared in advance so that strong type checking can be enforced for arguments as well as return values. This is called function *prototyping*. For example, the function **func1( )** is prototyped in this example:

```
#include "stdio.h"

float func1(int, float); /* declare the function */

void main(void)
{
  int x,
  float y;

  x = 10;
  y = 10.12;
```

```
   printf("%f", func1(x, y));
}

float func1(int a, float b)
{
   return (float) a + b;
}
```

Modern Versus Classic Function Declarations

The ANSI standard includes two ways to declare function parameters: the classic and the modern form. The classic form is used by the original C compiler. In this form, only function parameter names appear in the parenthesized list that follows a function's name. The actual type declarations appear after the parenthesized list and before the opening curly brace of the function. In the modern declaration form, the names and types of each parameter appear in the parenthesized list. (This book uses the modern form.) The ANSI standard specifies that either approach may be used, but strongly encourages the modern form.

For example, these declarations are equivalent:

```
/* classic form */
char f(a, b, c)
int a;
float b;
char c;
{

/* modern form */
char f(int a, float b, char c)
{
```

Standard Libraries

One of the most important aspects of the ANSI standard is that it defines a standard set of library functions that will be supplied with a C compiler. This enhances the portability of your programs.

Additional Preprocessor Directives

The following C preprocessor directives have been been added by the ANSI standard to those normally provided by the K&R standard:

#elif	#line
#error	#pragma

In addition, the standard defines these built-in macros:

Macro	Meaning
_ _LINE_ _	Number of current line
_ _FILE_ _	Name of source file
_ _DATE_ _	Current system date
_ _TIME_ _	Current system file
_ _STDC_ _	1 if a standard implementation

Apple®	Apple Computer, Inc.
AT®	International Business Machines Corporation
DEC™	Digital Equipment Corporation
FORTH®	FORTH, Inc.
IBM®	International Business Machines Corporation
Macintosh®	Apple Computer, Inc.
Microsoft®	Microsoft Corporation
PC®	International Business Machines Corporation
PC*jr*™	International Business Machines Corporation
Turbo C®	Borland International, Inc.
UNIX®	AT&T
XT®	International Business Machines Corporation

The manuscript for this book was prepared and submitted
to Osborne/McGraw-Hill in electronic form.
The acquisitions editor for this project was Jeffrey Pepper,
the technical reviewer was Eric Geyer,
and the project editor was Dusty Bernard.

Text design uses Century Expanded for text body and
Eras demibold for display.

Cover art by Bay Graphics Design, Inc. Color separation
and cover supplier, Phoenix Color Corp. Book printed and
bound by R.R. Donnelley & Sons Company,
Crawfordsville, Indiana.